MIMICRY AND DISPLAY IN VICTORIAN LITERARY CULTURE

Revealing the web of mutual influences between nineteenth-century scientific and cultural discourses of appearance, *Mimicry and Display in Victorian Literary Culture* argues that Victorian science and culture biologized appearance, reimagining imitation, concealment and self-presentation as evolutionary adaptations. Exploring how studies of animal crypsis and visibility drew on artistic theory and techniques to reconceptualise nature as a realm of signs and interpretation, Abberley shows that, in turn, this science complicated religious views of nature as a text of divine meanings, inspiring literary authors to rethink human appearances and perceptions through a Darwinian lens. Providing fresh insights into writers from Alfred Russel Wallace and Thomas Hardy to Oscar Wilde and Charlotte Perkins Gilman, Abberley reveals how the biology of appearance generated new understandings of deception, identity and creativity; reacted upon narrative forms such as crime fiction and the pastoral; and infused the rhetoric of cultural criticism and political activism.

WILL ABBERLEY is Senior Lecturer in Victorian Literature at the University of Sussex. His other books are *English Fiction and the Evolution of Language 1850–1914* (Cambridge University Press, 2015) and *Underwater Worlds: Submerged Visions in Science and Culture* (2018). He is a BBC New Generation Thinker and Philip Leverhulme Prize recipient.

CAMBRIDGE STUDIES IN NINETEENTH-CENTURY
LITERATURE AND CULTURE

General editor
Gillian Beer, *University of Cambridge*

Editorial board
Isobel Armstrong, *Birkbeck, University of London*
Kate Flint, *University of Southern California*
Catherine Gallagher, *University of California, Berkeley*
D. A. Miller, *University of California, Berkeley*
J. Hillis Miller, *University of California, Irvine*
Daniel Pick, *Birkbeck, University of London*
Mary Poovey, *New York University*
Sally Shuttleworth, *University of Oxford*
Herbert Tucker, *University of Virginia*

Nineteenth-century British literature and culture have been rich fields for inter-disciplinary studies. Since the turn of the twentieth century, scholars and critics have tracked the intersections and tensions between Victorian literature and the visual arts, politics, social organisation, economic life, technical innovations, scientific thought – in short, culture in its broadest sense. In recent years, theoretical challenges and historiographical shifts have unsettled the assumptions of previous scholarly synthesis and called into question the terms of older debates. Whereas the tendency in much past literary critical interpretation was to use the metaphor of culture as 'background', feminist, Foucauldian, and other analyses have employed more dynamic models that raise questions of power and of circulation. Such developments have reanimated the field. This series aims to accommodate and promote the most interesting work being undertaken on the frontiers of the field of nineteenth-century literary studies: work which intersects fruitfully with other fields of study such as history, or literary theory, or the history of science. Comparative as well as interdisciplinary approaches are welcomed.

A complete list of titles published will be found at the end of the book.

MIMICRY AND DISPLAY IN VICTORIAN LITERARY CULTURE

Nature, Science and the Nineteenth-Century Imagination

WILL ABBERLEY

University of Sussex

CAMBRIDGE
UNIVERSITY PRESS

University Printing House, Cambridge CB2 8BS, United Kingdom

One Liberty Plaza, 20th Floor, New York, NY 10006, USA

477 Williamstown Road, Port Melbourne, VIC 3207, Australia

314–321, 3rd Floor, Plot 3, Splendor Forum, Jasola District Centre, New Delhi – 110025, India

79 Anson Road, #06–04/06, Singapore 079906

Cambridge University Press is part of the University of Cambridge.

It furthers the University's mission by disseminating knowledge in the pursuit of education, learning, and research at the highest international levels of excellence.

www.cambridge.org
Information on this title: www.cambridge.org/9781108477598
DOI: 10.1017/9781108770026

© Will Abberley 2020

This publication is in copyright. Subject to statutory exception and to the provisions of relevant collective licensing agreements, no reproduction of any part may take place without the written permission of Cambridge University Press.

First published 2020

Printed in the United Kingdom by TJ International Ltd, Padstow Cornwall

A catalogue record for this publication is available from the British Library.

Library of Congress Cataloging-in-Publication Data
NAMES: Abberley, Will, 1984– author.
TITLE: Mimicry and display in Victorian literary culture : nature, science and the nineteenth-century imagination / Will Abberley.
DESCRIPTION: New York : Cambridge University Press, 2020. | Series: Cambridge studies in nineteenth-century literature and culture | Includes bibliographical references and index.
IDENTIFIERS: LCCN 2019040879 (print) | LCCN 2019040880 (ebook) | ISBN 9781108477598 (hardback) | ISBN 9781108725767 (paperback) | ISBN 9781108770026 (epub)
SUBJECTS: LCSH: English literature–19th century–History and criticism. | Literature and science–Great Britain. | Imitation in literature. | Nature in literature.
CLASSIFICATION: LCC PR468.S34 A22 2020 (print) | LCC PR468.S34 (ebook) | DDC 820.9/008–dc23
LC record available at https://lccn.loc.gov/2019040879
LC ebook record available at https://lccn.loc.gov/2019040880

ISBN 978-1-108-47759-8 Hardback

Cambridge University Press has no responsibility for the persistence or accuracy of URLs for external or third-party internet websites referred to in this publication and does not guarantee that any content on such websites is, or will remain, accurate or appropriate.

Contents

List of Figures		*page* vi
Acknowledgements		vii
Introduction: Adaptive Appearance in Nineteenth-Century Culture		1
1	Seeing Things: Art, Nature and Science in Representations of Crypsis	28
2	Divine Displays: Charles Kingsley, Hermeneutic Natural Theology and the Problem of Adaptive Appearance	65
3	Criminal Chameleons: The Evolution of Deceit in Grant Allen's Fiction	86
4	Darwin's Little Ironies: Evolution and the Ethics of Appearance in Thomas Hardy's Fiction	116
5	Blending in and Standing out, I: Crypsis versus Individualism in Fin-de-Siècle Cultural Criticism	149
6	Blending in and Standing out, II: Mimicry, Display and Identity Politics in the Literary Activism of Israel Zangwill and Charlotte Perkins Gilman	178
Conclusion: Adaptive Appearance and Cultural Theory		205
Notes		215
Bibliography		255
Index		285

v

Figures

1 'Protective Mimicry', *Punch*, 136 (28 April 1909), p. 299   *page* 14
2 Plate from Henry Walter Bates, 'Contributions to an Insect Fauna of the Amazon Valley. Lepidoptera: Heliconidæ', *Transactions of the Linnean Society of London*, 23 (1862), 495–566, plate LV   44
3 Hawk moth and hummingbird. From Henry Walter Bates, *The Naturalist on the River Amazons* 2 vols. (London: J. Murray, 1863), I, p. 181   45
4 Frontispiece to Bates, *The Naturalist on the River Amazons*, I   46
5 Camouflaged Kallima butterfly, from Alfred Russel Wallace, *The Malay Archipelago*, 2 vols. (London: Macmillan & Co., 1869), I, p. 131   48
6 Grouse specimen in cabinet, from Abbott Handerson Thayer, 'The Law Which Underlies Protective Coloration', *The Auk*, 13:2 (1896), 124–129, p. 126   55
7 Grouse specimen in vegetation, from Thayer, 'The Law Which Underlies Protective Coloration', p. 126   56
8 'Male Ruffed Grouse in the Forest', from Gerald Handerson Thayer and Abbott Handerson Thayer, *Concealing-Coloration in the Animal Kingdom* (New York: Macmillan, 1909), p. 38   59
9 Wood duck on pond, from Thayer and Thayer, *Concealing-Coloration in the Animal Kingdom*, p. 59   60
10 Kallima butterfly, from Grant Allen, 'Masquerades and Disguises', in *In Nature's Workshop* (London: George Newnes, 1901), 88–115, p. 95   89

Acknowledgements

First, I must thank the Leverhulme Trust, which, through its Early Career Fellowship scheme, enabled me to complete the bulk of the research for this book. I am also grateful to the English Faculty at the University of Oxford and School of English at the University of Sussex for hosting me during the fellowship. Among the many people who have helped me to refine my arguments, those deserving special mention include Sally Shuttleworth, Kirsten Shepherd-Barr, Michael Whitworth, Cathryn Setz, Bernard Lightman, Julie Codell, Linda K. Hughes, Lara Kriegel, Rae Greiner, Michaela Castellanos, Martin Willis, John Holmes, Ruth Livesey, Richard Adelman, Norman Vance, Piers Hale, Jim Endersby, Angelique Richardson, Philipp Erchinger, David Amigoni, Carolyn Burdett, Alex Murray, Kathrin McCann and Tiffany Watt-Smith. Portions of Chapter 2 first appeared in the article 'Animal Cunning: Deceptive Nature and Truthful Science in Charles Kingsley's Natural Theology', *Victorian Studies* 58:1 (2015), and I am thankful for permission to reuse this material. I also thank Bethany Thomas and my anonymous reviewers at Cambridge University Press for their help and advice. Among the academic networks that have nourished my research, I am particularly indebted to the British Society for Literature and Science and the British Association for Victorian Studies, whose conferences provided a space for me to test ideas. Equally important have been Oxford's literature and science research seminars and Sussex's eighteenth- and nineteenth-century literature series. I must also thank my friends and family for their love, support and encouragement.

Introduction
Adaptive Appearance in Nineteenth-Century Culture

Appearances matter. Thus contended the naturalist Henry Walter Bates in 1861 when he delivered a paper to the Linnean Society of London on curious patterns of resemblance among Amazonian flora and fauna. Bates had spent eleven years in the country studying animals (particularly insects) that took on the aspects of vegetation, terrain or other species. His interest in such resemblances ran against a growing tendency in science to disregard nature's impressive qualities as superficial distractions. The emerging discourse of objectivity advocated mechanised methods of observation supposedly purged of personal perceptions.[1] The scalpel and microscope promised to pierce through illusions that tricked the casual eye. Yet, instead of expunging illusions from his evidence, Bates placed them centre-stage. 'These imitative resemblances', he wrote, 'are full of interest, and fill us with the greater astonishment the closer we investigate them; for some show a minute and palpably intentional likeness which is perfectly staggering'.[2] Such appearances, Bates suggested, were not trivial but vital clues to evolutionary history.

This point was demonstrated by the interspecies resemblances which Bates called *mimicry*. These resemblances seemed to occur when two species with common foes lived side by side and one possessed some defence such as a noxious taste. Bates argued that, as predators learned to avoid the defended species, they were also likely to avoid other creatures that resembled it. This dynamic created a selective pressure favouring the survival of individuals that imitated the model species to ever-greater degrees. There might have been more to life's forms than met the eye, but how they met the eye could be key to their survival. Organisms, Bates suggested, were at once physical beings and clusters of signs that prospered and perished depending on other organisms' perceptions of them.

Protective mimicry was one of a web of theories in the second half of the nineteenth century that framed appearance as a factor in environmental adaptation. Camouflage and mimicry (now known collectively as *crypsis*)

2   Introduction

could also disguise predators to help them catch prey.[3] Mimicry depended on aposematism, that is, organisms signalling their defences via striking features.[4] In 1878, the German biologist Fritz Müller proposed that such warnings could also be mimetic. Species with similar defences, he claimed, evolved resemblances to each other to spread the cost of predators learning to avoid them (which often involved individuals being killed).[5] Charles Darwin had also argued in *On the Origin of Species* (1859) that many species developed conspicuous features to attract mates, rendering aesthetics a factor in adaptation.[6] Darwin highlighted the newly pronounced role of appearance in biology in an 1863 review of Bates's findings, commenting that, 'to the perplexity of naturalists ... Nature [has] condescended to the tricks of the stage'.[7] His view was echoed by the co-discoverer of natural selection, Alfred Russel Wallace, who had studied crypsis alongside Bates. Many animals, Wallace reflected, seemed 'like actors or masqueraders dressed up and painted for amusement, or like swindlers endeavouring to pass themselves off for well-known and respectable members of society'.[8]

As Darwin's and Wallace's images show, these theories of crypsis, aposematism and sexual display (which I collectively term *adaptive appearance*) were highly suggestive, spurring Victorians and Edwardians to rethink many aspects of life. Natural historians had long noted examples of organisms concealing themselves, resembling other species and standing out through conspicuous features. However, an intensified focus on survival adaptation and a new view of nature as dynamic and evolving gave a new resonance to such appearances. Representations of adaptive appearance troubled emerging divisions between objective and subjective knowledge, inviting readers to imagine the world through other species' eyes. Christopher Herbert finds many Victorians entertaining the thought that the world was only knowable as differences and relations rather than things-in-themselves, rendering knowledge relative.[9] Adaptive appearance extended this relativism by collapsing distinctions between illusion and reality: biological existence, it implied, was permeated to its core by interpretation and contingencies of perception. Adaptive appearance also encouraged new approaches to human deception and display. If nature was theatrical, then perhaps the theatricality of society could also be understood as natural. Jane Goodall and Kirsten Shepherd-Barr note that nineteenth-century drama could highlight the performativity of evolution through the physical-semiotic interactions of actors' bodies in the 'environment' of the stage.[10] I suggest that adaptive appearance further encouraged Victorians and Edwardians to reconceptualise human deceit, rhetoric and

Introduction

self-presentation as biological phenomena rather than moral choices. Adaptive appearance came to serve as a vehicle for burgeoning uncertainties about the role of signification in nature, the human/animal divide, the place of deceit in human evolution, and the possibility of individual agency and authentic identity.

I will trace how adaptive appearance mediated these tensions through a combination of cultural history and literary criticism, modelled on the pioneering work of Gillian Beer, George Levine, Sally Shuttleworth and Laura Otis.[11] Adaptive appearance was not just scientific theories but what Beer has called a 'shared discourse' of 'metaphors, myths and narrative patterns' that traversed scientific and non-scientific communities.[12] *Mimicry and Display* has no truck with views of science in culture as a one-way dissemination from expert-originators to passive audiences. It views adaptive appearance as a pliable set of images and concepts that were reshaped to suit different perspectives and agendas, much like evolution in general.[13] Greg Garrard defines ecocriticism as the rhetorical analysis of 'ways of imagining, constructing or presenting nature in a figure' or 'trope'.[14] I identify adaptive appearance as a cluster of such 'tropes' (namely mimicry, camouflage and conspicuous display) which circulated unpredictably through late nineteenth- and early twentieth-century Anglophone culture with myriad connotations. Like the organisms that inspired it, adaptive appearance signified different things to different perceivers, from divine presence to a Godless world, progress to degeneration, creative individuality to mindless conformity.

Ecocriticism is further characterised as part of an avowedly environmentalist and animal-liberationist politics that critiques anthropocentrism and seeks alternative, 'posthuman' ways of conceptualising life.[15] A subfield of such critical theory adopts the linguistic-biological terminology of *biosemiotics* and *zoosemiotics* to challenge traditional binaries between mindful, human semiosis and mindless, non-human mechanism. At the same time, some theorists advocate a framework of *zoopoetics*, which, by questioning the construction of art or literature as exclusively human activities, attacks oppositions between mindful humans and mechanical non-humans.[16] *Mimicry and Display* engages tentatively with these discussions by showing that discourse of adaptive appearance in the long nineteenth century could undermine such binaries and, thus, seem to anticipate the political resonances of contemporary bio- or zoosemiotics. For authors such as Grant Allen and Thomas Hardy, adaptive appearance also cohered with wider critiques of capitalism and biological essentialism. Jerome McGann argued that Romantic ideals of the transcendent power of the imagination obstructed progressive politics by downplaying life's material conditions.[17] By contrast, adaptive appearance could support a thoroughly materialist account of the mind, folding society, culture and biology into a single, dynamic whole characterised by contingency and potential change.

However, I am wary of smoothing out the complexities of the past by forcing it into teleological political metanarratives. Adaptive appearance certainly problematised human/non-human binaries, but this was not necessarily accompanied by an expanded sense of ethical responsibility toward non-humans. Imagining animals as sign-makers and interpreters inspired some Victorians to reinstate divisions between humans and non-humans (and, indeed, between different human groups) by hierarchising semiosis into ascending levels of mindedness. *Mimicry and Display* thus challenges the assumption that extending semiosis to non-humans necessarily extends agency and personhood to them as well. Indeed, I show that adaptive appearance could even deprive humans of these capacities, absorbing them into economies of advertisement and deception the same as non-humans. This perspective sometimes tended toward political pessimism, framing human behaviour as the inevitable product of fixed, amoral biology. Further, as Chapter 5 shows, conceptualising human society through the lens of adaptive appearance led some to regard the manipulation of the masses by elites as unavoidable and perhaps even desirable. Insofar, then, as this study contributes to an ecocritical (or, indeed, any progressive) politics, it shows that bio- or zoosemiotic discourse is not an automatic ally of such politics, and can bolster oppressive structures as well as resisting them.

English literature has long depicted human dissembling and dishonesty with metaphoric figures of chameleons and other elusive animals.[18] However, I argue that literary appropriations of adaptive appearance in the Victorian and Edwardian periods represented more than just updates of old metaphors. Beer notes that, through its revelation of common ancestry, evolutionary theory functioned 'to substantiate metaphor and particularly to find a real place in the material order for older mythological expression'.[19] Similarly, when applied to people, adaptive appearance could turn old metaphors into newly literal realities, suggesting that humans were embedded in the same dynamics of deception and display as their animal cousins.

At the same time, I recognise that scientific and literary or artistic communities defined themselves according to different goals, and developed different methods and identities, sometimes in conscious opposition to each other. Like Anne DeWitt, I view late nineteenth-century

Introduction 5

science and literature as not just overlapping activities but also tectonic tensions between rival, shifting centres of authority.[20] Some of this study's protagonists (notably Charles Kingsley and Abbott Handerson Thayer) often seem more concerned with defending or expanding their territories of expertise than uniting in a utopian 'one culture' of interdisciplinarity.[21] Adaptive appearance is particularly suited to interdisciplinary analysis since its theory and practice necessarily blurred the boundaries between science and the arts. However, this lineality could also problematise its status as oppositional models of art and science gained influence toward the end of the century (see Chapter 1).

I suggest that, as a shared discourse, adaptive appearance interacted with certain literary forms. Caroline Levine, Charlotte Sleigh, Peter Garratt and Adelene Buckland have analysed Victorian realism as a response to scientific epistemologies, characterised by doubt, uncertainty and epistemic modesty.[22] Catherine Gallagher further portrays Victorian realism as a dynamic tension between the rival truth claims of the typical and the particular.[23] Recently, Pamela Gilbert has argued that Victorian realism co-developed with a new emphasis on bodily surfaces as foci of identity and subjectivity, 'posited at once as radically transparent to interpretation and as obscure'.[24] I submit that natural historians' representations of adaptive appearance reflected these tendencies, critiquing their impressions of nature in a manner reminiscent of John Ruskin's theories of artistic vision. Such representations also depended on conventions of natural-historical memoir, which combined systematic data-gathering with personal anecdote and aesthetic impressions. I argue that novelists such as Allen and Hardy similarly foregrounded the unreliability of perception with various narration devices, and promoted the virtue of interpretive restraint through plots involving adaptive appearance. Equally, such tales could frame generic conventions such as poetic justice as deceptions to be exposed similarly as science penetrated the deceptions of animals. I claim that adaptive appearance existed in tension (at least in Hardy's fiction) with pastoral tradition, which tended to construct nature as honest and transparent. I also show that adaptive appearance could undermine detective fiction's conventional faith in the power of science to unmask deceptions. Further, I suggest that the biology of appearance energised cultural criticism that conceived of culture in biological terms.

Although the literary and cultural contexts of crypsis and aposematism in the nineteenth century have been relatively neglected by scholars, this study builds on and responds to works concerned with science and appearance more generally.[25] Sexual selection has received more sustained attention, with scholars exploring how this concept reshaped aesthetic experiences as material, transspecies phenomena.[26] *Mimicry and Display* argues that scientific naturalism similarly materialised deception and semiosis as activities that linked humans to animals instead of separating them. I expand on Margot Norris's claims that Darwinism influenced Modernist notions of mimesis, applying her concept of 'mimeophobia' to Victorian texts.[27] Sleigh has shown that studies of ants in the twentieth century evolved in dialogue with theories of communication such as semiotics and cybernetics.[28] I suggest that such discourse of communication-as-biology, and its problematisations of intentionality and individuality, were prefigured by nineteenth-century discourse of adaptive appearance. Srdjan Smajić and Martin Willis have highlighted Victorians' awareness of the hazards of inference, and I argue that adaptive appearance was built upon such problematising of perception.[29] I draw on Jonathan Smith's and George Levine's studies of Ruskin's opposition to Darwinism, but I also complicate this opposition.[30] Although Ruskin reviled materialism, I argue that his notion of apprehending nature 'innocently' unwittingly set a template for later representations of adaptive appearance. Anne Helmreich has shown that ideas of 'truth to nature' transformed through the nineteenth century as the virtues of accuracy and precision gave way to subjective impressionism, redrawing relations between art and science.[31] I contend that adaptive appearance contributed to this complication of natural truth, highlighting the importance of failures and partialities of perception in nature's economy. Tiffany Watt-Smith observes that the ideal of restrained, objective observation in the period was countered by physiologically responsive forms of scientific looking, notably in vivisection and psychology.[32] I extend her argument, suggesting that, in the case of adaptive appearance, embodied perception acted as a tool of interspecies empathy. The radical implications of adaptive appearance derived from its approach to the non-human world as a space of rhetoric and interpretation, so I will first sketch how this approach developed, before outlining its significance for human life.

Nature's Rhetoric and Primitive Interpretation

The framing of nature as rhetorical can be seen in the ways that researchers and popularisers of adaptive appearance evoked it. In 1897, the zoologist Edward Bagnall Poulton distinguished Bates's and Müller's theories of mimicry in terms of commercial branding. As mentioned previously, Batesian mimicry involved defenceless species passing themselves off as better-defended ones, while, in Müllerian mimicry, species with equal defences resembled each other to spread the cost of communicating their unpalatability to their foes. Hence, Poulton wrote that, in Batesian mimicry, the relation between mimic and model species 'may be compared to that existing between a successful well-known firm and another small unscrupulous one which lives upon its reputation'. Conversely, in Müllerian mimicry, 'the relation may be compared to that between two successful firms which combine to use a common advertisement'.[33] At around the same time, the science writer and novelist Grant Allen was also emphasising nature's manipulativeness, writing,

> Human life and especially human warfare are rich in deceptions, wiles, and stratagems ... Trade in like manner is full of shams ... But Nature we are usually accustomed to consider as innocent and truthful. Alas, too trustfully: for Nature too is a gay deceiver. There is hardly a device invented by man which she has not anticipated: hardly a trick or ruse in his stock of wiles which she did not find out for herself long before he showed her.[34]

Allen's gendered language draws on long-standing associations between femininity and dishonesty, presenting adaptive appearance as a shocking blow to nature's supposed moral purity and authenticity. Rousseauian celebrations of nature as unmediated presence and goodness seem to have abruptly given way to Machiavellian skulduggery.

Yet Allen's vision of an innocent natural world destroyed by Darwinian adaptive appearance was somewhat exaggerated. Appearance had long been recognised as having at least some role in non-human life. The famous dictum 'Nature loves to hide' descended from Heraclitus, while Pliny the Elder had noted examples of animal camouflage.[35] Ancient ideas of animals possessing cunning were symbiotic with observations of seemingly deceptive behaviour such as foxes hiding in their dens.[36] In the late eighteenth century, Christian Konrad Sprengel had argued (although with little impact) that flowers' eye-catching colours served to attract insects, which aided fertilisation.[37] Charles Darwin's grandfather Erasmus observed that 'the colours of many animals seem adapted to their purposes of concealing themselves'.[38] Early nineteenth-century naturalists were well aware of resemblances between unrelated species, although they usually called these resemblances 'analogies' instead of mimicries. What changed between then and the time of Bates and Poulton was less the kind of data being collected than how it was interpreted.[39]

Pre-Victorian researchers often presented interspecies resemblances as a kind of divine decoration, signalling an intelligent creator. William Sharp Macleay argued that resemblances between species of different taxa followed regular patterns. His quinarian system assumed that morphologically similar species occurred in rings of five, which overlapped symmetrically with other rings of kindred species. Such symmetry could be imagined as evidence of intelligent design, as in William Paley's comparison of the organic world to a watch, too perfect to have come about by chance.[40] However, zoologists increasingly doubted quinarianism toward the mid-century as examples mounted of species varying erratically. Prior to Darwin's evolutionary tree, asymmetrical 'maps' of species were replacing Macleay's rings.[41] Anthropocentric natural theology was giving way to a more ecocentric natural history that focussed on how organisms' traits adapted them for survival. This ecocentric orientation shifted the focus away from humans' aesthetic responses to nature and toward organisms' probable perceptions of each other.

Such ecocentrism undermined the tradition not only of admiring nature as divine art but also of regarding it as a legible text of the creator's mind. Notions of the 'book of Nature' had long figured organisms as moral allegories.[42] Although this symbolic view lost much of its potency through the Enlightenment, mild versions of it persisted into the nineteenth century. In 1824, for example, the entomologist John Oliver French described nature as 'a boundless theatre, in which moral and intellectual agency is ever active and employed'. The appearances and instincts of animals, he claimed, acted as 'a mirror' 'in which the various moral and intellectual powers of man are symbolically reflected', from 'industry, integrity, justice and order' to 'dishonesty, injustice ... selfishness and cowardice'.[43]

Susan Lorsch claims that Victorian culture witnessed a 'designification' of nature as secular science progressively emptied it of such spiritual meaning.[44] I argue that the change was more complex. Nature was not simply voided of significance; rather, signification was reduced to a material process within nature instead of being a spiritual process external to it. Rather than constituting a coherent statement of divine values, the world fragmented into a cacophony of signs and interpretations between organisms, which were bound up with the business of survival and reproduction. Chapter 2 explores this disturbance to divine nature symbolism through the parson-naturalist Charles Kingsley's engagements with adaptive appearance. Kingsley struggled to reconcile the phenomenon with his faith that nature expressed God's personality and instructions. His efforts to control nature's significations show that adaptive appearances interacted with wider anxieties in the period about the variability of interpretation and instability of meaning.

Nature's Rhetoric and Primitive Interpretation

The construction of nature as rhetorical placed its appearances on a spectrum with other forms of communication, culminating in human language. The sense of commonality between human and non-human communication was further aided by philosophers increasingly locating meaning in receivers' interpretations instead of senders' intentions. The ancient art of rhetoric approached language as a means of eliciting audience responses, but this had not usually been regarded as the essence of communication. John Locke had depicted words and, by extension, all signs, as arbitrary markers of thought which people used to transmit their ideas to each other.[45] Signs and the exchange of meanings (including deceitful ones) seemed to be primarily purposeful acts of transmission. However, the emergence of historical philology undermined this logic, showing that languages evolved through deep time regardless of human intentions. Humans seemed moulded by the specific histories of their mother-tongues, which were held to embody and shape unique national characters.[46] This new outlook rendered translation a matter of indefinite approximations between different collective experiences; and perhaps what applied on the national level also applied to individuals.

The logician Benjamin Humphrey Smart elaborated this point in *An Outline of Sematology* (1831), asserting that communication consisted not of transmitting one's thoughts outward but of 'touch[ing] the chords' and 'awaken[ing] the associations' in others. Rejecting the claim that rhetorical devices, or 'expedients', as he called them, were simply 'instruments of deception', Smart declared: 'It is only by expedients that mind can unfold itself to mind ... there is no such thing as an express and direct image of thought'.[47] He argued that speakers ascribed meanings to words through the contexts in which they heard them used, rendering signification associative and receiver-focussed. Language functioned, Smart concluded, 'rather to put other minds into a certain posture or train of thinking, than pretend to convey at once what the speaker thinks'.[48] Theories of adaptive appearance were similarly receiver-focussed. Wallace explained in 1867 that the term 'mimicry' denoted not 'the sense of voluntary imitation' but 'a particular kind of resemblance only ... As this kind of resemblance has the same effect as voluntary imitation or mimicry, and as there is no word in the language that expresses the required meaning, "mimicry" was adopted.'[49] Insect mimicry had struck Bates as 'palpably intentional'. Yet, similarly as Darwinism obviated the origin of a creator for the world, adaptive appearance obviated the origin of an intentional agent for signs, true or false.

Shifting the emphasis in signification from intention to reception placed humans and animals on a semiotic continuum. Smart claimed that beneath artificial language there was a 'Rhetoric of nature, namely, tone, looks, and gesture', as well as 'the inarticulate cries of the mere animal'.[50] Similar thinking underlay Henry Lord Brougham's observation that animals 'seem to have some knowledge of conventional signs. If I am to teach a dog or a pig to do certain things on a given signal, the process I take to be this. I connect his obedience with reward, his disobedience with punishment.'[51] The young Charles Darwin read both of these authors in the late 1830s when he was first working out his theory of evolution (and, aptly, worrying about how it might be received). Darwin's notes praised Smart's and Brougham's insights, and their influence can be seen in his later arguments that language had grown out of animal communication, and that humans shared a repertoire of emotional expressions with animals.[52] However, as Smart and Brougham had made clear, the crux of semiosis lay in interpreting signs rather than producing them. Hence, Darwin argued in *The Descent of Man* (1871), non-linguistic beings could still reason as they learned to interpret the world around them. 'Animals', he wrote, 'may constantly be seen to pause, deliberate, and resolve'.[53] Humans and animals could be conceptualised as fellow-interpreters of the world.

This view legitimised efforts to imagine the mental worlds that other species inhabited. From Lockean sensationalism, it followed that the closer animals were to humans anatomically, the more similar their nervous systems and, so, their mental lives would be. 'We are perfectly justified', Alexander Bain wrote in 1850, 'in conceiving of the feelings engendered in a flying bird, a cantering horse, or by the loiterings of a flock of sheep; our own bodily states can approach sufficiently near to any of these to enable us to form some estimate of the resulting sensations'.[54] Bain argued that the homology of the 'organs of sense' between vertebrate animals supported the inference that 'the outer world must impress the sentient organs in very nearly the same way'. Animals learned to associate these sensations with consequences, enabling them to be deceived, as Bain commented: 'the animal tribes, no less than humanity itself, come to know a whole class of things from a single specimen ... Both man and brute are liable to be misled by apparent similarities, and to miss such as are real.'[55]

Bain's levelling of human and animal perceptions recalls W. J. T. Mitchell's insight that depictions of animals being deceived have often emphasised these creatures' similarities to humans. Mitchell cites an anecdote in Pliny's *Natural History* in which birds fly at a painting of grapes, mistaking the image for real fruit. He notes that 'Pliny presents "being taken in" as consistent with a kind of judgment', a capacity for 'verdict (iudicio)'.[56] Animals' ability to be mistaken demonstrated their nonmechanical, agential nature. Far from being purely metaphysical, signification could be imagined as intrinsic to the processes of life, blurring the boundaries between mind and matter, agency and necessity. Jonathan Culler notes that, 'Traditionally, Western philosophy has distinguished "reality" from "appearance," *things* themselves from *representations* of them', rendering representations 'but a way to get at reality' that 'should be as transparent as possible'.[57] Adaptive appearances confounded this distinction, suggesting that being and representation were interwoven inextricably. As Chapter 1 explores, this mingling of mind and matter led investigators to treat their own embodied experiences of adaptive appearance as substitutes for the imagined perceptions of other non-humans.

However, animal misinterpretations could also reinscribe the human/non-human binary, opposing naïve animal interpreters to critical human ones. Mitchell notes that Pliny's anecdote of birds mistaking a painting for fruit frames the animal gaze as confined to literalness. While Pliny's animals associate objects with visual forms, they have no notion of representations existing apart from the objects they refer to. Although humans might be taken in by a trompe l'oeil the same as animals, only the former can '"take in" the image with self-conscious awareness that it is only an image'.[58] Animals might be deceived by mimicry, but only humans can comprehend mimesis. The biologist George Romanes asserted that most animal intelligence consisted of 'recepts' (associated impressions), not abstract 'concepts'. Only 'the human mind', he wrote, was able

> to stand outside of itself, and thus to constitute its own ideas the subject-matter of its own thought ... The diving bird, which avoids a rock and fearlessly plunges into the sea, unquestionably displays a receptual knowledge of certain 'things,' 'relations,' and 'truths'; but it does not know any of them *as such*: although it knows them, it does not *know that it knows them* ... it does not *think* them, or regard the things, the relations, or the truths which it perceives as *themselves the objects of perception*.[59]

Animals and humans might both be interpreters, but, perhaps, only humans reflected on their interpretations, recognising the difference between object and representation.

Such detachment from one's perceptions became closely identified with scientific authority through the nineteenth century. From geological cross-sections to Darwin's diagram of descent from a common ancestor, visualisations of physical phenomena became increasingly abstract, framing ultimate reality as lying beyond what could be sensed directly.[60] Developments in telescopes, microscopes and photography accentuated the limitations of unassisted vision. Simultaneously, optics, optometry and acoustics framed sensory perception as physiological processes which distorted and elided as much as they revealed.[61] Willis notes that Victorian scientific researchers understood vision as a precarious 'negotiation' between 'the actual and the imagined'.[62] Early psychology explored perception as a process not merely of registering facts but of inferring them, based on pre-existing ideas.[63] Herbert Spencer described this process in semiotic terms in 1862, writing that humans 'conceive as objects what are only signs of objects'.[64] Such statements framed psychology as a kind of self-conscious meta-interpretation that scrutinised perceptions as hermeneutic constructs. Science seemed to depend more than ever on the separation of facts from subjective experiences. These developments could produce tensions in naturalists' representations of adaptive appearance (see Chapter 1). Their efforts to recreate the effects of crypsis for readers conflicted with the wish to emphasise their critical detachment from the animal subjectivities they studied. Nonetheless, Bates's and others' construction of humans and animals as fellow-interpreters energised discussions about the possible roles of adaptive appearance in human life.

The Evolution of Deception

The idea of primitive interpretation, which adaptive appearance depended on, could be as much applied to humans as to animals. The associationist model of ideas as compound sensations framed thought as a spectrum of increasing perceptual detachment. G. H. Lewes commented that, while the vulgar theatre-goer became caught up in a play, forgetting its unreality, the 'critical' spectator occupied 'a double world', considering at once the action on stage and its artistic construction.[65] Like Pliny's birds that were unable to grasp the mimetic nature of a painting, working-class humans could be imagined as stupidly literal-minded, unable to separate representation from reality. Such notions of primitive interpretation aligned with anxieties about the expansion of reading among the masses and their susceptibility to manipulation. In 1850, the novelist Fanny Mayne had warned that sensational 'tales of imagination' might incite working-class readers to violence, since, for them, reading was not primarily intellectual but 'a sensual gratification'.[66] A decade later, H. L. Mansel similarly railed against 'sensation novels' for 'preaching to the nerves instead of the judgment'.[67] Near the end of the century, Gustave Le Bon further developed the concept of primitive interpretation in his theory of crowd psychology. Le Bon argued that large crowds, particularly of the uneducated, processed language and images as 'unconscious' 'suggestions', like people hypnotised.[68] Such anxieties about primitive literal-mindedness gave secular form to old notions of idolatry, the failure to distinguish material objects from abstract, spiritual meanings.[69]

Late Victorian anthropologists explicitly linked such superstitious gullibility with nature's parasitic deceptions when discussing the figure of the shaman. E. B. Tylor observed that the shaman depended on the gullibility of his followers, whose primitive 'animist' thinking caused them to interpret coincidences as the work of supernatural agencies. Tylor emphasised the shaman's economic reliance on his deceptions, writing of food offerings to the gods: 'more usually it is the priest who as minister of the deities has the lion's share of the offering or the sole privilege of consuming them'.[70] The American psychologist Norman Triplett later concluded that conjuring was a survival of such superstition, which was based on the twin 'atavistic tendencies' of the 'instinct of deception' and 'animistic' misinterpretation of phenomena.[71] As with animals, the possible intentionality of the shaman's deception was immaterial. What mattered was the gullibility of his interlocutors, which he subsisted upon. Triplett wrote that the shaman thus manifested the same 'biological tendency' as Batesian mimicry.[72]

Wallace figured protective mimicry as the refuge of 'weak and decaying species', and invocations of the phenomenon with reference to humans often carried this association of parasitic weakness.[73] Edith Wharton's short story 'The Eyes' (1910) uses the term to skewer the pretentions of an erratic young man who fantasises about becoming a writer. One character explains the youth's aspirations to literary greatness as 'simply protective mimicry – an instinctive ruse to get away from family life and an office desk'.[74] Protective mimicry could also feature in political satire. A 1909 cartoon in *Punch* by Edward Linley Sambourn with the title 'PROTECTIVE MIMICRY' depicted the Ottoman Sultan Abdul Hamid as a chameleon skulking cravenly on the 'Young Turkey Carpet'. Alluding to the Sultan's recent failed countercoup against the Young Turks, the cartoon highlights the insincerity of his support for constitutional reform as the caption states: 'I THOUGHT I COULD MANAGE SOMEHOW TO TAKE THE COLOUR OF MY SURROUNDINGS, BUT I'M NOT AT ALL SURE THAT THESE LIBERTY DESIGNS WON'T BE TOO MUCH FOR ME' (see Fig. 1). The Sultan-lizard's crypsis emphasises his political weakness, forced to falsely identify as a constitutionalist to survive.

Fig. 1 'Protective Mimicry', *Punch*, 136 (28 April 1909), p. 299.

Some Victorians viewed scientific progress as the cure for such parasitic deception and the primitive interpretation on which it relied. In an era when society was often conceptualised as a kind of organism, adaptive appearances could be seen as systemic inefficiencies to be overcome. Spencer claimed that societies and organisms alike developed through simultaneous 'integration' and 'differentiation', their parts becoming increasingly individuated and yet also 'mutually dependent'.[75] This orientation figured morality and science as advancing together teleologically. Similarly as critical interpretation was imagined as overcoming deceptive appearances, altruism promised to remove the motivation to deceive as humankind grew toward sympathetic cooperation.[76] Darwin posited that humans had evolved 'fidelity' incrementally since tribe members 'who were always ready to warn each other of danger, to aid and defend each other . . . would without doubt succeed best and conquer the other'.[77] Spencer argued that humans grew away from dishonesty with the development of commerce, depending on vast networks of trust, which 'the cunning selfishness of the savage' would render impossible.[78] This optimistic view

The Evolution of Deception

would seem to conform to the 'widespread belief' in the period, charted by Lionel Trilling, that the English national character exhibited unparalleled 'probity and candour'.[79] Spencer presented this supposed veracity as part of a more general civilising process as humans ceased to covet the fripperies of wealth. He wrote that such 'indiscriminate' reverence of 'external signs', which had no connection with inner worth, represented a primitive 'idolatry which worships the symbol apart from the thing symbolized'.[80] Scepticism of surface appearances seemed to fit into a wider model of progress.

However, it did not necessarily follow that increasing critical awareness of signs and interpretation should correlate with increasing altruism and aversion to deceit. The former might only enable more elaborate forms of deception as individuals continued to pursue selfish goals. In 1860, Darwin wrote with amusement that the press had represented his evolutionary theory as a vindication of 'every cheating tradesman'.[81] Nonetheless, his later discussions of human evolution suggested that, despite intragroup 'fidelity', deception remained valuable in struggles between groups. 'To lie to your enemy has rarely been thought a sin', he remarked, 'as the history of modern diplomacy too plainly shews'.[82] Further, as long as competition of some kind persisted between individuals, dishonesty would continue to have adaptive value. Although Triplett's work might seem to form part of civilisation exposing and, so, overcoming primitive deceit, his rhetoric often pointed toward deceit becoming ever-more sophisticated. The 'instinct to deceive' was 'blind enough at the beginning', he wrote, but 'in the higher orders [it] becomes implicated with an ever-increasing intelligence, ending with the conscious deceptions of man, which in him, find their widest range and their highest form'.[83]

Some Victorians defined progress as the elaboration of adaptive deceptions by evoking the history of hunting and warfare. In 1854, the science populariser J. G. Wood observed that human hunters often replicated animals' ruses. For example, Africans digging pits to catch fast mammals echoed insects' use of holes to trap prey. In such cases, Wood wrote, 'The reasoning operations of man are anticipated by the instinctive capacities of an insect.'[84] The development of military uniforms could further be interpreted as a human adaptation consciously modelled on natural ones. Colonial soldiers began to wear khaki uniforms in the 1840s, and this style became widespread among western infantry by the end of the century. In 1899, the Lieutenant-Colonel C. H. Powell wrote that advancements in the ranges and accuracy of firearms had produced 'the absolute necessity for dressing the soldier in a colour as invisible as it is possible to give him'.

16   Introduction

Thus, he wrote, 'Nature', with its animal concealments, 'teaches man a valuable lesson'.[85] The First World War saw the development of various forms of camouflage, and the painter Abbott Handerson Thayer (discussed in Chapter 1) would try to design military uniforms based on his theories of animal crypsis.

Notions of primitive cunning were also countered by depictions of westerners proving their superiority over colonised others by deceiving them. In Henry Rider Haggard's *King Solomon's Mines* (1885), white explorers win the support of Zulus by predicting a lunar eclipse and presenting it as an act of magic.[86] Similarly, the white protagonist of Rudyard Kipling's *Kim* (1901) grows into an adept servant of the British Empire through his ability to shape-shift through many disguises and apparent identities.[87] Kipling's earlier novel *The Jungle Book* (1894) also troubles the trajectory from primitive deception to civilised truthfulness. Animals in the tale exhibit various adaptive appearances, such as the python Kaa, who fascinates his prey with a 'dance' of hypnotic movements and 'could make himself look so like a dead branch or a rotten stump that the wisest were deceived, till the branch caught them'.[88] The boy Mowgli sometimes seems above such tricks, remaining unaffected by Kaa's dance. However, he ultimately conquers the jungle by using his intelligence to contrive a more complex trick, trapping the tiger Shere Khan in a valley amid a buffalo stampede. Such narratives framed western civilisation as not transcending deception but deploying it as a tool of domination.

It was also questionable whether 'civilised' humans' supposed higher intellect rendered them less gullible. Certainly, despite Spencer's claims, metropolitan modernity and international capitalism produced new opportunities for predatory deceit. Food adulteration scandals shared headlines with anxieties about 'Confidence Men' and imposters such as Arthur Orton of the Tichborne case.[89] Reflecting on such modern deceptions, the American showman P. T. Barnum opined: 'humbug is an astonishingly wide-spread phenomenon – in fact almost universal'.[90] Ruskin argued that humans viewed the world in a qualitatively different way to animals, seeing moral and spiritual significances behind literal phenomena. Yet the gaze of scientific materialism transcended primitive gullibility by suppressing hermeneutics, examining nature's objects as signifiers of nothing more than themselves. Perhaps, instead of being too literal, primitive interpretation was not literal enough, straying from concrete facts into imagined causes. The abstraction that enabled humans to outfox their rivals also created new possibilities of delusion from religious superstition to philosophical dogmatism. In *Middlemarch* (1872),

The Evolution of Deception

George Eliot's narrator noted sardonically 'this power of generalising which gives men so much the superiority in mistake over the dumb animals'.[91] Humans could overcome animals' basic misreadings only to be duped by more rarefied fancies. Indeed, a year after the publication of Eliot's novel, Friedrich Nietzsche would write that the ideal of truth was humankind's greatest delusion of all.[92]

Some late Victorians came to view deception as not just an inevitable evil, but, perhaps, fundamental to civilisation. John Kucich has shown that the period's novelists often problematised the ideal of sincerity, suggesting that the complex nature of modern life sometimes made hypocrisy necessary.[93] In 1874, the philosopher Henry Sidgwick and statesman John Morley both published books arguing that lying could be ethically justified.[94] Five years later, the satirical novelist Samuel Butler used imagery of adaptive appearance to explore the paradox of ethical dishonesty. Writing a series of hoax letters to the *Examiner* on the subject of clergymen concealing their religious doubts, Butler made up one correspondent who argued that such lying made people happy and (perhaps more crucially) provided clergymen with a living. Observing insect crypsis and plovers feigning injury, Butler's speaker echoes Nietzsche's as-yet-unpublished thoughts, commenting:

> What is truth? for there is no such thing apart from the sayer and the sayee. There is that irony in nature which brings it to pass that if the sayer be a man with any stuff in him, provided he tells no lies wittingly to himself and is never unkindly, he may lie and lie and lie all the day long, and . . . his lies will become truths as they pass into the hearer's soul.[95]

Butler's tongue-in-cheek reasoning gave voice to a widespread middle-class intuition that societal stability might require some massaging of the facts, particularly regarding religion. Concomitant with visions of the working class as primitive interpreters was the notion that they needed to be shielded from matter that they might harmfully misconstrue.[96] Authors such as Kingsley and Stephen feared that atheism would induce anarchy among the lower orders (see Chapters 1 and 5). By the 1890s, Benjamin Kidd was arguing explicitly that irrational religion was necessary for making the masses subordinate their individual interests to 'the larger interests of the longer-lived social organism to which they belong'.[97] H. G. Wells can be seen to toy with such thinking in his novel *Love and Mr. Lewisham* (1899) through the character of the spiritualist charlatan Chaffery. When the protagonist Lewisham exposes Chaffery's fakery and accuses him of 'cheating' people, Chaffery retorts that communities are held together and the progress of civilisation made possible only by vigorous and sometimes even, violent Lying; that the Social Contract is nothing more or less than a vast conspiracy of human beings to lie to and humbug themselves and one another for the general Good. Lies are the mortar that bind the savage Individual man into the social masonry.[98]

Although Lewisham dismisses Chaffery's words as sophistry, he can offer no counter-argument, leaving the text haunted by a Nietzschean nihilism. Indeed, Nietzsche argued that codes of politeness and social 'finesses' derived from the animal tendency to hide, to the extent that 'the entire moral phenomenon' derived from 'those instincts which teach us to search for food and to avoid our enemies'.[99] Far from transcending nature's deceptions, civilisation was perhaps built upon them.

Primitive 'mimicry' instincts could also be imagined more positively as the foundation of sympathy. In his famous lecture *Evolution and Ethics* (1893), Thomas Henry Huxley declared: 'Man is the most consummate of all mimics in the animal world . . . And there is no such another emotional chameleon. By a purely reflex operation of the mind, we take the hue of passion of those who are about us, or, it may be, the complementary colour.'[100] Yet, although Huxley's image frames primitive mimicry as the source of morality, it also relativises such moral passions, reducing them to adaptations to one's (social) environment. Huxley's sympathetic mimicry could easily shade into Le Bon's dangerous, emotional contagion.

This study traces the tensions between these competing narratives about adaptive appearance and human development through the writings of Charles Kingsley, Grant Allen and Thomas Hardy. Kingsley and Allen often envisaged primitive deception being overcome by the disinterested eye of science. Both authors tended to focus their moral opprobrium on the deceived as much as the deceivers, associating gullibility with stupidity, narrow-mindedness and egoism. Their idealisations of science sometimes made them ambivalent about fiction, viewing it as a kind of trick upon naïve, undiscriminating readers. Their notions of progress toward truth and transparency also became stuck upon the classic is/ought problem, conflating the ethics of what ought to be with the ontology of what is.[101] Allen, particularly, struggled to reconcile the optimistic Spencerian model of progressive veracity with a less teleological, Darwinian vision of increasingly complex deception. Hardy's fiction further problematised these themes by suggesting that deceit was both primitive and advanced, and could be altruistic and moral as well as selfish (such as through the noble lie). Adaptive appearance not only impacted on such large-scale visions of

Adaptive Appearance and Identity

In her study of membranes in science and culture, Otis posits that cell theory interacted with ideas of the self as having an '"inside" and "outside"'.[102] Similarly, discourse of adaptive appearance connected with notions of selfhood as inner essence versus outer display, authentic original versus derivative copy. Charles Taylor observes that Romantic thinkers such as Jean-Jacques Rousseau and Johann Gottfried Herder promoted 'expressive individuation', assuming that each individual possessed a unique inner nature that yearned to be nurtured and expressed.[103] Such thinking placed self-realisation in conflict with society as, Rousseau complained, the civilised man 'only knows how to live in the opinion of others, so that he seems to receive his consciousness of his own existence merely from the judgment of others concerning him'.[104] Artistic development shifted from imitating masters to escaping their influence.[105] Liberal economics also valorised individuality, framing the individual as a self-sufficient unit. John Stuart Mill's *On Liberty* (1859) celebrated expressive individuality and scorned social conformity as 'ape-like imitation'.[106] Victorians thus often revered individuality and sincerity as desirable, specifically masculine, traits. The ideal of manly sincerity framed discourse as a struggle between individual and environment, fitting with the Carlylean view of history as the actions of 'Great Men'.[107] While the weak yielded to and imitated external influences, the strong imposed their unique inner natures on the world.

This orientation reacted upon the biology of adaptive appearance to produce a general 'mimeophobia' (in Margot Norris's words) or, more generally, cryptophobia.[108] Protective mimicry clashed with both Romantic and economic individualism since it seemed to suppress self-expression and allowed the weak to survive parasitically, harming the efficiency of the social organism. Wallace's depiction of mimetic animals as 'weak and decaying' implied that they were on a downward path to extinction. Nietzsche traced a direct line from such animal mimicry to an imitative 'instinct' among the downtrodden human

> lower classes, who had to survive under changing pressures and coercions, in deep dependency ... always adapting themselves again to new circumstances, who always had to change their mien and posture, until they learned gradually to turn their coat with *every* wind and thus virtually to

> *become* a coat – and masters of the incorporated and inveterate art of eternally playing hide-and-seek, which in the case of animals is called mimicry.[109]

Nietzsche presents the chameleonic poor as the antithesis of his will to power. Instead of dominating their environment, they blend in with it, sacrificing their agency and inner natures. Such degenerate mimicry could be attributed to any groups regarded as unproductive such as criminals or the mentally ill. Cesare Lombroso claimed that criminals tended to fake mental illness in a survival strategy that resembled insect mimicry. In a summary of the criminologist's work in English, Lombroso's daughter Gina explained: 'Naturally inferior individuals tend to imitate characters of a terrifying nature (psychic in this case) which serve to protect them and enable them to compete with others who are better equipped for the battle of life.'[110] Mimicry seemed to prelude passing out of existence altogether. As Chapter 2 shows, Kingsley exploited such thought to salvage a sense of moral symbolism in nature, arguing that God ultimately punished deceitfulness through degeneration.

Yet the mimeophobic belief in an individual inner essence was countered by another philosophical tradition that regarded selfhood as relational rather than essential. Georg Wilhelm Friedrich Hegel argued that people formed identities through interacting with and being recognised by others. Although Hegel's development of mind involved rejection of and alienation from society, social relations nonetheless remained necessary in this process of self-actualisation.[111] His point that no identity could exist without the recognising gaze of others was reinforced by the biology of adaptive appearance. Even the appearance of aposematic creatures, standing out boldly from their surroundings, was highly rhetorical, protecting them from injurious attacks. Darwinian sexual selection further problematised fitness, suggesting that mate selection was directed by signs of fitness rather than fitness per se. Traits that served this semiotic function could be useless or even detrimental to individual survival; as Darwin wrote, the 'long train of the peacock and the long tail and wing-feathers of the Argus pheasant must render them more easy prey to any prowling tiger-cat'.[112] There could be no transparent self-display since display necessarily opened a gap between appearing and being. The imagined essence of fitness became lost in a play of signs, while organisms could win recognition only by conforming to semiotic conventions.

These tensions shaped critical writings by various fin-de-siècle authors who used adaptive appearance as a model for understanding creativity,

Adaptive Appearance and Identity

conformity and identity. Chapter 5 shows that Leslie Stephen, Theodore Watts-Dunton and Walter Pater all figured literature as a scene of protective mimicry with mediocre authors echoing popular styles and sentiments. This logic justified their elitist reverence of originality as a rare gift appreciated by few and exhibited by even fewer. Yet they also withdrew from advocating unrestrained expressive individualism, which they associated with degenerate solipsism and social destabilisation. Oscar Wilde stood out from these contemporaries by celebrating expressive individualism irrespective of its disruptiveness.

Adaptive appearance also coloured representations of group identity, which often similarly involved mimeophobic or cryptophobic ideals of self-sufficiency and authenticity. Scholars have noted how patriarchal, imperialist discourse reduced women and non-whites to mimics, echoing their white, male superiors from colonial servants to female typists.[113] Romanes averred that female 'inferiority displays itself most conspicuously in a comparative absence of originality'.[114] The anthropologist James Hunt stated that African 'savages' were incapable of invention, and 'What civilization they had was imitated.'[115] Such dichotomies between creative white masculinity and imitative non-whiteness or femininity fitted into a broader framework of biological fitness and self-sufficiency versus weakness and dependence. Just as insect mimicry was conceptualised as the refuge of the weak, nature was imagined as having 'armed women with the power of deception for her protection'.[116] Similarly, imperialist discourse frequently depicted races from the Irish to Indians as dishonest due to their supposed inadequacy.[117]

However, authors from subaltern groups sometimes appropriated tropes of adaptive appearance to subvert imperialist logic or explore possible routes to empowerment. In his 1904 play *John Bull's Other Island*, George Bernard Shaw inverted stereotypes of Irish dishonesty by presenting English disingenuousness as a form of adaptive mimicry. The Irishman Larry Doyle compares bumbling English colonialists to camouflaged caterpillars. As the caterpillar blends in with leaves, Doyle claims, the Englishman 'makes himself look like a fool, and eats up all the real fools at his ease while his enemies let him alone and laugh at him for being a fool like the rest. Oh, nature is cunning, cunning!'[118] Doyle's observation is confirmed in the play when his English colleague charms the residents of an Irish village into signing away their homes to be developed into a resort. Conversely, in 1897, the Irish author Alice Stopford Green invoked protective mimicry to reflect on women's historic marginality in literature. In an environment dominated by men, she wrote, the female author 'seeks safety in what is known in Nature as protective mimicry'. Instead of expressing women's inner 'eccentricity', 'originality' and 'passion', she claimed, women's writing had cloaked itself under the conventional 'maxims of duty and the laws of business'.[119] If historical oppression had suppressed such groups' authentic natures, then perhaps social and political liberation would help to revive them. This logic underlay the writings of Israel Zangwill and Charlotte Perkins Gilman, who portrayed Jews and women as forced into protective mimicry and sexual display, respectively, by their weak positions in society (see Chapter 6). Zangwill and Gilman imagined their identity groups casting off these adaptive appearances in tandem with the building of a Jewish state and the emancipation of women.

Overview of Chapters

The scope of *Mimicry and Display* could have easily been broadened to include many a text in the period that thematised imitation, imposture or self-presentation from Mary Elizabeth Braddon's *Lady Audley's Secret* (1862) to Henry James's *The Portrait of a Lady* (1880–1881). However, this book is not about mimicry or appearance in general but the construction of appearances as biological phenomena, and the ways in which this biologization of appearance responded to, and helped to shape, wider cultural currents. Adaptive appearance was a niche area within evolutionary theory, so I have focussed mainly on authors who were demonstrably aware of phenomena such as protective coloration, mimicry and sexual and aposematic display. Kingsley, Allen, Hardy, Stephen, Watts-Dunton, Pater, Wilde, Zangwill and Gilman all make explicit references to such phenomena or invoke its associated terminology in their writings, even if only occasionally. This places my argument for an interchange between the discourse of adaptive appearance and wider literary themes on a firmer basis than would be possible in a study of appearance in general. Charles Dickens, for example, was much occupied by appearance in human society, but he showed little interest in considering it more expansively as a factor in other species' fates. When his novella *The Battle of Life* (1846) makes a rare reference to the 'insect deriving its delicate colour from harmless leaves and herbs', it does so only to frame nature as innocent decoration, painted by 'the Almighty Hand' to please human tastes.[120] By contrast, the principal literary authors in this study were all intrigued by the idea that non-human economies of appearance could shed new light on human ones.

Overview of Chapters

Bates, Wallace and Poulton obviously command attention due to their central roles in the development of theories of adaptive appearance. Thayer's work (and its controversy) illustrates starkly how adaptive appearance problematised the increasing opposition of science and art, and the correlative binary of subjective and objective knowledge. Among defenders of natural theology, Kingsley stands out as a widely read author. He was also closely connected with England's scientific naturalists, corresponding with Darwin, Huxley and, most importantly for this study, Bates. His obsessions with truth and divine immanence, and his wish to preserve ecclesiastical authority in scientific matters, render him a revealing case study in the pressures that adaptive appearance placed upon natural theology. As authors of fiction, Allen and Hardy were both particularly well versed in the details of evolutionary theory, and their tales persistently thematise the adaptive dynamics of appearance (indeed, Allen also wrote popular science articles about crypsis). Stephen, Watts-Dunton, Pater and Wilde were similarly fascinated by evolution, finding in it a new materialist paradigm for understanding life, art and culture. Zangwill and Gilman were also knowledgeable about the biology of adaptive appearance and integrated it deeply into their visions of racial and sexual identity. For these reasons, and for their considerable fame in the period as author-activists, both warrant sustained attention.

The narratives of human deception, imposture, misperception or self-representation discussed here do not always directly invoke crypsis, aposematism or sexual display. Nonetheless, I suggest that these tropes still often haunt the texts via plots and rhetoric that rhyme strikingly with the logic of adaptive appearance, particularly in its relativising of meaning and identity. Devin Griffiths has observed that analogy, as a method of analysis, can be 'harmonic' as well as 'formal': while formal analogy is 'top-down', explaining one phenomenon in terms of another, which is already understood, harmonic analogy is 'reciprocal'.[121] By juxtaposing different phenomena, such analogies change our understanding of both. Beyond authors' direct allusions to adaptive appearance, this study offers several such harmonic analogies. For example, Allen's chameleonic criminals resonate suggestively with his descriptions of animals' 'false pretences'. Hardy's fictive meditations on the unreliability of bodies as indexes of ancestry evoke the deception of the cuckoo. Yet such analogising reveals divergences as well as convergences, showing how these authors imagined ways in which humans might transcend nature's deceptive dynamics. Juxtaposing the biology of adaptive appearance and literary explorations of the roles of appearance in human life thus reveals the richness and complexity of

24   Introduction

mimicry, concealment and display as pervasive tropes through which Victorians envisioned life.

This study's historical range begins in the 1850s, when Bates and Wallace were finding hundreds of mimetic species in the tropics and Kingsley was trying to balance ideas of adaptive deception with the world as a divine text in *Glaucus: Wonders of the Shore* (1855). It ends in 1915 when Gilman published *The Dress of Women* and *Herland*. I could have begun earlier in the nineteenth century when naturalists such as William Kirby, William Spence and John O. Westwood began to popularise examples of insect crypsis.[122] I could also have included Modernist engagements with adaptive appearance and culminated in Hugh Cott's landmark work *Adaptive Coloration in Animals* (1940).[123] However, I have chosen a narrower time span in order to focus on one network of theorists of adaptive appearance, and the context they inhabited (although Poulton and Thayer were decades younger than Bates and Wallace, they corresponded extensively with the latter). This approach enables me to explore the rich suggestiveness and multi-discursivity of adaptive appearance as it suggested different implications to different audiences. This study mostly focusses on Britain but crosses the Atlantic to include authors such as Thayer and Gilman, whose engagements with crypsis and sexual selection reflect the international culture in which these ideas developed.

Chapter 1 contends that theorists of adaptive appearance argued for its reality by recreating it on the page, and these simulations were influenced by Ruskin's theories of art and perception. I argue that Bates's and Wallace's evidence partly relied on anecdotes of their encounters with cryptic organisms. These anecdotes vacillated between impressionistic immediacy and detached analysis of how nature's illusions were produced, paralleling Ruskin's concepts of 'innocence of eye' and suspended judgement. I posit that later theorists of adaptive appearance further blurred the lines between science and art by simulating the phenomenon through illustrations and descriptions which drew on conventions of ekphrasis. The incompatibility of such efforts with hardening, dichotomous definitions of science and art was demonstrated most forcefully in Thayer's work, and the controversy it excited.

Chapter 2 explores how adaptive appearance clashed with theological views of nature as a divine text, demonstrated through close readings of Kingsley's writings. I argue that Kingsley struggled to reconcile adaptive deceptions with his belief that nature illustrated God's love of truth. This conflict sometimes led Kingsley to relocate divine truthfulness in the scientific study of nature. Envisaging science as a providential development, he presented nature's mendacity as a sort of trial though which humans could attain godly truthfulness. However, I suggest that Kingsley resisted fully abandoning the idea of moral symbolism in nature since doing so would undermine the clergy's authority in scientific matters. At stake for him was not only God's truthfulness but also nature's capacity to express transcendent meanings (and churchmen's authority to interpret them).

Chapter 3 examines interactions between theories of adaptive appearance and depictions of human deception through close readings of crime fiction by Allen. I show that tales such as 'The Curate of Churnside' (1884) and *The Devil's Die* (1887–1888) involve criminals outwitting their would-be detectors and, thus, extend the logic of evolutionary crypsis into modern human life. I suggest that these stories reflect the disturbing view that society progresses only to enable subtler forms of deceit. However, Allen's *An African Millionaire* (1896) is more conflicted, fluctuating between this pessimistic outlook and Spencer's optimistic one that humanity would evolve beyond deception through altruism and science. The latter possibility was tempered for Allen, though, by the capitalist status quo, which seemed to him rather to perpetuate short-sighted egoism. As an author by trade, Allen sometimes worried that he was supporting these conditions rather than combating them.

Chapter 4 proposes that adaptive appearance helped Hardy to think through his complex views about the morality (or amorality) of human deception. I suggest that Hardy's fiction often followed pastoral tradition, which associated humans' natural instincts (and, by extension, rural society) with honesty. Yet this tendency was contrasted with an acutely Darwinian view of humans' appearances and actions evolving to deceive as amoral adaptations. This wavering sense of deceit perhaps being as much natural as artificial problematises moral responsibility as Hardy equivocates on whether his characters' misrepresentations are intentional or not. I argue that Hardy's tales replace the ethical binary of truth and falsehood with the opposing biological tendencies of egoism and altruism, and judge deceptive acts according to which of these urges motivates them more. I further contend that Hardy's fiction applies the logic of adaptive appearance to humans through plots involving the misidentification of bodies, namely in judgements of kinship. I suggest that Hardy frames these misidentifications as products of egoism, thus salvaging the possibility of ethical progress. Humans will avoid such mistakes, he suggests, by learning to value people equally, regardless of genealogy.

Chapter 5 considers how concepts of crypsis energised discussions of individualism and creativity in fin-de-siècle cultural criticism. I argue that

26   Introduction

such discourse was often torn between competing biological models, presenting authors as both individual organisms struggling to survive and nodes in the larger organism of society. Stephen and Watts-Dunton invoked crypsis to attack bad faith in religious apologetics and imitativeness in literature, respectively. However, both also viewed culture as a collective entity that might be undermined by too much chaotic individualism, causing them to suggest that some 'mimicry' was necessary. Pater's art criticism took a different view, concluding that humans inevitably mimicked their surroundings, so that non-conformist self-actualisation inhered in constructing one's surroundings from eclectic sources. I argue that, while Pater withdrew from the radical implications of such mimetic individualism, his pupil Wilde embraced them. Wilde's writings on art idealised conspicuous obscurity as the paradoxical essence of individualism. By calling for art that defied straightforward signification, Wilde exposed the contradictoriness of cryptophobia and its implicit instrumentalist view of art.

Chapter 6 traces the themes of blending in and standing out in representations of group identity. I argue that crypsis and sexual advertisement shaped Israel Zangwill's and Charlotte Perkins Gilman's political writings, supplying models for articulating the marginalisation of Jews and women, respectively. However, adaptive appearance also undermined the essentialist logic of their visions of Jews and women recovering their authentic selves. Zangwill suggested that Jews' assimilative invisibility followed from their historical precariousness. Yet his vision of Jewish reinvigoration as an unmasking clashed with the realisation that all identities were mediated and relational. Gilman drew on sexual selection theory to critique women's fashion, arguing that women's subjection forced them into impractical clothing, sacrificing physical fitness to attract male providers. In contrast to Zangwill's model of powerful conspicuousness, she envisaged women becoming liberated by blending in with men, losing the exaggerated femininity forced upon them by the patriarchy. As with Zangwill, though, Gilman's ideal of authentic self-display was undercut by the reality, shown by adaptive appearance, that identities were always already mediated by signs and, so, inauthentic.

Finally, the Conclusion reflects on how this study intervenes in contemporary discussions in cultural theory. I suggest that current uncertainties about how to define signification and subjectivity beyond humans echo tensions that were manifest in nineteenth-century discourse on adaptive appearance. I also argue that *Mimicry and Display* offers a new angle on debates about the politics of visibility and mimicry. I explore the

Overview of Chapters

implications of my findings for discussions about the historic separation of science and the humanities, and possible future paths of research in the cultural and literary history of adaptive appearance. I further reflect on how the study's themes resonate with contemporary concerns in literary criticism about empirically robust forms of reading, and the relevance of adaptive appearance to environmentalist politics.

CHAPTER I

Seeing Things
Art, Nature and Science in Representations of Crypsis

Now, I want to know what the appearance is to an eagle, two thousand feet up, of a sparrow in a hedge, or of a partridge in a stubble-field. What kind of definition do these brown spots take to manifest themselves as signs of a thing eatable; and if an eagle sees a partridge so, does it see everything else so.

—John Ruskin[1]

We argue from the effect produced by certain colours, forms, or attitudes upon ourselves, to the effect that must be produced upon other animals.

—Edward Bagnall Poulton[2]

Crypsis was introduced to Victorian readers as a peculiarly visual phenomenon, which had only to be seen to be believed. Bates described protective mimicry as 'a most beautiful proof of the truth of the theory of natural selection'.[3] This visual emphasis fitted with the Linnaean tradition of reducing the animal world to static, isolated objects which could be minutely described, pictured and classified, seemingly from a transcendent vantage point.[4] Yet crypsis also problematised vision, foregrounding the limitations of sight and suggesting that nature shaped itself around these limitations. Lacking methods for systematically recording animals' behaviour in the wild, advocates of the theory were forced to place themselves and their readers in the position of the animals supposedly deceived. When naturalists saw deceptive resemblances between animals, they shared the imagined views of those animals' predators and prey, as Ruskin and Poulton advocate in the epigraph quotations above. Researchers such as Bates regarded these perceptual experiences as evidence for crypsis, and strove to simulate them through words and pictures. Such representations resisted the hardening dichotomy between science and the arts, mixing material facts with aesthetic impressions and evocations. I argue that these texts followed a pattern of perceptual self-scrutiny and suspended judgment that had been articulated by John Ruskin. As in Ruskin's discussions of nature's appearances, Bates, Wallace and others' representations of crypsis shifted between raw, momentary impressions and detached, methodical analysis of how these impressions were created.

However, this approach to knowledge as visual revelation clashed with the developing discourse of objectivity. This discourse framed the truths of the universe as lying beyond human perception and, therefore, associated scientific authority with the establishment of facts independent of sensory experience. The tensions between ideas of subjectivity and objectivity, science and art, would come to a head when the American painter Abbott Henderson Thayer intervened in discussions of crypsis in the 1890s and 1900s, sparking bitter controversy. I will outline how traditions of natural-history writing and Ruskin's art theory legitimised impressionistic representations of crypsis before showing how Bates, Wallace and others developed them. I trace the use of anecdote in Bates and Wallace's articles and memoirs on crypsis, arguing that personal narrative constituted an important form of evidence for the phenomenon. I also suggest that zoologists sought to simulate crypsis as a sensory-cognitive experience for readers through illustration and accompanying text which drew on conventions of ekphrasis. The uncertainty and debate excited by such representations of crypsis reflected the problematic status of subjectivity in late nineteenth- and early twentieth-century zoology (both human and animal).

Victorian Zoology and the Art of Seeing

Philosophers had long argued over where to draw the line between objective facts and sensory impressions. Galileo Galilei and Locke had distinguished between objects' intrinsic 'primary' features, such as their shape and size, and 'secondary' ones, such as their smell or colour, which varied between perceivers.[5] George Berkeley and Immanuel Kant questioned this distinction, positing that all knowledge was ultimately subjective.[6] Johann Wolfgang von Goethe later stressed that the mind constructed colours rather than discovering them.[7] Alexander von Humboldt had embodied holist epistemology in his memoirs of exploration, which treated his aesthetic responses to nature as inextricable from empirical understanding of it. Nature's appearances, Humboldt wrote, 'stand alike in an ancient and mysterious communion with the spiritual life of man', and he sought to capture this communion in evocative, poetic descriptions of natural environments.[8] Moreover, Humboldt dwelt repeatedly on the illusions that nature produced in the human observer.[9]

30   Art, Nature and Science in Representations of Crypsis

In jungles, he observed, 'by a continual interlacing of parasite plants, the botanist is often led to confound the flowers, the fruits, and leaves, which belong to different species'.[10] Humboldt's conviction that these impressive qualities of nature were important in their own right led him to praise art and literature for capturing them and thus 'linking together the outward and the inward world'.[11]

This view of nature as inherently subjective would combine in early to mid-nineteenth-century British art criticism with empiricist interests in accurately depicting nature's objects as they appeared in situ regardless of representational ideals or conventions.[12] John Constable commented in 1836, 'Painting is a science, and should be pursued as an inquiry into the laws of nature.'[13] Two decades later, Ruskin proposed a 'science of aspects' that would combine the 'accuracy' of material science with art's 'love of beauty' and 'tenderness of emotion'. The latter two faculties were by no means 'unscientific', he declared, for it was 'as much a fact' that organisms 'produce such and such an effect upon the eye or heart ... as that they are made up of certain atoms or vibrations of matter'.[14] Ruskin found this 'science of aspects' demonstrated in the paintings of J. M. W. Turner, who had been influenced by Goethe's colour theory.[15] Such art, Ruskin claimed, represented an 'innocence of eye' that drew attention to the partiality and contingencies of sight.[16] The mind's ability to fill in the gaps in ocular sensation and construct a unified, three-dimensional world was, in Ruskin's view, both illuminating and blinding. He suggested that, by inferring objects via salient features, humans navigated the world without really seeing it either in detail or in totality. 'Having once come to conclusions touching the signification of certain colours', he wrote, 'we always suppose that we *see* what we only know, and have hardly any consciousness of the real aspect of the signs we have learned to interpret.'[17] His programme for educating the eye, therefore, involved unlearning the shortcuts by which the mind avoided perceiving things in full. Ruskin contended that the greatness of artists like Turner lay in their ability to switch between conventionalised human vision and 'a sort of childish perception of these flat stains of colour, merely as such, without consciousness of what they signify'.[18]

Caroline Levine argues that Ruskin encouraged viewers to reflect on the gap between the world and its representation through 'a process of doubting and testing'.[19] Such aesthetics of epistemological 'suspense' cohered closely with the logic of scientific induction which sought constantly to test inferences. Ruskin can be seen using this aesthetics of suspense to study the animal world in an 1872 lecture when he recalls

Victorian Zoology and the Art of Seeing

an encounter with a snake in a wood. His description of the event is punctuated by perceptual gaps as the creature repeatedly eludes his gaze. Walking along, Ruskin 'came suddenly on a small steel-grey serpent, lying in the middle of the path', which, in spite of its position, had been invisible on his approach. After holding his gaze for a moment, 'with an almost imperceptible motion, it began to withdraw itself beneath a cluster of leaves', where

> it gradually concealed the whole of its body. I was about to raise one of the leaves, when I saw what I thought was the glance of another serpent, in the thicket at the path side; but it was the same one, which having once withdrawn itself from observation beneath the leaves, used its utmost agility to spring into the wood; and with so instantaneous a flash of motion, that I never saw it leave the covert, and only caught the gleam of light as it glided away into the copse . . . What was, indeed, a matter of interest to me, was just that which would have struck a peasant, or a child; – namely, the calculating wisdom of the creature's device.[20]

Ruskin's anecdote foregrounds the partiality of vision, which is fundamental to the 'device' of the snake's concealment, enabling it to hide both behind physical objects and in the gaps in spectators' perceptions. Ruskin has to withdraw from his immediate senses and infer the animal's movement away from him to dispel the illusion of one snake becoming two. His designation of the trompe l'oeil as a 'device' evokes Paleyan environmental adaptation, emphasising the intersection of science and art. The snake's artistic effect is also a factor in its material survival. Ruskin grasps and conveys this biological truth through his embodied encounter with the animal, live and in the wild. The anecdote justifies his scepticism of closet and laboratory science with its magnifying instruments and anatomical dissections. Ruskin complained that such studies were the work of 'human bats; men of semi-faculty or semi-education, who are more or less incapable of so much as seeing, much less thinking about, colour'.[21] Technical precision came at the cost of a narrowing of vision. As Dinah Birch comments, 'Ruskin undoubtedly thought that there was much to be learned from looking at animals. But the lessons were embodied in the living creatures, entire and whole, and not in the dissection of their corpses.'[22]

Bates and Wallace also spent much time looking at animals and contrasting their appearance as live (often moving) entities in the wild with their static specimens. Like Humboldt and Ruskin, these investigators offered impressionistic anecdotes of their field experiences as a form of data about organisms. Also like Ruskin, they challenged the authority of

32   Art, Nature and Science in Representations of Crypsis

the museum and laboratory with their measuring and amplifying instruments. By abstracting organisms from their living conditions, such hyper-controlled, artificial spaces might be said to obscure the networks of visibility that these life forms inhabited in the wild. As in Ruskin's aesthetics of suspense, researchers of crypsis switched between sensation and intellect, opposing nature's immediate appearances in situ to the deeper realities revealed by systematic comparisons and theorising. However, Ruskin differed from these investigators by imagining the science of aspects as an end in itself, discovering moral and spiritual significance in nature. Describing in 1869 how various species 'mocked' one another, Ruskin asserted that such matters were irrelevant to Darwinism: 'The aesthetic relations of species are independent of their origin.'[23] Yet theorists of crypsis denied this distinction, studying nature's appearances in order to infer non-humans' perceptual relations with each other. Instead of preserving vision from the Darwinian struggle, the science of aspects could be used to absorb the former into the latter.

Such appeals to embodied, phenomenal experience ran counter, though, to growing scientific concerns about the unreliable and inferential nature of sensory perception. Narratives of 'rambling' naturalists were haunted by the danger of visual 'skimming' and misapprehension.[24] James Krasner remarks that Darwin's diaries of his *Beagle* voyage frequently linked excitement at nature's beauties with 'the failure or confusion of physical vision'.[25] Of Brazilian rainforests, Darwin wrote:

> The delight one experiences in such times bewilders the mind, – if the eye attempts to follow the flight of a gaudy butter-fly, it is arrested by some strange tree or fruit; if wanting an insect one forgets it in the stranger flower it is crawling over, – if turning to admire the splendour of the scenery, the individual character of the foreground fixes the attention.[26]

The vivid immediacy of personal impressions came at the cost of scientific detachment.

The emerging ideal of objectivity associated epistemic authority with observation independent of personal perceptions. This ideal shaped the development of the museum closet and later laboratory as spaces of work characterised by exact measuring instruments and standardised methods. As early as 1807, Georges Cuvier had argued that his systematic studies of specimens in the cabinet yielded insights which were impossible in the field. The traveller's perceptions were 'broken and fleeting', Cuvier wrote, so that, 'it is only really in one's study that one can roam freely throughout the universe'.[27] Dorinda Outram notes that, for Cuvier, 'true knowledge of the order of nature comes not from the whole-body experience of crossing the terrain, but from the very fact of the observer's *distance* from the actuality of nature ... [O]ut of distance comes truth'.[28] The cabinet and laboratory could be considered more reliable sources of scientific knowledge than the field because they enabled naturalists to abstract from the sensory excess of nature, examining its objects precisely and methodically.[29]

Similarly, through the century, zoologists developed conventions of schematic illustration in order to enhance the factual authority of their images. While lavish illustration became a hallmark of popular natural history (particularly that written by women), nascent professional science often distrusted such aestheticised images for appealing to sensory pleasure and emotion.[30] By contrast, abstract images such as diagrams, maps and cross sections presented themselves as purely factual, unaffected by personal feelings or perceptions.[31] By reducing animals to static, mechanically measured objects isolated from their environments, schematic specimen images sought to minimise the subjectivity of zoologists.[32]

The effort to exclude perception also bred suspicion of language and narrative. While words remained necessary for communicating data and explaining theories, they often seemed to scientific investigators dubious tools requiring strict control.[33] This outlook was reflected by a growing emphasis in scientific writing on the 'precision' of 'quantifications' and 'technical vocabulary'.[34] William Whewell defended technical terms as a means of minimising the interference of personality in the transmission of 'intellectual' matter. 'Common language', he complained, reflected 'common knowledge' in which intellect was hopelessly mixed up with 'affection' and 'fancy'.[35] The personal nature of literary style and anecdote seemed to be opposed to science's aim of generating impersonal knowledge.[36] Darwin echoed this point when he wrote (to Bates of all people), 'I think too much pains cannot be taken in making the style transparently clear and throwing eloquence to the dogs.'[37]

Ideals of impersonal scientific observation and representation contrasted with views of the arts as emphatically subjective. Matthew Arnold argued that, while science focussed on the external world of 'fact', poetry was wholly internal, so that, 'for poetry the idea is everything; the rest is a world of illusion'.[38] In the same decade that he mooted a 'science of aspects', Ruskin also presented science and art as dichotomous activities concerned with incompatible objects. 'Science deals exclusively with things as they are in themselves', he wrote, 'and art exclusively with things as they affect the human sense and human soul. Her work is to portray the

34   Art, Nature and Science in Representations of Crypsis

appearance of things. The work of science is to substitute facts for appearances, and demonstrations for impressions.'[39] Ruskin conceptualised art as the revelation of a privileged seer in contrast to science's methodical fact-gathering.

Nonetheless, Ruskin's epistemology of suspense still had some continuity with the objectivity ideal, stressing critical distance from one's perceptions; and this logic underpinned Bates's and Wallace's use of anecdote in their writings on crypsis in the 1860s. While empathising with the animals that they imagined being duped by cryptic resemblances, the naturalists also abstracted from this naïve perspective to analyse how these deceptive appearances were produced. The tension between Ruskinian vision and depersonalised objectivity would become more explicit as naturalists sought to recreate crypsis for their readers through illustrations and analyse these images as though they were works of art.

Anecdotes of Crypsis: Sensory Immediacy versus Scientific Distance

In 1892, the London anatomist Frank Evers Beddard noted that naturalists' observations of insect mimicry had developed a conventional narrative mode. 'Every naturalist traveller', Beddard wrote, 'appears to have some instance to relate of how he was taken in by a protectively-coloured insect. These stories are told with a curiously exaggerated delight at the deception, and often with a framework of details tending to throw the deception into still greater prominence.'[40] Such anecdotes were rhetorically powerful, acting as a form of 'virtual witnessing' to the claimed phenomenon.[41] Bates and Wallace had placed anecdotes at the heart of their writings on animal crypsis. As in Ruskin's science of aspects, the naturalists' narratives of discovery shifted between immediate perceptions and detached reflection, examining nature as a system of visual effects. Their sensory responses to crypsis substituted for the reactions of animals that were supposedly duped by such appearances, a bestial 'innocence of eye'. Like Ruskin, they strove to establish the effects of nature's forms upon viewers as generalisable facts rather than mere personal taste, matching their responses with those of others. Bates and Wallace also abstracted from such qualia, deconstructing how nature formed these suggestive appearances similarly as Ruskin had deconstructed painters' techniques. This sense of abstraction was accentuated by anecdotes of indigenous people being deceived. Such supposed primitive viewers acted as foils to the perspicacious naturalists, and exemplified the naïve vision which crypsis depended on and science claimed to see through. Bates's and Wallace's writings thus shifted between

Sensory Immediacy versus Scientific Distance

the narrative perspectives of immediate, naïve impressions and detached, anatomical descriptions of organisms and their environmental relationships.

In his earliest writings on protective mimicry, Bates stressed the importance of first-hand field encounters with the organisms concerned. Resemblances between distinct species, he wrote, 'produce the most effective deception when the insects are seen in nature. The faithfulness of the resemblance, in many cases, is not so striking when they are seen in the cabinet.'[42] The cabinet (and the images it produced) also elided the variability of these creatures' appearances due to movement and perspective. Noting the likenesses between Amazonian *Ithomia* and *Leptalis* butterflies, Bates wrote: 'In fact I was quite unable to distinguish them on the wing.'[43] Cabinet workers like Cuvier would have regarded the flora, terrain, climate and neighbouring species mainly as obstacles to accurate anatomical scrutiny. Conversely, Bates suggests that these surrounding details are fundamental to understanding the creature's (in)visibility. 'When we see a species of Moth which frequents flowers in the daytime wearing the appearance of a Wasp', Bates wrote, 'we feel compelled to infer that the imitation is intended to protect the otherwise defenceless insect by deceiving insectivorous animals, which persecute the Moth, but avoid the Wasp.' The same explanation, he argued, applied to 'insects and other beings [which] are assimilated in superficial appearance to the vegetable or inorganic substance on which, or amongst which, they live'.[44] Bates implies that the zoologist hunting creatures in the field sees them much as other animals probably see them, as ambiguous shapes and colours. Anecdotes of being deceived by such 'superficial appearance[s]' were therefore vital clues to the deceptive dynamics that obtained between the environments' native organisms.

Bates's anecdotes emphasise the analogy between human and animal vision by describing his impressions in carnal, emotionally charged terms. Recall his statement, quoted in the Introduction, that 'staggering' insect mimicries 'fill us with . . . astonishment'. Bates stated that, whenever he realised he had confused an *Ithomia* for a *Leptalis*, 'I could scarcely restrain an exclamation of surprise.'[45] The naturalist's amazement stems partly from the dissonance between his intellectual understanding that the forms are different species and his sensory perceptions of them as one and the same. While anatomical studies of the captured specimens reveal their differences, the roving eye of the field naturalist remains gullible, as Bates confesses: 'Although I had daily practice in insect-collecting for many years, and was always on my guard, I was constantly being deceived by

36   Art, Nature and Science in Representations of Crypsis

them when in the woods.'[46] Bates's repeated mistakes, in spite of his knowledge to the contrary, echo the thousands of animal misperceptions which his theory assumes. He further reinforces the emotional, pre-rational nature of such responses through an anecdote of 'a very large Caterpillar' which emerged from some foliage and 'startled me by its resemblance to a small Snake'. Bates's immediate senses process the creature's dilatable segments, black eye-like spots and keeled scales as 'a poisonous or viperine species', an impression that is dispelled only by later, rational scepticism and testing of his perceptions.[47] Other snakes blend invisibly into the texture of bark before springing suddenly into the foreground. 'It was rather alarming', Bates recalls, 'in entomologising about the trunks of trees, to suddenly encounter, on turning round ... a pair of glittering eyes and a forked tongue within a few inches of one's head.'[48] Bates's depiction of the snake as a succession of body parts accentuates the fragmentariness of perception, which builds the semblance of unitary objects through bundles of impressions. Like Ruskin's art criticism, Bates's anecdotes foreground the disjuncture between represen-tation and reality, and the need to doubt and test appearances.

Bates's anecdotes of jungle illusions further alternated between imagined naïve animal apprehension and scientific scepticism through use of poetic simile and metaphor. In his memoir The Naturalist on the River Amazons (1863), he recalls seeing one butterfly, camouflaged by 'wings transparent as glass', flying low over foliage so that it 'looks like a wandering petal of a flower' (I, 104). Bates's imagery becomes more phantasmagorical when he encounters snakes which blend in with the vegetation. 'I was wandering one day amongst the green bushes of Gua-jara', he writes,

> when I was startled by what appeared to be the flexuous stem of a creeping plant endowed with life and threading its way amongst the leaves and branches. This animated liana turned out to be a pale-green snake, the *Dryophis fulgida*. Its whole body is of the same green hue, and it is thus rendered undistinguishable amidst the foliage of the Guajara bushes, where it prowls in search of its prey, tree-frogs and lizards. (I, 184)

The mention of the snake's usual victims at the end of the passage encourages the reader to imagine these animals' perceptions as similar to the naturalist's, mystified by a strangely animated plant. Bates's dramatic rendering of such moments frames them as vicarious insights into the experience of prey tricked by camouflage. Another snake catches him off guard by resembling 'a piece of whipcord', while he almost steps on a boa

Sensory Immediacy versus Scientific Distance

constrictor before watching it move away 'like a stream of brown liquid flowing over the thick bed of fallen leaves' (I, 184). Such figurative language highlights Bates's recognition of the difference between literal affinities and mere resemblances, a distinction supposedly beyond animals' comprehension. Humans' self-conscious mimesis enables them to doubt nature's misleading appearances.

Bates further complicates his narrative perspective by blending his descriptions of cryptic creatures in the field with subtle details of their structures revealed by later anatomical studies. He signals this spatiotemporal disorientation by shifting from the active to passive voice. One variety of disguised moth 'is seen flying about' on open commons, and another is found 'expanded over the trunks of trees, to the bark of which it is assimilated in colour' (I, 104). Further moths 'wear the livery of different species of beetles' by 'hold[ing] their wings in repose, in a closed position over their bodies, so that they look like the wing-cases of the beetles they deceptively imitate' (I, 105). The naturalist-narrator's depiction of the creatures in their habitats is shaped by his retrospective knowledge of their true affinities, gained through examination of captured specimens. Bates thus creates a temporal disjunction between his experiences hunting the insects and his narrative about them, eliding his initial misapprehensions. It is other animals that these insects deceive, not the naturalist.

Bates's omniscient description creates a sense of dramatic irony as the naturalist-narrators' knowledge of animals' deceptive mechanisms contrasts with the ignorance of their victims. Spiders 'double themselves up at the base of leaf-stalks, so as to resemble flower-buds, and thus deceive the insects on which they prey' (I, 106). A fly 'deposits the egg it has otherwise no means of providing for' in a bee's nest, bypassing the bees' defences thanks to its 'deceptive resemblance' to the bees (I, 298). Combining his emplaced impressions of Amazonian wildlife with retrospective reflection and taxonomic studies, Bates envisions a phenomenon (protective mimicry) which, by its very nature, could never be seen in situ. This shifting between sensory immediacy and intellectual detachment is most pronounced in Bates's description of his encounters with a hawk moth which resembles a hummingbird. Bates's initial misperceptions of the insect in the field merge with his later examinations of captured specimens:

> Several times I shot by mistake a humming-bird hawk-moth instead of a bird. This moth['s] . . . manner of flight, and the way it poises itself before a flower whilst probing it with its proboscis are precisely like the same actions of humming-birds. It was only after many days' experience that I learnt to distinguish one from the other when on the wing . . . The resemblance . . .

38 Art, Nature and Science in Representations of Crypsis

> strikes one even when both are examined in the hand. Holding them sideways, the shape of the head and position of the eyes in the moth are seen to be nearly the same as in the bird, the extended proboscis representing the long beak. At the tip of the moth's body there is a brush of long hair-scales resembling feathers, which, being expanded, looks very much like a bird's tail. But, of course, all these points of resemblance are merely superficial. (I, 181–182)

Bates's narration moves from fleeting impressions to prolonged, microscopic scrutiny which pierces through the 'superficial' similarities that previously beguiled him. While detailing the intricate parts of the resemblance, Bates's description is omniscient. What unreflective animals would see as a 'long beak' and 'a bird's tail' the zoologist recognises as an 'extended proboscis' and 'a brush of long hair-scales'. Bates offers not a single, raw snapshot of the creature but a condensation of many experiences with it, from sightings to capture, dissection and classification.

Bates further evokes the need for distanced vision through ambivalent depictions of indigenous Amazonian people in relation to crypsis. Unlike European colonists who master nature through farming and science, the natives in his travel memoir seem rather nature's subjects. Of one tribe, Bates writes: 'They had no fixed abode, and of course made no plantations, but passed their lives like the wild beasts, roaming through the forest, guided by the sun' (II, 126). The natives' closeness to nature sometimes seems to render them gullible to its deceits. Regarding the hawk moth which mimics the hummingbird, Bates reports that the natives

> firmly believe that one is transmutable into the other. They have observed the metamorphosis of caterpillars into butterflies, and think it not at all more wonderful that a moth should change into a humming-bird ... The negroes and Indians tried to convince me that the two were of the same species. 'Look at their feathers', they said; 'their eyes are the same, and so are their tails.' This belief is so deeply rooted that it was useless to reason with them on the subject. (I, 182)

Bates frames the non-whites' magical explanation of the resemblance as a more elaborate version of the delusion which animals form upon seeing the hawk moth. Lacking the naturalist's detachment, they trust their first impressions and ignore subtler, contradictive details. Similarly, in his paper on mimicry, Bates reports that, after encountering the caterpillar that resembled a snake, 'I carried off the Caterpillar and alarmed every one in the village where I was then staying, to whom I showed it.'[49] Although the natives' misperceptions replicate those of Bates, only he penetrates its deceptive exterior, discovering its true identity and the components of its

Sensory Immediacy versus Scientific Distance

illusion. This epistemic superiority is proved by his ability to frighten the natives with the specimen. To know nature's illusions is to master and reproduce them at will, and such mastery seems to require a measure of distance.

Yet, conversely, the natives' propinquity to Amazonian wildlife can also render them wise to its tricks and, perhaps, natural deceivers themselves. In his memoir, after a close encounter with a puma which blends in with the forest due to its deer-like hue, Bates remarks that 'the natives call it the Sassu-arana, or the false deer ... The hunters are not at all afraid of it, and speak always in disparaging terms of its courage' (I, 176–177). In this case, the natives' experiential knowledge of the local wildlife puts them at an advantage over the startled Bates, who is caught off guard by the puma's cryptic coat. The natives' close association with nature's imitations is echoed in their own talent for mimicry, a common marker of savagery in Victorian anthropological discourse. In a festive masquerade, Bates writes, 'They get up capital imitations of wild animals ... and act their parts throughout with great cleverness' (I, 89). At a similar event, Bates reports that one native disguised as a tapir made 'such a good imitation of the beast grazing, that peals of laughter greeted him wherever he went. Another man walked about solitarily, masked as a jabirú crane ... and mimicked the gait and habits of the bird uncommonly well' (II, 205). While Bates praises such performances as proof of the natives' ingenuity, these images nonetheless place them in obvious parallel with the animal mimics of Bates's studies. Bates further aligns the natives with nature's deceptive economy by describing their witch doctors as deceitful parasites. He writes that the witch doctor or 'pajé' diagnoses every illness without an obvious origin as

> caused by a worm in the part affected. This the pajé pretends to extract; he blows on the seat of pain the smoke from a large cigar ... and then sucks the place, drawing from his mouth, when he has finished, what he pretends to be the worm. It is a piece of very clumsy conjuring ... The pajé was with difficulty persuaded to operate whilst Senhor Joaõ and I were present. I cannot help thinking that he, as well as all others of the same profession, are conscious impostors, handing down the shallow secret of their divinations and tricks from generation to generation. (II, 132–133)

Bates's contemptuous dismissal of the pajé's supposed magic highlights again his sceptical detachment as a European naturalist. By contrast, for the gullible natives, seeing is believing. Although Bates is physically present to witness such deceits, he is able to recognise them as such only by

40   Art, Nature and Science in Representations of Crypsis

abstracting from his perceptions, realising their unreliability. Nonetheless, the dichotomy between naïve savagery and sceptical western science is destabilised by the apparent calculation of the pajé. Such fakery was, perhaps, not so different to the spiritualist séances that Bates's colleague Wallace would come to believe in.

Wallace's anecdotes of crypsis similarly shift between immediate impressions and detached analysis of how these impressions are produced. As in Bates's memoir, Wallace's *Malay Archipelago* (1869) depicts his field experiences of animal illusions as substitutes for the imagined perceptions of other species. Of one camouflaged butterfly, Wallace writes: 'I often endeavoured to capture it without success, for after flying a short distance it would enter a bush among dry or dead leaves, and however carefully I crept up to the spot I could never discover it until it would suddenly start out again and then disappear.'[50] The insect so closely resembles 'a dead leaf attached to a twig' that it vanishes before the naturalist's eyes. 'At length I was fortunate enough to see the exact spot where the butterfly settled', he continues, 'and though I lost sight of it for some time, I at length discovered that it was close before my eyes' (I, 130–131). Wallace's wavering vision of the butterfly reconstructs the experience of other animals chasing it as it enters their view while flying and vanishes when settled. Like Bates, Wallace then dispels the illusion by distancing his narration from the moment he is taken in. Having 'captured several specimens on the wing', he is able to delineate the minute structures of their body which produce the likeness. 'The end of the upper wings terminates in a fine point, just as the leaves of many tropical shrubs and trees are pointed', he explains, while from top to bottom 'there runs a dark curved line exactly representing the midrib of a leaf, and from this radiate on each side a few oblique marks which well imitate the lateral veins' (I, 132). In such passages, Wallace's description shifts from blurred impressions to sharp anatomical detail, reflecting the movement from sighting in the field to long, methodical scrutiny of static specimens.

Like Bates, Wallace sometimes shows his scientific detachment from nature's appearances by presenting indigenous people as contrastingly too close to nature to view it correctly. Although natives help Wallace to find and capture specimens, he suggests that they fail to understand the deceptions involved. Noting that some birds protect their eggs by burying them under earth and rubbish, he admits that the natives always know which mounds contain eggs. Yet he claims that they attribute these eggs to some magical agency, 'for it almost always appears to them the wildest romance to be told that it is all done by birds' (I, 156). Despite living

Sensory Immediacy versus Scientific Distance

alongside the birds, the natives, in Wallace's view, are unable to perceive them correctly because they lack systematic methods of observation. Their vision is acute but unreflective. Similarly, in an article published two years before, Wallace relates his encounters with uncannily deceptive stick insects, only to contrast his distanced, rational view with that of a fooled native. One specimen, he states, 'was covered over with foliaceous excrescences of a clear olive green colour, so as exactly to resemble a stick grown over by a creeping moss'. Writing of himself in the third person, Wallace continues: 'The Dyak who brought it assured him it was grown over with moss although alive, and it was only after a most minute examination that he could convince himself it was not so.'[51] Although the Dyak servant was able to distinguish the stick insect from its surroundings, he is still taken in by its cryptic exterior, through which only the detached, impersonal eye of science can pierce.

Wallace also catalogued other people's reactions to mimetic animals in an effort to enhance the perceived objectivity of the anecdotal evidence. This technique mirrored his defence of spiritualism, which he honed in the 1860s, at the same time as his theories of crypsis. Wallace asserted that too many had reported the same experiences for supernatural phenomena to be simply delusions. He stressed the diversity of testifiers, suggesting that the objective reality of the supernatural was confirmed by aristocrats, men of science and uneducated labourers all reporting the same events.[52] Likewise, his writings on crypsis cite other naturalists' accounts of being startled by uncanny resemblances, as well as the general reactions of local human populations. For example, he references John Abbot and James Edward Smith's observations of the American 'hickory-horned devil' caterpillar which resembled and moved like a rattlesnake. Wallace takes on trust Abbot and Smith's racially loaded claim that local 'negroes believe it to be as deadly as a rattlesnake'.[53] It is, of course, ironic that Wallace believed so strongly that eyewitness testimony proved supernatural phenomena while, simultaneously, his work on crypsis revolved around vision's fallibility. However, the two research areas were also similar, in Wallace's view, since both involved abstracting from (seemingly) visible phenomena to theorise unseen causes. 'To a race of blind men, how utterly inconceivable would be the faculty of vision', Wallace declared, and, in the same way, there might be 'intelligences uncognisable directly by our senses, and yet capable of acting more or less powerfully on matter'. Wallace regarded individual sightings of spirit manifestations as data for him to develop his theory of 'etherial motion' beyond human perception.[54] Equally, while the naturalist finds corroborative use in black

42   Art, Nature and Science in Representations of Crypsis

fieldworkers' reputed perceptions of a caterpillar, he also claims to transcend their limited view, revealing the hidden processes behind it.

Wallace sometimes exhibits this distanced perspective on crypsis by depersonalising his depictions of animals deceiving humans, shifting from individual witnessing to generalised models of perception. Of the ptarmigan bird, he writes: 'Its summer plumage so exactly harmonizes with the lichen-coloured stones among which it delights to sit, that a person may walk through a flock of them without seeing a single bird.'[55] The naturalist abstracts from specific examples to authoritatively define the typical human field of vision. The colours of a South American goatsucker 'so closely resemble the rock and sand that it can scarcely be detected till trodden upon'.[56] While Wallace's description seems to transcend humankind's imperfect perceptions, it also emphasises the role of embodied experience in achieving such transcendence. Tactile encounter with the bird contradicts his initial, visual impressions, and thus enables him to abstract from them, understanding the creature as an object of perception. The same shifting narrative orientation is discernible in Wallace's reference to beetles 'which generally rest on the midrib of a leaf, and the naturalist often hesitates before picking them off, so closely do they resemble pieces of bird's dung'.[57] By identifying the insects *as insects* before depicting the observer mistaking them for excrement, Wallace seems to penetrate the illusion with a God's-eye view. Yet, as the passage suggests, he unmasks the beetles' superficial appearance only by touching them. As in Ruskin's contrasting of paintings with real vegetation, scientific distance proceeds, paradoxically, from coming closer to the sources of one's senses and representations (artistic or mental).

No amount of aggregation or generalisation, however, could transcend the subjective, and so disputable, basis on which such evidence rested. At the turn of the century, at Brown University, the mimicry-sceptic Alpheus Spring Packard listed numerous experts' statements that they had seldom or never witnessed birds pursuing any kind of butterfly.[58] Packard offered these testimonies as evidence for his Lamarckian theory that butterflies' resemblances proceeded from them sharing common environments, not from such resemblances deterring predators. He further inverted the implications of anecdotal observation by using the technique to suggest that observations of birds chasing butterflies were exceptional instead of commonplace. 'For the first time in my life', he wrote, 'having for over forty years observed and collected insects ... I actually saw a bird chase a butterfly ... I watched the procedure ... from the piazza of my summer cottage on the shores of Casco Bay, Me., at noon of a bright sunny day early in July, 1901.'[59] The form of the momentous anecdote here functions to highlight the event's atypicality, whereas natural selection depended on steady, regular patterns of interspecies activity. Similarly, Packard countered the claims that model species were unpalatable by performing his own smell and taste tests, which he related in the article. Of one supposedly repellent butterfly, he wrote: 'I caught one, and pinching it between my fingers I could not detect any odor, nor could three other members of my family ... I tasted two pieces cut from the middle of the abdomen, but the taste was hardly perceptible and not unpleasant, neither bitter, acid, or in any way pungent.'[60] Personal testimony could be used to undermine crypsis as well as support it, similarly as it was used both to defend spiritualism and to claim to expose it as charlatanry.

Equally, as with spiritualism, anecdotes of animal misperception could be dismissed as only evidence of the observers' wild imaginations. Beddard's mention of 'exaggerated delight' in naturalists' crypsis anecdotes signalled his discomfort with such evidence, implying that it was distorted by the naturalists' feelings. Beddard argued that the widespread existence of crypsis had been too hastily asserted and that personal anecdotes were insufficient to settle the matter. Perhaps to counter such doubts, Bates, Wallace and others sought not just to narrate their experiences of crypsis but also to recreate these experiences for their readers through visual and verbal evocation. Such ekphrastic simulations borrowed concepts and techniques from art to encourage readers to reflect on sight as a process. In this way, paradoxically, they sought to objectify crypsis by foregrounding its subjective mechanics.

Crypsis Illustration and Ekphrasis

Naturalists in the period frequently attempted to simulate crypsis on the page, combining illustrations with ekphrastic analysis. As with the anecdotes, such simulations strove to replicate animals' (or, rather, zoologists') fleeting impressions of crypsis while also replicating the naturalist's anatomical scrutiny which pierced through the illusions. This extension of the Ruskinian aesthetics of suspense can be seen in the illustrations in Bates's and Wallace's travel memoirs, and became more pronounced in the writings of the Oxford entomologist Edward Bagnall Poulton. Poulton evoked crypsis by analysing animals' appearances as ingenious combinations of lines, colours and shades which tricked the eye. Ruskin's emphasis on variety, illusion and perceptual contingency had established a formal mode which, I argue, Poulton used to analyse examples of crypsis. Schooled in the latest knowledge of optics, Poulton viewed crypsis as a matter of aesthetic effects which could be parsed in a similar manner to the mimesis of a painting. However, this systematic approach could not remove the inherent subjectivity of investigating nature's appearances, and Poulton's efforts amplified the friction between the field and ideals of objectivity.

The difficulty of visualising crypsis was evident in its earliest theorisations. Bates's 1862 paper on protective mimicry contained only one set of images: coloured plates of butterfly mimics and models arranged in rows on a plain background (see Fig. 2). The anatomical detail of these pictures

Fig. 2   Plate from Henry Walter Bates, 'Contributions to an Insect Fauna of the Amazon Valley. Lepidoptera: Heliconidæ', *Transactions of the Linnean Society of London*, 23 (1862), 495–566, plate LV.

showed the fine differences between species, but Bates's argument was more concerned with their gross resemblances when seen momentarily and in motion. Ironically, while Bates complains in the paper of zoologists focussing too much on cabinet specimens instead of appearances in the wild, his illustrations replicate this problem. In his memoir, a similar excess of precision dogs the illustration of the hawk moth which mimics the hummingbird. E. W. Robinson's engraving tries to give the impression of the model and its mimic being glimpsed in the wild as they hover side-by-side in front of a flower (see Fig. 3). The caption further wrong-foots the reader by listing the hummingbird and hawk moth in opposing sequence to their positions in the left and right of the picture. However, the image is still clearly based on anatomical drawings which have been superimposed upon a scenic background. This static picture accentuates the differences between the species which the motion of their wings would blur out. The illustration is too accurate to effectively simulate a first-hand sighting in the field.

However, not all of Bates's illustrations were so anatomical. Alongside Robinson, Bates also employed Joseph Wolf and Johann Baptist Zwecker to make more dramatic images of key moments in the narrative. The most

Fig. 3   Hawk moth and hummingbird. From Henry Walter Bates, *The Naturalist on the River Amazons*, 2 vols. (London: J. Murray, 1863), I, p. 181.

Fig. 4   Frontispiece to Bates, *The Naturalist on the River Amazons*, I.

notable of these is the frontispiece which depicts Bates's anecdote in which he shot a toucan, only to be ambushed by the rest of its flock which had been concealed by vegetation (see Fig. 4). When the wounded toucan squawks for help, Bates writes:

> In an instant, as if by magic, the shady nook seemed alive with these birds, although there was certainly none visible when I entered the

Crypsis Illustration and Ekphrasis

thicket . . . After killing the wounded one I rushed out to fetch my gun, but, the screaming of their companion having ceased, they remounted the trees, and before I could reload, every one of them had disappeared. (II, p. 344)

More impressionistic than the previous image, this one attempts to visualise the 'magic' moment when the toucans abruptly reveal themselves. Wolf and Zwecker suggest the birds' elusiveness by distributing them across different depths, so that some are half-hidden by shadow and blend in with nearby vegetation. In the background, the forest melts into a dark blur, heightening the impression of embodied, subjective perception rather than technical accuracy. The illustration coheres with Ruskin's arguments for visual art which reflected nature as imperfect vision constructed it. 'The true work represents all objects exactly as they would appear in nature', Ruskin had written in 1854, while the 'false work' 'represents them with all their details, as if seen through a microscope'.[61] Wolf and Zwecker's non-microscopic view cohered with a wider tendency in popular natural history illustration, paralleled in Pre-Raphaelite art, which sought to combine painstaking accuracy with sophisticated visual effects.[62] The non-panoramic nature of the image is further emphasised by Bates appearing as a character in the frame. Instead of gazing down on organisms and seeing through their superficial camouflage, Bates is dazzled by it, just like other animals, and his readers. This levelling of naturalist and animal is reinforced by Bates's and the toucans' opposing lines of sight. Bates is not only limited in his perceptions but an object of perception himself, demonstrated by the toucans' ability to attack and then hide from him.

Wallace similarly tried to simulate crypsis as a phenomenological experience through illustration. His anecdotes in *Malay Archipelago* about the camouflaged Kallima butterfly which posed on branches like a leaf were accompanied by two juxtaposed figures of the insect by T. W. Wood. The images depict the butterfly both in conspicuous flight and in almost-invisible repose (see Fig. 5). Perched on a tropical shrub with its wing's folded, only the insect's tiny, just protruding legs differentiate it from the surrounding leaves upon close inspection.

The problem remains of the static, anatomically accurate image rendering the insect too precisely so that the reader is unlikely to be fooled like the field naturalist. However, the illustration replicates the effect of the disguise more successfully than Bates's examples, since the disguise depends on stasis rather than motion. Further, the figure of the butterfly

Fig. 5   Camouflaged Kallima butterfly, from Alfred Russel Wallace, *The Malay Archipelago*, 2 vols. (London: Macmillan & Co., 1869), I, p. 131.

with wings spread sets an example of salience that contrasts with the perching, cryptic butterfly, which emerges only under finer scrutiny. Wallace's text guides this simulated experience for the reader, as he declares: 'All these varied details combine to produce a disguise that is so complete and marvellous as to astonish every one who observes it' (I, 132). Readers need not rely on the testimonies of naturalists, Wallace implies, but can experience the illusion themselves.

Wallace further bolstered the credibility of such simulations by presenting the recognition and imitation of crypsis as a matter of artistic sensitivity. In an 1867 article aimed at popularising crypsis, Wallace commentated on a series of illustrations by his long-term collaborator T. W. Wood.

Wood was a member of the diminishing artist-naturalist class, and enjoyed Darwin's and Wallace's respect as a fellow-theorist of protective coloration.[63] In the article, Wallace suggests that Wood's combination of scientific induction and artistic intuition enables him to capture the essence of crypsis and recreate it for the reader. Wallace once praised Ruskin as a writer and thinker 'in the front rank' whose 'influence is increasing' and 'ought to increase'; and Wallace's depiction of Wood perhaps owes something to Ruskin's notion of the visionary artist.[64] Like Ruskin's Turner, Wallace's Wood is no passive copier but a privileged seer. Wallace writes:

> We owe the discovery of one of the most beautiful examples of 'disguise' in a native insect to the talented young artist and close observer of nature who has furnished the illustrations for this article. He tells us that one fine afternoon in May, being overtaken by a shower, he sought shelter under a hedge ... While observing the light and elegant forms of these plants, he noticed what appeared to be a small bunch of flowers projecting beyond the rest; and a closer examination led him to the interesting discovery that our beautiful little 'Orange-tip,' one of the gayest and brightest of our native butterflies, was reposing among these flowers in such a manner as to gain a complete protection by its resemblance to them.[65]

The passage is not merely an anecdote of Wood's perceptions but an origin story for his illustration. Wallace implies that Wood's developed aesthetic sense as a 'talented young artist' enhances his insight into nature's displays, and enables him to share his discovery pictorially with others. Discriminating organisms' 'light and elegant forms' occurs in tandem with detecting their disguises, which are not merely functional but also 'beautiful'. By imitating the appearances of natural objects, the artist might offer useful insights into the ways that these objects imitate each other.

The analogy between art and nature would be further developed by Poulton in *The Colours of Animals* (1890). The book summarised research on animal coloration for a wide readership, and documented many forms of crypsis, all formed by natural selection. Although Poulton used frequent illustrations, his innovation lay in verbal description which presented crypsis as an aesthetic phenomenon. He applied to animals a similar style of ekphrasis as that which Ruskin had applied to art, analysing the subtle optical tricks which created each illusion. Working in Oxford for decades, Poulton recalled having 'regularly attended' the Slade Professor's lectures 'and greatly enjoyed them'. He even lent a hand in 1874 when Ruskin rallied scholars to dig a road at the city's outskirts to improve the lives of local workers.[66]

Art, Nature and Science in Representations of Crypsis

Introducing his book, Poulton echoed Ruskin's calls to look at nature afresh, declaring that 'my object ... is ... to stimulate observation' (vii). This meant challenging conventional representations of nature as Ruskin had done. Ruskin observed, counterintuitively, that moss attained its brightness through contrasting 'dark hollows' around each tiny leaf which 'makes them much clearer and brighter than if they were of dead green'.[67] Poulton similarly argued that, while some animals' exteriors may seem conspicuous, 'We cannot appreciate the meaning of the colours ... apart from their surroundings, because we do not comprehend the complicated artistic effect of the latter. A caterpillar in the midst of green leaves may have many brilliant tints upon it, and yet may be all the better concealed because of their presence' (25). As in Ruskin's commentaries, Poulton's natural environments present the viewer with a dazzling kaleidoscope of shapes, tones and depths, which cannot be taken in all at once. 'The appearance of the foliage is really less simple than we imagine', he states: 'for changes are wrought by varied lights and shadows playing upon colours which are in themselves far from uniform' (25). As Ruskin stressed the minute differences between every leaf, Poulton draws attention to vegetative diversity to show how insects blend in with it. 'Dead and withered leaves are not all alike', Poulton comments; 'they may be almost any shade of brown, grey, or yellow ... Similarly the under sides of the wings of the butterfly are excessively variable, the different colours and markings only agreeing in that they all represent some familiar appearance presented by withered or decayed leaves' (53). Like Turner's paintings, protective resemblances mirror nature's variety and harness the impressionistic dynamics of vision.

Poulton's ekphrastic commentaries parse the elements of an animal's appearance to reveal how the ensemble tricks the eye. For example, as Turner contrived the appearance of distance, a butterfly's round pupa mimics the flatness of a leaf. On the pupa's sloped points, Poulton states,

> the whole effect of the roundness is neutralised by increased lightness, so disposed as just to compensate for the shadow by which alone we judge of the roundness of small objects. The degree of whiteness is produced by the relative abundance of white dots and a fine white marbling of the surface, which is everywhere present mingled with the green ... The degree of lightness produced in this way exactly corresponds to the angle of the slope, which, of course, determines the depth of the shadow. (38)

Poulton cannot help describing such effects in the language of artistic invention. The dissipating shade, he writes, constitutes a 'beautiful and simple method' for producing 'the impression' of flatness, 'a process exactly analogous to stippling' (38). Poulton again resembles an art critic, praising the aesthetic and evocative power of a work, when he describes a caterpillar which disguises itself as an impenetrable cocoon. The creature 'is covered with very long beautiful hair which is brilliantly white, and bends over on all sides so as to touch the leaf, forming a wide margin round the caterpillar. Hence all we can see is an oval convex mass of a substance resembling white cotton wool, an appearance very suggestive of a cocoon' (43–44). Poulton's aesthetic appreciation of the larva's beauty and brilliance cements the association between crypsis and artistic contrivance. While the effect may be experienced subjectively, its causes can be analysed into objective formal properties. Further, the zoologist discovers subtle details behind the eye-catching foreground, like a critic instructing an audience in how to view a painting. 'The caterpillar's body is almost invisible', he writes, 'but on looking carefully we can just make out a dim curved shape beneath the white covering, just as a caterpillar or chrysalis appears through the walls of its cocoon' (44).

Poulton's connoisseur-like scrutiny of animals' appearances seems to yield further rewards as he describes resemblances of a 'General' or 'Variable' order. Some of his subjects shape-shift into the likenesses of numerous inanimate things. For example, one caterpillar 'resembles such very different objects as a twig and the excrement of a bird, the whole difference being made by a modification of attitude alone' (33). Elsewhere, moths resemble 'splinters of wood' and 'surfaces of rock' (58). Some resemblances also seem highly nuanced and specific, such as moths that rest upon leaves with their wings spread out. 'In this position', Poulton asserts, 'they forcibly suggest the appearance of birds' excrement which has fallen on to a leaf from a great height, and has therefore become flattened into a wide patch'. He again adopts the authority of the Ruskinian art critic, dictating not only the ideas that an image evokes but also the feelings. He assures the reader (somewhat bizarrely) that, 'In spite of a faithful resemblance to such an object, these moths possess very great beauty' (57). This authoritative stance is necessary as Poulton's examples of resemblance become increasingly elaborate. He claims to have seen a moth resting on a plant which 'forcibly suggested the appearance of a small piece of leaf which had been accidentally torn, and had turned brown and curled up, remaining attached to the uninjured part of the leaf by one end' (33). Another moth, he assures us, is 'very perfectly concealed by resembling a broken piece of decayed and lichen-covered stick'. Poulton pre-empts the objection that a stick cut off cleanly at both ends is not a common natural

52   Art, Nature and Science in Representations of Crypsis

object by hypothesising natural causes which could produce such a stick. 'The purple and grey colour of the sides of the moth', he writes, 'together with the pale yellow tint of the parts which suggest the broken ends, present a most perfect resemblance to wood in which decay has induced that peculiar texture in which the tissue breaks shortly and sharply, as if cut, on the application of slight pressure or the force of an insignificant blow' (57). Poulton implies that sceptics who deny the existence of such objects fail to appreciate nature's immense variety.

However, such arguments underlined the dangerously speculative and subjective nature of Poulton's ekphrasis, based on his personal responses to nature's displays, which he assumed were mirrored in other species. Although verbal and visual simulations of cryptic deception were striking and memorable, they did not prove that crypsis was a factor in evolution. Of course, Bates's, Wallace's and Poulton's claims rested upon not only human encounters with animals but also exhaustive bio-geographic surveys of species populations across environments. The strongest evidence for adaptive crypsis lay in the correlations found between these geographic distributions and varieties' morphological differences. Nonetheless, rival zoologists argued that different species came to resemble each other through hybridisation or diet, climate or other environmental conditions.[68] Conversely, the anti-evolutionist J. O. Westwood wrote that the theory of insects acquiring such resemblances through natural selection required 'a wide stretch of imagination' beyond reasonable probability.[69] Darwin's *Origin* had been attacked as 'a mere idle play of the fancy', and crypsis was even more prone to this charge, depending on the hypothetical perceptions and actions of thousands of animals.[70]

Further, the rise of laboratory physiology had induced a new imperative for investigators to avoid 'anthropomorphism', and public objections to vivisection encouraged practitioners to challenge the assumption that animals experienced the world the same as humans.[71] Hence, the naturalist John Lubbock observed: 'The familiar world which surrounds us may be a totally different place to other animals. To them it may be full of music which we cannot hear, of color which we cannot see, of sensations which we cannot conceive.'[72] With this in mind, physiologists began to study the different structures of animals' eyes and to design experiments to test their visual capacities such as light sensitivity.[73] Eventually, such studies would complement ethological investigations of adaptive appearance, but, from a late Victorian perspective, they highlighted the speculative anthropomorphism of Poulton's methods. Beddard thus chastened Poulton for too hastily pronouncing animals mimetic or cryptic. 'We must get out of the way of judging instances of this kind from the human standpoint', Beddard counselled, complaining that 'there is always too great a tendency to endow animals with senses exactly similar to those possessed by ourselves'.[74] Non-humans' vision might be both too acute to be fooled (such as in birds) and not acute enough for such resemblances to affect their actions (such as in insects).

From the late 1860s onward, occasional experiments were made in aviaries and menageries, testing animals' reactions to mimetic and model insects. However, such studies were tentative and did not always support crypsis.[75] A question mark thus hovered over the theory which no amount of vivid images or descriptions could dispel. France's most famous fin-de-siècle entomologist Jean-Henri Fabre always denied the existence of protective mimicry, comparing it to the 'naïve belief' of children fancying they saw a monster that 'mixed himself up with a boulder, a tree trunk, a bundle of boughs'.[76] In 1913, the American ornithologist Waldo Lee McAtee similarly excoriated Poulton's suggestion that the lobster moth (*Stauropus fagi*) mimicked a spider when in a certain attitude. This supposed resemblance was in addition to its other likenesses to an ant, earwig, lobster and leaf noted by previous observers. McAtee sneered:

> Thus the larva of *Stauropus* is supposed to mimic more or less closely, objects in both the vegetable and the animal kingdoms ... representatives of five orders ... It is evident that the predaceous foes of *Stauropus*, had they only the imaginative powers of its human observers, could have a banquet of many diverse courses, each of which would be merely *Stauropus* in disguise.[77]

Poulton fought such scepticism throughout his long career, even into the 1930s.[78] By presenting crypsis as a pseudo-artistic matter, he had gifted sceptics with the accusation that his investigations were too subjective to qualify as science. Poulton parried this criticism by designing experiments to observe animals' reactions to different colours in controlled environments.[79] However, art and science would be blurred still more by another investigator whose work foregrounded the subjectivity involved in simulating crypsis on the page.

Animal Canvases: The Strange Case of Abbott Handerson Thayer

Abbott Handerson Thayer was a New England painter who came to believe that natural selection evolved all animals to blend in with their environments. He developed this theory by photographing and painting animal specimens against natural backgrounds, claiming to expose the complicated optical effects that concealed them. In a process he called 'counter-shading', Thayer argued that animals' bodies transitioned from darker to lighter tones with increasing exposure to sunlight, reducing their visibility. Thayer suggested animals' appearances were also obliterated by 'disruptive coloration': strongly contrasting patterns which diminished their outlines. Further, he hedged that such invisibility was not always constant; rather, animals vanished at crucial moments when viewed from particular vantage points.[80] Thayer's efforts to depict such 'concealing coloration' through text and image were paradoxical 'attempts to visualize invisibility'.[81] He pursued this aim by inverting artistic conventions that highlighted objects to achieve the opposite effect: counter-shading, for example, was chiaroscuro reversed, contriving the appearance of flatness instead of depth. Thayer thus argued that animals evolved into literal 'pictures' of their surroundings. Thayer was a much-sought-after portrait artist, having painted such luminaries as Mark Twain and Henry James, and he leveraged his connections to propound his ideas about animal coloration to both zoological specialists and the wider public. He evidenced his theories through demonstrations with mocked-up specimens and backgrounds, and published articles in the American Ornithologists' Union's journal *The Auk*, as well as a book on animal concealment co-written with his son Gerald.

At the heart of Thayer's theorising lay the Ruskinian notion of the artist as a privileged seer. Thayer insisted that his artistic eye gave him a unique insight into crypsis. His intervention demonstrated the potential of crypsis to blur imagined boundaries between science and art. Yet the controversy of his work also showed how scientific authority at the turn of the century was increasingly defined by the rejection of the epistemic value of vision (and thus art). While Bates, Wallace and Poulton tried to corroborate their crypsis theories with bio-geographic or experimental data, Thayer's claims about animals' perceptions were wholly inferred from his own. Regarding the apprehension of crypsis as equivalent to proof of it, he made increasingly far-fetched claims about animals' supposed invisibility. His work thus highlighted, ad absurdum, crypsis theory's incompatibility with the ideal of objectivity due to its conspicuous reliance on phenomenological experience.

Thayer's writings further extended Ruskin's epistemology of suspense, foregrounding the gap between representational conventions and nature. This anti-conventionality can be seen in his first article on protective coloration, published in 1896. Through a succession of photographs,

Fig. 6   Grouse specimen in cabinet, from Abbott Handerson Thayer, 'The Law Which Underlies Protective Coloration', *The Auk*, 13:2 (1896), 124–129, p. 126.

Thayer claimed to demonstrate the effect of counter-shading on a grouse. The images depict the specimen first in a cabinet, then posed, as though alive, among vegetation (see Figs. 6 and 7).

Guiding the reader's viewing, Thayer explains that the bird's inconspicuousness in the latter picture shows how its black and white patterns cancel out the 'gradation of light and shade, by which opaque solid objects manifest themselves to the eye'.[82] Further photographs show the grouse more and less conspicuous as Thayer poses it in different positions and paints its body parts darker or lighter. Thayer's manipulations of the bird visualise the imagined operation of natural selection: individuals whose exteriors stand out from the background will be seen, and killed, while those that blend in go unremarked, and survive. Artifice is required to

Fig. 7   Grouse specimen in vegetation, from Thayer, 'The Law Which Underlies Protective Coloration', p. 126.

make wild animals conspicuous because nature works constantly against conspicuousness. Indeed, the distinction between nature and artifice breaks down as Thayer frames his actions as exposures of nature's illusion-making. Painted with new colours, he writes, the grouse 'is completely unmasked'.[83] Paradoxically, in Thayer's formulation, wild animals can be seen truthfully only when falsified by art.

Thayer undermined the art/nature dichotomy, though, by claiming that nature itself was representational, crafting animals into uncanny 'pictures' of their surroundings. What Poulton had presented as an analogy became in Thayer's hands literal reality. 'Nature has evolved actual Art on the bodies of animals', he wrote in 1903, 'and only an artist can read it.' Parsing wild animals into arrangements of lines, colours and shading, Thayer viewed them as accurate images of their surroundings. 'Let us take the widest possible survey' of animals' movements, he continued, and all will 'prove to be actual *animated pictures* of their environment ... Tigers and zebras are resolved into pictures of tall, strong flags, grasses, and bamboos, while the lion is a picture of the desert.'[84] Thayer opposed this model of self-obliteration to theories of protective mimicry and warning colours, arguing that most examples of supposed conspicuousness really promoted concealment. Butterflies, he sweepingly asserted, 'are mainly either flying pictures of various combinations of flowers and their

The Strange Case of Abbott Handerson Thayer

backgrounds, pictures of *shadow under foliage* ... [or] wonderful representations of flowers themselves'.[85] Echoing Bates's rhetoric (although not his arguments), Thayer claimed that these insect disguises had been overlooked because too many entomologists spent more time in the cabinet than the field. Furthermore, Thayer suggested that even field naturalists misperceived the matter due to their insensitivity to art's subtleties. Only a painter could recognise the delicate varieties of shadow which such patterns resembled.

These comments show how Thayer's insistence on the literal artistry of nature reflected his wish to stake out his expertise as an artist in debates over protective coloration, and wrest authority away from empirical zoologists. Thayer corresponded with Wallace and won (qualified) praise from Poulton.[86] Yet, while eager for such validation, he also resisted the idea that men of science were qualified to judge his work. 'It seems necessary', Thayer wrote in 1903,

> to establish the artist's claim as *the* judge of all matters of visibility, and the effect, upon the mind, of all patterns, designs, and colours. If even the artist is limited in this, his own field, what hope is there for others? Fullest wisdom on the part of naturalists would make them adjourn all matters of animals' appearances to us artists.[87]

Similarly, in his and Gerald's book *Concealing-Coloration in the Animal Kingdom* (1909), Thayer asserted that universal cryptic coloration had passed unnoticed for so long because

> [t]he entire matter has been in the hands of the wrong custodians. Appertaining solely to animals, it has naturally been considered part of the zoölogists' province. But it properly belongs to the realm of *pictorial art*, and can be interpreted only by painters. For it deals wholly in optical illusion, and this is the very gist of a painter's life. He is born with a sense of it; and, from his cradle to his grave, his eyes, wherever they turn, are unceasingly at work on it, – and his pictures live by it. What wonder, then, if it was for him alone to discover that the very art he practices is *at full* – beyond the most delicate precision of human powers – on almost all animals?

Thayer's rhetoric echoes Ruskin's criticism of scientific materialists as 'one-eyed bats', claiming nature's appearances as the domain of aestheticians like him. Thayer similarly frames protective coloration as an elusive phenomenon brought into sharp focus by a privileged mediator. 'Although this search, like all others, requires a specialist', he states, 'the beautiful *things discovered* are appreciable by all men.'[88] Thayer's artistic eye enables

58 Art, Nature and Science in Representations of Crypsis

him to glimpse nature innocently, like a wild animal, and so reveal its unremarked techniques of illusion.

Thayer's dismissal of zoology as a discipline all but blind to protective coloration was breathtakingly arrogant, given that his own theories were founded on the prior work of zoologists. Nonetheless, Thayer needed to assert his authority as a viewer to justify his approach, which focussed almost wholly on human perceptions. Whatever details Thayer noticed were assumed to be significant for other species too. Animals needed to blend in only momentarily with certain backgrounds for Thayer to claim that evolution had adapted them to do so. Moreover, conceptualising nature as art legitimised Thayer's technique of appropriating and rearranging its materials to create illusions supposedly illustrative of those in nature. He carved and painted wooden 'eggs' with counter-shading and challenged audiences to spot them in the distance, presenting such exercises as demonstrations of natural concealing-coloration. Taking for granted the universality of animal concealment, he regarded his task as simply discovering how organic forms could be made to disappear. Thayer's assumption of purposiveness in nature emerges in his ekphrastic descriptions of crypsis, which anthropomorphise nature as a cunning illusionist. 'Any one who has tried to catch a snake in the grass', Thayer wrote in 1903, 'will see at a glance why Nature tries to direct an enemy's attention behind the animal he is hunting. The snake forever proves to be further on. It is hard to set one's foot far enough ahead as he moves ... Now Nature, realizing this, offers the enemy the utmost inducement to strike too far back.'[89] Indeed, Thayer came to view nature as not only an ingenious illusionist but the standard and source of all illusion. His and Gerald's book declared that 'the essential realism' of the 'pictures' which nature painted on animals' bodies 'is such as the keenest artist among men could never hope to match. Nay, for Nature herself has made them – Nature herself has discovered and applied, to a point utterly beyond human emulation, the art of painting pictures.'[90] Art's optical illusions could be imagined as not departures from nature but reflections of it, and, therefore, valid materials for studying nature.

Thayer exemplified this circular reasoning most strongly in his and Gerald's 1909 book, which reproduced oil paintings they had made of animals as evidence of these animals' supposed invisibility. Although outdoor wildlife photography had developed considerably by this point, its lack of colour limited its capacity to reproduce the effects of adaptive appearance.[91] Thayer thus presented his and Gerald's ability to make animals blend in with certain backgrounds on canvas as proof of nature's

Fig. 8   'Male Ruffed Grouse in the Forest', from Gerald Handerson Thayer and Abbott Handerson Thayer, *Concealing-Coloration in the Animal Kingdom* (New York: Macmillan, 1909), p. 38.

ability to do the same. For example, Gerald's 'Male Ruffed Grouse in the Forest' was based on a specimen of the bird, painted over background copied from photographs and outdoor sketches of its habitat (see Fig. 8). Proffering the painting as an accurate glimpse of the grouse in the wild, the Thayers wrote: 'The transverse barring of its breast and flanks ... closely imitates the appearance of horizontal branches seen at rather short range.' The bird's oval-spotted rump 'looks like a several yard distant patch of pine-needle-covered ground, peppered with small dead leaves ... or dappled with broken flecks of sunlight'.[92] The Thayers' description presents the image as a painting of a painting, nature being a canvas of optical manipulations and corresponding patterns. The painting's artifice, which

Fig. 9 Wood duck on pond, from Thayer and Thayer, *Concealing-Coloration in the Animal Kingdom*, p. 59.

would seem to remove it from nature, becomes a means of highlighting nature's own artifices. Life not only imitates art but sets the standard of artistry. Another painting, of a wood duck floating on a pond, claims to prove that the duck mimics not only the rippling water around it but also the reflections on the water (see Fig. 9). The duck is a 'combination of softly blended with clean-cut, sharp-edged markings', which render the creature a bundle of evanescent images of its surroundings. Its stripes and bars of contrasting colours

> picture bright and sharp reflections of the sky (their sharpness of outline caused perhaps by straggling wavelets which cut and border them) lying on

The Strange Case of Abbott Handerson Thayer 61

the dark, translucent water, tinted by vague reflections from the shore. Or, again, the white and dark marks, all together, suggest a definite, fixed, reflection-picture of a fringe of bushes along the shore, with the bright sky cutting in among their crowns.[93]

Further, the duck's 'chestnut' breast echoes 'the muddy bank and brown-stemmed bushes', while its brightly coloured bill blends in with flowery backgrounds. So certain were the Thayers of the accuracy of these resemblances that they admitted to having 'copied' the background of the painting, 'color-note for color-note, from the bird himself'.[94] The evidence thus closes into a deductive circle in which animals' appearances are treated as reliable images of the environments which supposedly camouflage them. Thayer's view of nature as a fellow-artist with consistent intentions enables him to postulate and depict animal concealments which have never been witnessed.

Thayer's book stirred much controversy, particularly in the pages of *The Auk*. Reviewers poured scorn on Thayer for his dogmatic insistence on the universality of concealing colours. However, the opprobrium stemmed from not only Thayer's dogmatism but, more fundamentally, his Ruskinian idea of knowledge as vision, which clashed with the ideal of objectivity. The preface to his and Gerald's volume indicated this conflation of seeing with knowing as it declared: 'Our book presents, not theories, but revelations, as palpable and indisputable as radium or X-rays.'[95] Yet, for Thayer's scientifically minded critics, truth was to be inferred by methodical testing of material facts, not glimpsed by special sages. 'We do not see with the eye of an artist', remarked Thomas Barbour and John C. Phillips in response to Thayer's book. 'We are, however, far from convinced as to how valuable an attribute this artistic eye really is; and are inclined to wonder whether, from a scientific point of view, a more open-minded conservativism would not be more persuasive in the end.'[96] Thayer's inspired vision, they wrote, caused the logical problems in his theory to be 'ignored or glossed over with an artistic haze'.[97] Theodore Roosevelt, freshly returned from hunting in Africa and fancying himself an authority on wild animals, was blunter. He condemned Thayer's book as a series of 'misstatements of facts, or wild guesses put forward as facts', generated by 'the wild enthusiasm of a certain type of artistic temperament'.[98] As in Beddard's criticism of Poulton, Roosevelt regarded Thayer's visions as obstacles rather than vehicles to understanding other animals' perceptions. 'The fact that Mr. Thayer's eye and brain make him regard a crow on its nest as having concealing color', the ex-President continued, 'merely shows

62 Art, Nature and Science in Representations of Crypsis

that his comments are of interest chiefly from a subjective and not an objective standpoint, that he has permitted himself to become obsessed by his subject'.[99] Thayer was like a city-dweller amazed by his inability to spot creatures in the wild, Roosevelt claimed, so that, 'instead of realizing that it is his own vision and attitude of mind which are at fault, he thinks that there is some peculiar attribute of invisibility in the animal itself'.[100] Barbour, Phillips and Roosevelt accepted that animal concealment existed in many forms, and praised Thayer's concept of counter-shading. Yet his epistemology of artistic vision was anathema to inductive objectivity or, as Roosevelt brashly termed it, 'common sense'.[101]

Thayer's model of vision as proof was further problematised by the invisibility of the fundamental processes behind crypsis. Like evolution in general, the phenomenon involved changes and influences over thousands of generations and so could not be captured in a single image, but only hypothesised abstractly. As Barbour and Phillips commented, 'The processes and steps by which these phases of coloration have been reached are ignored.'[102] The ornithologist J. A. Allen similarly commented that Thayer's paintings of cryptically coloured objects were 'all very striking and very interesting', but 'the effects were produced through artificial environment, and really proved very little as to the effect of color patterns as a means of concealment in living animals in the actual or natural environment of the species'.[103] The mechanics of variation and predation which would determine concealing-coloration could not be glimpsed or imaged but must be delineated indirectly through experiments and field surveys. Such criticisms of Thayer paralleled complaints in Britain of 'museum-made mimicry'. The entomologist George F. Hampson coined this phrase at the turn of the century to describe the reduction of protective mimicry 'to the matching of specimens in a drawer like ribbons in a store, being a nice easy subject to philosophise on and entailing a minimum of work'. Such artificial displays, he lamented, ignored the fact that 'protective mimicry entirely depends on community of habit' and therefore could be established only by 'accurate field observations'.[104] The artistic imagination could be useful for imaging facts already proved, but it could not, apparently, be relied upon to discover or test facts external to itself.

However, was not objective induction also a chimera which elided the inevitable, and sometimes generative, role of imagination in science? The ornithologist Francis Allen argued so in an article which defended Thayer, despite his overreaching claims. Roosevelt's dichotomy between the 'wild absurdities' of the 'artistic temperament' and 'common sense' of inductive science was false, Allen contended, for '[a]ny science that goes deeper or

The Strange Case of Abbott Handerson Thayer   63

soars higher than the mere accumulation of facts must make use of the imagination'.[105] Roosevelt had been equally dogmatic in his dismissals of Thayer's claims, Allen noted, baldly asserting that many animals' colours promoted 'advertisement' instead of concealment based purely on his impressions from hunting. Allen contended that Thayer's arguments could be more usefully treated as 'suggestions' than 'facts', offering promising starting points for future investigation. 'Mr. Thayer has shown us several things that we had not seen before', Allen asserted, and scientific research would be stagnant without such creative reflections.[106] Further, while experiments and surveys strove to study crypsis objectively, they usually originated in humans being deceived, and speculating that other creatures were similarly affected. Scientific classifications could blind the inquirer to the variability and ambiguity of organic objects, as Allen counselled, echoing Ruskin's 'innocence of eye': 'We must cultivate the artist's power of seeing only what appears on the surface, if we would see things as the wild creatures see them.'[107]

Nonetheless, Allen stood largely alone among America's professional ornithologists in his defence of Thayer and the principle that art might contribute to zoology.[108] Replying to Allen's defence of Thayer, Barbour dismissed the artist's claimed proofs as 'mathematical demonstrations in human optics, pure physics and nothing else'. He continued: 'As aesthetic, physical demonstrations, they are of great interest, but as to their interpretation in terms of the organic universe they are of little interest and of no value.'[109] The dispute was then abruptly halted by *The Auk*'s editor, Witmer Stone, who, siding with Thayer's opponents, announced that the journal would debate the matter no further.[110] Matthew Brower argues that Thayer constituted a 'last' embodiment of the tradition of the 'artist-naturalist', who claimed to enhance knowledge of animals through his depictions of them.[111] Scientific authority had become too closely tied to ideals of objectivity for many professionals to accept personal perceptions as valid evidence of anything external.

The trajectory from Bates's and Wallace's impressionistic anecdotes and images to Thayer's ekphrasis and paintings shows how crypsis problematised the emergent standards of professionalising scientific culture. Modern zoology sought to base itself upon facts that were materially verifiable. By contrast, Thayer refused to recognise the problematic anthropomorphism that was inherent in simulating crypsis for readers. Thayer's conflation of human and animal vision would be further underlined during World War I, when he tried to promote military camouflage designed according to his theories of animal invisibility.[112] Although

64   Art, Nature and Science in Representations of Crypsis

Thayer made lasting contributions to the science of animal coloration, and framed some theories which later studies would confirm, his insistence that human perceptions could be used to infer those of animals ran dead against the ascendant discourse of objectivity. For professionalising scientists, such anthropomorphic projection was too personal, too disputable and too resistant to falsification to qualify as a legitimate method and belonged to the separate realm of artistic imagination.

Yet, at the same time, the use of artistic techniques and ideas to investigate adaptive appearance highlighted the reality that such phenomena could never be fully reduced to the quantifiable elements and mechanical operations associated with 'objectivity'. The biologist E. R. Lankester hinted at this problem in 1910 when he remarked on the semantic slipperiness of nature's signs. 'What are "concealment markings" when viewed by an aggressive bird or lizard at a distance', he wrote, 'may be recognised as "warning marks" when seen by the same observers at close quarters, and it is also possible that the latter may have become the more important or only important result of the colour marks of a given butterfly which were once useful as "concealment".' Lankester compared this semantic drift to 'the effect on human beings of the burglar's crêpe mask', which was originally invented to help intruders 'to escape observation' but had become, through convention, 'a "mark" or "sign" of evil, not to say violent intentions'.[113] By extending semiosis to nature, adaptive appearance compromised science's ability to comprehensively map it, since the possibilities of semiosis were infinite. As linguists could only broadly indicate the endlessly changing contexts of verbal meaning, scientific investigators could only scratch the surface of the organic world's endless play of signification.

Despite its uncertain status in professionalising circles, adaptive appearance, by materialising semiosis, could also embody the most radical implications of scientific modernity. Ruskin, whose art theory had laid the groundwork for representations of adaptive appearance, had insisted that nature embodied God's moral and spiritual values. Yet phenomena such as crypsis and sexual display reconfigured organic semiosis as a matter of perceptual contingency, not divine intention. As the next chapter shows through its examination of Charles Kingsley's natural theology, adaptive appearance problematised science's relationship with religion as well as art.

CHAPTER 2

Divine Displays
Charles Kingsley, Hermeneutic Natural Theology and the Problem of Adaptive Appearance

Can nature lie? This question weighed upon the parson-naturalist Charles Kingsley in 1857 as he read with horror a new book by his friend Philip Henry Gosse. Gosse's *Omphalos* argued that the Earth's record of changing species was an illusion caused by fossils and strata appearing ready-made in the beginning, along with creatures possessing signs of parentage (such as navels). 'Each organism', Gosse wrote, 'was from the first marked with the records of a previous being. But since creation and previous history are inconsistent with each other ... it follows, that such records are *false*.'[1] Kingsley had earlier praised Gosse's work, which framed nature studies as religious worship. *Omphalos*, however, dismayed Kingsley. In an 1857 letter to Gosse, he confided:

> For twenty-five years, I have read no book which has so staggered and puzzled me ... Your book tends to prove this – that if we accept the fact of absolute creation, God becomes a *Deus quidam deceptor* ... You make God tell a lie. It is not my reason, but my conscience which revolts here; which makes me say, 'Come what will, disbelieve what I may, I cannot believe this of a God of truth, of Him who is Light and no darkness at all, of Him who formed the intellectual man after His own image, that he might understand and glory in His Father's works.'... I cannot ... believe that God has written on the rocks one enormous and superfluous lie for all mankind.[2]

Kingsley's language shows that his objection to Gosse's book stemmed from his belief that nature was a readable expression of God's personality. To call nature false was to impugn God's honesty, raising the spectre of Descartes's deceptive demon.[3]

Kingsley's nature was truthful in the sense that it did not contradict its own laws. He reasoned that God intended humans to master nature, so nature's facts, discovered through careful, systematic study, should not be inherently misleading. In 1850, Kingsley had written: 'God never does ... break the Laws of Nature, which are His Laws, manifestations of the eternal ideas of His Spirit and Word.'[4] This conviction led Kingsley to

65

support Darwin's evolutionary theory since disregarding the weight of evidence for it would have seemed to him theologically unsound. However, his description of natural laws as 'manifestations' of God's 'eternal ideas' also framed nature as truthful in a moral and spiritual sense. In Kingsley's view, nature was a text, on which the creator's values and instructions to humans were 'written' just as in the Bible. 'Truth' for Kingsley signified not only verified facts but also Christian doctrine, which was revealed in both scripture and (less explicitly) nature. Further, Kingsley regarded truthfulness as one of God's most cherished virtues and, therefore, expected to find it preached in nature.

Adaptive appearance problematised such hermeneutic natural theology, suggesting that nature's aspects served purely to promote organisms' survival. If nature was a text of divine values, then God would often seem to endorse Machiavellian deceitfulness. This chapter examines how Kingsley struggled to reconcile nature's deceptiveness with the idea of a divine symbolism through analysis of his book of seaside studies *Glaucus: Wonders of the Shore* (1855), his evolutionary fairy tale *The Water-Babies* (1863) and other scientifically oriented writings. I argue that Kingsley sometimes accepted nature's apparent lack of truthfulness and located this virtue instead in the rise of science, which he regarded as a providential realisation of God's values. However, Kingsley also sought to preserve vestiges of moral symbolism in nature since this notion underlay both his religious faith and the Church's authority in knowledge of the natural world. Kingsley's belief in immanent divinity depended on nature expressing God's mind similarly as the Bible was imagined doing. If nature's appearances were only biological adaptations with no transcendent significance, then perhaps human perception and thought were merely adaptations as well. Kingsley's insistence on nature's symbolism thus cohered with his insistence on the spirituality of the body, preserving a link between matter and divinity. This rhetorical strategy would be echoed by other religiously committed commentators who sought to reconcile adaptive appearance with the notion of nature as a divine text. I will first set out the tradition from which Kingsley developed his hermeneutic natural theology before showing how adaptive appearance obstructed his efforts.

The Victorian Book of Nature

Victorian studies of the organic world were marked by a progressive, long-term shift in authority from natural theology to secular natural history.[5] While the former sought evidence of God in nature, the latter ignored first

The Victorian Book of Nature 67

causes and sought only to understand proximate causes of physical phenomena. Natural theology and natural history, then, can be distinguished as different attitudes toward the relevance of hermeneutics to understanding the physical world. To the natural theologian, nature's facts were signs of an unseen creator, while, for the natural historian, physical facts signified nothing other than themselves. Peter Harrison argues that empirical science involved a methodological 'liberation' from Biblical interpretation as the natural world was 'evacuated of order and meaning'.[6] However, the transition from natural theology to natural history occurred unevenly across communities of researchers and writers, and Jonathan Smith argues that some Victorian naturalist-authors wavered for a long time between the two modes.[7] Theologians continued to engage with the findings of natural historians (including Darwin) to the end of the century and beyond, interpreting science through the lens of religion.[8] In addition, Victorian science was not a monolithic entity but, in Roger Luckhurst's words, 'a fragile edifice' with numerous, disputed 'fault-lines'.[9] This point would be illustrated by Wallace, who, alongside his work on adaptive appearance, fervently defended the existence of spirit phenomena (see Chapter 1). For many Victorians, the questions of whether and how nature signified a creator remained far from settled.

Nature had long been imagined as a second Bible filled with moral–spiritual allegories from the industrious ant and bee to the obedient sheep. The persistence of such thinking in the nineteenth century is discernible in William Kirby's 1835 *Bridgewater Treatise*, which declared: 'The *Works* of God and the *Word* of God may be called the two doors which open into the temple of Truth; and, as both proceed from the same Almighty and Omniscient Author, they cannot, if rightly interpreted, contradict each other.'[10] Kirby believed that animals' appearances were formed to suggest moral types to humans. He wrote with his colleague William Spence that the beautiful butterfly 'borne by radiant wings through the fields of ether ... gives us some idea of the blessed inhabitants of happier worlds, of angels, and of the spirits of the just arrived at their state of perfection'. Conversely, Kirby and Spence wrote, insects with 'threatening jaws of fearful length' that dwelled in 'dens of darkness' and lived on 'predatory habits and cruelty' were symbols of 'evil demons, the enemies of man, or of impure spirits for their vices and crimes driven from the regions of light into darkness and punishment'.[11] Every fibre of life seemed to point to higher, divine meanings.

Alongside the idea that nature's objects symbolised Biblical morals was the notion that nature as a whole embodied truthfulness. Anthony

68 Kingsley, Hermeneutic Natural Theology & Adaptive Appearance

Pilkington has traced such thinking back to the Earl of Shaftesbury and Jean-Jacques Rousseau framing nature as transparent in contrast to human mendacity.[12] The endurance of this idea in the Victorian period can be seen in comments by the preacher and art critic George Dawson, whom Kingsley once dubbed 'the greatest talker in England'.[13] 'I look at Nature', Dawson wrote in 1849,

> and it becomes to me a preacher. I watch all its details and I find written upon every one – truthfulness . . . The body tells of the soul and the soul of the body . . . Every form is made up of particles, each of which bears the true form of the whole . . . There is no show, no 'appearance,' no 'getting up,' as there is in many of our lives . . . Nature never does lie. It is only man that lies; and in proportion as man lies, he departs from Nature.[14]

Animal bodies might be imagined as similarly transparent, as Kingsley's friend Ruskin showed when contrasting them with 'deceptive' modern architecture. 'That building will generally be the noblest', he wrote, 'which to an intelligent eye discovers the great secrets of its structure, as an animal form does, although from a careless observer they may be concealed.'[15] Nature seemed to parallel the Bible as the standard of truthfulness.

However, such rhetoric masked long-growing doubts about nature's capacity to convey moral truths. While science had discovered natural laws that were empirically verifiable, their possible symbolic meanings were, like those of the Bible, open to question. Deism had shown how ambiguous nature could be when read independently of scripture. Thomas Paine implied that nature favoured republican democracy and rejected artificial aristocracy.[16] Conversely, David Hume noted that if nature did proclaim a creator, its gratuitous violence and suffering hardly suggested a moral one.[17] Such dangerous deism and scepticism caused evangelicals to stress the primacy of scripture and nature's moral inscrutability.[18] These problems had likewise prompted the influential natural theologian William Paley to emphasise practical evidence of design over less certain moral symbolism. Paley concluded that nature testified to a creator through its ingenious adaptations, which maximised happiness. Kingsley was immersed in Paley's work as an undergraduate and described him, in later years, as one of the 'greatest natural theologians'.[19] However, Paley's utilitarian effort to calculate the world's goodness undermined the claim that it *taught* goodness. As naturalists followed Paley's lead, studying organisms' adaptions to their environments, examples multiplied of creatures surviving not through superior strength or skills but by deceptive camouflage and parasitism. Gosse commented: 'A very vast amount of the

The Victorian Book of Nature 69

energy of animal life is spent either in making war, or in resisting or evading it . . . Various are the arts and devices, the tricks and stratagems . . . employed in that earnest strife which never knows a suspension of hostilities.'[20] As evidence mounted for species extinction, nature seemed to reward deceit and to consign the honest to oblivion.

These influences suffused mid-century English nature writing with a profound ambivalence about the moral significance of its objects. Although Gosse regarded his studies of nature as a kind of worship, he believed that natural religion could be no substitute for the revelation of scripture, writing: 'When an anxious conscience demands to know something more of God, something of his feelings towards offenders, of his way of dealing with rebels, whether there is forgiveness with Him, and mercy, – the creatures are mute. One says. It is not in me! and another says. It is not in me! All are ominously dumb on such questions.'[21] If Nature spoke, it perhaps spoke only of its own internal workings.

Nonetheless, many Victorians continued to believe that studying nature somehow connected humans to some spiritual reality. The theologian and friend of Kingsley Frederick Denison Maurice refused to distinguish between natural and revealed religion, arguing that humans naturally saw God in the world: scripture had simply sharpened their vision.[22] The Wordsworthian notion that nature and the human mind were adapted to each other lived on in Ruskin's claim that humans' aesthetic responses to nature derived from their spiritual link with the creator. Hence, Ruskin claimed, creatures such as crocodiles and sheep evoked for man 'in a quite inevitable way . . . states of moral evil and good, and becoming myths to him of destruction, redemption, and, in the most literal sense, "word" of God'.[23] Echoing scholars such as Friedrich Max Müller, who studied myths as pseudo-organic growths, Ruskin framed religion as created by humans in reaction to the natural world.[24] Biblical inspiration, then, might have derived from the providential interaction of the human spirit with a world designed to excite it. God's messages were, perhaps, not printed explicitly on the creation; but they might be glimpsed elusively through interactions with it.

Such statements resisted the reduction of nature to mechanism, preserving a role for hermeneutics in understanding it. Thomas Carlyle, one of Kingsley's heroes, voiced a similar sentiment through his fictional philosopher Diogenes Teufelsdröckh, who calls nature 'a Volume written in celestial hieroglyphs, in the true Sacred-writing; of which even Prophets are happy that they can read here a line and there a line'. Academies of science had managed to translate individual letters of this script,

Teufelsdröckh claimed, 'and therefrom put together this and the other economic Recipe'. Yet the notion '[t]hat Nature is more than some boundless Volume of such Recipes, or huge, well-nigh inexhaustible Domestic-Cookery Book . . . the fewest dream'. Science's reading of nature might be accurate, Carlyle implied, but it was also shallow, while, in Teufelsdröckh's words, 'Nature remains of quite *infinite* depth.'[25] The image of nature reduced to a 'Domestic-Cookery Book' frames physical science as a vulgar, literal reading of a text that is, in reality, rich, polysemous and symbolic (however cryptic its meanings). Let us now consider how Kingsley's writings inhabited this context of natural–theological uncertainty, and how adaptive appearance specifically compounded this uncertainty for him.

Mixed Messages

Kingsley was a well-connected, middle-class parson of wide-ranging interests, as concerned about politics and social questions as he was nature and theology.[26] As a young clergyman, he co-founded the Christian Socialist movement, which aimed to reconcile Chartists with the establishment but caused some clerical leaders to view him as a radical. Blocked from advancement in the Church, Kingsley achieved fame as a novelist and commentator before becoming a professor of history at Cambridge and, finally, a cathedral canon before he died in 1875. A Broadchurch Anglican, Kingsley sought to preserve the fundamentals of Christian belief in an era when Higher Criticism was undermining literal readings of the Bible. Kingsley also defended the traditional bridge between science and religion, which new theories of the history of the Earth and its life forms were putting under strain.

As a young curate, Kingsley echoed the rhetoric of natural theologians such as Kirby, who viewed nature as a second Bible. In an 1842 letter to his future wife Fanny, he instructed: 'Do not study matter for its own sake, but as the countenance of God! . . . Study the sky! Study water! Study trees! . . . Study all these . . . as allegories and examples from whence moral reflections may be drawn.'[27] Kingsley also voiced his feelings about the holiness of nature through his early social-problem novel *Yeast* (1848), in which the protagonist Lancelot anticipates Kingsley's later dispute with Gosse. Lancelot declares at one point that the 'laws of Nature must reveal Him, and be revealed by Him', and if these laws contradict Biblical ones, then 'God is a deceiver, and His universe a self-contradiction'. Refusing to accept this possibility, Lancelot asserts, 'my priests and preachers are every

Mixed Messages

71

bird and bee, every flower and cloud', the messages of which do not clash with scripture when read correctly.[28]

Kingsley's insistence upon nature's veracity derived from his Protestant idealisation of sincerity and wish to reconcile sexual desire with spirituality. Protestantism's removal of the priest as a holy mediator placed the burden of responsibility for salvation on the individual worshipper. Worshippers needed to reveal their innermost thoughts and feelings to God, and such thinking encouraged sincerity to be revered as a general attribute of the godly.[29] Kingsley often evoked this ideal in his discourse. 'I will not be a liar', he wrote to Fanny in 1848 when encouraged to distance himself from the controversial Christian Socialists: 'I will speak in season and out of season. I will not shun to declare the whole counsel of God.'[30] His public dispute with John Henry Newman in the 1860s stemmed from Kingsley's contention that the Catholic author had encouraged priests to lie.[31] Kingsley also opposed celibacy and the Catholic logic that underlay it of the body being inherently sinful. Conversely, Kingsley came to believe that the body, and its sexual desire, could be sacred, at least within marriage.[32] These ideas are reflected in *Yeast* when Lancelot defines Protestantism as the 'universal symbolism and dignity of matter, whether in man or nature'.[33]

Kingsley's concerns with sincerity and the holiness of physical matter shaped his view of the natural world as a truthful statement of God's mind. His hermeneutic natural theology fitted with an author-centric view of literary and artistic creation. In an 1848 lecture, 'On English Composition', he argued that God had intended language to serve not concealment but 'the expression of thought'. True literature, then, expressed 'the character of the writer's mind and heart', since, 'Expression is literally the pressing out into palpable form that which is already within us.'[34] From this perspective, Kingsley imagined nature as a divine text, not only indicating the existence of a designer, but realising the designer's character in material form.

Kingsley made his name as a parson-naturalist with *Glaucus*, first published as an article and then expanded into a book. The work presents nature as a kind of text imbued with divine morals and a love of truthfulness. Narrating his rambles around Devon's coastline, Kingsley reflects: 'How easily a man might, if he would, wash his soul clean by going out to be alone a while with God in heaven, and with that earth which He has given to the children of men ... as a witness and a sacrament that in Him they live and move.'[35] Nature seems to reveal its creator just as Kingsley imagined books revealing the souls of their authors. The beaches and rock

72 Kingsley, Hermeneutic Natural Theology & Adaptive Appearance

pools, he writes, display 'the finger-mark of God' (16). Amy King notes that the popular genre of the seaside-study book followed the novelistic logic of discovering general truths by scrutinising tiny particulars.[36] Kingsley frames his narrative in this way, instructing the reader 'to see grandeur in the minutest objects . . . estimating each thing not carnally . . . by its size or its pleasantness to the senses, but spiritually, by the amount of Divine thought revealed to him therein' (45). His sense of nature having a deeper symbolism beneath its sensual effects echoes Ruskin's distinction between 'aesthesis', or bodily gratification, and 'theoria', the apprehension of a moral, spiritual reality beyond the material.[37] Similarly as literature is at once visible words and invisible authorial ideas, Kingsley's nature is both physical objects and ideas of God.

Kingsley particularly finds the divine values of duty and social responsibility preached by nature's life forms, such as in crabs that prevent the spread of diseases by eating carrion.[38] The crab's scavenging of decayed fish offers a morality play, as the narrator states: 'The evil was there, – and there it should not stay; so having neither cart nor barrow, he just began putting it into his stomach, and in the meanwhile set his assistants to work likewise' (179). Nature appears a righteous foil to 'the carelessness, and laziness, and greed of sinful man', preaching morals to humans wise enough to listen (174). 'All the invaluable laws and methods of sanitary reform', Kingsley writes, 'at best are but clumsy imitations of the unseen wonders which every animalcule and leaf has been working since the world's foundation; with this slight difference between them and us, that they fulfil their appointed task, and we do not' (175). Kingsley's description of nature's actions as 'unseen' suggests that its language is indirect, requiring an attentive observer to interpret moral significances from crucial details. He continues, 'The sickly geranium which spreads its blanched leaves against the cellar panes . . . had it a voice, could tell more truly than ever a doctor in the town, why little Bessy sickened of the scarlatina, and little Johnny of the hooping-cough' (175). Kingsley presents disease as a consequence of humans' alienation from God through unnatural industrial capitalism. The moral, divine path, he suggests, lies in observing and imitating nature.

Such moral symbolism was countered, however, by apparently wanton destruction and deceit. In 1856, Kingsley wrote to Maurice of his disappointment in nature studies:

> I have long ago found out how little I can discover about God's absolute love, or absolute righteousness, from a universe in which everything is

Mixed Messages

73

eternally *eating* everything else – infinite cunning and shift (in the good sense), infinite creative fancy it does reveal; but nothing else, unless interpreted by moral laws which are in oneself already, and in which one has often to trust against all appearances, and cry out of the lowest deep (as I have had to do) ... Art thou a 'Deus quidam Deceptor,' after all? – No. There is something in me – which is not nature, but Thou must have taught me ... I know that my Redeemer ... will justify me, and make me right, and deliver me out of the grasp of nature ... But beetles and zoophytes never whispered *that* to me ... [Nature] can teach no *moral theology*. It may unteach it, if the roots of moral theology be not already healthy and deep in the mind. I hinted that in 'Glaucus'.[39]

Kingsley's qualification of the phrase 'cunning and shift' betrays his anxiety that nature might show creative ingenuity but not a truth-loving God. *Glaucus* often implies this possibility by discovering God's 'love' in animals' adaptations to their environments. The whelk, for example, 'burrows in the sand in chase of hapless bivalve shells, whom he bores through with his sharp tongue (always, cunning fellow, close to the hinge, where the fish is), and then sucks out their life' (75). The whelk's amoral 'cunning' testifies merely to its practical adaptation to its surroundings. Kingsley similarly avoids moral symbolism when discussing the parasitic sea anemone that rides on a crab's back, stealing its food. The only lesson Kingsley draws here is that 'kind Nature' always provides, as it fits the anemone 'with a stout leather coat' to shield the creature when the blundering crab collides with rocks (76). The rhetoric of moral symbolism gives way to literal utility in the struggle for survival.

Kingsley's anthropomorphic descriptions of sea life paradoxically accentuate nature's amorality. Depicting prey as pitiable victims and predators as devious villains, he highlights nature's injustice as its crimes go unpunished and, indeed, are rewarded through the offenders' survival. In one memorable passage, the reader is encouraged to empathise with a fish lethally duped by a camouflaged sea worm. Kingsley's description hovers between the perspectives of naturalist and fish as the worm

hangs, helpless and motionless ... it may be a dead strip of sea-weed, *Himanthalia lorea*, perhaps, or *Chorda filum*; or even a tarred string. So thinks the little fish who plays over and over it, till he touches at last what is too surely a head. In an instant a bell-shaped sucker mouth has fastened to his side. In another instant, from one lip, a concave double proboscis ... has clasped him like a finger; and now begins the struggle: but in vain. (137)

The Gothic horror continues as the fish descends into a 'cave of doom' (the worm's stomach). The 'black murderer' curls up to digest its kill,

74 Kingsley, Hermeneutic Natural Theology & Adaptive Appearance

'motionless and blest', the latter adjective showing Kingsley's effort to preserve some sense of divine morality in the proceedings (138). He retreats to Paley's view of nature as a system that maximises happiness, suggesting that he is unable to read any divine instructions in such phenomena.[40] 'This planet was not made for man alone', Kingsley reflects. Hence, 'if there were ... final moral causes for their existence, the only ones which we have a right to imagine are these – that all, down to the lowest Rhizopod, might delight themselves, however dimly, in existing; and that the Lord might delight Himself in them' (88–89). Even this claim seems overly optimistic, though, in light of nature's cruel tricks and wastefulness of life. Kingsley characterises the underwater world by:

> wild flux and confusion, the mad struggles, the despairing cries of the world of
>   spirits which man has defiled by sin, which would at moments crush the naturalist's heart, and make his brain swim with terror, were it not that he can see by faith, through all the abysses and the ages, not merely
>   'Hands,
>   From out the darkness, shaping man';
>   but above them a living loving countenance, human and yet Divine. (125)

Nature might be empirically 'truthful' insofar as its facts were consistent. However, as a model or allegory of *moral* truthfulness, it often failed to deliver. As Romanes would remark near the end of the century, the seeming contradiction between the facts of biology and traditional ideas of God could 'only be overcome by supposing, either that Nature conceals God, while man reveals Him, or that Nature reveals God while man misrepresents Him'.[41]

Science Transcends Deceitful Nature

Kingsley sometimes managed this problem by focussing on the habits of naturalists, framing their commitment to empirical truth as a providential realisation of divine veracity.[42] Such an approach was justifiable in natural–theological terms on the basis that the Fall had created a degenerate world.[43] Divine morals might thus be found in the providential development of civilisation, by which humans came to control and improve nature. The theologian Thomas Chalmers had claimed that the existence of a 'moral designer' was proved by society's dependence upon 'honour and integrity'. Anticipating Spencer's later secular argument for ethical progress, Chalmers stated that, if falsehood were the rule instead of

Science Transcends Deceitful Nature

the exception 'the world of trade would henceforth break up into a state of anarchy', along with 'every social and every domestic relationship'.[44] Morality could be imagined as a progressive transcendence of amoral, animal nature.

Kingsley frequently presented human veracity with this progressive logic. While civilised people made and obeyed laws, he declared in one sermon, savages 'have little or no property, for they have no laws to protect property; and therefore every man expects his neighbour to steal from him, and finds it his shortest plan to steal from his neighbour'. Crimes such as tax evasion, smuggling and poaching represented vestiges of this savage dishonesty, he proclaimed, going 'hand in hand' with 'lying, and idling, and sneaking'.[45] *Yeast* promotes this view by portraying poaching as symptomatic of the moral degradation of the rural working class. One character comments that poverty 'makes men beasts', and this truth is illustrated through the selfish, animal cunning of poachers, who sneak invisibly over private land to steal game.[46] Kingsley foregrounds the animal deceptiveness of poaching through one poacher disguising himself in a river so that the middle-class protagonist Lancelot mistakes him for an otter. As the virtuous gamekeeper Tregarva arrests this poacher, Lancelot finds it 'hard to believe' that the two men are 'even animals of the same species'. Kingsley further emphasises the dichotomy between civilised honesty and bestial mendacity with Tregarva reprimanding the poacher when he tries to deny his crimes: 'Don't lie, you were setting night-lines. I saw a minnow lie on the bank as I came up. Don't lie; I hate liars.'[47] By thus focussing on individual morals, Kingsley glosses over the history of enclosure, which had criminalised the common use of land, and presents poaching as simply degenerate, selfish dishonesty.

In contrast, Kingsley imagined science's disinterested search for truth as the providential realisation of divine truthfulness, ushering in a new spirit of altruism. This vision echoed scientific investigators who sought cultural authority by associating their methods with moral discipline. The Cambridge geologist Adam Sedgwick (whom Kingsley praised in *Glaucus*) had claimed that inductive research embodied the Christian values of humility and restraint.[48] In 1854, the physicist John Tyndall stated that the man of science's avoidance of personal bias rendered him 'a heroic, if not indeed an angelic, character'.[49] Kingsley echoed such sentiments in *Glaucus*, depicting the naturalist as rising above the physical world through his bodily self-control. 'For his moral character', Kingsley declares, 'he must, like a knight of old, be first of all gentle and courteous ... He should be brave and enterprising' (44). The naturalist 'must keep himself free ...

76 Kingsley, Hermeneutic Natural Theology & Adaptive Appearance

from haste and laziness, from melancholy, testiness, pride, and all the passions which make men see only what they wish to see' (45). Kingsley conflates science's search for factual truths with Christian self-abnegation: both involve transcending the mortal body, subjective feelings and animal urges. Science, in his view, both demonstrated human veracity and inculcated it. He wrote that the naturalist's habits 'of general patience, diligence, accuracy, reverence for facts for their own sake ... are not merely intellectual, but also moral habits, which will stand men in practical good stead in every affair of life'.[50] While nature might often be deceitful, studying it could form part of humankind's elevation toward godly truthfulness.

Glaucus's rambling narrative form foregrounds the naturalist-narrator scrutinising his perceptions and, in the process, abstracting from nature, viewing it from a higher, more spiritual altitude. As in Gosse's popular books, the narrative begins not with systematic taxonomies but subjective impressions that the truth-seeker must filter and interrogate. Approaching a bed of shells washed up on the beach, the narrator exclaims:

> What a variety of forms and colours are there, amid the purple and olive wreaths of wrack. What are they all? What are the long white razors? ... What the tufts of delicate yellow plants like squirrels' tails, and lobsters' horns[?] ... What those tiny babies' heads, covered with grey prickles instead of hair? ... What are the red capsicums? and why are they ... rattling about the huge mahogany cockles, as big as a child's two fists, out of which they are protruded? (63–64)

Structuring his description as a series of questions and visual metaphors, Kingsley foregrounds problems of perception and perspective. These creatures are, of course, neither razors, squirrels' tails nor human body parts, but our minds process these unfamiliar objects through comparisons that can mislead. Kingsley urges his readers to gather corallines on the beach, 'and think long over them before you determine whether the oat-like stems and spongy roots belong to an animal, or a vegetable. Animals they are, nevertheless, though even now you will hardly guess the fact, when you see at the mouth of each tube a little scarlet flower' (169). Through Kingsley's narration, the reader vicariously experiences the confusion of the naturalist duped by one organism's resemblance to another. He asks: 'What is that little brown thing whom you have just taken off the rock to which it adhered so stoutly by his suckingfoot? A limpet? Not at all: he is of quite a different family and structure' (128–129). The sea snail serves as an object lesson, Kingsley explains, 'of the way in which a scientific knowledge of objects must not obey, but run counter to, the impressions of sense' (129). Although nature's deceptions would seem to render it morally meaningless, Kingsley rationalises them as spurs to humans' innate will to truth, inviting us to dispel nature's tricks and ambiguities with science. While animals might deceive each other, God seems to express his love of truth through the providential rise of science, by which humans see through such deceit.

Kingsley extends this moralisation of science in *The Water-Babies*, suggesting that humans are destined to remodel nature into something more truthful. By mastering nature technologically, they can remove or ameliorate its cruel deceits. In the process of this work, they perfect themselves. The protagonist Tom begins life as a devious, blackened chimney sweep, but eventually develops into an honest 'great man of science' who 'can plan railroads, and steam-engines, and electric telegraphs, and rifled guns'.[51] Tom realises this destiny after he is transformed into a magical 'water-baby' who repairs marine environments and safeguards their inhabitants. Victorian aquarium-keepers were often depicted as moral managers, as they prevented fights between sea creatures and obviated predation by feeding them.[52] Tom acts similarly, protecting prey and foiling predators' deadly deceptions. He warns salmon of a 'wicked otter' lying in wait for them and tries to protect them from poachers, who lure the fish to the surface with lights (140). Kingsley was no vegetarian and accepted the necessity of predation in nature's economy, but his vision suggests that predation might at least be made more honest, echoing fox-hunters' justification of their 'blood sport' as a fair contest between noble opponents.[53] Kingsley also emphasises the theme of humans making nature honest through imagery of purification. The water-babies render rock pools 'neat and clean', similarly as Tom washes off his camouflaging soot. The tale's claim that 'people's souls make their bodies' (171), not vice versa, presents virtues as supernatural, elevating them above brute nature. Although humans develop truthfulness in themselves through their interactions with the physical world, the virtue seems to transcend the material.

However, Kingsley's rhetoric of souls making bodies also left room for some moral symbolism in nature. Although bodies could be understood in wholly physiological terms, he suggested, such an understanding would be incomplete, omitting the deeper, spiritual realities they represented. Counter to the argument that the Fall had destroyed nature's moral symbolism, decay and disease could be imagined as part of God's system of signs. Kirby had written that such unpleasant phenomena were designed

78 Kingsley, Hermeneutic Natural Theology & Adaptive Appearance

> to hold the mirror to man, that he may see how ugly and disgusting an object he becomes, when he gives himself up to vice and the slave of his passions . . . and the sloth and the glutton may be added to the mandril and baboon as equally calculated to cause him to view vice with disgust and abhorrence.[54]

Kingsley deployed this logic in his aforementioned association of disease with the sinfulness of urban life in *Glaucus*. He further equated bodily degeneration with immorality and, particularly, dishonesty.[55] As Kingsley imagined texts expressing their authors' characters, he viewed bodies as expressions of their owners' moral–spiritual states.

We have already seen this dynamic at work in *Yeast*'s animal-like poachers, and it is further exemplified in Tom's physical evolution in *The Water-Babies*. At the tale's beginning, Kingsley repeatedly associates Tom with concealment. As a dirty chimney sweep, he blends into urban environments as well as Bates's insects, and throws stones at passing horses while ducking behind a wall (6). When he identifies a rich potential client on one such horse, Tom cunningly hides the missile he was about to throw (7). His master Grimes is similarly associated with deceit, as he examines clients' grounds for poaching opportunities and hides rabbits in his soot bag. As in *Yeast*, Kingsley associates this dishonesty with primitive animality. When Tom flees after being mistaken for a thief, the narrator states: 'Now, Tom was a cunning little fellow – as cunning as an old Exmoor stag . . . He knew as well as a stag, that if he backed he might throw the hounds out' (28–29). As a water-baby, Tom at first torments aquatic creatures with tricks, putting stones in their mouths. The narrator laments these actions and spurns the excuse that they are natural to boys, for 'if they have naughty, low, mischievous tricks in their nature, as monkeys have, that is no reason why they should give way to those tricks like monkeys, who know no better' (72). Kingsley's suggestion that evolutionary regression is the embodiment of divine moral judgment is crystallised in the tale of the Doasyoulikes, who degenerate into apes through their parasitic laziness and egoism. The dishonest and selfish become trapped by their vices and unable to survive without them – not unlike weak insect species that survive by mimicry.

Kingsley further emphasises the moral, teleological symbolism of evolutionary laws by personifying them in the matriarch Mrs. Bedonebyasyoudid. This Mother Nature figure punishes wrongdoers by relegating them to lower levels of animal existence. All sin will be reckoned with, she explains, through her 'machinery' of justice (154), echoing Paley's image of nature as a vast machine. She particularly punishes dishonesty, caning schoolmasters for 'telling lies' (158) and reducing Tom to an echinoderm after he secretly steals from her. Tom's recovery from this degeneration begins only when he confesses his sin, as she explains: 'I always forgive every one the moment they tell me the truth of their own accord' (172). Tom's odyssey imports into biological evolution Maurice's notion of an immanent God directing history. The providential rise of civilisation and truth-loving science, Kingsley suggests, is as much part of nature's laws as the degenerate states associated with deceitfulness.

The dynamic of dishonesty-as-degeneration is particularly pronounced in Kingsley's depiction of the Irish. In a letter to his wife in 1860, he notoriously described impoverished Irish people as 'white chimpanzees'.[56] His similarly animalistic portrayal of them in *The Water-Babies* associates such primitivism with mendacity. The narrator refers to the Irish as 'gorillas' who 'would not learn to be peaceable Christians' (146–147). Elsewhere, in a digression on rivers, the narrator imagines an Irish servant named Dennis who is incapable of answering questions without lying:

> So you must not trust Dennis . . . but, instead of being angry with him, you must remember that he is a poor Paddy, and knows no better . . . [than to] tell you fibs . . . a hundred an hour; and wonder all the while why poor ould Ireland does not prosper like England and Scotland, and some other places, where folk have taken up a ridiculous fancy that honesty is the best policy. (90–91)

Kingsley frames the colonisation of Ireland as truthful civilisation policing mendacious primitives. Furthermore, Ireland's famine and poverty are sanitised as consequences of its people's dishonesty, and symbols of God's hatred of this trait.

The Cultural Stakes of Kingsley's Hermeneutic Natural Theology

Kingsley's contradictory stance on the natural world, portraying it as at once infused with moral-spiritual meanings and bereft of them, reflected the embattled state of both his faith and his authority as a liberal Anglican churchman. Arguing that nature was a text of divine values compensated for the diminished truth value of the Bible in an era of Higher Criticism and geology that had contradicted literalist accounts of the Earth's history. It also parried the arguments of humanists such as Matthew Arnold that the truths of scripture were purely symbolic and moral in contrast to science's literal facts.[57] Suggesting that nature and scripture both contained elements of symbolic and literal truth protected theology's authority as a

80 Kingsley, Hermeneutic Natural Theology & Adaptive Appearance

method for understanding the material universe. Nature and scripture could be imagined as mutually explanatory, nature clarifying the Bible's factual truth and the Bible clarifying nature's moral truth. This strategy resisted the creeping materialisation of morality and mind by secular science, placing these faculties at once inside and outside physical nature. Kingsley was fighting to save not just spiritual meaning in nature but the very concept of meaning as a metaphysical phenomenon. Adaptive appearance constructed meaning as material effects instead of spiritual presence, undermining Kingsley's model of both divine and human expression.

Locating divine truthfulness in the study of nature instead of its phenomena tended to separate factual truth from moral truth. Such a separation, exemplified in Tyndall and T. H. Huxley's agnosticism, would split science and ethics (along with religion) into what Stephen Jay Gould called 'non-overlapping magisteria'.[58] As Baden Powell wrote in 1860, science answered to 'matters *of external fact*' and religion to matters 'internal, moral, and spiritual'. Theologians and men of science confused questions of 'right or wrong' with 'truth or error', Powell concluded, through being 'forgetful of their own professions'.[59] His comments reflected the growing divergence of the clergy and scientific researchers into separate professional identities produced and trained by different institutions.[60] For those committed to natural theology, though, this trend could seem less like an amicable division of labour and more like a land grab by secular science of territory previously shared with the Church. George Levine suggests that Ruskin's objections to Darwinism boiled down to a refusal to accept that physical matter could be considered apart from spiritual values. Accepting this, Levine notes, would have weakened Ruskin's authority in natural history since his claimed expertise rested on the supposed inseparability of material life from mental–spiritual subjectivity.[61] Kingsley's engagements with science followed the same pattern, treating facts as the tips of icebergs, the hidden depths of which could be glimpsed only via his theological hermeneutics.

This strategy can be seen in a letter that Kingsley wrote to Bates in 1863, praising the naturalist's discovery of insect mimicry. Having proposed an alternative mechanism to explain part of the phenomenon, Kingsley yielded to Bates's rebuttal, stating: 'I honestly bow to your superior knowledge.' However, Kingsley was also quick to circumscribe this knowledge, explaining:

> I have been trying to bring my little logic and metaphysic to bear – not on physical science herself, for she stands on her own ground, microscope in

> Cultural Stakes of Kingsley's Hermeneutic Natural Theology   81

> hand, and will allow no intruder, however venerable; but on the nomen-
> clature of physical science, which is to me painfully confused, from a want
> in our scientific men of that logical training by which things are rightly
> named, though they cannot be discovered thereby.

Kingsley argued that although physical science discovered 'laws' of nature, these laws were external to its material facts, 'the result of a strictly immaterial and spiritual agency'.[62] He demonstrated this point by remarking that Batesian mimicry 'looks most like an immensely long chapter of accidents', while it 'is really, if true, a chapter of special Providences of Him without whom not a sparrow falls to the ground'.[63] While men of science decided the facts that made up nature's laws, Kingsley implied that only theologians had the authority to discover meanings in these laws.

Such assertions of authority not only defended the idea of nature preaching moral messages but also resisted efforts by secularists to usurp the role of interpreter. Spencer had conceptualised ethics as a material evolution and suggested renaming morality 'moral physiology'.[64] His vision of humanity developing toward increasing truthfulness (see the Introduction) thus required no Christian metaphysics. At the same time, scholars have made much of Kingsley's correspondence with Huxley in the 1860s, in which the men found common ground in spite of their different beliefs.[65] Huxley's statements during this exchange sometimes seem to place him in agreement with Kingsley on the universe being morally as well as physically ordered. In 1860, he wrote of his conviction that 'the wicked does not flourish nor is the righteous punished . . . The gravitation of sin to sorrow is as certain as that of the earth to the sun.'[66] Huxley echoed Kingsley's prioritising of veracity, praising the parson's 'truthfulness and sincerity' and declaring: 'One thing people shall not call me with justice and that is – a liar.'[67] Yet these comments also illustrate how the rhetoric of natural morality could be secularised. While Kingsley imagined nature echoing biblical truths, Huxley conceived of an agnostic ethics founded on natural laws alone. In 1868, he claimed that nature offered humans an 'education' in how to live, stating that 'all artificial education ought to be an anticipation of natural education'.[68] Like the deists before them, Spencer and Huxley implied that nature's moral text might be read independently of Christian scripture.

Kingsley met this threat to his interpretive authority by presenting nature and the Bible as mutually dependent. Each acted as a key to unlock the meaning of the other, he suggested. In this case, his argument was

82 Kingsley, Hermeneutic Natural Theology & Adaptive Appearance

helped by the seeming elusiveness of nature's moral symbolism. In 1863, he wrote in a collection of sermons on the Pentateuch: 'Those whom I have to teach want a living God, who cares for men, forgives men, saves men from their sins: – and him I have found in the Bible, and nowhere else, save in the facts of life, which the Bible alone interprets.'[69] Kingsley's argument takes advantage of the past disunity created by natural religion, warning that mere instinctive 'religious sentiment', which secularists sought to harness, was 'apt (to judge from history) to develop itself into ugly forms ... into polytheisms, idolatries, witchcrafts, Buddhist asceticisms, Phoenician Moloch-sacrifices, Popish inquisitions, American spirit-rappings'.[70] Kingsley's examples of religion gone awry reveal the national, racial and religious hierarchy implicit in his natural theology. Liberal Anglicanism derives its interpretive authority, Kingsley implies, from its peculiarly British moderation, as it carefully balances traditional belief with recognition of science's discoveries.

While scripture illuminated nature's moral meanings, Kingsley also suggested that science illuminated the facts of scripture. He claimed that the Bible did not conflict with evolution, but was merely vague on such matters. 'How God created', he wrote, 'the Bible does not tell us. Whether he created ... this world suddenly out of nothing, full grown and complete; or whether he created it ... out of things which had been before it – that the Bible does not tell us ... It is not a book of natural science.'[71] Having told Maurice in the same year of his hope that science and religion would 'shake hands at last', Kingsley depicted science and scripture as shading into one another, along with factual and moral truth.[72] The Bible began with the origins of 'man' and the Earth, Kingsley claimed, because these formed the first question of science: 'And if man takes up with a wrong answer to that question, then the man himself is certain to go wrong in all manner of ways. For a lie can never do anything but harm, or breed anything but harm.'[73] Kingsley's rhetoric blends scientific and moral truth, describing its opposite not simply as error but as 'a lie'. Kingsley highlights the factual indefiniteness of scripture and the moral-symbolic indefiniteness of nature to suggest that the two become fully intelligible only when combined.

Yet such efforts to align science and scripture as two parts of a single, moral–physical 'truth' did not dispose of the more ominous notions that nature was amoral and morality a mere biological adaptation. After Kingsley's death, Huxley would renounce his earlier claims for natural moral laws. Ethics, Huxley argued in 1893, emerged through not conformity but 'combat' with the ruthless 'cosmic process'.[74] As early as 1863, Huxley had

Cultural Stakes of Kingsley's Hermeneutic Natural Theology   83

written to Kingsley of his despair at 'the impassable gulf between the anthropomorphism (however refined) of theology and the passionless impersonality of the unknown and unknowable which science shows everywhere underlying the thin veil of phenomena'.[75] The material universe was, perhaps, not an anthropocentric text but a nexus of mindless, mechanistic processes. Conversely, Darwin's *Descent* argued that moral sentiments had developed from the natural selection of groups over individuals (see the Introduction). Materialising morality in this way barred it from existing outside the material world as a higher, governing law for interpreting nature. Truthfulness might be no more intrinsically moral than deceitfulness, representing only adaptive utility.[76] Kingsley showed his awareness of this problem in his response to *Descent*, voicing 'regret' that this 'most illustrious man of science' had 'entangled' his studies with a questionable 'metaphysic', particularly regarding 'the origin of Morality'.[77] This criticism misrepresented Darwin's argument in order to downplay its threat to Kingsley's position: Darwin had not so much misused metaphysics as removed it entirely from the equation.

Kingsley defended his belief that truth and truthfulness flowed from an immaterial source by dividing the natural world into what he called 'the How' and 'the Why', representing separate spheres of authority. This rhetoric of division paradoxically maintained links between science and theology, suggesting that each needed the other. In 1863, he had written to Darwin that, although their occupations were different, 'Your work, nevertheless, helps mine at every turn. It is better that the division of labour should be complete, and that each man should do only one thing, while he looks on, as he finds time, at what others are doing, and so gets laws from other sciences which he can apply, as I do, to my own.'[78] Kingsley's politico-economic vocabulary ('division of labour') presents science and natural theology as different points in the pursuit of a single truth. By 1871, he had developed this division into 'the How' and 'the Why', telling secular researchers that 'you have no business with final causes, because final causes are moral causes, and you are physical students only. We, the natural theologians, have business with them.'[79] By insisting that nature had a 'Why', he preserved the model in which natural laws signified divine values. Simultaneously, by dividing the 'moral' from the 'physical', he presented the latter as proceeding from the former instead of vice versa. Beneath the material phenomena of science, he declared, lay an invisible 'vital force' that eluded reduction to mechanistic principles and could only be 'the Breath of God'.[80]

84 Kingsley, Hermeneutic Natural Theology & Adaptive Appearance

So what morals did God's 'Breath' preach? In another lecture of 1871, Kingsley admitted that 'Nature's text at first sight' seemed 'to say – not the righteous, but the strong shall inherit the land'. The world appeared ruled by 'selfish competition, over-reaching tyranny, the temper which fawns and clings, and plays the parasite as long as it is down'. Nonetheless, he demanded, 'is this all which the facts mean?' The law of 'mutual competition', he claimed, was offset by 'a law of mutual help', as every organism relied on others to feed and protect it, however unconsciously. Hence, 'self-sacrifice, and not selfishness, is at the bottom the law of Nature . . . as it is the law of all religion and virtue worthy of the name'.[81] Just as many Victorians assumed that the Old Testament prefigured the New, Kingsley presents nature as symbolically prefiguring the morality that scripture would crystallise.[82] His rhetoric of moral symbolism frames theology's textual interpretation and science's empirical observation as complementary methods. While science reveals nature's hieroglyphs, only the theologian can glimpse moral meaning in them. Kingsley recognised that such meanings were often unclear and questionable, like many textual interpretations. In 1870, he wrote to the geologist William Pengelly: '"Life is certain," say I, because God is educating us thereby. But this process of education is so far above our sight, that it looks often uncertain and utterly lawless.'[83] Yet, no matter how inscrutable nature seemed, Kingsley always insisted that higher, moral meanings lay behind it.

At stake in the argument was not only Kingsley's relationship with a personal God but all human communication, which he conceptualised as a meeting of spirits. As the following chapters explore, Darwinian adaptive appearance rendered meaning a matter of receiver interpretation instead of authentic self-expression. Ironically, Kingsley's own public persona illustrated this model, projecting an image of bullish confidence in the stability of Christian orthodoxy while he privately fretted over the foundations of his belief. John Hawley concludes that, while Kingsley always publicly insisted on nature's divine legibility, in his later years, he 'turned to the "book" of nature as one might view a Rorschach blot: as a suggestive invitation to discern meaning'.[84] Louise Lee argues that Kingsley crafted a public voice that suppressed his doubts in many areas, hiding the nervous, stuttering clergyman behind rhetoric of affected self-assurance.[85] Kingsley occasionally voiced the fear that he was failing to embody his ideal of sincere expression, such as in an 1857 letter to the critic George Brimley in which he regretted writing fiction. The activity, Kingsley complained, was 'a farce and a sham', since 'the best things' in humans 'are too good to be told. So nobody will ever know them, save a little of the outside'.[86]

Kingsley's reverential language evokes ideas of immaterial spirit, too lofty to be conveyed by worldly discourse. Yet Kingsley is unclear about how such souls might come to know each other, the same as he struggled to explain how humans could come to know God. The novelist was perhaps not so different to the animal imposter whose false colours were contrived to induce reactions in its audience rather than reveal its inner essence. In this way, Kingsley's struggles prefigured Allen's more explicit anxieties, discussed in the next chapter, that fiction-writing replicated nature's dynamics of deceit.

Nonetheless, Kingsley's efforts to read divine morality in nature, despite its seemingly amoral deceptions, would be echoed by other religiously committed evolutionists through to the end of the century. In his polemical treatise *Natural Law in the Spirit World* (1883), the Scottish evangelist and naturalist Henry Drummond argued that protective mimicry was a vehicle of divine moral symbolism. Drummond claimed that the physical weakness often associated with such 'parasitic' deceptions showed God's displeasure at sloth and dishonesty. He wrote that, as with Kingsley's Doasyoulikes, mimetic creatures became dependent on and defined by their 'clever ruse[s]', losing the ability to develop to 'higher things'. This parasitism, Drummond averred, breached 'the law of Evolution', which commanded: 'Thou shalt evolve, thou shalt develop all thy faculties to the full, thou shalt attain to the highest conceivable perfection of thy race.'[87]

Such projection of moral meanings onto adaptive appearance shaded into Social Darwinist concepts of biological efficiency. As the following chapters show, ideas of health and degeneration continued to fill discourse of adaptive appearance with implicit moral valences even among writers who had largely abandoned traditional religious belief. Yet they also reimagined deception in amoral terms, inviting readers to consider such acts as the outcomes of material, biological laws. Such representations further broke with the past by reimagining meaning, in line with adaptive appearance, as a matter not of intentions but of interpretation. Kingsley had figured expression as an externalisation of inner essence. Conversely, adaptive appearance functioned through a logic of non-essentialist semiosis in which meanings arose in networks of interaction, *between* interlocutors rather than from *within* them. Adaptive appearance threatened Kingsley's faith in an authorial God that gave meaning to the universe. Similarly, for writers such as Stephen, Watts-Dunton, Zangwill and Gilman, it would threaten their desires for authentic, autonomous human expression, for both individuals and groups.

CHAPTER 3

Criminal Chameleons
The Evolution of Deceit in Grant Allen's Fiction

In 1887, Grant Allen published an article in *The Cornhill Magazine* which compared animals' disguises with human criminality. For example, a spider duping insect prey by mimicking a flower bud evoked the invisibility of clandestine murderers. The arachnid, Allen writes, 'reminds one of that charming and amiable young lady in Mr. Robert Louis Stevenson's "Dynamiter", who amused herself in moments of temporary gaiety by blowing up inhabited houses, inmates and all'. He is similarly struck by mantises which have evolved to resemble termites, enabling them to move among termite society and devour victims, unremarked. Allen imagines the termites baffled by 'the frequent mysterious disappearance of a fellow-townswoman, evaporated into space, like the missing young women in neat cloth jackets who periodically vanish from the London suburbs'. Such comparisons between human and animal disguises were well worn, but Allen added a newer, Darwinian feature. After the termites repeatedly noted the appearance of 'their suspicious friend' at the time of these vanishings, he wrote, they

> would carefully avoid all doubtful looking mantises; but, at the same time, they would only succeed in making the mantises which survived their inquisition grow more and more closely to resemble the termite's pattern in all particulars. For any mantis which happened to come a little nearer the white ants in hue or shape would thereby be enabled to make a more secure meal upon his unfortunate victims ... The more cunning you get your detectives, the more cunning do the thieves become to outwit them.[1]

Allen's comparison of humans and insects remodels criminal deceit and concealment from individual sins into mechanical, probabilistic phenomena following predictable patterns. At a time when social theorists were increasingly conceptualising crime as a statistical phenomenon determined by naturalistic laws, Allen suggests a continuum between human society and the Darwinian masquerades observed in nature.[2]

The Evolution of Deceit in Grant Allen's Fiction 87

This chapter argues that Allen's fictional visions of criminal deceit and imposture were similarly shaped by his fascination with adaptive appearance. Pamela Gilbert notes that the dialogue between materialist physiology and Victorian realist narrative as a 'discursive mode' produced a 'realist body' that seemed at once transparent and opaque, and invited a 'close and even suspicious' mode of 'reading'.[3] Peoples' inner natures were imagined as written on their bodies, but often in subtle ciphers that only exceptional viewers could decrypt, through either scientific or intuitive insight. In tales such as 'The Curate of Churnside' (1884) and *An African Millionaire* (1896), Allen exploited this modal concern with bodily readability to depict wily, elusive criminals as examples of evolution's arms race between concealment and detection. These criminals expunge evidence of their crimes while projecting respectable public personas or shape-shifting between fabricated identities. Their stories challenge the conventions of sensation fiction by departing from, and even mocking, the melodramatic tradition of fate intervening to foil villains. In Allen's universe, providence often cannot be expected to expose hidden evil. Instead, as in adaptive appearance, the outcomes of criminal deceptions frequently depend on their relative sophistication versus the perspicacity of their victims or pursuers. This practical, poetically unjust orientation imbues Allen's tales with moral ambiguity. Allen sometimes implies that criminal deceptions succeed only through people's gullibility. These human traits constitute environmental conditions to which the perpetrators adapt. Allen suggests that, instead of simply condemning such elusive criminals, readers might reflect on what their success reveals about the perceptual habits of society. Like cryptic organisms, Allen's undetected criminals are not isolated aberrations but elements in a wider structure of relationships following consistent, often amoral, laws.

However, Allen's fiction of chameleonic criminality was also torn between opposing models of evolution. On the one hand, Allen envisioned a non-teleological, Darwinian trajectory in which growing intelligence and societal complexity generated ever-more-elaborate predatory deception. Texts such as 'Curate' and 'The Next Presentation' (1902) demonstrate this trajectory, depicting middle-class men who murder for personal gain and evade punishment. These tales contradict theories of identifiable criminal types and detective fiction's usual faith in science's power to expose criminals. On the other hand, Allen sometimes suggested a more optimistic, Spencerian view in which science and rationality promised to overcome both the egoism that motivated criminal deception and the

88 The Evolution of Deceit in Grant Allen's Fiction

primitive interpretation that it exploited. His serial novel *Millionaire* suggests, through its tale of a chameleonic fraudster, that such deception proceeds from modern society's dysfunctionality. Depicting the fraudster's victims as naïve, ignorant and selfish, Allen implies that they deserve to be defrauded and exemplify capitalism's tendency to elevate mediocre philistines to the top. Their vulnerability to fraud exposes capitalism's replication of nature's egoistic competition and primitive perceptions. Allen suggests that predatory deceit would be neither necessary nor possible in a society that valued science and reason. Nonetheless, Allen was pessimistic about such a utopia coming to pass in the near future, and his fiction generally presents the status quo, and its dynamics of deceit, as inescapable. Allen's satire was further complicated by the feeling that his writing was not above the primitive economy of deception. Complaining that popular demand forced him to silence his radical convictions and produce conventional potboilers, Allen sometimes imagined his fictions as examples of human crypsis as much as explorations of it.

Allen's journalism on crypsis paralleled the naturalists' writings discussed in Chapter 1, conveying the phenomenon by inviting readers to reflect on their perceptions. In one article, for example, he directs us to study an illustration of a Kallima butterfly perched on a plant stem, where it blends in with the leaves. Challenging readers to locate the missing insect, Allen writes: 'No. 5, if you look close, contains the explanation of this "mysterious disappearance of a gentleman." But you *must* look close ... The branch, you see, has four leaves on it: well, the uppermost left-hand leaf is our vanishing butterfly' (Fig. 10).[4] Allen uses similar techniques of disorientation in his crime fiction, experimenting with narrative perspectives to foreground the unreliability of perception (and thus its susceptibility to misdirection). Some of these tales involve an omniscient narrator observing the criminals' private actions and thoughts, alongside other characters' erroneous perceptions of them. Such dramatic irony recalls how narratives of animal crypsis shifted between naïve credulity of mimetic forms and detached, scientific knowledge of their true affinities. Allen's example thus reveals parallel tensions in studies of crypsis and Victorian fiction. Similarly as naturalists vacillated between immediate impressions of cryptic forms and distanced reflection on them, fiction writers such as Allen struggled to reconcile traditional narratorial omniscience with empiricist ideas of the corporeality and situatedness of knowledge.[5] Conversely, *Millionaire* uses first-person narration, placing the reader in the position of the criminal's dupes who are misled by contrived appearances and false inferences. In these ways, Allen's fictions of criminal

Fig. 10   Kallima butterfly, from Grant Allen, 'Masquerades and Disguises', in *In Nature's Workshop* (London: George Newnes, 1901), 88–115, p. 95.

deception preach the value of scientific scepticism. At the same time, though, they also idealise science as a means of making the world transparent, overcoming the gap between being and appearance.

Further, Allen's tales of invisible criminals complicate the relationship between visibility and power. Foucault famously identified the Enlightenment's search for panoramic, all-penetrative vision with desire for control, emblematised in Jeremy Bentham's penal Panopticon, a regime of 'compulsory visibility'.[6] Critics have applied this model to the Victorian novel, arguing that its common use of omniscient narration reflects a dynamic in

90 The Evolution of Deceit in Grant Allen's Fiction

which 'seeing without being seen becomes the measure of power'.[7] Allen's crime fiction at once subverts and reinstates this Panopticism. While his omniscient narrators penetrate criminals' deceptive exteriors, other characters are not privy to this knowledge and often remain like the naïve animals duped by crypsis. Conversely, *Millionaire*'s first-person narration and episodic, picaresque structure reinforces its anti-hero's evasion of compulsory visibility. Indeed, for much of the novel, Panoptical power is inverted as the elusive fraudster Colonel Clay almost always anticipates his antagonists, appearing to see all and never be seen. However, Allen also suggests that such criminals would be visible to more intelligent and rational viewers. Far from critiquing Panopticism, then, his tales idealise it and lament current society's failure to attain it. I will first outline how Allen's interests led him to imagine the dynamics of crypsis extending into human life, before exploring how this thinking inflected his fiction.

From Animal Crypsis to Cryptic Criminality

Although Allen's work is little read now, his versatile knowledge, wry humour and prolific output rendered him a leading voice in popular science writing while his fiction showed his sharp nose for the market. His prize-winning thriller *What's Bred in the Bone* (1891) and scandalous New Woman novel *The Woman Who Did* (1895) captured large audiences and were translated into several languages. Peter Morton notes that Allen serves as 'an interesting study in the sociology of authorship', shifting from scientific dilettantism to popular journalism and fiction in response to commercial pressures.[8] His first books *Physiological Aesthetics* (1877) and *The Colour-Sense* (1879) explored the evolution of perceptions, and their effects upon the organic world. While cataloguing examples of sexual selection and protective mimicry, he also made original speculations, claiming fruits had acquired bright colours to attract animals and, so, spread their seeds.[9] As a science writer, he returned repeatedly to the utility of misperception in the organic world, stressing 'the large part which such disguises play in the balanced and complicated scheme of nature ... Unobservant people see only the obvious ... But the world about us teems with unobtrusive, skulking life.'[10] A personal friend of Bates and Wallace, Allen presented himself as an authority on protective mimicry, publicly taking to task other popularisers for misrepresenting it.[11] He even wrote the definition of biological 'mimicry' for the ninth edition of the *Encyclopædia Britannica*.[12] Allen was thus uniquely well versed in theories of crypsis among fiction writers of his time, and his work represents a fascinating example of popular literature appropriating these ideas to rethink human life.

Like Spencer, whom he praised as 'the greatest mind' of the age, Allen identified human progress with growing honesty and disinterested love of truth.[13] He can be seen to associate deception with primitiveness when comparing non-human disguises with accounts of 'when a savage dresses up in the skin of a wild animal, in order to approach others of the same kind without being noticed'.[14] Critiquing conservative fears about science undermining religious belief and with it, social stability, he wrote: 'Most people imagine that if we cease to believe a Lie it will be all "up" with us ... I have no such craven fear of the Truth or its consequences. I hold rather, with the Apostle, that the Truth will make us free.'[15] Allen suggested, like Stephen (see Chapter 5) that intellectuals were morally obliged to confront the discoveries of scientific naturalism, however disturbing they might be. He conceived such fearless honesty as part of a more general advancement in which humans grew toward physical, mental and societal perfection. Allen wrote: 'To be sound in wind and limb; to be healthy of body and mind; to be educated, to be free, to be beautiful – these things are ends towards which all should strain, and by attaining which all are happier in themselves, and more useful to others.'[16] In Allen's future society of mentally, physically and morally perfect humans, adaptive deception, associated with weakness, decay and selfish competition, would no longer be necessary. Like Kingsley, Allen identified progress toward truthfulness with an increasingly detached, restrained gaze. Unlike primitive organisms driven impulsively toward vague stimuli, scientific humankind, in Allen's view, strove to render its perceptions more objective. While lower life forms relied more on the 'indefinite' data of smell, Allen hailed 'the man of science, accurately measuring everything in the last resort by an appeal to the delicately discriminative sense of sight, employing microscopes and micrometers'.[17] Allen also argued that perception advanced via growing 'disinterestedness', separating sensory data from vulgar, physical desires.[18] Instinctive attraction to food and mates gave way to intellectual appreciation of the abstract beauty of art and critical reflection on one's impressions. Humans seemed destined to outgrow primitive deception.

This progressive view conflicted in Allen's thinking with Darwin's more open-ended model of evolution in which humankind might not transcend nature's deceits but replicated and even extended them. Darwin had suggested that, even as honesty increased within groups, intergroup mendacity could continue (see the Introduction). The American sociologist

92   The Evolution of Deceit in Grant Allen's Fiction

Lester Ward agreed that society had evolved through the refinement of nature's law of 'deception', writing:

> Primitive man had early to learn that to live he must deceive ... [T]here exists every-where a merciless competition in these arts by means of which the more sagacious and powerful are perpetually circumventing and destroying the more simple and feeble. It has been previously pointed out that, whatever human ideas may prevail, the law of nature is the 'right of might'. But the normal influence of the intellect, the schemes, contrivances, wiles, and deceptions which are the marks of sagacity and even of intelligence, can not be omitted from this notion of 'might', since, when fully understood, they show themselves as the mightiest of all agencies.[19]

Allen reviewed the book in which Ward wrote these words, praising its 'immense amount of novel and very suggestive matter'.[20] His popular science writing echoed the notion of deceit being continuous through animal and human life by humorously comparing animal ruses to various crimes. The *Volucella* fly's resemblance to the bees it steals from, Allen writes, is a 'gross case of impersonation for purposes of burglary'. The flower's enticement of insects with a nectar-coloured stamen is 'a flagrant case of obtaining services under false pretences'.[21] Allen also questioned humans' supposed transcendence of nature's deceits by suggesting that their apparent honesty was merely maladaptation. One of his articles on crypsis ends with the ironic remark: 'Nothing could more beautifully prove the noble superiority of the human intellect than the fact that while our grouse are russet-brown to suit the bracken and heather, and our caterpillars green to suit the lettuce and the cabbage leaves, our British soldier should be wisely coated in brilliant scarlet to form an effective mark for the rifles of an enemy.' Allen compares the soldiers' uniformed conspicuousness to the old idea that God gave fish bright colours to help predators catch them. He rejects this notion, however, as 'worthy of the decadent school of natural history', explaining: 'Nowadays we all know that the carp are decked in crimson and blue to please their partners, and that soldiers are dressed in brilliant red to please the aesthetic authorities who command them from a distance.'[22] Allen punctures the prestige of showy uniforms, implying that they merely reflect the expendability of the lower classes. With the British army increasingly wearing khaki, Allen frames deception as a link instead of a division between wild animals and human civilisation.

Allen's sense of the potential for increased deception among humans was intensified by his interest in illusions. Contributing to the psychology journal *Mind* acquainted him with James Sully and William James's work on this topic.[23] Sully argued that illusion was an inevitable by-product of

From Animal Crypsis to Cryptic Criminality 93

perception, which combined visual stimuli with a 'store of mental recollections' of past experience. Illusions, Sully concluded, 'depend on the general mental law that when we have to do with the infrequent ... and the exceptional, we employ the ordinary, the familiar, and the well known as our standard ... Illusion in these cases always arises through ... the application of a rule ... to an exceptional case'.[24] This model of illusion as perceptual pattern-seeking plus phenomenal novelty chimed closely with the logic of crypsis. The predators of mimetic insects were duped because the mimics were scarcer than their models, rendering them exceptions to the rule. Indeed, humans were more susceptible to such deception, as their greater association of ideas created more inferential links. James noted that 'we perceive a wrong object because our mind is full of the thought of it at the time, and any sensation which is in the least degree connected with it touches off, as it were, a train already laid and gives us a sense that the object is really before us'.[25] Allen illustrated this unreliability of inference in his first published story, 'Our Scientific Observations on a Ghost' (1878). The tale depicts a man of science, Harry, who encounters an apparition but refuses to concede that he has *seen* a ghost, since he is unable to test his perception. Harry tells the ghost: 'You have merely convinced me that a certain visible shape exists apparently unaccompanied by any tangible properties ... At the best we can only say that we saw and heard Something.' The humorous tale links such illusions with contemporary interest in imposters, as Harry explains he must doubt the ghost as he would 'a living person [who] introduces himself to me as ... Sir Roger Tichborne of Alresford'.[26] The unreliability of perception applies not only to supernatural seemings but also to the appearances that structure everyday identity.

This example also shows Allen critiquing the conventions of sensation fiction, encouraging readers to question its epistemology instead of passively consuming it. Allen hoped for a future of 'purposive' literature that would stimulate love of truth and 'philosophic and ethical thinking'.[27] Writers, he asserted, ought to be 'prophets of progress'.[28] However, he complained that market demand forced professional authors to indulge readers' primal emotions instead of engaging their intellect. When he treated fiction as a vehicle for his Socialist and evolutionary beliefs in the early novel *Philistia* (1884), the result was a commercial failure. Smarting from this setback, he expressed a more cynical attitude the following year in a letter to his friend George Croom Robertson. With the help of the *Cornhill*'s editor James Payn, Allen wrote,

> I am learning to do the sensational things that please the editors. I am trying with each new novel to go a step lower to catch the market ... Payn's advice

is ... 'Never mind your own ideas and wishes: write strictly for the *Cornhill* public. I know what they want, and I can teach you how to supply them.'[29]

The masses, Allen later argued, demanded fiction that comforted them by reinforcing conventional morality rather than challenging it, perpetuating '*banal* and immoral lies'.[30] Commercial survival seemed to consist of indulging the public's unreflective desires and delusions.

Allen seems sometimes to have regarded this work as a kind of adaptive appearance, involving the repression of one's convictions to earn a living. In his letter to Croom Robertson, Allen presented his apprenticeship in sensation fiction in biological terms, writing: 'I'm almost sure I have ability enough to accommodate myself to the environment.' He echoed this evolutionary logic in a later article, commenting that successful writers adapted to their audience's expectations. 'If you don't supply what the public wants, somebody else will step in and oust you', he wrote, 'and the somebody else will survive in the struggle for life, while you go to the wall or into the workhouse. That is the gospel according to Darwin and Malthus applied to art.'[31] Allen paints himself as a kind of *Volucella* fly, surviving through mimicry of the bee population around it. 'I never write what I really think about anything', an interview quotes him in the same year: 'For years I have been trying hard as a matter of business to imitate the tone of the people from whom I differ in every possible idea, religious, social, political, ethical, psychological, biological, philosophical, and literary.'[32] Commercial print culture seemed to replicate the deceitful dynamics of nature.

However, I argue that Allen did not simply repress his evolutionary view of life in his fiction. Rather, his evolutionary outlook existed in tension with the narrative and moral conventionality that Allen often felt compelled to follow. This tension emerges in his fictions of hidden and chameleonic criminals through their erratic relationships with poetic justice. The rise of scientific materialism had undermined traditional belief in a divine moral balance determining human fates, causing some Victorian novelists to regard poetic justice as delusional. Eliot mockingly observed that it distributed 'rewards and punishments ... according to those notions of justice on which the novel-writer would have recommended that the world should be governed if he had been consulted at the creation'.[33] While Allen's narrative resolutions sometimes conformed to poetic justice, these conventional endings were often incongruous with the wider worlds of the stories, which were characterised by amoral, Darwinian struggle.

Invisible Murderers

Allen's fictions of cryptic criminality challenge the common implicit assumption in sensation and detective fiction that malignant deceit must inevitably be punished or, at least, exposed. Novels of clandestine criminals such as Wilkie Collins's *No Name* (1862) and Mary Elizabeth Braddon's *Lady Audley's Secret* (1862) responded to rising anxieties about hidden criminality stimulated by cases such as the 'Road Murder' of 1860.[34] Such fiction tended to partly allay these anxieties as their hidden criminals were usually made visible, if not caught, by the end. As faith in cosmic justice weakened, early detective fiction such as Arthur Conan Doyle's Sherlock Holmes stories offered the penetrative eye of science as a substitute. However, entrusting justice to expert detectives generated the possibility of equally expert criminals evading justice, personified in Conan Doyle's Moriarty and E. W. Hornung's Raffles.[35] Allen's fictions of clandestine gentleman murderers explore this problem. They moot the possibility that criminal concealment and detection depend upon not a cosmic balance of justice but an amoral, economic calculation of variables. Cryptic organisms avoided notice through their deceptions being subtler than their spectators' perceptions. Allen's 'The Curate of Churnside', *The Devil's Die* (1887–1888) and 'The Next Presentation' apply this logic to human criminals, emphasising their murderer–antagonists' superior intelligence and discrimination. These men's evasions of justice illustrate the progressive refinement of deception with the development of society.

Allen's omniscient narration of these events, like a naturalist gazing down knowingly on animal mimicries, encourages readers to reflect on the superficiality and manipulability of public appearances. 'Curate' and *Devil's Die*, particularly, thematise the public's failure to do this as people are overwhelmed by sensational effects and gulled into drawing false inferences. Whereas poetic justice determines characters' fates according to their inner, moral condition, adaptive appearance depends on spectators' views of them from the outside. By contrasting criminals' private acts and thoughts with other characters' mistaken perceptions of them, Allen foregrounds the latter orientation. Simultaneously, even though these narratives' denouements sometimes conform to poetic justice, they also undermine it via characters and narrators questioning the realism of such conventions.

'The Curate of Churnside' depicts an Oxford-educated curate and aesthete who forges a will and murders his uncle to secure an inheritance. Allen first published the tale in the *Cornhill* in 1884, with a morally

96 The Evolution of Deceit in Grant Allen's Fiction

conventional ending in which the curate, Walter, loses his sweetheart Christina and kills himself, half-mad with guilt. Allen seems to have written this version under pressure from Payn, since he later republished the tale with a more disturbing ending in his collection *Strange Stories* (1884). In the second version, Walter inherits the money, marries Christina and becomes a respected Church leader who 'has almost forgotten all about' the murder.[36] Allen used this second version in collections thereafter and endorsed its conclusion in the preface to *Strange Stories*, writing:

> I have tried to present a psychical analysis of a temperament not uncommon among the cultured class of the Italian Renaissance, and less rare than many people will be inclined to imagine among the colder type of our own emancipated and cultivated classes. The union of high intellectual and aesthetic culture with a total want of moral sensibility is a recognized fact in many periods of history, though our own age is singularly loth to admit of its possibility in its own contemporaries. (iv–v)

Allen's vision of rational intellect coexisting with criminal amorality fitted with the diagnostic category of 'moral insanity' that had been coined by J. C. Prichard and prefigured later concepts of psychopathy.[37] Walter's aesthetic refinement, forgery and subtle murder method would have evoked the case of the poet and poisoner Thomas Griffiths Wainwright, who seemed a case study in moral insanity. Wainwright had re-entered the popular imagination recently through a published volume of his art criticism, which later inspired Oscar Wilde to ironically assess the man's murders as artworks.[38] Allen originally wanted to call his story collection 'Nightmares', and its version of 'The Curate' confronts the nightmarish possibility of signs of civilisation camouflaging a ruthless murderer.[39] The tale also chimes with an earlier essay by the *Cornhill's* former editor Leslie Stephen (who mentored Allen) that characterised modern murder by its inconspicuousness. In contrast to the flamboyant killings of the past, Stephen wrote, modern murderers worked 'to enable them to escape all notice in a crowd'.[40]

From the beginning, Allen foregrounds how appearances can be contrived, introducing Walter by his impeccably clothed exterior. The man's 'faultless Oxford clerical coat and broad felt hat' render him 'an idyllic young curate' in visual harmony with the 'idyllic village' of his curacy (66). Later, we see him in church, listening to his uncle, the parish vicar, and deciding to murder him. Yet, to his parishioners, Walter displays a 'beautiful clear-cut face … seen to great advantage from the doctor's pew, set off by the white surplice, and upturned in quiet meditation towards the elder priest in the pulpit' (77). The narrator's attention to visual perspective and contrast reflects how Walter exploits these effects. Prefiguring Wilde's *Picture of Dorian Gray* (1890), the curate exemplifies the paradoxical depth of surfaces, producing rich impressions upon others with superficial devices. He moves his congregation with sermons plagiarised from past essayists, while his solipsistic love of art causes Christina to imagine deep sympathy within him. When her father worries that Walter's rhapsodies on his feelings indicate selfishness, she reassures him that Walter 'has more feelings to display than most men, and I'm sure that's the reason why he displays them so much' (72). Christina's praise highlights, with dramatic irony, Walter's manipulation, as she states that 'whenever he's talking with one, he seems so anxious to make you feel happy and contented with yourself. He has a sort of little subtle flattery of manner about him that's all pure kindliness; and he's always thinking what he can say or do to please you' (71). Walter's apparent innocence also depends on Darwinian chance, as people interpret his emotional expressions out of context. When servants bring in his uncle's corpse, Walter's grief stems not from his bereavement but the ugliness of a mark left on the body's head by a passing boot. Even this seemingly authentic emotion (however misinterpreted) becomes a device as Walter keeps one eye on his audience: '"This day's work has been too much for my nerves," he thought to himself between the sobs; "but perhaps it is just as well I should give way now completely"' (87). Wilde would comment in his preface to *Dorian Gray*, 'It is the spectator, and not life, that art really mirrors'; and spectatorship works similarly in Allen's tale.[41] Walter's neighbours think they see humane sympathy in him when they are only projecting their own onto contrived appearances.

Walter's deceptions extend beyond his public image to the manipulation of physical evidence. Like a Ruskinian fine artist, Walter is sensitive to the nuances of appearance and the chains of inference that grow from them. He calculates his crimes to avoid detection, reflecting, through free indirect discourse: 'It was only bunglers and clumsy fools who got caught' (79). He forges his uncle's will by having the same solicitors make one for him, studying the clerk's handwriting and practising mimicking it for a week. Like a student of William De Quincey's satirical lecture on murder as a 'fine art', Walter plans his uncle's killing to avoid self-incrimination.[42] He considers poison 'the cleanest and neatest way of managing the thing', but realises procuring it will leave a trail of evidence against him. Reasoning also that 'shooting makes an awkward noise, and attracts attention', he decides to stab his uncle in the back (79). He studies human

98 The Evolution of Deceit in Grant Allen's Fiction

anatomy to target the right spot, and observes his uncle's regular walks so as to intercept him at a secluded place. He then lets the body fall before smoothly withdrawing the knife, instead of 'pulling it out carelessly so as to get himself covered needlessly by tell-tale drops of blood, like ordinary clumsy assassins' (82). Allen's free indirect discourse shows Walter constantly comparing his methods with those of past, convicted murderers so as to avoid their mistakes. Similarly, as cryptic animals refined their concealments through many generations, Walter's hidden murder develops out of countless antecedents. When disposing of the knife, he reflects, 'A fool of a fellow would throw it into the river ... They always dredge the river after these incidents. I shall just stick it down a hole in the hedge a hundred yards off. The police have no invention, dull donkeys; they never dredge the hedges' (84). Walter's ability to anticipate the naïve views of investigators places him in the position of Ruskin's Turner, manipulating viewers with an innocence of eye.

Walter's belief that his aesthetic refinement enhances his ability to cover his tracks is confirmed when the poacher Joe Harley blunders upon the vicar's body and incriminates himself. Examining the body, he stains his clothes with blood, for 'Joe was not so handy or dainty with his fingers as the idyllic curate' (86). Joe is subsequently indicted for the murder and avoids conviction only through Walter inventing an alibi for him. Allen frames justice as a matter of superficial impressions as police prosecute and jurors convict based on ambiguous facts and visible traits associated with guilt. Joe's blood-stained clothes (due to his poaching) are wrongly interpreted as proof that he stabbed the vicar, while his prior experience of standing in the dock for petty crimes 'made him at once assume the hang-dog look of the consciously guilty' (91). Walter's avoidance of punishment, and Joe's near-conviction in his place, contradicts the conventional wisdom of poetic justice often invoked by Victorians that 'murder will out'.[43] Contrary to this dynamic of inner guilt projecting outward, Allen's sustained attention to appearances frames murder, and its possible discovery, as matters of external perception. Sally Shuttleworth comments: 'The [Victorian] diagnosis of moral insanity was not a straightforward affair of decoding outer signs, but rested crucially on the observer's *interpretation* and assessment of the relationship between outward behaviour and inner motivation.'[44] Allen's tale confirms this view, suggesting that exposure depends entirely on spectators' abilities to avoid erroneous inferences and pierce contrived veneers of innocence. As Walter reflects before forging his uncle's will, evoking the algorithmic nature of adaptive appearance, 'the

Invisible Murderers 99

true philosophy of life consists in invariably minimising the adverse chances' (75).

Allen softened this amoral Darwinism in the *Cornhill* version of the tale through Walter suffering Macbethian guilt after the murder, which Christina intuits. Meeting him again, we are told, Christina 'could not disguise from herself the fact that she did not like Walter Dene quite so well that day as formerly. There was something about him that did not please her; an indescribable shrinking from him'.[45] Allen defers to the generic convention of sensation fiction in which intuition helps to foil the guilty. Brooke Taylor notes that the discovery of hidden criminality in *Lady Audley's Secret* hinges on 'non-empirical apprehension'. Such premonitions (which 'are almost always correct') impel Robert Audley to distrust appearances and seek empirical evidence to corroborate his suspicions.[46] Allen was fascinated by notions of intuition, particularly in women, and claimed possessors of this faculty 'can often read like an open book' such hidden matters as 'character, motive, or passing mood, fetches of insight into the mind of others'.[47] However, Christina's intuitive knowledge of Walter's crime contradicts her earlier susceptibility to his charms. Her new-found penetration and Walter's suddenly conventional (and, so, transparent) feelings act as *dei ex machina*, restoring moral order. Fate also intervenes to expose Walter's forgery as the clerk who drew up the will hears of his inheritance and plans to question its legitimacy. Allen almost seems to acknowledge the inconsistency of the resolution by accentuating its poetic justice in his narration. Throughout the story, Walter reflects that he is no slave to 'conventional morality', but, in the final line, after his suicide, the narrator states: 'after all, that despised conventional morality had had its revenge'.[48] It is tempting to interpret Allen's unnecessary foregrounding of this cosmic moral balance as a subtle invitation to question the ending's plausibility.

In any case, Allen's final version of the story removes the incongruous poetic justice. The narrator states that, after marrying Walter, 'Christina believed in him always, for he did his best to foster and keep alive her faith'. Walter's conscience remains untroubled, 'for those who think a murderer must feel remorse his whole life long, are trying to read their own emotional nature into the wholly dispassionate character of Walter Dene' (99). The second version also removes the discovery of Walter's forgery as the clerk hears of the inheritance and doubtfully reflects: 'I wonder if I can have gone and copied the wrong names in the wrong places?' Darwinian chance combines with the fallibility of perception and memory to prevent

Walter's detection. Modern society, mediated by faceless bureaucracy, enables further chains of inference for criminals like Walter to hide behind, as the narrator states of the solicitor's office: 'in a big London business, nobody notes these things as they would have been noted in Churnside' (99). As deception and misapprehension form part of the universal struggle, the narrator dispassionately observes these factors at work upon humans as Bates and Wallace had upon insects. The tale reworks Allen's image of an eternal struggle between criminals and detectives from a metaphor for animal crypsis into a literal example of it.

Amoral adaptive appearance further clashes with conventional poetic justice in *The Devil's Die* in which the homicidal doctor Harry Chichelle uses his medical knowledge to hide his murders. Harry is an expert in cholera, who pushes a working-class woman suffering the disease toward death so he can observe all of the virus's stages. Murdering her enables him to complete his germ theory, become a tenured professor and marry his sweetheart Olwen. However, he later falls in love with another woman and plots to murder Olwen so that he can remarry. Harry avoids suspicion by contriving his murders to resemble natural deaths. While claiming to treat the woman with cholera, he chills his hand in ice before touching her bare back. This action reverses her recovery and she soon dies, while the murder weapon, ice, melts away. Later, he plans to murder Olwen in an equally undetectable way by planting cholera germs in her medicine, infecting her with the disease. The challenge that Harry's example poses to conventional poetic justice is made explicit through an idle comment that he makes in conversation with a friend:

> There's a precious lot of rubbish talked everywhere ... [about] the utter certainty of the discovery of murder. Pure artificial bolstering up of the conventional morality – that's what I call it. Murder will out, they say – of course it will, my dear fellow, when it's done so clumsily that everybody can see at a glance it's murder. But how about the thousand and one gentle removals which must always be happening, but which never come out as murders at all?[49]

Harry's vision of murder as a large-scale phenomenon, 'the thousand and one gentle removals which must always be happening', evokes statistical approaches to crime that challenged traditional views of it as a moral aberration. Conversely, crimes, even murder, could be imagined as constants of life following amoral, mathematical patterns. Stephen observed that, if murder was produced by heredity and environment, it followed that, 'given a fixed social order, a certain crop of murders will be produced

Invisible Murderers

as naturally as a certain crop of potatoes'.[50] Similarly, Allen suggests, the exposure of such deeds depends wholly upon the relative subtlety of the perpetrators and investigators.

As in 'The Curate', Allen implies that some criminals are partly able to conceal their crimes because the judicial system hinges upon the judgements of impressionable, uncritical spectators, that is, the jury. The novel makes this point through the inquest and trial that follow Harry's murder of the woman with cholera. Because the woman was admitted to hospital after being beaten by her husband, inquest jurors conclude that his violence must have caused her death, and the husband is subsequently convicted of murder. Harry tries to show the jurors that the woman died of fever, but they are too dazzled by her visceral injuries to listen to him. The woman's daughter gives a 'graphic description' of the husband's attack, which (although medically irrelevant) proves more persuasive than Harry's academic description of invisible germs. Harry's friend comments: 'It's a fine sensational scene, as she describes it – the fellow smashing in the sick wife's head with the empty gin bottle – and it loses nothing from that queer little imp's straightforward small mouth and theatrical manner. She'll produce an effect, I'll bet you a quid, upon any jury in all England' (67–68). While the detached scientist infers invisible causes, the jurors are overwhelmed by the sensory stimuli of visible wounds and dramatic testimony, and, so, confuse correlations with causes. Like beasts duped by crypsis, they seem unable to reflect critically on their sensations. No tell-tale signs can be attached to Harry's murders, so they go undetected.

The novel's sense of the adaptive utility of appearance also complicates criminological and racial typologies that claimed to read humans' inner natures from their bodily surfaces. Allen was interested in such typologies and remarked in an early article that traditional 'Hellenic' standards of facial beauty seemed often to correlate with 'physical, mental, and moral excellence'.[51] He dabbled in racist notions of non-white features indexing lower stages of evolutionary development. However, he also sometimes condemned racial prejudice and expressed scepticism about eugenics.[52] Allen further cautioned that 'a lovely and lovable soul may be unworthily housed; [and] a beautiful face may be a false index to the spirit within'.[53]

The novel suggests that such bodily inscrutability can help the morally insane to evade detection. As with Walter the curate, handsome features mask Harry's moral insanity. Allen further signals the unreliability of surface traits for gauging character through Harry's friend the Indian doctor Mohammad Ali. Despite his medical expertise and impeccable morals, Ali suffers prejudice against his dark skin, causing him to lament: 'Brain and soul and spirit may be civilized and European as you please; but none of them will weigh one grain in the scales against a wrong sort of epidermis! I wonder, now, why the epidermis should be considered, socially speaking, such a very important part of human anatomy' (8). The novel's discourse on race is contradictory: such apparent anti-essentialist sentiments sit alongside rhetoric of monolithic peoples that are innately civilised or barbaric. Ali attributes his cultured, moral disposition to his 'pure unadulterated Semite' heritage while associating Hindus with primitive sadism (38). In an ironic twist, Harry's white, English features hide Hindu ancestry, which is the source of his evil disposition. With rigid biological determinism, the narrator describes Harry as 'a complex of jarring elements. On the one side, the sensitiveness, the delicacy, the refinement, the sympathy of European moral ideas; on the other side, the unscrupulousness, the treachery, the suppressed and concealed but ever-present cruelty of the Hindoo native' (66). Although Harry's racial 'passing' seems, initially, to soften racial identities, it ultimately hardens them, implying that race runs deeper than visible surfaces.[54] Allen's reduction of character to race renders mixed heritage a potential means of adaptive concealment. The hybrid's barbaric elements hide under a white (supposedly civilised) exterior.

Again, Allen seems to have compromised his vision of amoral Darwinian struggle for the sake of serial publication as supernatural intuition exposes Harry's attempted second murder. Contrary to the portrayal of Ali as a westernised man of science, Allen abruptly transforms him into an exotic telepath gifted with 'oriental intuitions' for the purpose of revealing Harry's guilt. Through mystical inference, Ali realises that Harry is a murderer, sensing the spirit of the ruthless Hindu ancestor in his friend's 'keen, cold, scientific deliberateness' (88). The narrator states that, as Harry prepares to poison his wife Olwen, Ali's 'instincts told him, and correctly told him, that Harry Chichele was planning foul play' (148). When Olwen sickens, Ali confronts Harry and reduces him to a trembling wreck, the narrator noting: 'It was terrible thus to be confronted with the man who knew all, who had guessed all, who had read everything in his features beforehand' (165). Allen's salvaging of poetic justice requires him to temporarily endow Ali with the omniscient narrator's panoptical gaze in order to reveal Harry's cryptic criminality.

However, Allen's reliance on this fanciful conceit also accentuates the likelihood of Harry escaping detection in the everyday, factual universe.

Allen draws attention to this disjuncture by Ali failing to stop Harry because his suspicions do not qualify as credible evidence for the authorities. Reporting Ali's thoughts, the narrator notes, 'if he had imparted his suspicions to anyone else in all England, they would only have laughed at him for a romantic idiot. What possible evidence had he to allege? None, none, absolutely none – save the intangible evidence of his own keen and rapid oriental intuitions' (148). In spite of his discomposure when confronted by Ali, Harry denies his friend's accusations as 'false, or inferential only', showing that his clandestine crimes are adapted to the logic of empiricism. He defiantly tells Ali: 'What I did, and whether I did it or not, no man knows' (170), and legal standards of proof support him. Indeed, Harry plans to frame Ali for poisoning Olwen and is prevented from doing so only by conveniently catching and dying of cholera while Olwen recovers. This providential intervention jars with the amoral world hitherto depicted in the novel, and reinforces the point that science cannot be relied upon to expose cryptic criminals. G. B. Shaw noted in his review of the novel that Allen avoided following through with his own Darwinian philosophy. Harry was not a 'villain', Shaw wrote, but a 'scientific hero', embodying the 'remorseless struggle for existence', thwarted only by fate.[55] Harry's hidden murders are, after all, adaptations to his environment, enabling him to secure a future for his offspring with his most well-suited mate. From a Darwinian perspective, the gentleman murderer merely embodies certain laws of nature.

In one of his last stories, Allen further depicted clandestine murder in amoral, adaptive terms as a predictable outcome of environmental pressures. 'The Next Presentation' involves another curate who poisons his superior's coffee in order to secure a rectory. The poison, derived from an exotic plant, creates the appearance of heart failure, incurred naturally by old age. Like Walter and Harry, the curate Leonard is intensely aware of appearances, and this sensitivity aids the concealment of his crime. The tale opens with free indirect discourse reflecting Leonard's calculations of how to project the best public image. Leonard frets that visiting the diocese for which he is next in line will expose his unchristian desire for the old Canon to hurry up and die, as the narrator states: 'It looks a trifle obtrusive, you see, to loiter about casually in the neighbourhood of a cure of the souls to which you happen to possess the next presentation.'[56] When Leonard visits a public garden and sees a plant that, he has read, can kill without being detected, he furtively pockets some of its leaves,

104   The Evolution of Deceit in Grant Allen's Fiction

glancing about 'to reassure himself that nobody had seen him' (262). He later surreptitiously spikes the Canon's drink with the plant.

As in the previous stories, the gentleman-murderer adapts his crime to fit into the blind spots of societal surveillance while the omniscient narrator reveals his unseen acts and thoughts. Allen suggests that social manners serve to hide the primitive selfishness of people like Leonard. When the Canon taunts the curate that he must resent the old man's continuing good health, Leonard's discomfort stems from the mortifying accuracy of this inference. Reporting Leonard's thoughts, the narrator wonders,

> what are we to do if people insist upon stripping off these decent disguises of convention from our inmost thoughts in all their hideous nakedness? The police won't allow one to parade the public streets without the ordinary modicum of respectable clothing. Why be more lax in your treatment of our thoughts and ideas which often stand in far greater need of a decorous covering? (347–348)

The image points to the layered, calculated nature of the self, shaped to produce the best impressions upon others rather than authentically expressing inner feelings. At the same time, Allen's vocabulary of 'hideous nakedness' recalls the anatomical gaze of his writing on crypsis that penetrated superficial appearances.

However, unlike in the other stories, Allen suggests that there is nothing unusual in Leonard's constitution that causes him to harbour homicidal intentions behind a respectable public image. The alienist Henry Maudsley had concluded that moral insanity was spectral, rather than categorical, writing that 'everybody may, I suppose, be said to truly be a potential liar, a potential thief, a potential adulterer, even a potential murderer'.[57] Allen echoes this sentiment as Leonard prepares the poison, the narrator asserting: 'It is a common error to believe there exists such a thing as a class of murderers. Nothing could be more untrue. A murderer is anybody. A murderer is you and me, acting under the influence of exceptionally strong motives, or giving way at the moment to the suggestion of exceptionally favourable circumstances' (266–267). Leonard blends in with the general population because he is broadly similar to it, only placed in extraordinary circumstances. Leonard's father-in-law bought the rectory's next presentation fourteen years before with the understanding that the Canon would soon die. The Canon has continued in rude health, though, while Leonard and his wife struggle to support a growing family on a paltry curacy. The narrator depicts Leonard's situation in terms of Malthusian population pressure, stating that Leonard's 'family had increased in regular parsonical progression, at the rate of one in every two years, till there were now just seven of them, with power, as he feared, to add to their number' (242).

Meanwhile, events conspire with uncanny convenience to enable Leonard to secretly kill the Canon. During his visit to the diocese, Leonard happens to read a medical journal that describes the exotic plant's poisonousness and resistance to post-mortem detection. He then finds the said plant in a public garden during a stroll the next day – just before he is due to lunch with the Canon. The tale thus upends poetic justice, creating a set of improbable circumstances that tempt an otherwise average man to murder with impunity. Allen reinforces this irony through Leonard interpreting the opportunity before him as providential. As he stands before the plant he has just read about, the narrator reports his thoughts: 'Providence itself seemed to be throwing the Means to an End in his way! . . . And for Louisa's sake and the children's – was it not surely his duty?' (261). However, contrary to God endorsing murder, the wider sweep of Allen's narration suggests that the concept of providence is a self-justifying mechanism. It enables people like Leonard to avoid acknowledging the amoral selfishness by which they prosper. The concatenation of events begins with Leonard visiting the diocese because he has been invited to deliver a sermon in a neighbouring town, a development that the narrator designates 'chance or providence'. Yet the curate, we are told, 'set it down to providence' (238). Such fatalism works in tandem with Leonard's exaggeratedly Malthusian view of his family's (relative) poverty to justify the murder. Allen suggests that humans extend nature's deceptiveness by hiding their selfish motives not only from others but also from themselves to alleviate guilt.

Nonetheless, the tale also suggests that Leonard's self-justifications are not wholly delusional. Regarding the curate's economic precariousness, the narrator comments, 'He was the victim of a system' (241). While this comment clearly reflects Leonard's biased view, the story also highlights the injustice of ecclesiastical careers, which depend more on nepotism than merit. Although the Canon might not deserve to be killed, he benefits from an unequitable system in which childless old men like him live in luxury while families like Leonard's struggle. Leonard is no hero, but his crime, which leads to him rapidly ascending the Church hierarchy, is presented as a symptom of a dysfunctional society. Leonard, in his normality, exemplifies adaptation to a system that replicates nature's brutal competition, waste and parasitism. As the next section explores, for Allen, cryptic criminality could function as much as an indictment of the status quo and its irrational, topsy-turvy values as of criminals themselves.

Human Crypsis and Social Satire in *An African Millionaire*

An African Millionaire fits some of the conventions of detective fiction, recently consolidated by Allen's friend Conan Doyle.[58] The novel is narrated by the Watsonesque Wentworth, private secretary to the mining and finance magnate Sir Charles Vandrift. The tale begins with the pair holidaying at the Monte Carlo, where they hear of a fortune-telling Mexican seer, and plan to expose him as a fraud. However, the seer turns out to be a persona of the chameleonic imposter Colonel Clay, who goes on to outwit and defraud Vandrift and Wentworth in a series of disguises. The pair's gullibility forms the locus of Allen's social satire, demonstrating the egoism, avarice and philistinism of the bourgeoisie. The men's powerlessness to detect the shape-shifting Clay demonstrates their unworthiness of the high position to which capitalism had elevated them (particularly Vandrift). This satirical element partially restores a sense of cosmic moral balance as Allen presents Clay's deceptions as correctives to an unjust distribution of wealth and power. Further, Allen suggests that such deceptions are made possible by capitalism, which promotes the selfish competition and vulgar perceptions required for adaptive appearance. Allen's social critique implies that deceit need not be the eternal law of human life: a more just, meritocratic and scientific society could remove both the means and motivation of deceit. However, the novel also reflects Allen's pessimism about the likelihood of this ideal being realised in the near future.

Superficially, *Millionaire* would seem to frame Clay as a manifestation of nature's primitive laws of deception, which science promises to overcome in an arc of Spencerian optimism. Wallace had classified mimetic insects as 'polymorphic' when they resembled multiple different species, and the same adjective is applied to Clay twice in the novel.[59] Having worked in a wax model museum, Clay transforms his appearance with make-up, wax additions, costumes and acting skills, causing one police official to lament, 'he appears to possess an India-rubber face, and he can mould it like clay in the hands of the potter' (19). He defrauds Vandrift by appearing variously as a young curate, an old German chemist, a Mexican mind-reader, an Austrian prince, an American doctor and an English poet. Many of these personas are not merely disguises but precise mimicries of living people, as Vandrift discovers when Clay is finally caught and tried. The imposter

Human Crypsis and Social Satire in An African Millionaire   107

defends himself in court by asking Vandrift to identify a photograph of him disguised as a curate. When Vandrift confirms that the curate is Clay, the man pictured in the photograph rises to his feet in the court gallery. Wentworth comments: 'It was – to all outer appearance – the Reverend Richard Brabazon *in propria persona.* Of course I saw the trick. This was the real parson upon whose outer man Colonel Clay had modelled his little curate. But the jury was shaken. And so was Charles for a moment' (304). The passage echoes popular representations of crypsis as astonishing, vertiginous illusions. Allen's own journalism on crypsis reproduced this trope, exhorting readers to view illustrations of animal mimicries and 'see for yourselves here just how far the imitation goes ... Often enough, indeed, I have seen ladies scream at the approach of a perfectly harmless fly, because he came to them in wasp's clothing'.[60] Again, the courtroom, with its emphasis on sensation and spectacle, seems to provide the naïve viewing that crypsis exploits.

   This deceit is halted in the end by the disinterested gaze of science. The hired detective Beddersley reveals the Colonel's identity by comparing photographs of him in accordance with Alphonse Bertillon's system of criminal biometry. Like the naturalists who discovered mimic-insects' true taxonomic affinities by comparing their minute structures, Beddersley isolates the small commonalities between different faces. Wentworth notes that 'though he [Clay] could make up so as to mask the likeness to his other characters, he could not make up so as to mask the likeness to his own personality. He could not wholly get rid of his native build and his genuine features' (281). The photographs echo naturalists' method of unmasking mimics by dissection, probing beneath their surfaces. Allen wrote of insect mimicry: 'the disguise is always external only; it affects nothing but outer appearances, leaving the internal organs and underlying structure of the beast unaltered ... Visible parts undergo modification: invisible parts are never altered'.[61] The investigators in Allen's story similarly dissect Clay by using a fictional photographic process redolent of recently discovered X-rays. The process, we are told, 'reveals textures', discovering the organic structures of Clay's face beneath the make-up and India rubber (276). Like an anatomist exposing the contents of a speci-men's body, Beddersley states: 'Look here; that's an artificial scar, filling up a real hollow; and this is an added bit to the tip of the nose; and those are shadows, due to inserted cheek-pieces, within the mouth, to make the man look fatter!' (280). Clay echoes the notion of science superseding the deceptions of primitive nature, remarking when the protagonists arrest him: 'If you've tracked me strictly in accordance with Bertillon's methods,

I don't mind so much. I will not yield to fools; I yield to science' (286). Science seems to promise to expose impostures by making bodies transparent.

This progressive trajectory is obstructed, however, by capitalism, which, Allen argued, promoted the wrong people and rewarded the wrong behaviours. Insisting on 'natural inequality', Allen suggested that socialism would not abolish hierarchy but 'strive to prevent little men from masquerading as big ones' and enable 'big men to show their natural bigness'.[62] The image of little men appearing bigger than they are recalls Allen's accounts of animals' ruses to intimidate rivals in his journalism on adaptive appearance.[63] *Millionaire* illustrates this dysfunctionality of capitalism through Clay (who turns out to be a lowly office worker) physically outclassing his social superiors Vandrift and Wentworth. When the conman maroons the pair on an island, he skips sure-footedly between boat and land while, Wentworth reports, 'clumsily Charles and I followed ... treading gingerly on the thwarts' (123). After Clay jumps back into the boat and rows away, the two men are stranded because they cannot swim, as Wentworth explains: 'Charles hates the water; while, as for myself, I detest every known form of muscular exercise' (119). The episode shows Vandrift's helplessness among rugged nature as Wentworth observes the millionaire throwing 'himself on the bare rock in a wild access of despondency. He is accustomed to luxury, and cannot get on without his padded cushions' (133).

Vandrift and Wentworth are also shown to be intellectually inferior to Clay. Indeed, it is often Vandrift who more resembles a mimetic animal, puffing up his status by quoting literature he has not read. His posing as an art connoisseur also fails when he embarrassingly mistakes a genuine Rembrandt painting for a forgery and its promoter for Clay. When Clay pretends to be an Austrian prince selling an old castle, Vandrift again feigns erudition, parroting facts about the place from his Baedeker guide. However, his and Wentworth's ignorance of German causes them to fall for Clay's disguise, even though the latter's accent is imperfect. After scamming Vandrift in a fake sale of the castle, Clay later taunts him and Wentworth in a letter, writing: 'MR. VENTVORTH ... Ha, ha, ha; just a W misplaced sufficed to take you in, then! And I risked the TH, though anybody with a head on his shoulders would surely have known our TH is by far more difficult than our W for foreigners!' (103). Clay's superior mind enables him to manipulate Vandrift with the same detached, scientific gaze with which Beddersley ultimately catches Clay. As Beddersley admits, Clay is difficult to identify because '[a] man so ingenious as this ...

Human Crypsis and Social Satire in An African Millionaire   109

would no doubt have studied Bertillon's principles himself, and would take every possible means to prevent recognition by them' (272). Clay demonstrates his scientific perspective earlier in the tale when he poses as another detective promising to catch Clay. In this disguise, he shows Vandrift the commonalities between two specimens of Clay's handwriting, pointing out 'certain persistent twists in the formation of his capitals, and certain curious peculiarities in the relative length of his t's, his l's, his b's, and his h's' (177). Vandrift and Wentworth's blindness to such details demonstrates their perceptual bluntness as well as their ignorance. Like animals duped by mimetic forms, they fail to discriminate fine differences.

Allen sometimes suggested that capitalism promoted such indiscriminateness through commodity fetishism that appealed to primitive impulses. In one essay, he presented the public's reverence for diamonds (the basis of Vandrift's wealth) as symptomatic of their lack of discernment and critical reflection. Diamonds had no special lustre that could not be replicated by paste, Allen stated, as most people's inability to distinguish the two showed. The popularity of diamonds, then, proceeded from a 'vulgar', 'barbaric' attraction to eye-catching objects and 'monopolistic' urge to possess anything rare.[64] Socialism would be achieved, Allen wrote, only when humans had transcended these primitive 'monopolistic instincts': 'The test of a man's place in the scale of being is how far he has outlived them. They are surviving relics of the ape and tiger.'[65] By linking lack of discrimination with avarice, Allen frames the consumer as the opposite of the disinterested scientist: while the scientist cares only for truth, consumers care only for their primitive, egoistic desires for power, status and sensory pleasure. Allen's vision of humans evolving toward disinterested appreciation of beauty and truth constructed primitive organisms' perceptions as contrastingly entwined with physical urges. 'Babies', he wrote, 'automatically strive to place every bright object which they see between their lips.'[66] Such indiscriminate omnivorousness is paralleled in Allen's vision of the public's consumption of jewellery. Presented with paste, he wrote, they would still declare, 'How it shines! How it sparkles!,' like magpies attracted to any lustrous object.[67] The naïve, uncritical primitive mind seems to live anew in capitalist philistinism.

The satire of *Millionaire* revolves around this comparison as Vandrift's vulnerability to Clay stems from his monopolistic impulsiveness. His urge to dominate others renders him unable to assess situations calmly and objectively, and sends him rushing into Clay's traps. For instance, Clay steals diamond cuff-links from Vandrift and then wears them in his persona as a curate, who claims that they are mere 'paste' (36). This ruse causes Vandrift to buy the diamonds back, believing he is cheating the innocent curate out of their true value, while failing to notice discrepancies in the curate's story. Vandrift's deception over the Austrian castle is similarly afforded by his impetuous greed. His desire to possess the old building overwhelms any doubts about Clay's aristocratic persona as he surveys the castle and abruptly exclaims, 'I must and will have it!' (88). Allen further highlights Vandrift's primitiveness when the magnate seizes Clay's hair, mistaking it for a wig, during one of the Colonel's impostures. With tufts of torn-out hair in his fist, Vandrift can only stammer the apology: 'It was an impulse ... An instinctive impulse!' Clay's persona rebukes him with the Spencerian dictum, 'Civilised man restrains his impulses' (229). The notion that Vandrift's gullibility proceeds from his barbaric hunger for power and status is voiced explicitly when Clay strands Vandrift on the island. Clay explains:

> I can catch you just where you are trying to catch other people ... I lead you on, where you think you are going to gain some advantage over others; and by dexterously playing upon your love of a good bargain, your innate desire to best somebody else – I succeed in besting you. There, sir, you have the philosophy of our mutual relations. (129)

Vandrift resembles an animal pouncing at illusions, unable to hold back and evaluate his perceptions; and Clay adapts around these features.

Allen further emphasises the superficiality of the capitalists' perceptions through Wentworth's unreliable narration. He performs the Watsonesque role of missing crucial clues, but without a Sherlockian counterpart to correct him.[68] Clay's ruses are revealed only retrospectively after the conman has disappeared (usually with Vandrift's money). The novel's episodic structure, with Clay reappearing, transformed, in each chapter, prompts the reader to search for him with Vandrift and Wentworth. Yet what seem like objective facts about the Colonel are later revealed to be contrived impressions. When Clay appeared as an old chemist, we learn retrospectively, he 'produced the illusion of a tall bent man' through 'imitating a stoop with padding at his back' (169). This insight gleaned after the episode invites the reader to re-examine Wentworth's description of the chemist, seeing how ambiguous impressions gave way to false inferences: 'He was a remarkable-looking man, once tall, I should say, from his long, thin build, but now bowed and bent with long devotion to study and leaning over a crucible' (143). Wentworth's perceptions of Clay are shown to be vague and relative, noticing mainly deviations from population norms. When the police sketch 'the Colonel in his simple

Human Crypsis and Social Satire in An African Millionaire   111

disguise', Wentworth uselessly describes the image as 'a bland-looking young man, with no expression worth mentioning' (19). Under such an unobservant gaze, Clay can hide in plain sight.

Wentworth's narration also shows how he and Vandrift are always behind Clay in the arms race between deceivers and detectors as they expect him to resemble previous incarnations. Wentworth laments that the pair are 'slaves of preconceptions', and this is demonstrated in the afore-mentioned scene when Vandrift mistakes Clay's hair for a wig and tries to pull it off. Realising his mistake, Vandrift fails to grasp that the man before him might still be Clay. The fact that Clay wore a wig in the past causes Vandrift to infer that a person without a wig must, therefore, not be Clay. Similarly, Clay's heavy use of make-up in his seer persona causes Wentworth subsequently to rivet his attention upon people with exaggerated features. While the narrator is thus diverted, Clay's new persona registers only in his peripheral vision. Dining with Vandrift at a hotel, Wentworth describes in great detail a man sitting nearby whose large, bushy eyebrows have aroused his suspicion, barely noticing the curate who joins their company in the meantime. Amid this description, Wentworth only parenthetically mentions the 'nice little parson' as a background figure who joins in their observations: 'My attention was first called to the eyebrows in question by a nice little parson who sat at our side, and who observed that they were made up of certain large and bristly hairs' (28). Like the camouflaged insects which vanish with the beat of a wing, Clay shapes himself around his victims' perceptions. In his journalism on mimicry, Allen invited readers to interrogate their perceptions, expecting organisms to elude their notice. *Millionaire* revolves around its narrator failing to follow this lesson, to 'look' with sufficient precision or scepticism.

Allen fills Vandrift and Wentworth's lack of such critical awareness with moral significance. Clay's swindling of them would seem to represent a cosmically just redistribution of wealth according to natural inequality. Allen emphasises this justice by underlining the victims' unscrupulousness and dishonesty, confirming Linen Peach's claim that fictional 'Criminal masquerade and performance . . . raise questions about the extent to which so-called "respectable" society is ultimately a masquerade.'[69] During Clay's trial, Vandrift and his wife are often unable to give evidence for fear of publicly exposing their own immoral behaviour. Similarly, Wentworth is prevented from foiling Clay when he tries to engineer a commission for himself in a deal between Vandrift and one of Clay's personas. Clay later exploits this attempted embezzlement to discourage Wentworth from giving away another of his disguises. In contrast to science's collective, altruistic search for truth (in Allen's ideal vision), capitalists such as Vandrift view knowledge only as a means of enlarging or harming their wealth. Hence, when Clay poses as a chemist claiming to manufacture diamonds artificially, Vandrift tries to bribe him to hide the discovery, fearing for the value of his mining shares. This attempt to obstruct the progress of knowledge (however false) frames Vandrift as a regressive force, his dishonesty motivated by primitive egoism. Allen's denouement, in which Clay is caught and jailed, thus represents a reversal of poetic justice as society intervenes to halt Clay's (evolutionarily just) persecution of Vandrift. As the imposter is led away from court, an onlooker voices the implied view of the author, muttering: 'I'd a jolly sight rather it had been old Vandrift. This Clay chap's too clever by half to waste on a prison!' (316). Christopher Pittard argues that Clay partly embodies Emile Durkheim's notion of the heroic criminal who helps society to improve by revealing its dysfunctionalities.[70] Certainly, by exposing capitalism's recapitulation of nature's chaotic deceptions and inefficiencies, Clay embodies a kind of socialist progressivism.

Nonetheless, Allen struggled to articulate how primitive capitalism might be replaced by a new order of cooperation, discernment and disinterested intellectual inquiry. However scientifically detached Clay might seem, he remains embedded in capitalism's primitive struggle. He proposes no alternative to this system in which he has carved out a niche. Clay revels in his criminal deceptions, taunting Vandrift: 'we are a pair of rogues. The law protects *you*. It persecutes *me*. That's all the difference' (136). Indeed, Vandrift at one point confesses to wishing that he could employ the man as a stock broker, so perfectly suited is he to the profession. Clay's combination of advanced intelligence with deceitful parasitism resonates more with Darwin's non-teleological evolution than Spencer's progress toward perfection. As long as humans are forced to compete with each other, the novel seems to imply, their perceptual and mental acuity will only produce subtler forms of deception. To break this cycle, humans will need to exorcise their selfish 'monopolistic instincts'.

Yet Allen was often pessimistic about the attainability of this end by mere education and social engineering. Primitiveness was as much hereditary as societal, he maintained, and therefore could not be overcome in one generation. Allen expressed this sentiment in his review of Ward's *Dynamic Sociology* (1883), which argued that a better society could be built through universal scientific education. Currently, Allen declared, too many people were too mentally dull to recognise the value of such education or to benefit from it. He concluded: 'Only by gradual increase of the knowing

Human Crypsis and Social Satire in An African Millionaire   113

few at the expense of the ignorant or wrong-headed many can a public opinion arise which would even tolerate a national system of scientific education.' This change would be a matter not of changing minds, he wrote, but of allowing the duller ones to die out in 'the slow action of that wasteful genetic process'. Although interested in eugenics, Allen was sceptical of its feasibility. Progressive social critics, he claimed, could, therefore, observe the world around them only with 'an attitude of "refined despair"'.[71] Capitalism, and the deceptive replications that came with it, seemed to Allen inescapable, at least in his lifetime.

Millionaire's political pessimism fitted with Allen's general cynicism about his work as a novelist. The tale followed two other novels that Allen had presented as radical challenges to political and moral conventions, *The Woman Who Did* and *The British Barbarians* (1895). Allen had dubbed these texts 'hill-top' novels, which conveyed his 'sincere and personal convictions', uncompromised by serialisation.[72] However, *Barbarians* sold poorly and Allen published no more fiction with the 'hill-top' label, returning to the stifling but lucrative serial format with *Millionaire*. Three years later, Wallace exhorted Allen to write a didactic, socialist story, but Allen demurred, explaining: 'I have to write stories which editors will accept and the public will buy. Now no editor will take a socialist story – I have tried and failed: and the public will not buy such stories to a sufficient extent to pay for the trouble.'[73] Allen had, perhaps unconsciously, laid the groundwork for this self-justification in an early science article when he commented that 'it is a fact in nature as in human life that to be successful is to have many imitators'.[74] Forced to hide his controversial beliefs under potboiler conventions, Allen found himself in a position uncannily similar to the mimetic organisms he wrote about. At the same time, his contemptuous view of the reading public framed such people as akin to the undiscriminating beasts that were duped by such displays. 'Most novelists are bursting with ideas which they wish to impart to the world', he told one interviewer, 'but the world doesn't want their ideas; it wants a good, rousing, rattling, sensational story.'[75] Popular authors seemed to capture audiences with purple prose and melodramatic incident, as unsubtle in their way as the dazzle-colours on an animal's body.

Allen further regarded such literary titillation as a form of parasitism, perhaps not so different to that practised by Clay or Vandrift. Popular writers like him, he wrote in one essay, were essentially 'tootlers; that is to say, the good folk who write a tootle about nothing in particular for the mere gratification of idle people'. Although market demand sustained such useless literature, its producer remained, Allen wrote, an 'idle guest at the

114 The Evolution of Deceit in Grant Allen's Fiction

banquet of nature'. What, then, would happen to such authors if a future revolution demanded efficiency and value from everyone? Allen doubted his survival

> if some sea-green, incorruptible readjuster were suddenly to begin lopping off the useless branches from the social organism . . . For ours, after all, is a serious world of struggling, hungry mortals, governed by natural selection and the survival of the fittest – in other words, by ever-pressing famine which picks out on the whole the weakest and least successful members . . . If such a community, composed mainly of real workers and producers, of men and women who raise the bread and weave the garments that feed and clothe me, were seriously and solemnly to ask me what I had ever done for them and theirs that I should not be hewn down and cast into the fire like the barren fig-tree, could I really give them any solid and satisfactory excuse for my continued existence? I fear not.[76]

Allen envisions socialism producing true 'survival of the fittest' by weeding out the wily parasites that endure in wild nature and capitalism. As an author, Allen saw himself as living off the bourgeoisie's mindless impulses, similarly as Clay lives off Vandrift's, who, in turn, lives off the public's idiotic love of diamonds. The professional writer with radical sympathies had to be careful what he wished for.

Allen's laments about the tyranny of the market sometimes verged on bad faith. Framing himself as a helpless victim of circumstance enabled him to insist that he had no choice but to sacrifice his integrity for filthy lucre.[77] Allen was perhaps not so different to the curate-poisoner Leonard, who abdicated responsibility for his clandestine murder by imagining it as cosmic necessity. Yet Allen's protesting was not just self-reassurance, but also a working-through of his ideas about adaptive appearance in human life. Far from being easy, he suggested, sincere self-expression perhaps ran against the natural order of things or, at least, the level of development attained thus far. His crime fiction conveyed this idea by depicting criminal concealment and exposure as often determined by mere practical ability and chance environmental conditions. Although Allen yearned for a future of collective endeavour and sincere intellectual exchange, present society seemed to him to compel selfish insincerity. His omniscient narrations, and the fictional technology that catches Clay in *Millionaire*, represent fantasies of an all-penetrative gaze that would overcome these conditions. However, transcending nature's deceitful dynamics would be as much an ethical as intellectual development. As his tales show, Allen was keenly aware that these faculties did not necessarily advance in tandem. His hope of humans overcoming the biology of deceit was offset by a

Human Crypsis and Social Satire in An African Millionaire   115

darker vision of endlessly more complex skullduggery. The contradictoriness of Allen's vision partly derived from the difficulty of positioning deceit in a simple model of progress. It seemed to represent at once primitiveness and advancement, organic necessity and self-conscious agency. The next chapter considers how Allen's contemporary Thomas Hardy probed these uncertainties in his fiction.

CHAPTER 4

Darwin's Little Ironies
Evolution and the Ethics of Appearance in Thomas Hardy's Fiction

Like Kingsley and Allen, Thomas Hardy was much concerned with truthfulness, and often lamented that conventionality and market demand stifled authors' abilities to exercise this virtue. In 1888, he wrote, 'The besetting sin of modern literature is its insincerity.' Potentially divisive comments on 'morals and religion', he complained, were carefully 'qualified, even contradicted, by an aside' to avoid condemnation.[1] Hardy had learned to repress his radical convictions as a writer after George Meredith advised him to shelve his first novel, warning that it would scupper his commercial prospects. A few years later, when Leslie Stephen requested changes to the serialised version of *Far from the Madding Crowd* (1874), Hardy replied: 'The truth is that I am willing, and indeed anxious, to give up any points which may be desirable in a story when read as a whole, for the sake of others which shall please those who read it in numbers.'[2] However, success and financial security later emboldened Hardy to court controversy in novels such as *Tess of the d'Urbervilles* (1891) and *Jude the Obscure* (1895).

Hardy justified his challenges to orthodox views about marriage and sex as matters of conscience. He told an interviewer in 1892, 'I only try to give an artistic shape to standing facts ... I do feel very strongly that the position of man and woman in nature, things which everybody is thinking and nobody saying, may be taken up and treated frankly.'[3] Hardy praised the naturalist school as 'conscientious and well-intentioned authors ... [who] attempt to narrate the *vérité vraie*'.[4] Conversely, he condemned authors who avoided uncomfortable issues such as marital discontent by following 'the regulation finish that "they married and were happy ever after"'. Such conventions, he wrote, were mendacious 'false colouring' that ran against fiction's obligation to offer an 'honest portrayal' of 'Life' as 'a physiological fact'.[5]

However, as John Kucich has shown, Hardy's ethics of sincerity were complex. While he eviscerated modern society's hypocrisy and called for

116

Evolution and the Ethics of Appearance in Thomas Hardy 117

greater candour in public life, much of Hardy's fiction offers 'a systematic diagnosis of honesty's inadequacy as an ethical ideal'.[6] Although some of his characters stand as paragons of honesty, his tales also raise questions about the possible necessity of dissimulation in a society ruled by dogmatic prejudice and superficial appearances. Kucich observes that Hardy further undermines rationalist moral judgments of lying by exploring 'the gray area between deliberate dishonesty and accidental deception', and problematising the intentionality of many misrepresentations.[7]

This chapter argues that Hardy's ambivalence about the moral status of deceit was strongly shaped by his interest in adaptive appearance. His fiction was influenced by the pastoral tradition, which tended to associate mendacity with artificial, urban society and to frame the natural world (and, by extension, rural people) as contrastingly honest and transparent. Yet this pastoral mode clashed with an equal tendency toward naturalism, which approached humans as products of the amoral material influences of heredity and environment. As he matured as a novelist, Hardy's knowledge of adaptive appearance increasingly upset the pastoral dichotomy between natural honesty and artificial mendacity. Many of his characters survive and perish, reproduce and remain issueless due to not cosmic morality but chance circumstances favouring certain traits over others.[8] Misperception and dissimulation could be decisive in this struggle. Hence, Hardy's tales often depict deceit as less a corruption of humans' innate goodness than a development of amoral survival mechanisms.

This orientation complicated Hardy's view of how much humans chose to be deceitful and what motivated such choices. By depicting deceptive behaviour as partly instinctive, Hardy causes it to shade into nature's amoral dissimulations. Apparently agential human actions blur with the more mechanised displays of natural and sexual selection. Such representations would seem to frame truthfulness as an artificial virtue which humans could acquire only by mentally separating from and transcending nature's processes.[9] However, Hardy did not so straightforwardly equate moral agency with mentality, often suggesting that goodness derived from primordial instincts rather than logical reasoning. In this way, Hardy refigured mendacity and veracity from abstract vice and virtue into manifestations of opposing sociobiological tendencies: egoism and altruism. The path from egoistic deceit to altruistic truthfulness consisted for him not of simply repressing or giving free reign to natural impulses, but of a combination of the two. Further, the utilitarianism behind Hardy's altruism/egoism dichotomy complicated the moral status of deception. Instead of being an unqualified vice, deception became ethically ambiguous, depending on

118   Evolution and the Ethics of Appearance in Thomas Hardy

the selfish or selfless aims it served. Hardy's fiction further biologized deception by depicting physical bodies that hid or falsified their owners' identities. Random variations and chance resemblances cause characters to interpret erroneous ancestral histories in each other, sometimes with disastrous consequences. Similarly to Kingsley and Allen, Hardy made moral sense of such organic deception by focussing on the deceived party. Humans were tricked by family resemblances, he suggested, because they egoistically sought to elevate or extend themselves. Hardy was uncertain, though, whether such egoistic gullibility could be overcome.

Pastoral Honesty versus Darwinian Deceit

I will first outline Hardy's pastoralism before showing how it was compromised by his knowledge of adaptive appearance. As an author mostly focussed upon rural communities, who sought to challenge conventional Victorian morality, Hardy followed the pastoral tradition of opposing rural, supposedly natural, innocence to dishonest civilisation.[10] Hardy's early fiction, particularly, tends to associate rural seclusion and labour with natural honesty, in contrast to the artifice and contrived appearances of the urban middle class. A devoted reader of John Stuart Mill, Hardy felt that modern life enforced hypocritical conformity through intense public scrutiny.[11] Simultaneously, urban anonymity and social mobility enabled people to fabricate identities as never before. In 1888, Hardy observed that 'social refinement operates upon character in a way which is oftener than not prejudicial to vigorous portraiture, by making the exteriors of men their screen rather than their index, as with untutored mankind. Contrasts are disguised by the crust of conventionality'. By contrast, he continued, the unlettered peasant's 'nerves and muscles' and, therefore, his inner feelings, 'can be seen as in an *écorché*'.[12] Hardy can also be seen to equate naturalness with transparency in an 1892 interview, which quotes him as stating: 'One often notices in the woman of position the same transparency of passions, the same impulses, the same gentle, candid femininity that you meet with in dairymaids. The higher or lower you go, the more natural are the people – especially the women. Hence, perhaps, they are deceived more easily.'[13] Hardy's social criticism, then, drew energy from the pastoral tradition, condemning modern society for its deviation from wholesome, truthful nature. As Hardy's characters grow more self-conscious through education and city life, the more opaque and calculating they frequently become.[14]

Pastoral Honesty versus Darwinian Deceit

This tendency is exemplified in Hardy's third published novel, *A Pair of Blue Eyes* (1873), through its tragic heroine Elfride Swancourt. Growing up in the rectory of a remote Cornish parish, where 'idle men had not flattered her', renders Elfride an ingénue whose 'emotions lay very near the surface': 'she had a tongue so frank as to show her whole mind, and a mind so straightforward as to reveal her heart to its innermost shrine'.[15] By contrast, her suitor, Stephen Smith, is rendered opaque and calculating by his exposure to London's intense competition and public scrutiny. He conceals his humble origins through mimicry of the wealthier classes, learning chess by watching others play it and acquiring Latin through a correspondence course. Even Elfride's efforts at coyness underline her readability in contrast to Stephen. She rebuts his proclamations of love 'with coquettish hauteur of a very transparent nature', and is unable to wholly suppress her feelings when he tries to kiss her, blurting out: 'I didn't mean to stop you quite' (54, 61). The narrator comments that she fails to receive his kiss with the conventionally virginal manner: 'None of those apparent struggles to get out of the trap which only results in getting further in ... That graceful though apparently accidental falling into position, which many have noticed as precipitating the end and making sweethearts the sweeter, was not here. Why? Because experience was absent.' Hardy emphasises the artifice of love's rituals by linking them with games. The narrator compares such kisses to 'forcing a card', directing one's lover through pretended passivity (61). Hardy further contrasts Elfride's emotional transparency with the inscrutable restraint of her later lover, Henry Knight, when the two play chess. Her heart beats so strongly it sets the flowers on the table quivering, while she blushes, gasps and runs from the room in tears when he checkmates her. Henry's victory in the game parallels his emotional victory over Elfride, setting off the process of bewitching her. Forever displaying her inner life, Elfride's rustic body could not be more transparent.

By ironic contrast, Hardy frames urban life as generating a contrived naturalness. Worldly city women are able to appear innocent and virginal by mimicking the signs of these attributes. This point is accentuated when Elfride visits London with her step-mother Charlotte, who points out the affected naturalness of the people they see. Of the flowers people wear, she observes:

> Some of them are even more striking in colour than any real ones. Look at that beautiful rose worn by the lady inside the rails. Elegant vine-tendrils introduced upon the stem as an improvement upon prickles, and all

120   Evolution and the Ethics of Appearance in Thomas Hardy

> growing so naturally just over her ear – I say *growing* advisedly, for the pink of the petals and the pink of her handsome cheeks are equally from Nature's hand to the eyes of the most casual observer. (141)

Henry reflected the paradoxical idea of artificial naturalness and naivety in his notebook, writing, a propos of Elfride, that self-consciousness developed in women through 'the art of hiding itself' (176). Elfride's relative natural innocence is demonstrated, ironically, by her amateurish attempts at deceit. Having briefly eloped with Stephen, only for their marriage plans to fizzle out, she avoids informing Henry of this twist in her history during their courtship. When he learns of the elopement, Henry wrongly imagines that she is no longer a virgin, a misapprehension which she fails to correct when he cross-examines her and breaks off their engagement. Elfride is a victim of her own truthfulness, her 'simplicity', in the narrator's words, preventing her from perceiving the crux of Henry's suspicion (335). Her unselfconscious transparency blinds her to the ways in which she might be misperceived.

A pastoral logic further shapes Hardy's contrasts between veracious agricultural labourers and devious, urban sophisticates. In *Madding Crowd*, the shepherd Gabriel Oak's transparent character is associated with his closeness to the natural world. He nurses lambs, tells the time by the stars, saves bloated sheep by expertly pricking their stomachs and reads approaching storms in the landscape. He uses this knowledge selflessly, protecting his lover–employer Bathsheba's property regardless of his own interests. He extinguishes a fire in her barn before she has employed him, saves her sheep after she has dismissed him and protects her corn from storms when she has just married another man. His honesty is similarly selfless as he condemns Bathsheba for playing cruel pranks upon another, even though doing so does nothing to aid his own suit. Gabriel's very body seems to transparently proclaim its value, as the narrator states: 'Fitness being the basis of all beauty, nobody could have denied that his steady swings and turns in and about the flock had elements of grace.'[16] Perfectly adapted to his environment, Gabriel has no need for dissembling.

He thus contrasts with the educated, cosmopolitan Troy who dazzles Bathsheba with eye-catching dress, fluent French and assured flirting. We are told that 'to women [he] lied like a Cretan' and had learned to be 'a male dissembler, who by the simple process of deluging her with untenable fictions charms the female wisely' (146–147). While Gabriel speaks bluntly, Troy uses polished 'epithets' calculated to seduce, and fabricates stories to display himself in a better light, such as the lie that he is never seen in church because he modestly enters at the back (155). Hardy presents this dishonesty in tandem with Troy being out of step with the natural world. Lacking Gabriel's sensitivity to its signs, he wrongly predicts that there will be no storm on his wedding night and, so, neglects to protect the farm's corn. In contrast to Gabriel's bodily transparency, Troy's dashing figure and exterior charm is divorced from his internal machinations; as the narrator explains, he could 'be one thing and seem another: for instance, he could speak of love and think of dinner; call on the husband to look at the wife; be eager to pay and intend to owe' (147).

Hardy would rework this dichotomy a decade later in *The Woodlanders* through the characters of the rural woodsman Giles and cosmopolitan doctor Fitzpiers. Like Gabriel, Giles has a mysterious intimacy with the natural landscape in which he lives. He exhibits 'a marvellous power of making trees grow . . . [T]here was a sort of sympathy between himself and the fir, oak, or beech that he was operating on; so that the roots took hold of the soil in a few days'.[17] His association with nature is even more pronounced in the perceptions of his unrequited lover Grace, whose urban education has alienated her from her rural heritage. In one meeting between them, the narrator conveys Grace's impressions: 'He looked and smelt like Autumn's very brother, his face being sunburnt to wheat-colour, his eyes blue as corn-flowers.' This vision of 'chivalrous and undiluted manliness', seemingly 'arisen out of the earth', causes Grace to feel herself losing 'the veneer of artificiality which she had acquired at the fashionable schools' and reverting, momentarily, to 'the crude, country girl of her latent, early instincts' (185–186). Hardy's choice of words associates civilisation with concealment, while natural, rural life renders bodies instinctive and transparent. This opposition is reinforced by Giles's inaptitude for urban commerce. Venturing into town to sell his trees and cider, he fails to beguile customers, 'his habit of speaking his mind . . . militating against this branch of his business' (34). Giles's transparency derives from his unreflectiveness about his appearance. It had only 'sometimes dimly occurred to him', the narrator states, 'that external phenomena – such as the lowness or height or colour of a hat, the fold of a coat, the make of a boot . . . may have a great influence upon feminine opinion of a man's worth' (34–35). Like a naked, prelapsarian Adam, the woodsman is almost oblivious to other's perceptions of him.

Giles acts as a foil to the metropolitan Fitzpiers, who is full of stratagems to seduce other women and then hide his infidelities. When Grace catches him leaving the house of his lover Suke Damson, Fitzpiers quickly fabricates a tale of Suke having an aching tooth, which he removed. 'It was all

122   Evolution and the Ethics of Appearance in Thomas Hardy

so plausible – so completely explained!' the narrator states, verbalising the effect on Grace of Fitzpiers's well-crafted narrative (153). Fitzpiers embodies civilised falseness most fully in his affair with the widow Felice Charmond, a former actress from the city who entices him by wearing a wig made from another woman's hair. The affair develops through him offering her fake treatment for fictitious illnesses, before they elope to the continent, Fitzpiers so disguised with make-up 'that his own wife would hardly have known him' (241–242). Again, Hardy associates deceit with modern alienation from natural environments and instincts.

Yet this pastoral dichotomy of natural truthfulness versus conscious, civilised artifice was contradicted by realist and naturalist tendencies that framed nature's processes (involving animals and humans) as amoral. Hardy doubted Émile Zola's claim that novelists were scientific experimenters, and observed that truthfulness in fiction was more complicated than just mirroring reality.[18] Art, he wrote, necessarily involved 'cunning manipulation' of one's audience and 'a disproportioning ... of realities'. Nonetheless, Hardy also clarified that such 'disproportioning' served only 'to show more clearly the features that matter in those realities'.[19] Fiction might not be the same as science or history, but its depictions of 'human nature and circumstances' must still agree with 'the codified law of things as they really are'.[20] Reading deeply in the scientific naturalists, particularly Darwin, from early adulthood, Hardy lost his faith and came to regard humans as products of evolution, the same as other organisms. Thus in 1880, copying out the words of Leslie Stephen, he wrote: 'Darwinism is as fruitful in its ... bearing upon sociology as in its bearing upon natural history.'[21]

One possible area in which Hardy considered Darwinism might throw new light on social life was adaptive appearance. As a young man, he recorded his fascination at reading of parasitic crabs, camouflaged flies and the devil's coach-horse beetle, which masqueraded as a scorpion.[22] In 1885, he reflected on the 'Hypocrisy of things', concluding: 'Nature is an arch-dissembler.'[23] Darwin had suggested that adaptive appearance shaped human fates, comparing sexual selection among animals to 'young rustics at a fair courting a pretty girl, and quarrelling about her like birds at one of their places of assemblage'.[24] Hardy was similarly intrigued by the idea that human displays and deceptions might have deep biological roots. In the 1880s, he took notes on Maudsley's claims that dishonesty was partly hereditary. 'The individual's evil heritage', Hardy copied, descended 'from a line of ancestral development ... The outcome is ... a lack of wholesome unity & veracity of nature.'[25] In the original text, Maudsley

Pastoral Honesty versus Darwinian Deceit

continues by comparing the pathological liar to the protective mimic. Similarly as mimicry compensated for and exacerbated animals' degeneration, Maudsley wrote, the liar's 'suspicion and guile are a sort of natural protection, as they are a natural consequence, of his constitutional infirmity of mental structure'.[26] Influenced by scientific naturalism, George Eliot had earlier challenged pastoral idealisations of human nature, supposedly embodied by rustics. She critiqued 'the conventional countryman of the stage . . . who is too simple even to know that honesty has its opposite'. She continued: 'It is quite true that a thresher is likely to be innocent of any adroit arithmetical cheating, but he is not the less likely to carry home his master's corn in his shoes and pocket.'[27] Eliot's biologization of dishonesty as the product of 'selfish instincts' complicates the pastoral opposition between nature and artifice. Although people might become better dissemblers through practice and encouragement, Eliot suggests, these environmental factors only develop innate potentialities.

Although Hardy denied being much influenced by Eliot, critics have questioned this claim, and his fiction also erodes the equation between nature and honesty as often as invoking it.[28] Some rustics in *Madding Crowd* are less honest than Gabriel, such as the bailiff Pennyways, who steals barley (60–61). In *The Woodlanders*, Suke Damson hides her affair with Fitzpiers from her husband, who proves himself equally cunning by setting a man-trap for Fitzpiers when he discovers the affair. More than this, rural folks' proximity to nature acquaints them with the powers of appearance and misperception in the struggle for life. Fieldworkers in the novel are amused by nature's 'changeful tricks' when a bout of warm winter weather causes organisms to behave as if spring has arrived, with fatal consequences. The labourers delight in 'the strange mistakes that some of the more sanguine trees had made in budding before their month, to be incontinently glued up by frozen thawings now; the similar sanguine errors of impulsive birds in framing nests that were now swamped by snow-water' (113). Not only do the fieldworkers feel no sympathy for the organisms affected, but they harness nature's deceptions for their own purposes. Hardy depicts Giles and his helper Marty as able to penetrate organisms' misleading surfaces, writing: 'They knew by a glance at a trunk if its heart were sound, or tainted with incipient decay, and by the state of its upper twigs the stratum that had been reached by its roots. The artifices of the seasons were seen by them from the conjuror's own point of view, and not from that of the spectator' (298). Similarly, in *Madding Crowd*, Gabriel's intimacy with nature enables him to exploit its tricks, encouraging an ewe whose lamb has died to adopt another. This is achieved by

124 Evolution and the Ethics of Appearance in Thomas Hardy

skinning the dead lamb, wrapping its hide around the substitute and penning it in with the ewe 'till the old sheep conceived an affection for the young one' (107). Deception appears less a vice than a random by-product of perception, occurring through the organic world and utilised by humans.

Hardy sometimes appeals to adaptive appearance to reframe human dissimulation in amoral, Darwinian terms. In *Blue Eyes*, Stephen's class-concealment is described as comparable to animal camouflage. The narrator notes:

> Quickly acquiring any kind of knowledge he saw around him, and having a plastic adaptability more common in woman than in man, he changed colour like a chameleon as the society he found himself in assumed a higher and more artificial tone. He had not an original idea, and yet there was scarcely an idea to which, under proper training, he could not have added a respectable co-ordinate.

The rising classes mimic the established ones as threatened insects mimic well-defended ones. Hardy suggests that civilisation replicates the conditions of nature with its pressure toward homogeneity. People like Stephen become more common, the narrator states, 'as a nation gets older, [and] individuality fades', along with 'creativeness' (94). Like many animals, modern humans avoid persecution by blending in with their surroundings, eschewing eccentricity (a frequent comparison in the period that will be further explored in Chapter 5).

Chameleon imagery also appears in *The Return of the Native* (1878) as a figure of romantic inconstancy. When the outcast Eustacia Vye finds her lover Wildeve wavering between women, she reprimands him: 'You are a chameleon, and now you are at your worst colour.'[29] Yet Eustacia is also depicted in terms of animal display. The narrator notes 'a certain obscurity' in her beauty, meaning that, 'she was like the tiger-beetle, which, when observed in dull situations, seems to be of the quietest neutral colour, but under a full illumination blazes with dazzling splendour' (89). The comparison frames human beauty and insect coloration as ruled alike by perceptive contingency and sexual selection. This sense of appearance as a powerful force in nature is deepened by Eustacia's changeable feelings toward Wildeve. When told that his would-be wife Thomasin has another admirer, she feels less attracted to him, on account of '[t]he sentiment which lurks more or less in all animate nature – that of not desiring the undesired of others' (99). Ironically, the second suitor who harms Wild-eve's attraction value, Diggory Venn, tries to persuade Thomasin's mother to overlook his scruffy appearance, pleading: 'Looks are not everything' (94). Yet the tale's events and recurring imagery suggest, conversely, that appearance is fundamental to the success of all organisms that see and are seen.

More literally, several of Hardy's rustic characters show uncanny powers of invisibility, disappearing into nature's backgrounds like stick insects. This motif is exemplified in *Return* when Venn withdraws from society after suffering romantic rejection. He becomes a reddleman, coloured red by the ochre he sells and living nomadically on the heathland, connoting regression to more primitive life.[30] The narrator foregrounds this primitiveness, writing of Venn's movements: 'Rejected suitors take to roaming as naturally as unhived bees' (80). His new appearance conceals his identity, as one labourer states after conversing with Venn: 'I fancy I've seen that young man's face before . . . But where, or how, or what his name is, I don't know' (35). Venn is also able to camouflage himself when he spies on other characters, hiding under cut turf and crawling around 'quite invisible, even by daylight'. He becomes like subterranean fauna, as the narrator remarks: 'approaching thus, it was as though he burrowed underground' (81).

Similarly, when the would-be schoolmaster Clym takes up furze-cutting, Hardy's describes him blending in visually with the heath, to the extent that its creatures no longer fear him. In leather work clothes, Clym becomes 'a brown spot in the midst of an expanse of olive-green gorse, and nothing more'; 'his closest friend might have passed by without recognizing him'. He is surrounded by usually elusive animals, as though absorbed into their world of concealment:

> Tribes of emerald-green grasshoppers leaped over his feet . . . Huge flies, ignorant of larders and wire-netting, and quite in a savage state, buzzed about him without knowing that he was a man. In and out of the fern-dells snakes glided in their most brilliant blue and yellow guise, it being the season immediately following the shedding of their old skins, when their colours are brightest. Litters of young rabbits came out from their forms to sun themselves upon hillocks, the hot beams blazing through the delicate tissue of each thin-fleshed ear, and firing it to a blood-red transparency in which the veins could be seen. (244–245)

The animals' appearances are rendered doubly striking by their usual elusiveness near humans. Hardy highlights the relationship between concealment and predation through the heath flies' ignorance of 'wire-netting' (in which entomologists would catch them). As Bates and Wallace had observed, natural variation renders organisms brilliantly conspicuous, but

126   Evolution and the Ethics of Appearance in Thomas Hardy

this conspicuousness is checked by constant persecution. The animals' conspicuousness around Clym depends on his vegetative hue, stillness and passivity. The fact that he eludes the attention of both animals and humans accentuates the commonality of their perceptual processes. Hardy further accentuates Clym's affinity with animal concealment when his mother passes the heath and fails to recognise him, his 'russet hue' rendering him 'not more distinguishable from the scene around him than the green caterpillar from the leaf it feeds on' (267). His return to nature is a journey into invisibility.

Hardy continues to describe concealment among his rustic characters in animal terms in his later novels, imagining such elusiveness as environmental adaptation. In *The Woodlanders*, when Grace's father Melbury begins to doubt his son-in-law Fitzpiers's fidelity, the old man exhibits a talent for invisibility, as the narrator comments: 'No man so furtive for the time as the ingenuous countryman who finds that his ingenuousness has been abused' (195). He spies on Fitzpiers with 'a feline stealth', following the doctor unnoticed to a clandestine meeting in a wood with Felice Charmond, where Melbury keeps 'out of sight' among the vegetation (197). Hardy's rustic and urban characters are perhaps not more or less truthful but only adapted to blend in and stand out in different environments.

Similarly, when the heroine of *Tess of the d'Urbervilles* blends into her surroundings as a survival strategy, Hardy often compares her to a bird, evoking Wallace's arguments for camouflage among avian populations. Estranged from her husband and out of work, Tess encounters a predatory man on the road, and flees into a plantation where she hides in 'a sort of nest' assembled from dead leaves.[31] This act directly precedes her discovery of a flock of pheasants, injured by a shooting party, which she mercifully kills. The birds are victims of their conspicuous exteriors, as the narrator implies by noting their 'rich plumage', which attracted the hunters' rifles (278). Tess's eye-catching beauty can be similarly maladaptive, drawing unwanted sexual attention. Under Alec d'Urbervilles's gaze, the narrator states, this beauty 'amounted to a disadvantage', leading to her pregnancy and social disgrace (42). Later, destitute on the road, Tess protects herself against 'aggressive admiration' by covering and defacing herself. With her eyebrows snipped and her hair, chin and cheeks hidden under a dirty old field dress, she becomes camouflaged: 'a figure which is part of the landscape . . . [An] exterior, over which the eye might have roved as over a thing scarcely percipient, almost inorganic' (280). This effort is ultimately futile, though, as her next employer turns out to be her previous harasser, leaving her 'like a bird caught in a springe' (291). Again, concealment and exposure are imagined as matters of amoral, animal survival. Yet, in spite of this Darwinian emphasis on utility, deception and concealment would still seem to be incorporable into a moral framework, since they remain conscious, intentional acts. However, as the next section will explore, Hardy's fiction frequently suggested that deceitful display or concealment sprang from the borderland between rational intellect and unconscious instinct.

Instinctive Deceit (and Honesty)

Hardy's reading of Arthur Schopenhauer and Eduard von Hartmann consolidated his belief that humans were propelled by biological urges that might contradict rational wishes or interests.[32] Schopenhauer described sexual desire as a 'stratagem' of nature, which tricked individuals into reproducing, thereby helping the race rather than themselves.[33] Von Hartmann agreed that instinct deviously propelled the average man 'to establish a household, and to fulfil his destiny as father of a family, although he thereby ruins and makes unhappy himself and the girl whom he marries'.[34] Hardy can be seen thinking along similar lines in an 1882 notebook entry: 'Write a history of human automatism, or impulsion – viz., an account of human action in spite of human knowledge, showing how very far conduct lags behind the knowledge that should really guide it.'[35]

Hardy was also well aware of arguments for deceitful instincts relating to sexual attraction. Reading Darwin would have drawn his attention to how animals posed and displayed themselves in mating rituals. Francis Galton's *Inquiries into Human Faculty and Its Development* (1883), which Hardy read closely, claimed that women had evolved to be instinctively 'capricious and coy' in order to charm male suitors, and displayed 'a cohort of allied weaknesses and petty deceits'.[36] Women's physical weakness compared with men seemed to necessitate that they survive by deceit, like Bates's and Wallace's weak lepidoptera. Hardy was clearly considering such notions in the early 1890s, when he made paraphrased notes on Schopenhauer: '[Women] Dependent not upon strength but upon craft – tendency to say what is not true ... Dissimulation innate in woman, & almost as much a quality of the stupid as of the clever.'[37] This summary of Schopenhauer's assertions shows Hardy's interest in the possible independence of deception from intellect. Perhaps the tricks of romantic entrapment were not wholly intentional but stemmed from primitive instincts.

128   Evolution and the Ethics of Appearance in Thomas Hardy

The entrapped or deceived might also lack agency, succumbing through unconscious suggestion. In 1894, Hardy recorded having dined with E. R. Lankester and discussing hypnotism: 'Of willing, for example, certain types of women by speech to do as you desire – such as "You *shall*, or you *are to*, marry me", he seems to have had not much doubt. – If true it seems to open up unpleasant possibilities.'[38] These ideas permeated Hardy's tales through descriptions of his characters which blurred the lines between conscious and unconscious action.

Hardy's association of dissimulation with instinctive self-preservation and reproduction recalls Kingsley's and Allen's views of humans evolving from natural egoism to selfless candour. However, Hardy avoids framing truthfulness as artificial or transcendent, suggesting, like Darwin, that honesty also originated in primordial instincts, only altruistic rather than egoistic ones. He wrote in 1890: 'Altruism, or The Golden Rule, or whatever "Love your Neighbour as Yourself" may be called, will ultimately be brought about I think by the pain we see in others reacting on ourselves, as if we and they were part of one body. Mankind in fact, may be and possibly will be viewed as members of one corporeal frame.'[39] Critics have used such comments to argue for an 'evolutionary meliorism' in Hardy's vision, particularly in his later life as a poet.[40] Yet the outlandishness of the image also highlights humanity's remoteness from such altruism in its present condition. Conversely, Hardy's fiction often suggests that honesty and deceitfulness depend on people's chance (possibly hereditary) temperaments: some incline toward altruism and, so, truthfulness; others toward egoism and, so, deceit. More often, though, these contradictory instincts coexist within the same characters, causing them to vacillate between transparency and dissimulation. Hardy's characters thus embody Spencer's model of egoism and altruism as not successive states but an eternal dialectic.[41] By seemingly reducing morality to Darwinian utility, Hardy suggests that nature passes judgement on deceit and honesty by survival or extinction. However, such judgement is capricious and inconsistent, reflecting the tension between the interests of individual and group, a tension which could be solved, Hardy implies, only by the dissolution of the individual. Further, Hardy's absorption of deception and truthfulness into sociobiological tendencies complicates their traditional moral opposition. Instead of being right or wrong in principle, the two behaviours derive their moral import from utilitarian calculations of the general happiness or suffering they are likely to cause.

Many of Hardy's comparisons of human deceit to animal behaviour emphasise the actions' instinctiveness and, therefore, their possible

Instinctive Deceit (and Honesty)

unconsciousness. When *Blue Eyes* describes Stephen as a chameleon, it traces this adaptability to his physical body. Stephen's shape-shifting derived, the narration states, from his 'constitution', the 'extraordinary receptive powers' of 'his brain' (94). Similarly as naturalists assumed that chameleons' colour changes were reflexes rather than rational choices, Stephen's concealment of his origins seems unthinking and automatic.[42] Hardy further equivocates on the intentionality of deceit when Elfride exhibits a newly guarded demeanour around Henry, who becomes her second love interest. The change would seem to indicate Elfride growing away from her honest instincts as experience renders her self-conscious. Yet, conversely, the narrator states that '[a] complexity of instincts checked Elfride's conventional smiles of complaisance and hospitality' (157). Hardy implies that experience does not simply counter instincts but awakens and refines them.

Similarly, in *Madding Crowd*, Troy's seductive talk and displays derive from primitive instincts, apart from his education and intellect. The narrator explains: 'His reason and his propensities had seldom any reciprocating influence, having separated by mutual consent long ago.' Troy fluctuates between 'vicious phases ... the offspring of impulse' and 'virtuous phases of cool meditation' (146–147). By thus dissecting Troy's constitution, Hardy's omniscient narrator minimises his agency. When Troy flirts with Bathsheba on a whim, Hardy suggests that he is as much beguiled by her animated 'beauty' as she is by his glib love talk, which acquires an unplanned emotional momentum as he delivers it. By playing the part of a sincere lover, Troy momentarily becomes one. The narrator states: 'Her beauty, which, whilst it had been quiescent, he had praised in jest, had in its animated phases moved him to earnest; and though his seriousness was less than she imagined, it was probably more than he imagined himself' (175–176). Hardy's parsing of Troy's emotions problematises the dichotomy between sincerity and insincerity, which assumes that speakers know their inner selves and choose to express or conceal them.

Conversely, Troy's impulses run free of his conscious ego, sometimes derailing his intentions. Although he arguably tricks Bathsheba into a doomed marriage, the trick is not wholly intentional. As a husband, Troy is parasitic, gambling away Bathsheba's wealth, but his wooing of her does not seem to be motivated by financial calculations. Indeed, he passes up his love rival Boldwood's offer of an annuity in exchange for jilting Bathsheba, which would have gained him the financial stability of marriage without its restraints. Troy is true to his impulse to sexually possess Bathsheba, while

130   Evolution and the Ethics of Appearance in Thomas Hardy

the prosaic reality of marriage to her barely registers in his mind. Similarly, although he neglects his other lover, Fanny, while she is alive, the sight of her corpse ignites powerful feelings of loyalty toward her, causing him to abandon Bathsheba. He is incapable of lying in the sense of protracted calculation because he lives so in the moment. As the narrator comments: 'He was a man to whom memories were an encumbrance, and anticipations a superfluity. Simply feeling, considering, and caring for what was before his eyes he was vulnerable only in the present' (145). The aforementioned wooing scene ends with Bathsheba exclaiming of his professed love, 'I wish I knew how much of it was true!' (156). Hardy's descriptions of her husband's inner states suggest that Troy is perhaps none the wiser himself.

A Laodicean (1881) similarly problematises female concealment by eroding the boundaries between individual will, education and biological promptings. The novel's heroine, Paula Power, is a bourgeois heiress denounced for her lack of perceptible passion. Sometimes, her coolness seems symptomatic of educated insincerity. While entranced by her beauty, the young architect Somerset worries that she is 'a finished coquette and dissembler' due to her 'inscrutable' reserve.[43] The narrator also sometimes describes Paula's reticence as calculated, stating that, at a dance, 'like all wise maidens, Paula never ventured on the game of the eyes with a lover in public; well knowing that every moment of such indulgence overnight might mean an hour's sneer at her expense by the indulged gentleman next day' (196–197). This sense of artifice is countered, however, by the diction of biological imperatives. Earlier in the scene, when Paula sees Somerset for the first time, emotion flashes briefly on her face before disappearing, since '[t]he habit of self-repression at any new emotional impact was instinctive with her always' (193). The repression is so rapid that it seems to precede thought and is, perhaps, no less automatic than the expression it hides. Paula endorses this view, explaining to Somerset that she cannot help hesitating when he declares his love, for 'it is a natural instinct to retain the power of obliging a man to hope, fear, pray, and beseech as long as we think fit, before we confess to a reciprocal affection' (239). The supposedly agential actions involved in dissimulation recede into the uncertain penumbra of 'instinct'.

Hardy implies even less agency in female characters who dissimulate in spite of their conscious wishes. Such dissonance emerges in his first published novel *Desperate Remedies* (1871), when the woman Cytherea is forced into a loveless marriage. Nonetheless, she still carefully attends to her bridal appearance, causing the narrator to remark: 'here was Cytherea,

Instinctive Deceit (and Honesty)   131

in the bottom of her heart almost indifferent to life, yet possessing an instinct with which her heart had nothing to do, the instinct to be particularly regardful of those sorry trifles, her robe, her flowers, her veil, her gloves'.[44] Cytherea's imagined womanly impulse to maximise her attractiveness continues to drive her actions even when they contradict her conscious wishes.

Equally, in *Tess*, the heroine's characteristic honesty is countered by primordial urges to dissimulate before her prospective mate. After accepting Angel's marriage proposal, Tess withholds from revealing her non-virginity to him, the narrator commenting: 'her instinct of self-preservation was stronger than her candour' (189). Hardy downplays Tess's choice, stating that, in the moment when she plans to reveal all, the 'woman's instinct to hide' overcomes her (196). Although dissimulation makes use of intelligence, Hardy suggests that it is motivated by unconscious drives. He accentuates this point by describing Tess's concealment as the outcome of physiological processes, not abstract reflection: 'Every see-saw of her breath, every wave of her blood, every pulse singing in her ears, was a voice that joined with nature in revolt against her scrupulousness.' Like a beast motivated by immediate sensory attractions and aversions, she is compelled 'to snatch ripe pleasure before the iron teeth of pain could have time to shut upon her' (178). Hardy's language implies that, far from being calculated, impulsive dissimulation can derail premeditations.

Hardy's representation of deceit as partly instinctive even absolves his most unsympathetic characters of some moral responsibility, such as the ruthless Arabella in *Jude the Obscure* (1895). The pig-farmer's daughter lures the aspiring scholar Jude from his studies with false hair and dimples, before ensnaring him in marriage by falsely claiming to be pregnant. Yet Hardy depicts her deceptions as more impulsive than premeditated. Arabella first enters Jude's attention by throwing a pig's penis at him, initiating the conversation which leads to them courting. The thoughtlessness of the action is indicated by her afterward realising its vulgarity and lamenting, 'I wish I had thrown something else than that!'[45] Instead of Arabella planning to seduce Jude, the narrator states that her 'personality' uttered the 'unvoiced call of woman to man'. Hardy emphasises Arabella's bestial unreflectiveness by depicting her as 'a complete and substantial female animal – no more, no less', and her allurement of Jude as 'her game' (40–41). She gives no thought to the marriage that will satisfy neither party. Her actions are motivated by spontaneous desire, as she admits to her friends: 'I want him to have me – to marry me! I must have him. I can't

132   Evolution and the Ethics of Appearance in Thomas Hardy

do without him. He's the sort of man I long for. I shall go mad if I can't give myself to him altogether! I felt I should when I first saw him!' (50). Hardy further undermines Arabella's agency in her deceits through her denying to her friends that she intentionally faked pregnancy. While admitting to the 'trick' of seducing Jude with the intention of becoming pregnant, she claims to have been 'mistaken' and made no conscious 'sham' (60).

Arabella's ruses continue to spring from impulse rather than calculation later in the tale after Jude has divorced her, when she tricks him into remarrying her while drunk. The scheme disadvantages Arabella, burdening her with a sick, penniless husband, and Hardy indicates that it is motivated more by sexual jealousy than logic. Seeing Jude with his lover, Sue, provokes Arabella to throw off her religious, mourning persona (her other husband having recently died) and declare: 'I'd take him from her if I could! ... Feelings are feelings!' Ironically, Arabella views this yielding to instinct, which drives her deception, as sincere self-expression. Discarding her religious tracts, she states: 'I won't be a creeping hypocrite any longer ... I must be as I was born!' (315–316). From Arabella's perspective, deceiving others is being true to herself.

Hardy's late fiction further problematised moral responsibility in deception by presenting truthfulness as another product of instinctive impulse, albeit a different one to the selfish egoism behind deceit. As the Introduction showed, honesty could be imagined as deriving from the altruistic tendency to cooperate in ever-expanding groups. Hardy read Spencer avidly, and sometimes echoed the latter's vision of egoism and altruism as a timeless dialectic.[46] In 1893, he wrote: 'The doctrines of Darwinism require readjusting largely; for instance, the survival of the fittest in the struggle for life. There is an altruism and coalescence between cells as well as an antagonism. Certain cells destroy certain cells; but others assist and combine. – Well, I can't say.'[47] Hardy's indeterminacy resists both idealising nature as morally pure and disregarding it as totally amoral. While wary of taking nature as a moral guide, he still suggests that morality originates in nature rather than reason, deriving from instinctive emotions.

Hardy illustrates this point through characters being impulsively truthful, even though doing so contradicts their individual biological interests. Tess's egoistic instincts are usually conquered by her altruistic ones, causing her to be honest even at great personal cost. She feels no desire to play the coquette, as the narrator states of her courting period with Angel: 'in her honest faith she did not disguise her desire to be with him'. Such romantic reticence is at odds with 'the sum of her instincts ... since it must in its very nature carry with it a suspicion of art' (193). She is equally open about her feelings with her fellow milkmaids, despite their being love rivals for Angel. Over other women, Tess exercises 'a warmth and strength quite unusual, curiously overpowering the less worthy feminine feelings of spite and rivalry' (296). Indeed, Hardy frames the selfless companionship between Tess and her workmates as a high development of altruism, to the extent that they almost resemble one body: 'The differences which distinguished them as individuals were abstracted by this passion, and each was but portion of one organism called sex ... [Each one] did not delude herself with any vain conceits, or deny her love, or give herself airs, in the idea of outshining the others' (147). Tess's veracity is equally self-sabotaging, as she points out to Angel the beauty of her workmates and then, after the wedding, dispels his idealisation of her as a virgin. Even after she has been forced to marry Alec, killed him and gone on the run with Angel, Tess still sacrifices herself in the cause of altruistic honesty. Instead of planning any 'effectual escape, disguise, or long concealment', she asks Angel to marry her sister Liza-Lu, who fits his ideal of virginal peasant girl (386). By tracing honesty and dissimulation to contrasting instincts, Hardy undermines their supposed transcendent moral significance. Such behaviours seem more like adaptations evolved to serve the group or the individual, respectively.

Jude and Sue's impulsive veracity is similarly selfless and maladaptive individually, wrecking their prospects of material security. When Jude realises that he loves Sue, who is already married, he abandons his plans for a Church career, feeling, the narrator states, that 'he had made himself quite an impostor as a law-abiding religious teacher' (217). After Jude burns his theology books, 'the sense of being no longer a hypocrite to himself afforded his mind a relief which gave him calm' (218). The desire to be honest trumps pragmatic considerations of personal advantage. The same effect follows from Sue's insistence on the pair openly living together unmarried to avoid supporting an institution they no longer believe in. When she falls in love with Jude while married to another man, Phillotson, she refuses to be false to her marriage oath by committing adultery. She also loathes being forced to lie about doing so to obtain a divorce, complaining after the dissolution of her marriage: 'my freedom has been obtained under false pretences!' (258). Her subsequent refusal to marry Jude, or to hide their extramarital status, causes the pair and their children to be constantly thrown out of boarding houses. During one such eviction, Sue's impulsive truthfulness seals the destruction of their family as she tells their son, adopted from Arabella, that the family will split up because they

134 Evolution and the Ethics of Appearance in Thomas Hardy

are too numerous to find lodgings. The dour boy subsequently kills himself and his siblings with the mistaken belief that he is lightening his parents' burden. Blaming herself for the tragedy, Sue laments: 'it was that I wanted to be truthful. I couldn't bear deceiving him as to the facts of life' (338). In Hardy's Darwinian universe, selfless honesty is as likely to be punished as rewarded.

Yet Hardy also complicates the supposed evolutionary adaptability of deceitfulness through the fate of Arabella. Arabella's selfish dishonesty initially seems supremely adaptive, enabling her to survive Jude and his children with Sue, while Sue also appears likely to die soon from grief. Yet Arabella's dishonesty leaves her childless. Although she is adept at attracting sexual partners (lining up a replacement for Jude even before his death), she views such partners as means of raising her social standing and attractiveness, not reproducing. Her one thought upon marrying Jude is that 'she had gained a husband; that was the thing – a husband with a lot of earning power in him for buying her frocks and hats' (58). When she appears with her second husband at the fair, she is 'covered with beads from bonnet to skirt, that made her glisten as if clad in chain-mail' (290). By rejecting motherhood in favour of never-ending sexual display, Arabella is evolutionarily maladaptive, failing to procreate. Richard Kaye argues that Darwinian sexual selection amplified the disturbing possibility that desire might be derailed from its purpose of reproduction as the figure of the 'flirt' extended the play of attraction perpetually.[48] Arabella's childlessness exemplifies this paradox, demonstrating that dissimulative egoism is not necessarily advantageous from an intergenerational perspective.

Nor are the honest necessarily doomed. Hardy's vision of the universe as chaotic and random contradicted the assumption that it offered any model for society. The fact that Jude and Sue's altruistic candour often works against them is, perhaps, more a condemnation of Victorian society than an argument that the trait leads to extinction. Hardy once wrote that *Jude* aimed, like all of his fiction, to 'state . . . cases in which natural & human laws create tragic dramas'.[49] His division of 'human laws' from 'natural' ones allows for the possibility that such tragedies could be avoided if society was organised differently. Egoistic dishonesty is less the way of the universe than the way of capitalism and the traditional institution of the family. Jude voices this insight near the end of the tale when he reflects that his 'impulses' were mismatched with an age when one 'should be as cold-blooded as a fish and as selfish as a pig to have a really good chance of being one of his country's worthies' (326). The oppressive taboos of respectability force people to live dishonestly, as Sue sadly remarks while

Instinctive Deceit (and Honesty)

pondering her and Jude's work prospects: 'even a baker must be conventional, to get customers' (307). Of course, the massacre of their children follows as much from these hypocritical taboos as it does Sue's candour. Constantly reviled as a burden, the murderous son comes to regard himself as such, despairing: 'I troubled 'em in Australia, and I trouble folk here. I wish I hadn't been born!' (333). The final cause of the tragedy is perhaps not too much candour but a deficit of it. Sue avoids confronting the Malthusian pessimism which the boy has absorbed, later despairing that 'with a false delicacy I told him too obscurely . . . It was my want of self-control, so that I could neither conceal things nor reveal them!' (338). Hardy presents egoistic deceitfulness and altruistic truthfulness as equally adaptive in different social contexts: the fact that current society favours the former need not rule out another order favouring the latter.

Hardy's reduction of truth and lies to manifestations of egoism and altruism not only reduces his characters' agency; it redefines the moral import of candour and deceitfulness on purely utilitarian grounds. Sidgwick had recently argued that deceit could be altruistic when performed in the interests of others (see the Introduction). Likewise, Hardy's fiction explores the possibility of deceit being justified when it increases happiness. Regretting her honesty with her son, Sue laments: 'Why didn't I tell him pleasant untruths, instead of half-realities?' (338). Hardy's notebooks transcribe Comte's wry summary of the 'sincere hypocrisy' of Immanuel Kant, who, 'after having decisively demonstrated the unreality of supernatural beliefs, had made an attempt to reestablish them on the plea of their necessity to society'.[50] Hardy sometimes tentatively endorses this view, such as when Tess seeks reassurance from a parson that her impromptu baptism of her dying, illegitimate baby was valid. While the parson's intellect inclines him to tell the distressing truth, Tess's grief 'affect[ed] his nobler impulses' so that '[t]he man and the ecclesiastic fought within him, and the victory fell to the man' (96). A similar impulse restrains Angel from catechising Tess too deeply on religious questions, since her 'confused beliefs' harm no one and disturbing them would only distress her (172).

Conversely, the fates of Hardy's characters also question the supposed benevolence of religious illusions. While Tess's religious innocence seems to be comforting, it really compounds her suffering. Sexually exploited by Alec, she imagines creation condemning her: 'The midnight airs and gusts, moaning amongst the tightly-wrapped buds and bark of the winter twigs, were formulae of bitter reproach.' The narrator observes that such fancies were, in fact, 'a cloud of moral hobgoblins' conjured by social convention (85).

136   Evolution and the Ethics of Appearance in Thomas Hardy

Similarly, in *Jude*, Sue's hysterical, newfound religiosity after the death of her children exacerbates her misery, forcing her to repress her desire for Jude and return to Phillotson. When the latter kisses her in bed, the narrator notes, 'A quick look of aversion passed over her face, but clenching her teeth she uttered no cry' (398). Hardy further doubts the benevolence of religious lies by highlighting their promulgators' self-interest. While Angel's brothers in *Tess* uphold religious orthodoxy to advance their careers, Phillotson supports it out of sexual possessiveness. When Sue returns to him, the narrator notes that Phillotson indulges her delusions out of a 'human instinct' quite opposed to 'the humane instinct which had induced him to let her go' (366, 369). Hardy is less concerned with ideal moral principles than with how discourse affects the sum of suffering.

The next section argues that Hardy further problematised the ethics of deception through tales of people misreading signs of ancestry on each other's bodies. Such organic illusions have no deceiving agent, placing responsibility for them solely upon the deceived parties. Like Kingsley and Allen, Hardy finds moral significance in adaptive appearance by focussing on what makes the deceived parties gullible to such tricks. I suggest that these tales of bodily misreadings satirise the shallow egoism of valuing others as vehicles for biologically extending or socially enhancing oneself.

Illusory Ancestries

Hardy was much interested in how bodies could reveal and conceal lineages.[51] For him, the idea of proximate family features existed in tension with a more expansive view of the human family, whose ultimately shared ancestry was reflected in broad continua of features. In this sense, *ancestry* was what one made of it, characterised as much by what it excluded as what it included. Tess O'Toole notes that Hardy's fiction repeatedly dramatises the 'imaginative' nature of genealogy, suggesting that its 'effects' are partly produced by descendants' 'intellectual and emotional response[s]' to ambiguous bodies.[52] An obvious example of bodily misreading with biological consequences in the animal world was birds mistaking cuckoo chicks in their nests for their own offspring. Hardy's tales of misleading bodily features sometimes evoke this phenomenon as characters' fates revolve upon their resemblances or lack of resemblances to ancestors (real or imagined). Such plots would have echoed the Tichborne case, which Hardy took an interest in.[53] The example of a working-class man attaching himself to a rich, aristocratic mother by posing as her son might have seemed

Illusory Ancestries

a human equivalent of the cuckoo's deception. Hardy was acutely conscious of the biological and folkloric analogies between cuckoos and cuckoldry, transcribing in his notebook an account of the bird's song reportedly alerting a man to his wife's infidelity.[54] However, Hardy's fictions of bodily misreading also question the usefulness of the Darwinian arms race between masquerade and detection for understanding human relations. The moral of such tales is not that humans must establish others' ancestry scientifically to avoid being tricked (à la Allen) but that they should reconsider their valuation of ancestral lines, and its foundation in egoism. Hardy's characters are often doomed or thwarted not so much by their inability to read others' ancestry than by their obsession with doing so, which blinds them to people's individual characters and value.

Galton speculated that 'if a considerable number of variable and independent features could be catalogued, it might be possible to trace kinship with considerable certainty'.[55] Bodies are often revelatory of family history in this way in Hardy's writing. Tess's face displays uncanny resemblances to portraits of her aristocratic ancestors. Conversely, in the short story 'Squire Petrick's Lady' (1890), a young boy's features reveal his lack of aristocratic blood. The boy's father, a squire, nurtures the quixotic belief that his son is a nobleman's love child after the boy's dying mother confesses to infidelity. However, the boy fails to develop the nobleman's features, apparently confirming a doctor's judgement that his mother's affair was a hysterical delusion.[56] In the poem 'Heredity' (1917), Hardy depicts the recurrence of family features across generations as so pronounced that they diminish the significance of individual lives. The speaker gives a voice to genetic transmission, declaring, 'I am the family face . . . Projecting trait and trace/Through time to times anon.'[57] People's seemingly unique lineaments are reduced to links in repeating patterns. Similarly, in 'The Pedigree' (1916), the speaker envisions himself as a composite of elements from his predecessors, despairing, 'I am merest mimicker and counterfeit!'[58]

Nonetheless, bodies could also be unreliable records of lineage. Galton conceded that one could 'inherit a large number of minor and commonly overlooked features from many ancestors', and the features of distant, forgotten relations could spring to the fore unexpectedly.[59] In *Return of the Native*, we see the young Christian Cantle failing spectacularly to replicate his grandfather's masculine physique and dominant presence. Exhibiting a 'thin jibbering voice', 'reedy hair, no shoulders, and a great quantity of wrist and ankle', Christian causes Granfer Cantle to stare at him 'as a hen stares at the duck she has hatched' (28). Christian might, of

138   Evolution and the Ethics of Appearance in Thomas Hardy

course, have another biological father, but no evidence is given for this in the text. Hardy further foregrounds nature's caprice by suggesting Christian is a hermaphrodite. Characters' speculations that this abnormality was caused by lunar movements evoke environment's possible power to deflect individuals away from ancestral types. Most of Hardy's fiction preceded the development of genetics at the turn of the century, which promised to impose some predictability on the expression of inherited traits.[60] As biologists debated the vagaries of heredity, Hardy depicted the links between generations as fraught with unexpected divergences.

Further, familial resemblances might not be stable but could appear and vanish under different physiological conditions. Maudsley noted that 'the son who calls to mind his mother at twenty years old perhaps calls his father to mind at forty'.[61] Johann Caspar Lavater had also claimed that animation hid people's features, while the stillness of sleep and death made them 'much more prominent'.[62] Hardy's interest in such views of the face as a surface of shifting, elusive resemblances emerges in *The Mayor of Casterbridge* (1886). The protagonist Henchard sells his wife and young daughter to another man, Newson, only for mother and daughter to apparently return eighteen years later. However, after his wife's death, Henchard discovers a letter claiming that his own daughter perished and the living Elizabeth-Jane is Newson's. When Henchard sneaks into Elizabeth-Jane's chamber to examine her features, Hardy writes: 'In sleep there come to the surface buried genealogical facts, ancestral curves, dead men's traits, which the mobility of daytime animation screens and overwhelms. In the present statuesque repose of the young girl's countenance Richard Newson's was unmistakably reflected.'[63] Similarly, in the short story 'For Conscience' Sake' (1891), seasickness reveals previously invisible similarities between a father and daughter, who have kept their consanguinity secret to hide the daughter's illegitimate birth. The daughter's love interest, who thinks her father is only a step-father, is sailing on a yacht with the pair when he notices their uncanny resemblance. The narrator notes:

> Nausea in such circumstances . . . brings out strongly the divergences of the individual from the norm of his race, accentuating superficial peculiarities to radical distinctions. Unexpected physiognomies will uncover themselves at these times in well-known faces; the aspect becomes invested with the spectral presence of entombed and forgotten ancestors; and family lineaments of special or exclusive cast, which in ordinary moments are masked by a stereotyped expression and mien, start up with crude insistence to the view.[64]

Illusory Ancestries 139

Like mimetic animals' true taxonomic affinities that emerged under the anatomist's lens, Hardy's family features can lie half-hidden, becoming visible only in special conditions. O'Toole observes that mismatches in Hardy's writing between lineages and their expected features frame the 'genetic process' 'as a textual system in which "traits" are signifiers connoting, but not necessarily denoting, a signified "quality"'; in short, 'a breeder of fictions'.[65]

Yet, in contrast to the speaker in 'The Pedigree' who feels diminished by his resemblance to his ancestors, many of Hardy's fictional characters view family resemblance as a vehicle of self-assertion or advancement. They place high value on chance bodily traits, embracing or rejecting people based on the ancestry apparently signalled in their lineaments. Such bodily signs sometimes mislead, however, with tragic consequences. Hardy thus harnesses nature's tricks of resemblance to make a moral point. These tricks have the power to deceive, he suggests, only due to the small-minded prejudice and egoism that drives people to value certain genealogies over others. Such tragic misapprehension can be avoided by valuing humans irrespective of ancestry, rendering resemblances inconsequential.

Hardy's fiction persistently ridicules preoccupations with lineage, associating them with delusional pomposity. He depicts ancestral pride as the refuge of underachievers. The most obvious example of this tendency is Tess's father, John Durbeyfield. This poor, feckless haggler becomes fixated upon his imagined nobility after learning that he is descended from the old d'Urberville family. His childish notion that the current, rich d'Urbervilles will favour their long-lost 'kin' sets the novel's tragedy in motion (26). The fact that these d'Urbervilles descend from a bourgeois capitalist who adopted the name to enhance his reputation reinforces the fatuity of John's ancestral pride. The villainous Alec d'Urbervilles taunts the powerless Tess by reminding her that he is a 'sham d'Urbervilles', a mimetic creature adapted to his environment (364).

However, Hardy also lampooned genealogical snobbery earlier, in *Blue Eyes*, through Elfride's father, Swancourt. This genteel-poor parson is obsessed with his connection to the aristocratic Luxellian family. Hardy emphasises the asininity of Swancourt's snobbery by him mistakenly identifying Stephen as a man of 'blue blood' and, on this basis, allowing him to court Elfride (20). Swancourt's failure to notice clues to the young man's humble upbringing, such as his mispronunciations of Latin and inexperience at chess, demonstrate Swancourt's failure to grasp that class status is a social acquisition and performance. When Stephen's origins are revealed, Swancourt angrily forbids the romance with Elfride, valuing imagined ancestral status over the actual qualities individuals display. The dramatic irony of Swancourt asserting that Stephen's nobility 'is as plain as the nose in your face' suggests that origins are anything but plain when judged on features alone (20). Hardy accentuates this implication through the parson's later, unconvincing claim to have always doubted Stephen's gentility. The young man expressed no preferences when offered condiments, Swancourt recalls, and '[a]n unedified palate is the irrepressible cloven foot of the upstart' (87). The bathetic absurdity of Swancourt's statement highlights his desperate wish for genealogy to always reveal itself. Hardy hints that Swancourt is perhaps lucky that it does not as other characters mention a local legend that the Luxellians secretly descended from a peasant. The narrator ironises Swancourt's notion of visible ancestry by implying that his body proclaims his commonness. Of the parson's muscular physique and ruddy features, we are told: 'His *tout ensemble* was that of a highly-improved class of farmer, dressed up in the wrong clothes' (26). Hardy further links the reading of ancestry upon bodies with vain self-importance through the figure of the local sexton. Digging up long-dead villagers, the man claims to recognise each skeleton individually 'by some little sign', although, the narrator confides, 'in reality he had never recognized any' (79–80). The macabre image underlines the futility of genealogical snobbery: death reveals how little these distinctions matter.

Hardy further satirises reverence of nobility and its imagined features in *A Laodicean* through identifications (and misidentifications) of members of the De Stancy family. This aristocratic line gives its name to the castle that the bourgeois Paula now owns. Sometimes Hardy presents the modern De Stancys' bodies as transparent indexes of their illustrious genealogy. When the middle-aged Captain De Stancy appears before Paula in De Stancy castle, he seems to become one with its paintings of his ancestors. As the Captain positions himself beneath one particular portrait, the narrator observes: 'the De Stancys were a family on whom the hallmark of membership was deeply stamped, and by the present light the representative under the portrait and the representative in the portrait seemed beings not far removed' (166).

Yet this apparent genealogical transparency of the Captain's body is also a mask, hiding his differences from the ancient De Stancys, biological and economic. The modern De Stancys have lost most of their wealth, and the Captain is an undistinguished military man of modest means. His posing before the portraits is part of a cynical plot to win Paula's heart and regain the castle. Hardy suggests that, far from revealing his essential self, the

Illusory Ancestries 141

Captain's resemblances to the paintings are contrived illusions. He displays, the narrator states, a 'Protean quality . . . by means of which he could assume the shape and situation of almost any ancestor' (170). The Captain exaggerates the resemblances by donning a suit of armour, arranging the room's lighting and mimicking the figures' stances. He talks authoritatively about the family history when, in reality, he has just skimmed a memoir like a 'crammed . . . candidate for a government examination' (166). In a further irony, Hardy casts doubt on the accuracy of the old De Stancy portraits as Somerset reflects: 'Some were willfully false, no doubt; many more so by unavoidable accident and want of skill. Somerset felt that it required a profounder mind than his to disinter from the lumber of conventionality the lineaments that really sat in the painter's presence' (21). The images regarded as authentic benchmarks of the De Stancy line are, perhaps, as contrived as the Captain's mimicry of them.

The novel further undermines the idea of bodies reliably indexing ancestry through the Captain's daughter, Charlotte, and secret illegitimate son, William Dare. Charlotte's features illustrate nature's tendency toward variation and, perhaps, also the reality that all heritages are mixed, rendering a single, pure bloodline an impossible fantasy. When Somerset first sees her, the narrator reports, Charlotte displays, 'not the De Stancy face with all its original specialities: it was, so to speak, a defective reprint of that face: for the nose tried hard to turn up and deal utter confusion to the family shape' (23). The reification of fixed familial features is further problematised by Dare, who passes among the other characters unidentified and plots the Captain's romance with Paula. At one point, Hardy seems to suggest that Dare might bear some De Stancy family resemblances as Paula comments vaguely that he is 'something like' Charlotte and 'one or other of the old pictures about the house'. However, she and the others disregard this apparent commonality, Somerset declaring, 'People's features fall naturally into groups and classes . . . To an observant person they often repeat themselves; though to a careless eye they seem infinite in their differences' (63). Dare appears to exemplify such averageness, and hides behind it as others struggle to classify even his nationality or age. When Somerset suspects the young man of foul play, he tries to sketch Dare's features for the police, only to find that 'he could not make a drawing that was a satisfactory likeness' (131). Indeed, Dare needs to tattoo his chest with his family name as an insurance policy, since his body cannot be relied upon to identify his lineage.

The De Stancys' inconsistent, sometimes contrived, bodily resemblances serve to expose the perceptual biases of others, notably Paula, whose idealisation of nobility renders her vulnerable to Dare and the Captain's manipulations. The narrator remarks that, seeing the Captain standing by his ancestors' portraits, 'a new and romantic feeling that the De Stancys had stretched out a tentacle from their genealogical tree to seize her by the hand and draw her in to their mass took possession of Paula' (166). The Captain's meticulous mimicry of his ancestors' portraits is crafted to appeal to her fantasies. Indeed, the narrator suggests that the spectacle puts Paula into a trance in which her rational faculties are disabled: 'Paula was continually starting from a reverie and speaking irrelevantly, as if such reflections as those seized hold of her in spite of her natural unconcern' (166). Like an animal fooled by protective mimicry, Paula is unable to abstract critically from her immediate sensations and the primitive desires they trigger. Paula's reverence of the De Stancy lineage (and thus her gullibility) is driven by a desire for elevated social status. Her story thus fits into a pattern in Hardy's fiction in which attempting to read history in bodily traits and being misled by apparent family resemblances are seen to proceed from egoistic motives.

The same pattern emerges in *The Mayor of Casterbridge* when Henchard realises that Elizabeth-Jane is not his biological daughter. Initially, he imagines his previous belief in their consanguinity the 'impish trick' of some 'sinister intelligence'.[66] Henchard sees himself as a cuckold, hoodwinked by nature's ambiguous signs into supporting another man's child. However, the story subsequently implies that such concerns are irrelevant. Far from abandoning Elizabeth-Jane after discovering her parentage, Henchard cleaves to her, lying to Newson that she is dead to prevent the latter taking her away. Hardy suggests that human bonds depend more on the performance of familial roles than consanguinity. Having acted as Elizabeth-Jane's father, Henchard develops an emotional dependence on her which knowledge of her true paternity cannot extinguish. From this perspective, the ambiguity of family resemblances loses its import, concerning only egoistic minds which value their relations as extension of themselves (although, admittedly, Henchard's possessiveness of Elizabeth-Jane is hardly altruistic).

This lesson is exemplified more sharply in Hardy's short story 'The Marchioness of Stonehenge' (1891), in which a poor woman, Milly, raises a noblewoman's secret illegitimate son. When the son grows up, the Marchioness begins to crave a relationship with him, and visits Milly to demand him back. The noblewoman assumes that the son will transfer his affections to his biological mother, telling Milly, 'He is my own flesh and

Illusory Ancestries 143

blood.' However, Milly boldly retorts, 'flesh and blood's nothing!', and her son proves her right when he coldly rejects the Marchioness.[67] His reaction illustrates how adoptive love can trump consanguinity, redefining family as a social acquisition rather than a fixed biological given. He states of Milly: 'She, dear devoted soul ... tended me from my birth, watched over me, nursed me when I was ill, and deprived herself of many a little comfort to push me on. I cannot love another mother as I love her. She *is* my mother, and I will always be her son!'[68] Milly and the son's relationship acquires an emotional reality which renders its fictitious origin irrelevant.

Hardy countered this conclusion with another tale in the same collection, 'Lady Mottisfont', in which a woman adopts Dorothy, the illegitimate daughter of a countess, only for the countess to later return and win the child back. The narrator suggests that Dorothy feels an intuitive affinity for her biological mother, taking to the Countess 'with a strange and instinctive readiness that intimated the wonderful subtlety of the threads which bind flesh and flesh together'.[69] However, this apparently instinctive bond does not last, as the Countess later jettisons Dorothy again in order to marry a new suitor. The resemblances between Dorothy and her biological mother, which inspire Dorothy's affections, prove misleading, causing Dorothy to lose a more devoted adoptive mother (although, after falling pregnant, the adoptive mother also refuses to take her back). In both stories, the desire of the biological mothers to reunite with their estranged children proceeds from egoistic possessiveness rather than altruistic concern for their children as independent beings. The Marchioness in the first tale tells the adoptive mother proprietorially, 'He is *my* son ... You must give him back to me' (125). Yet the son reminds the noblewoman that she 'cared little for me when I was weak and helpless' (126). The Marchioness becomes interested in the son only when she is a lonely widow and he a handsome, successful soldier who can enhance her status. Similarly, in the other tale, the Countess yearns for Dorothy only during her lonely widowhood. Having found a rich, new husband, she no longer refers to Dorothy as her child but 'the dear foundling I have adopted temporarily'.[70]

These tales undermine the model of bodies falsifying affinity or otherness by redefining family as social, as well as biological, bonds. In this way, Hardy's fiction reflected wider, emerging notions of family as an artificial institution. The legal historian Henry Maine had recently argued that all society depended on 'the Fiction of Adoption which permits the family tie to be artificially created'.[71] Similarly, Hardy suggests that bodies are

144   Evolution and the Ethics of Appearance in Thomas Hardy

deceptive only to those who view their relations as self-extensions. Hence, when Arabella abandons her child to Jude's care, Jude disregards the question of whether the boy is his biological son, declaring:

> The beggarly question of parentage – what is it, after all? What does it matter, when you come to think of it, whether a child is yours by blood or not? All the little ones of our time are collectively the children of us adults of the time, and entitled to our general care. That excessive regard of parents for their own children, and their dislike of other people's, is, like class-feeling, patriotism, save-your-own-soul-ism, and other virtues, a mean exclusiveness at bottom. (274–275)

One could be deceived by family (non)resemblances only if one valued others egoistically by their biological proximity to oneself.

Hardy implies this conclusion most directly in his late short story 'An Imaginative Woman' (1894), in which a mysterious variation in a child's face causes his father to erroneously conclude that the boy is another man's. The mother, Ella, conceives the child during a holiday, when the family stays in the lodgings of the poet Robert Trewe. Although Ella never meets Trewe, she becomes obsessed with him, treating his imagined personality as a surrogate for the emotions which her loveless marriage fails to satisfy. She spends the holiday gazing at Trewe's photograph, reading his poetry and touching his possessions. Ella subsequently becomes pregnant, is devastated by news of Trewe's suicide, and then dies in childbirth. Years later, her husband finds the poet's picture and a lock of his hair (obtained through a mediator) among Ella's possessions, causing him to suspiciously examine his young son. The narrator states: 'By a known but inexplicable trick of Nature there were undoubtedly strong traces of resemblance to the man Ella had never seen; the dreamy and peculiar expression of the poet's face sat, as the transmitted idea, upon the child's, and the hair was of the same hue.'[72]

It is debatable how realistic this event would have appeared to Hardy's initial readers, evoking old ideas that a mother's psychological 'impressions' during pregnancy could visibly influence the child.[73] Such notions were increasingly doubted in the 1890s, most notably by August Weismann (whose work Hardy had read).[74] However, the 'trick of Nature' might equally be a chance coalescence of variations, which cause the young boy, at that moment, to display features somewhat resembling Trewe. More significant than the uncertain biological mechanism to which the boy owes his features is the proprietorial attitude with which his father reacts to them. He immediately declares: 'Then she did play me false with

Illusory Ancestries 145

that fellow at the lodgings! ... Get away, you poor little brat! You are nothing to me!'[75] In Darwinian terms, the husband's search for his own features in his offspring proves maladaptive, causing him to mistakenly reject his own child. Hardy suggests that nature's 'tricks' of resemblance afflict humans only because they are yet to progress beyond selfish egoism, valuing ancestors and offspring merely as ways of elevating or extending themselves.

Hardy further linked misreading of family resemblance with egoism in his last published novella, *The Well-Beloved.*[76] The tale follows the sculptor Pierston, who falls in love with three successive generations of women from the same family. Having jilted Avice Caro as a young man, the middle-aged and sexagenarian Pierston pursues her daughter and grand-daughter, who fail to return his love. The man views these unrequited infatuations as a kind of cosmic prank. Pierston imagines nature playing a 'queer trick' on him by drawing him back to his homeland where he encounters the second Avice as a 'perfect copy' of her mother.[77] However, Hardy suggests that the deception lies less in the Caro family's bodies than in Pierston's obsessive fetishising of Avice, which stems from an egoistic sense of affinity with her. Descending from the same inbred island as Avice, he imagines that union with her (or one of her descendants) will unite him with himself. Only the Caro family, he reflects, 'possessed the materials' to 'furbish up an individual nature which would exactly, ideally, supplement his own imperfect one and round with it the perfect whole' (251).

This fixation causes him to overlook the differences between the successive Avices, blinded by his vision of an ideal type. The narrator observes that, regarding the second Avice, Pierston 'could not help seeing in her all that he knew of another, and veiling in her all that did not harmonize with his sense of metempsychosis' (244). Hardy emphasises the irrational, brute nature of Pierston's infatuation, remarking, 'Honest perception had told him that this Avice, fairer than her mother in face and form, was her inferior in soul and understanding ... But it was recklessly pleasant to leave the suspicion unrecognized as yet, and follow the lead' (240). Similarly, he knows that a 'hereditary persistence' of lineaments can exist 'without the qualities signified by the traits', but 'unconsciously hoped that it was at least not entirely so here'. Although Pierston has the intelligence to question his perception of Avice as her mother reincarnated, his desire for this to be the case suppresses his critical faculties.[78] As with Bates's predators, unthinking impulse impels him toward superficial resemblances. Further, he

146   Evolution and the Ethics of Appearance in Thomas Hardy

nurtures his delusion by avoiding becoming deeply acquainted with the second- and third-generation Caro girls. When the second Avice, now middle-aged, encourages him to court the third, Pierston assures her: 'Virtually I have known your daughter any number of years. When I talk to her I can anticipate every turn of her thought, every sentiment, every act, so long did I study those things in your mother and in you. Therefore I do not require to learn her; she was learnt by me in her previous existences' (295–296). He is proved spectacularly wrong when the young woman agrees to marry him, only to elope with a secret lover.

Nature's 'trick' of seeming to replicate the same person in different bodies depends on the biases of the observer, who seeks to confirm his desired preconceptions. Hardy's narration reflects this bias, stating of mother and daughter: 'the lost and the found Avice seemed essentially the same person. Their external likeness to each other – probably owing to the cousinship between the elder and her husband – went far to nourish the fantasy' (239). Unable to separate his perceptions of the women from the impossible replication he desires, Pierston is the engineer of his own deception. Annette Federico claims that *The Well-Beloved* argues for the necessity of detaching aesthetic perception from selfish desire in order to see others clearly. Perception is morally and intellectually stunted by egoistic possessiveness and self-projection, as Feredico states: 'Pierston's is another Pygmalion story, the love of the creator for his creation – in other words, the love of the creator for himself.'[79]

Only when Pierston is old and his libido moribund does he begin to view the Caros unselfishly, providing money for the third Avice and her husband. He perceives her as an individual with a mind and life of her own instead of the manifestation of a subjective ideal, responding to praise of her looks: 'I suppose she is handsome. She's more – a wise girl who will make a good housewife' (330). The evaporation of Pierston's desire enables him to overcome nature's apparent trickery, since he no longer ignores the Caro women's deviations from an imagined type. His motivation changes from possession to sympathy. The narrator notes Pierston's new concern for the middle-aged second Avice: 'Once the individual had been nothing more to him than the temporary abiding place of the typical or ideal; now his heart showed its bent to be a growing fidelity to the specimen, with all her pathetic flaws of detail; which flaws, so far from sending him further, increased his tenderness' (286). Pierston now wishes to see people as they are rather than use them as 'material' for gratifying his aesthetic fantasies. Marrying another old woman, Marcia, to make amends for jilting her as a youth, he insists on her removing all cosmetics to reveal the ravages of age.

Illusory Ancestries 147

This resolution highlights how the 'trick' of Pierston's infatuations lay not only in the human flesh he perceived but in his blinkered, self-centred processing of it. Objectivity emerges in tandem with sympathy. Hardy further emphasises this point through the aged Pierston throwing himself into town-planning, improving sanitation for the inhabitants of his native island. Instead of being manipulated by nature, chasing phantoms of resemblance, he manipulates nature for the common human good, laying water pipes and building ventilated houses (not unlike Tom at the end of Kingsley's *Water-Babies*). Pierston replaces carnal, selfish subjectivity with altruistic detachment. Yet such detachment comes at the price of personal extinction as Pierston abandons his search for a viable mate (his marriage to Marcia being a mere sterile, loveless companionship).

Like Kingsley and Allen, Hardy preserved some moral significance in deception as a natural phenomenon by focussing on the deceived. He suggested that humans were misled by nature's illusions due to their egoistic desires. Humans would overcome such gullibility, he implied, only when altruistic self-detachment replaced the urges to elevate or advance oneself, socially and biologically. Yet, in Darwinian terms, this development would be a dead end, as Tess exemplifies with her self-sacrificing attitude. Her disinterest in tracing her features in portraits of her noble ancestors coincides with her wish that '[she] had never been born' and her reluctance to produce children who might suffer as well (76). The struggle for existence will continue without her, and those who remain focussed on carnal, egoistic satisfaction often seem more likely to prevail.

Hardy was less optimistic than Kingsley, and perhaps even Allen, about the universe bending inevitably toward truth and altruism. He tended to view these ideals and, indeed, all thought, as at odds with the physical cosmos rather than in harmony with it. In 1883, he reflected that 'we have reached a degree of intelligence which Nature never contemplated when framing her laws and for which she consequently has provided no adequate satisfactions'.[80] Seeing nature's phenomena accurately involved recognising one's own insignificance, and thus ran against the instincts of self-preservation and reproduction. In tension with Hardy's insistence on candour's moral necessity was his consideration that some delusion was, perhaps, necessary for survival. 'The best', Tess counsels herself, 'is not to remember that your nature and your past doings have been just like thousands' and thousands', and that your coming life and doings'll be like thousands' and thousands'' (126). Similarly, the speaker in 'The Pedigree' parries his fears of being 'merest mimicker and counterfeit' by thundering

148   Evolution and the Ethics of Appearance in Thomas Hardy

the attempted denial: 'I AM I/AND WHAT I DO I DO MYSELF ALONE.'[81] Instead of liberating humans from nature's cycle of deception, the development of mind perhaps only internalised it. Humans had overcome animals' literal (and, therefore, gullible) perceptions only to be gulled by ideations, such as God or a sovereign self, which enabled them to ignore the randomness of existence.[82] In Hardy's poem 'God's Funeral', a chorus of voices, representing humankind, laments:

> [T]ricked by our own early dream
> And need of solace, we grew self-deceived,
> Our making soon our maker did we deem,
> And what we had imagined we believed.

The means by which humans were able to see beyond nature's illusions were also the means of more complex (perhaps emotionally necessary) delusion; a parallel that would also concern Lesley Stephen, as the next chapter explores.

Hardy's fiction drew on adaptive appearance to problematise the conventions of the pastoral mode and the ethics of human deceit. His tales undermine the traditional association of nature, and rustic ways of life, with uncorrupted honesty and transparency. They also blur the lines between intentional deception and unconscious actions and bodily states that have deceptive effects. Hardy further uses the tendency of bodies to mislead viewers through intra- and extra-familial resemblances to align the pursuit of truth with inclusive altruism. Yet Hardy was uncertain whether altruistic indifference to ancestry was humankind's inevitable destiny. He sometimes suggested that this aim ran against the tendencies of the universe, similarly as Huxley argued that the 'ethical process' conflicted with the 'cosmic process'. Hardy's problematising of natural transparency accorded with fin-de-siècle discourse about authentic identity that appropriated the language of adaptive appearance. As the next two chapters show, various authors used such biological tropes to think through the difficulties of being true to oneself, on both individual and group scales. Further, Hardy's depiction of women as natural dissimulators would be both echoed and countered in Charlotte Perkins Gilman's political writings, which regarded sexual selection as a central mechanism of women's oppression (see Chapter 6).

CHAPTER 5

Blending in and Standing out, I
Crypsis versus Individualism in Fin-de-Siècle Cultural Criticism

As the discussions of Kingsley, Allen and Hardy have indicated, adaptive appearance resonated with concerns about literary sincerity and authenticity. These imagined virtues were intrinsic to ideologies of intellectual and artistic individualism. Blending in with one's environment or mimicking others represented negative mirror-images of such individualism. This chapter contends that crypsis acted as a versatile trope by which several fin-de-siècle literary and cultural critics thought through and complicated ideals of self-expression and originality. Norris argued that several Modernist authors exhibited a Nietzschean 'mimeophobia', associating mimicry and concealment with weakness and heteronomy. For such authors, Norris claims, conspicuous self-display embodied vigour and autonomy, following one's inner promptings regardless of external influences.[1] I suggest that such mimeophobia (or, more generally, *cryptophobia*) also permeated critical discussions of the previous generation in the 1870s to 1890s, who often invoked animal crypsis as a figure of conformity and bad faith.

However, the ideal of authentic self-expression, on which cryptophobic individualism relied, was incongruent with the semiotic logic of adaptive appearance. As the Introduction discussed, adaptive appearance pointed to the effectual, receiver-focussed nature of communication, framing meaning as interpreted rather than expressed. This emphasis aligned with growing doubts among critics about the possibility of purely sincere or authentic self-expression. Some conformity and imitation were, perhaps, required in order to connect with audiences. Fin-de-siècle cultural and literary critics thus tempered their individualist cryptophobia by warning that too much expressive individualism would promote social disintegration. The tension between individualism and collectivism reflected opposing narratives of what literature and art were for: expressing oneself or strengthening societal bonds?

149

The four authors discussed here exemplified this tension in various ways. Leslie Stephen's agnostic writings attacked theology as a form of human crypsis while simultaneously worrying that too much candid discussion of the crisis of faith would foment violent revolution. Theodore Watts-Dunton's literary criticism hailed originality as a rare, progressive force against common imitation. Yet he also feared that too much of it was socially destructive and, therefore, immoral. Walter Pater, conversely, concluded that all art was inherently mimetic, reworking elements from pre-existing sources. He suggested that individualism was attained by mixing eclectic influences, generating novel recombinations. It would take Pater's pupil, Oscar Wilde, though, to fully realise the radical implications of such mimetic individualism. Wilde's critical rhetoric prioritised self-expression over mental and moral conventionality, and the societal stability associated with it. His vision of artistic authenticity required eluding recognition so that, paradoxically, the artist truly stood out by blending in. I will preface this discussion with an outline of how cryptophobia, and its biologized ideals of sincerity and authenticity, undergirded individualism in fin-de-siècle literary culture.

Culture, Biology and Cryptophobic Individualism

'Individualism' was often invoked in nineteenth-century intellectual and literary culture, but with ambiguous connotations.[2] Steven Lukes distinguished separate traditions of Romantic 'German Individualism', which revered 'uniqueness, originality, [and] self-realization' from 'Victorian individualism', which advocated laissez-faire economics.[3] These different traditions cohered and conflicted at different points. The idea that art expressed its maker's unique personality was intrinsic to intellectual property. Yet the free market also seemed to militate against individualistic expression by compelling professional artists to adapt their works to audiences' tastes (as Allen complained). At the same time, political economy and scientific naturalism undermined personal autonomy, absorbing individuals and their actions into vast processes of gradual change.[4] Nonetheless, many late Victorians continued to revere self-directed individuality as an ideal, however unattainable it might seem. Individuality was associated with masculine vigour and independence, while imitation seemed to bespeak effeminate weakness and dependence.[5]

Sincere and authentic self-expression were fundamental to this ideal. Since the eighteenth century, 'masculine sensibility' had been closely identified with 'brisk sincerity, candour and spontaneity'.[6] Trilling argued

Culture, Biology and Cryptophobic Individualism

that, as social mobility grew, British society increasingly valorised sincerity as a substitute gauge of personal worth.[7] This reverence of individual transparency gradually evolved from a means of social stability to an end in itself, manifested in late nineteenth- and twentieth-century notions of 'authenticity' which framed individual and society as inevitably antagonistic.[8] Authentic man was true not only to others but also to himself, following his internal promptings and voicing his convictions regardless of convention. The Baptist pamphleteer William Landels wrote in 1859 that men were made 'not by passively yielding to an internal pressure, but by the putting forth of an internal force, which resists and masters, if it cannot change, the outward'.[9] Such rhetoric of outward-moving force echoed sincerity and authenticity's logic of dissolving the boundary between inner life and outer display.

This muscular individualism (and accompanying cryptophobia) dovetailed with notions of literary creativity. The emergence of modern copyright law in the early eighteenth century had redefined texts as the personal property of authors and encouraged a 'shift from a poetics of imitation to a valorization of originality'.[10] Early nineteenth-century critics such as William Hazlitt, Leigh Hunt and Carlyle helped to consolidate the view of literary originality as an inborn quality separate from society and history.[11] Carlyle depicted original authors as heroes who struggled physically to break through verbal convention and express their unique visions. Conversely, he prefigured Nietzsche's view of mimicry as inadequacy, stating of poetry: 'Imitation is a leaning on something foreign; incompleteness of individual development, defect of free utterance.'[12] Vigorous writers seemed to stand out from their fellows, while weak ones merged with them.

However, the ideal of individual autonomy was increasingly undermined in the second half of the century by political economy and scientific naturalism, which absorbed individuals and their actions into vast processes of gradual change. Herbert Spencer observed that 'great men are the products of their societies ... If their society is to some extent re-moulded by them, they were, both before and after birth, moulded by their society – were the results of all those influences which fostered the ancestral character they inherited, and gave their own early bias, their creed, morals, knowledge, aspirations'.[13] The growth of comparative philology and anthropology further impinged upon individual agency. These disciplines framed languages and beliefs as cultural structures which evolved autonomously through history, shaping individuals' thoughts and actions.[14] Hence, Tylor declared that the arts, religion and customs of any given

152   Blending in and Standing out, I

people developed in predictable patterns according to 'laws of human nature'.[15]

In this atmosphere, notions of the sovereign imagination gave way to ideas of collective cultural or racial inheritance. Critics increasingly conceptualised writing as 'the inventive reuse of the words of others' instead of creation *ex nihilo*.[16] Imitation, while apparently weakening individuality, also now seemed fundamental to it, enabling the social life and culture on which identity and thought were founded. Walter Bagehot argued that humans' capacity to cooperate in groups depended on mimetic instincts, writing: 'A gregarious tribe, whose leader was in some imitable respects adapted to the struggle for life, and which copied its leader, would have an enormous advantage . . . [I]t would be coherent and adapted, whereas, in comparison, competing tribes would be incoherent and unadapted'. The beliefs and behaviours of communities were largely uniform and predictable, Bagehot suggested, because people were so dominated by an 'extreme propensity to imitation'.[17] Toward the turn of the century, psychologists such as James Mark Baldwin stressed that imitation was crucial to mental development, laying the foundations of identity and abstract thought.[18] Far from transcending imitation, humans were perhaps the most imitative creatures of all.

Furthermore, individuality was not always imagined as an unqualified good since an excess of it threatened to place people at odds with wider society. Benjamin Kidd contended that advancement perhaps required some reduction of average intelligence as people's roles became more rigidly defined.[19] Paul Bourget famously designated 'decadence' as the sacrifice of the whole for the development of the part, a process applying as much to literature as to organisms. Just as a life form disintegrated when its cells ceased to subordinate themselves to the wider whole, he wrote, so '[t]he social organism . . . succumbs to decadence as soon as the individual has begun to thrive'. The more sensitive and idiosyncratic individuals became, Bourget claimed, the less well they fulfilled collective roles. Likewise, in literature, as authors' visions and idiolects became more individuated, their work grew more 'unintelligible' to most readers. Bourget viewed such decadence as consciously incompatible with the logic of Darwinian adaptation and survival, writing: 'The great argument against decadences is that they have no future, and that barbarity crushes them. But is it not the inevitable fate of what is exquisite and rare to succumb to brutality?'[20] Although cryptophobic rhetoric identified distinctiveness with natural fitness, the opposite could be argued when individuals were viewed as parts of larger systems and networks.

Culture, Biology and Cryptophobic Individualism 153

Cultural criticism in the period thus frequently depicted excessive individuality as dangerous and degenerate. Classifications of cultural degeneration tended toward cryptophobia, framing Aestheticism and Symbolism's penchants for allusion and quotation as reflections of their proponents' morbid enervation. However, degeneration as a concept depended on abnormality, meaning that any pronounced individuality could be classed as degenerate. Max Nordau complained that poets such as Paul Verlaine sacrificed semantic clarity for the sake of novelty, undermining language's communicative purpose. The 'mystic' poet, Nordau wrote, 'either use[s] recognised words, to which he gives a meaning wholly different from that which is generally current, or else ... he forges for himself special words which, to a stranger, are generally incomprehensible, and the cloudy, chaotic sense of which is intelligible only to himself'.[21] Similarly, Lombroso classified 'genius' in art and literature as 'a form of degenerative neurosis', since 'craziness' inevitably accompanied any wide deviation 'from the average'.[22]

A more considered view of the dangers of too much originality would be offered in 1906 by the American scholar Francis B. Gummere, who commented: 'Solitary man has no literature ... [L]iterature shows beyond doubt that an excess of invention spells sterility; while nearly all great writers, who serve as rallying points for a school of literature, have been, in the deep sense of the word, strongly conventional'.[23] He further reinforced the biological analogy by summing up the 'literary process' as a 'formula' of 'invention and imitation, corresponding to the Darwinian formula of heredity and variation'.[24] Gummere suggested that conventionality was linked with the wider social tendency of 'altruism', involving 'a partial surrender' of self to social unity.[25] Gummere's martial language implies ambivalence about the situation: literature's mimetic conformity involves, perhaps, not noble self-sacrifice but humiliating reliance on and absorption into external agencies. Cryptophobic individualism clashed with an uncomfortable awareness that mimicry was intrinsic to cultural production.

These tensions surfaced in the critical writings of Stephen, Watts-Dunton and Pater, all of whom used crypsis as a trope of intellectual and literary imitation and conformity. These three influential writers revered individualism as a force of human and artistic progress. As educated members of the middle and upper class, they saw popular print culture as the enemy of such progress, pressuring authors to imitate whatever sold and to reinforce conventional beliefs. Similarly, they reasoned, as nature could not be relied upon to favour the best forms, so mass audiences could not be relied upon to favour the best art or ideas. However, such rhetorical treatment of individualism as a fixed biological trait collided with parallel views of literature and culture as collective structures that were easily broken. Consequently, Stephen and Watts-Dunton qualified their celebrations of originality and attacks upon imitation, suggesting, like Gummere, that a balance needed to be struck between these tendencies. Even Pater, who advocated self-development through eclecticism, moderated his doctrine with elements of conventionality. Such balancing acts agree with Jason Camlot's claim that late Victorian critics often appealed to a paradoxical, 'critically mannered sincerity', which implicated 'an ideal of immediate truth with a model of rhetorical artfulness'.[26]

Norris notes that pursuing Nietzschean mimeophobia to its logical conclusion led to anarchistic politics and violent assaults upon language and logic such as Surrealism. Stephen, Watts-Dunton and, in his later years, also Pater feared such destabilisation and defended the maintenance of social authority and tradition. Wilde, though, was bolder, pursuing artistic individualism to its logical, socially disruptive conclusion. He suggested that art attained individuality only by resisting straightforward signification, disrupting the chains of recognition by which sentient creatures stereotyped the world. Animal mimicry functioned through its obviousness and unambiguity, reliably transmitting consistent messages to its audiences. By contrast, Wilde idealised semantic instability, regarding directness in literature as similar to mimicry in nature: a surrender of one's individuality to external processes. Art transcended nature's cycle of mimicry, he implied, by rejecting the goal of mimesis.

Lesley Stephen: Theology as Crypsis

Cryptophobia formed a strong undercurrent in the intellectual criticism of Lesley Stephen. As an agnostic, Stephen used imagery of crypsis to attack theologians who clothed their religious beliefs in the rhetoric of scientific naturalism. He argued that, similarly as weak animals survived by mimicking the appearance of stronger creatures, religious apologetics endured by blending in with the secular science which threatened to supplant it. However, Stephen's view of ideas as collective, historical sedimentations fitted with a Burkean fear of radical change. He thus demurred from attacking religious institutions too aggressively and conceded that some theological adaptive appearance was necessary. Indeed, he sometimes

Lesley Stephen: Theology as Crypsis

looked to apologetics as a model for managing the masses, lest intellectuals like himself became their prey.

Stephen was a prominent critic and biographer, best known today as the father of Virginia Woolf and Vanessa Bell. As a young man, Stephen had been a tutor and chaplain at Cambridge, but reading Comte and Mill caused him to renounce holy orders and pursue a career in journalism.[27] He consistently defended 'free thinking' and 'plain speaking', claiming that ignoring tensions between traditional belief and modern science would be dishonest. Like Spencer, he imagined humans progressing toward ever-greater autonomy, and defended free speech and laissez-faire capitalism. In an 1892 address to the freethinking West London Ethical Society, Stephen asserted that men should 'cultivate the virtue of strenuous, unremitting, masculine self-help', taking control of everything from their economic position to their mental and emotional states.[28] Stephen saw himself as an exemplar of such individualism, having found Christian doctrine wanting, and expressed his doubts regardless of majority opinion.

Stephen outlined his view of intellectual history as a Darwinian struggle between strong, honest individualists and weak dissemblers in his 1872 article 'Darwinism and Divinity'. The article compared theologians to mimetic insects, surviving amid secular modernity by resembling scientific materialists. Citing Wallace's work, Stephen wrote:

> A butterfly which precisely suits the palates of certain birds would be speedily exterminated if it were not for an ingenious device. It cleverly passes itself off under false colours by imitating the external shape of some other butterfly, which the bird considers as disgusting. A very similar variety of protective resemblance may be detected in the history of opinions. The old-fashioned doctrine remains essentially the same, but it changes its phraseology so as to look exactly like its intrusive rival.

Such 'protective resemblances' were exemplified, Stephen claimed, by 'orthodox Catholics' such as St. George Jackson Mivart, who newly conceded that apes had gradually evolved into humans: 'only they must save themselves by calling the process miraculous, and thus, for a time at least, the old theory may be preserved'.[29] Stephen found another instance in Newman's argument that faith was justified by resemblances between the world's religions. Newman had suggested that these similarities pointed to a universal, innately known wisdom. Stephen noted that 'in simpler times the resemblances between the heathen and the orthodox religion would have been indignantly denied'. Now, however, as secular anthropology exposed Christianity as an irrational superstition, Stephen's Newman strategically rehabilitated superstitions into 'a dim reflection of revealed truths'. By such wily dodges, Stephen wrote, theologians dressed up their indefensible creeds as scientific reasoning: 'Just as the sceptic rashly fancies that he has brought matters to a conclusive issue, the theologian evades his grasp by putting on the external form of the very doctrines which he has been opposing'.[30] By dividing theology into inner being and 'external form', Stephen opposes it to his own 'plain speaking' agnosticism. While the theologian survives by dissimulation, the agnostic is transparent about his doubts and would (as Stephen's combative language implies) defeat the theologian in a fair contest.

Stephen's dichotomy of strong individualists and weak mimics reflected his elitism. The masses were inherently conservative and mimetic, he implied, because they lacked the mental power to think for themselves. Similarly as variation vied with persistence of type in biology, Stephen claimed that societal innovation conflicted with a more common conservativism. In a reflection on the failure of secular philosophy to usurp religious tradition in the eighteenth century, he commented:

> The intellectual activity of the acuter intellects ... is the great force which stimulates and guarantees every advance of the race. It is of course opposed by a vast force of inertia ... Mankind resent nothing so much as the intrusion upon them of a new and disturbing truth. The huge dead weight of stupidity and indolence is always ready to smother audacious inquiries.[31]

Stephen imagined originality as an energy which enabled people to break with convention and forge new mental paths, while those who lacked it took refuge in the thoughts of their predecessors. He regarded the possessors of such originality as heroic patricians, 'the genuine thinkers', who stood above the weak-minded, mimetic plebeians.[32]

However, Stephen recognised that ideas were not created *ex nihilo* by individuals but grew through collective social life. He was also forced to admit that the best ideas did not always triumph, just as the strongest organisms did not always survive. Like mimetic animals, ideas endured through adaptation to their environments, namely, communities' mental–emotional needs. He wrote: 'A theory spreads from one brain to another in so far as one man is able to convince another.'[33] Stephen claimed that in the 'natural selection' of religions, 'those which provide expression for our deepest feelings crush out their rivals, not those which are inferred by a process of abstract reasoning. To be permanent, they must bear the test of reason; but they do not owe to it their capacity for attracting the hearts of men'.[34]

He also wrote that the success of new theories of life depended on the 'social conditions' in which they were received, warning: 'Truths have been discovered and lost because the world was not ripe for them.'[35] He posited that the eighteenth century had witnessed such a false start when Deism anticipated aspects of scientific naturalism. Christian apologists had defeated Deism, Stephen claimed, not because they had stronger arguments but because their creed was emotionally appealing. Deism proved too 'weak' to thrive because its 'metaphysical deity was too cold and abstract a conception to excite much zeal in his worshippers'.[36] Now, in the late nineteenth century, Stephen's rhetoric of crypsis pointed to the logical weakness of theological evolutionism and, yet, also, its likely success. By indulging emotional needs for certainty and meaning in life, such apologetics seemed advantaged over scientific agnosticism.

This realisation drove Stephen to temper his cryptophobia and even to advocate cryptic strategies for promoting agnosticism. Similarly as he accused theologians of aping science, Stephen proposed clothing agnosticism in religious garb to placate the masses. The materialist view, he wrote, 'must find some means, though it is given to nobody as yet to define them, of reconciling those instincts of which the belief in immortality was a product. The form may change – we cannot say how widely – but the essence, as every progress in the scientific study of religions goes to show, must be indestructible.' Channelling Comte's idea of a religion of humanity, Stephen warned that a new, science-based creed 'will not take root till in some shape or other it has provided the necessary envelopes for the deepest instincts of our nature. If Darwinism demonstrates that men have been evolved out of brutes, the religion which takes it into account will also have to help men to bear in mind that they are now different from brutes.'[37] The passage resonates with the theological evolutionism of Kingsley, whom Stephen had met during his Cambridge years and admired greatly.[38]

Yet the possibility of intellectual elites spreading such a new religion to the masses would have seemed increasingly unrealistic as the popular print market undermined traditional cultural authorities. Like Allen, Stephen complained that commercial print culture encouraged authors '[t]o reproduce the opinions of the average reader; to dress them so skillfully that he will be pleased to see what keen intelligence is implied in holding such opinions'.[39] This issue perhaps motivated the older Stephen to moderate his criticism of apologetics, seeing them as a more viable method of crowd control than a secular religion. He suggested that agnostics and liberal religious leaders might 'become allies in promoting morality'. It was undeniable, he stated, that '[e]normous social forces find their natural channel through the churches', and, regardless of one's position on its dogmas, Christianity had been and continued to be 'one great organ of civilisation'. In order to unite the intellectuals with the masses, Stephen mused, 'It is possible enough that the creed of the future may, after all, be a compromise, admitting some elements of higher truth, but attracting the popular mind by concessions to superstition and ignorance.'[40] Stephen thus moved from attacking theological crypsis to endorsing it as a necessary means of maintaining social stability. Religion posed little 'harm', Stephen concluded, since the independent-minded elite would inevitably outgrow it while the masses gradually followed them. Citing his own childhood of Anglican indoctrination, he claimed that in adulthood 'the obsolete exuviae of doctrine dropped off my mind like dead leaves from a tree'. He therefore urged: 'Let the wheat and tares be planted together, and trust to the superior vitality of the more valuable plant.'[41] Stephen's emphasis on the mental strength and independence of his class downplayed its weak position, forced to indulge religious sentiments to avoid violent upheaval.

Further, Stephen did not specify how, unlike everyone else, 'educated' men like him should transcend the influences of history and society to think as individuals. By his own admission, Stephen outgrew his religious upbringing through not just personal reflection but exposure to secular writers. He thus exhibited the common liberal contradiction of positing an autonomous individual who, simultaneously, is shaped by society. At the heart of this contradiction, for Stephen, was a confused metaphor. His vision of intellectual history as a Darwinian struggle vacillates between depicting the units of struggle as individual thinkers, who fight against mental convention, and ideas, of which people are mere conduits. What is the triumphant 'plant' in Stephen's rhetoric: the 'freethinking' agnostic or agnosticism as a body of thought, assembled and consolidated by many minds? Stephen's battle of ideas exemplified Nietzsche's claim that thought had eroded rather than enhanced humans' self-possession, since philosophising necessarily relied on the society of others.[42] Perhaps all thinkers resembled animal mimics, dependent on supplementary models and interlocutors. Despite his rhetoric of individualist candour, Stephen valued social stability more, advocating in the end a bad-faith theological agnosticism. His vacillations, and contradictory biological metaphors, would be mirrored in the literary criticism of Theodore Watts-Dunton.

Theodore Watts-Dunton: Literary Crypsis

Theodore Watts (he added his mother's maiden name Dunton to his surname in 1896) came from a middle-class East Anglian family and was educated in the physical sciences before working as a solicitor in London.[43] He served such literary clients as Algernon Swinburne, who ended up living with Watts-Dunton for years after falling into alcoholism. From the 1870s onward, Watts-Dunton regularly reviewed poetry in the *Examiner* and *Athenaeum*, and contributed the entry for 'Poetry' in the 1902 edition of the *Encyclopædia Britannica*. Watts-Dunton's scientific knowledge encouraged him to conceptualise literature in biological terms. Like Allen, he compared consumerist print culture to Darwinian nature, its conditions favouring adaptive imitation and resemblance rather than individual distinctiveness. Framing originality as 'health', Watts-Dunton lamented imitative poets ousting innovative ones because the former were better adapted to dull, conservative readerships. While the reading masses resembled animals duped by mimicry, Watts-Dunton's elite critic resembled a selective breeder, promoting 'vital' poetry and filtering out weak imitations. However, as in Stephen's criticism, Watts-Dunton's thinking on poetry wavered between different scales, which could frame originality as, conversely, healthy or morbid. Considering poetry as individual self-expression, originality seemed an unqualified sign of health. Yet, when Watts-Dunton regarded poetry as part of the social organism, he suggested that excessive idiosyncrasy would harm the wider body like a cancerous organ.

Watts-Dunton compared originality to organic variation, and society's conventions to the environmental pressures that checked such variations, enforcing cryptic homogeneity. He celebrated Tennyson for resisting the 'natural instinct of self-protective mimicry' that caused most people 'to move about among their fellows hiding their features behind a mask of convention'. He continued: 'So infinite is the creative power of Nature that she makes no two individuals alike ... To break down the exterior signs of this variety of individualism in the race by mutual imitation, by all sorts of affectations, is the object not only of the civilization of the Western world, but of the very negroes on the Gaboon river.' Watts-Dunton's racial comparison, drawing on associations of non-Europeans with supposedly primitive mimicry, accentuates the evolutionary nature of his argument. Amid eternal pressure for 'mutual imitation', Tennyson's great achievement, Watts-Dunton claimed, was to defiantly cultivate and display his 'individualism'.[44] Originality seemed to exist in tandem with vigour and

160   Blending in and Standing out, I

self-sufficiency as individualist-poets stood out boldly from their surroundings. Watts-Dunton thus dubbed the lesser-known Charles Wells 'perhaps the healthiest man that has ever written in English verse since Chaucer'.[45] Similarly, he praised Augusta Webster for 'being quite uninfluenced ... by the poetic fashions of the day', at a time when 'the press is now pouring forth a flood of so-called poetry which is something less than a weak dilution of the poetry of Mr. Swinburne and Mr. Rossetti'.[46] Resemblance to one's contemporaries is identified with weak self-concealment, while idiosyncrasy bespeaks autotelic authenticity.

Yet, equally as variation was checked by natural selection, Watts-Dunton concluded that literary individualism was suppressed by capitalist print culture. The verse drama *Joseph and His Brethren* by Charles Wells (1824), whom Watts-Dunton praised so highly, had languished out of print for half a century before Swinburne celebrated it, leading to a new edition being published. The supreme 'health' of Wells's verse, Watts-Dunton observed, had not saved it from 'oblivion', while more formulaic poetry had become canonical.[47] Reviewing the work, Watts-Dunton took it as an object-lesson in the randomness of survival, writing:

> the prosperity of any work of art ... depends upon the mood of the public to which it is addressed. For, there is a tide in the affairs of books which must be taken in at the flood. And it is a popular error to suppose that, in a good book, there is some fate-compelling power which will save it from perishing ... Science tells us that, in the struggle for life, the surviving organism is not necessarily that which is absolutely the best in an ideal sense, though it may, and indeed must, be that which is most in harmony with surrounding conditions. It is the same in art. Therefore, good books may perish, and do.[48]

Failure to adapt meant failure to resemble the popular poets which one's audience had been primed to consume. Watts-Dunton depicts the newly literate masses as fickle and unreflective, consuming texts based on superficial sensation, much as animals responded to eye-catching mimetic forms. He made this view more explicit in a notice of Dante Gabriel Rossetti's private letters, complaining: 'we do not so much blame the editors of such books as we blame the public, whose coarse and vulgar mouth is always agape for such pabulum'.[49] In another review, he complained that competition for the public's attention had so demeaned poetry that 'the poet's quest is little more than that of discovering a line by one poet which will rhyme with a line by another and joining them together. And the marvel is that the public seems to prefer the mocking-bird to the defrauded singer whose note has been stolen and burlesqued.'[50]

Theodore Watts-Dunton: Literary Crypsis 161

Watts-Dunton's animal metaphor reinforces his view that modern print culture reproduces nature's parasitic mimicries.

Watts-Dunton positioned critics as selective breeders, intervening in this chaotic struggle for survival with intelligent selection. Similarly as breeders nurtured grand variations that would otherwise go extinct, Watts-Dunton's critical elite nourished strains of original poetry. Progress in poetry, he wrote, depended on the creations and criticism of 'the few who, partly by temperament and partly by education, are sensitive to the true beauties of poetic art'. By contrast, he continued, 'success in finding and holding an audience is almost damnatory' to poets, so predictably vulgar and superficial was the public's taste.[51] Failing to find an audience might be a necessary consequence of originality, as Wells's case, perhaps, demonstrated. It seemed to be 'in the nature of things', Watts-Dunton lamented, 'that, in England at least, "the fit though few" comprise the audience of such a poet until the voice of recognized Authority proclaims him ... And was it always so? Yes, always'.[52] The philistinism of modern mass culture, he suggested pessimistically, both crushed original talent and disempowered appreciative critics from saving it. Commercial modernity was, he wrote, a 'complex web' in which the 'out-speaking' individualist formed a 'troublesome and discordant thread'.[53] As in selective breeding, the work of the critical elite, however successful on a small scale, could not overcome the universe's tendency toward homogeneity. Tennyson, in his wide acclaim, seemed to be the exception that proved the rule.

Yet Watts-Dunton's paradigm of original variation versus environmental homogenisation was complicated by his awareness of the collective and historical nature of languages and literatures. 'What do we mean by "originality"?' he mused in 1902: 'Scott did not invent the historic method. Dickens simply carried the method of Smollett further, and with wider range. Thackeray is admittedly the nineteenth-century Fielding.'[54] Watts-Dunton also praised Edgar Allan Poe as 'one of the most original' storytellers of the nineteenth century while simultaneously tracing Poe's tales to influential predecessors. Read texts such as Coleridge's 'Rime of the Ancient Mariner', Watts-Dunton instructed, 'and you will see at once the suggestions for Arthur Gordon Pym, and the way in which they crystallized into new forms in Poe's mind'. Anyone who interpreted such influences as disproving Poe's originality, Watts-Dunton warned, 'would be a poor psychologist indeed'.[55] His imagery stresses the incremental nature of literary development by evoking the long-term processes of geology, processes that had also lent credence to theories of the gradual evolution of species.

Further, as with Stephen, Watts-Dunton's sense of literature as a collective, historical organism, and part of a wider social organism, checked his celebration of individuality. Poetry needed to remain in harmony with the society in which it lived, he implied, lest it become a morbid growth in need of amputation. Watts-Dunton hinted at this idea in his criticism, stating: 'The poetical endowment is a superfluous organ in the economy of the struggles.'[56] That such statements were not wholly ironic is suggested by Watts-Dunton rejecting poetic individuality when he felt that it threatened the health of the race. This move can be seen in his review of Percy Bysshe Shelley's 'Laon and Cyntha', which publishers had originally refused to print due to its anti-theism and positive depiction of incest (causing Shelley to write a new version, 'The Revolt of Islam'). Watts-Dunton agreed with this suppression, arguing that the poem's promotion of incest was 'immoral' because such 'teaching' was 'harmful to the commonweal' and 'incompatible with the healthy movement of *any* social organism in a state of society above that of savagery'. The poem seemed to exemplify the danger of a poet pursuing only his individual imaginative vision, regardless of wider societal needs. Watts-Dunton lamented that Shelley had celebrated incest for its sheer non-conformity, 'the good force against which the conventions of society are cruelly and wickedly at war'. Yet society was not merely artificial conventions, Watts-Dunton contended, but a kind of organism that was 'built' upon 'the great eternal laws of nature'.[57] Like Stephen, Watts-Dunton vacillated between presenting poets as independent organisms and parts of a larger organism that would be harmed by excessive individuation. In the latter moments, he suggests that poets' responsibility is more to society's collective fitness than authentic self-expression.

Watts-Dunton's organicist, collectivist vision of poetry also caused him to associate pronounced individuality with unhealthy solipsism. 'All vital literary work is, we believe, a compromise, more or less, between idiosyncrasy and the general temper of the time in which it is produced', he wrote. 'What becomes of the poet when he is a law unto himself we see in Sidney Dobell and the Spasmodists.'[58] Critics had earlier characterised the work of Dobell and his associates by introspective soliloquies, focussed on particular rather than common experiences, which alienated readers.[59] While Watts-Dunton admired these poets, he also viewed them as cautionary examples of morbid individualism. The Spasmodists, he later wrote, had produced 'Bedlamite poetry', so 'that nothing will ever now persuade the reader of this generation that they were not each more or less mad'. The 'perfect mind' for poetry, Watts-Dunton claimed, was 'in accord with

Theodore Watts-Dunton: Literary Crypsis

the healthy mind of general humanity', as opposed to 'that mind which is in accord with nothing, not even with itself and the phantasms of its own conjuring'.[60] He conceived of poetry as a communicative bridge between people and, therefore, requiring common ideas. While a healthy, advanced organism was complex and possessed diverse, individuated parts, it seemed to him undesirable that any part should stand out so much as to disrupt the functioning of the whole.

Watts-Dunton's anxieties about poetry degenerating into unintelligible obscurity pointed to wider, growing uncertainties in the period about the nature of aesthetics and semiosis. The aesthetic value ascribed to objects, he wrote in his later years, was not fixed but 'associative', formed by the constitution and experiences of the perceiver. 'Beauty itself is entirely a relative term', Watts-Dunton asserted, 'depending for its acceptance upon the relations existing between the admirer and the object admired, as Darwin has proved'.[61] Such aesthetic relativism paralleled discussions of language that increasingly defined meaning as social conventions and subjective mental associations (see the Introduction). Watts-Dunton's friend Swinburne reflected such thinking when he wrote that poetry worked through its effects upon readers, not its makers' intentions: 'The rule of art is not the rule of morals; in morals the action is judged by the intention ... in art, the one question is not what you mean but what you do.'[62] Such semantic relativism undermined the idea of poetry as a meeting of minds, even among Watts-Dunton's imagined cultural elite. The commonality of language might prevent it from being able to fully convey individual subjectivity.

Watts-Dunton touched upon this idea in a notice of William Morris's *The Water of the Wondrous Isles* (1896) when he despaired that no criticism could capture the essence of Morris's imagination. 'To endeavour to reproduce in colourless language any notion of the beauty of the story', he wrote, 'was to confront a task as hopeless as that of the gipsy girl whose first effort on being taught to write was to represent by phonetic signs, cut on the bark of a tree, the nightingale's song.'[63] While original art could move audiences profoundly, its effects varied with each spectator. Watts-Dunton generally avoided this vortex of aesthetic–semantic relativism by cleaving to the Spencerian rhetoric of a social organism in which readers and writers intermeshed. Nonetheless, his visions of esoteric self-expression tended in the opposite direction, framing poetry as the ever-finer differentiation of subjectivities and, thus, perhaps, also their alienation from each other. Such radical, socially disruptive individualism would be developed more boldly by Wilde. However, Wilde's arguments would be built upon

164 Blending in and Standing out, I

the ideas of the more reserved Pater. While Stephen and Watts-Dunton described art and ideas as extensions of organic processes, Pater envisaged them transcending these processes. He concluded that humans escaped nature's mimetic adaptations through not physical health but self-consciousness. In this formulation, the opposite of individuality was not weakness but automatism.

Walter Pater: Aesthetic Self-Obliteration

Pater was an Oxford don and journalist who came to see art as a refuge of agency. Paterian AESTHETICISM has sometimes been described as a flight from Darwinian nature.[64] However, I contend that Pater sought not simply to escape nature (since all existence might be contained in this term) but to realise its imagined telos in conscious self-fashioning.[65] Accepting that humans had evolved from lower life forms, Pater meditated on how they might attain some autonomy from the twin grips of heredity and environment. He argued that art's non-instrumentality marked humans' liberation from material automatism. Kant had earlier written that art stood out from other activities and modes of representation because it was simultaneously a means and an end, being 'purposive for itself'.[66] Pater concluded that artists' ability to create such autotelic work demonstrated their agency and self-awareness, 'the most luminous and self-possessed phase of consciousness'. Accordingly, he dismissed models of artistic creativity as intuitive inspiration. In this view, Pater objected, 'the artist has become almost a mechanical agent ... the associative act in art or poetry is made to look like some blindly organic process of assimilation'.[67] Pater's aversion is less to organic processes per se than to their assumed blindness.

Mimetic crypsis struck Pater as a vivid example of this blind automatism, which he imagined extending into civilised life through human imitation. In a lecture series on Plato that used the Greek philosopher's observations as a basis to develop his own ideas, Pater declared that imitation

> enters into the very fastnesses of character; and we, our souls, ourselves, are for ever imitating what we see and hear, the forms, the sounds which haunt our memory, our imagination. We imitate not only if we play a part on the stage but when we sit as spectators, while our thoughts follow the acting of another, when we read Homer and put ourselves, lightly, fluently, into the place of those he describes: we imitate unconsciously the line and colour of the walls around us, the trees by the wayside, the animals we pet or make

use of, the very dress we wear ... Let us beware how men attain the very truth of what they imitate ... Like those insects, we might fancy, of which naturalists tell us, taking colour from the plants they lodge on, they will come to match with much servility the aspects of the world about them.[68]

Pater's characterisation of camouflaged insects and humans by 'servility' highlights their lack of autonomy. Such imitativeness fitted with a general argument made repeatedly by Pater that human actions and even ideas perhaps evolved as necessarily as physical traits and instincts. Each organism, he explained, was shaped by its 'physical conditions', 'remote laws of inheritance', and (for humans) 'the mind of the race, the character of the age' and 'the medium of language and current ideas'.[69] Evoking Ruskinian optical innocence, Pater stated: 'Our failure is to form habits: for, after all, habit is relative to a stereotyped world, and meantime it is only the roughness of the eye that makes any two persons, things, situations, seem alike.'[70] The deadening influence of habit, he suggested, automatised behaviour, perception and ideation. Conventionalised ways of seeing, thinking and acting seemed as predictable as glacial formations.

Pater envisaged humans transcending such cosmic automatism through self-consciousness, declaring that 'the end of life is not action but contemplation – being as distinct from doing – a certain disposition of the mind'. He regarded art as the means of this emancipation, defining the task of poetry as 'not to teach lessons, or enforce rules, or even to stimulate us to noble ends, but to withdraw the thoughts for a while from the mere machinery of life'.[71] How, though, could such autonomous 'contemplation' be attained when one's intellect was also formed by the 'machinery of life', that is, heredity and environment? Pater addressed this problem by suggesting that mental autonomy came from ever-finer receptiveness to external stimuli, not resistance to them. Experience, he wrote, constituted 'a world of fine gradations and subtly linked conditions, shifting intricately as we ourselves change – and bids us, by a constant clearing of the organs of observation and perfecting of analysis, to make what we can of these'.[72] Individualism consisted in taking control of the influences that acted upon one, seeking out fresh and eclectic sources of sensory and intellectual stimulation. 'The supreme artistic products of succeeding generations', Pater wrote, 'form a series of elevated points, taking each from each the reflection of a strange light, the source of which is not in the atmosphere around them, but in a stage of society remote from ours'.[73] By appropriating models from distant times and places, the artist abstracts from his immediate milieu and is no longer 'servile' to its influence. Channelling

166   Blending in and Standing out, I

Plato, Pater envisaged a highly controlled artistic 'manliness' characterised by 'a full consciousness of what one does'.[74] While the insects imitate whatever happens to surround them, Pater's artists aspire to choose and modify their surroundings (material and intellectual) in order to reflect and develop their unique personalities.

Pater would apply this philosophy to language, contending that the best writer was 'of necessity a scholar' who diverged from the common language of his time, unearthing subtle, forgotten shades of meaning from words' histories. Such an author, Pater declared, 'will resist a constant tendency on the part of the majority of those who use them to efface the distinctions of language ... [H]e will be apt to restore ... the finer edge of words ... [which] it has been part of our "business" to misuse'.[75] The Roman protagonist of Pater's novel *Marius the Epicurean* (1885) exemplifies this approach to language in his writing. 'Latin literature and Latin tongue', the narrator states, 'were dying of routine and languor.' Marius counteracts this tendency by 'going back to the original and native sense of each [word], disentangling its later associations, restoring to full significance all its wealth of latent figurative expression'.[76]

Such etymological excavations would seem to cohere with long-running notions of language change as decay from pure, vital origins. Pater's diction further strengthens this association as he describes Marius's effort 'to restore to words their primitive power', as though words were organisms charged with a life force of their own. However, the rest of the passage depicts Marius as concerned less with returning Latin to some imagined origin than with analysing its connotative hinterland to control it more precisely and, so, express more fully his individuality. 'For words, after all', the narrator comments, 'words manipulated with all his delicate force, were to be the apparatus of a war for himself.' By tracing the histories of words, Marius subdues them to his will, seeking 'to re-establish the natural and direct relationship between thought and expression'.[77] Similarly, in his essay 'Style' (1889), Pater implied that the writer gains control of language, and thus autonomy from it, by discrimination. He comments: 'any writer worth translating at all has winnowed and searched through his vocabulary, is conscious of the words he would select in systematic reading of a dictionary, and still more of the words he would reject'. Through this painstaking process, Pater writes, the author-scholar 'begets a vocabulary faithful to the colouring of his own spirit, and in the strictest sense original'. Pater's ideal author combines words from diverse sources, crafting a unique idiolect: 'Racy Saxon monosyllables, close to us as touch and sight, he will intermix readily with those long, savoursome, Latin

Walter Pater: Aesthetic Self-Obliteration 167

words, rich in "second intention".'[78] By combining vocabulary from across history and traditions, Pater's writer partially escapes the conformist influence of his own society. He consciously selects models of thought and art instead of passively submitting to those around him.

Yet Pater qualified and restrained this individualism, particularly after he found himself embroiled in controversy and potential scandal. His 'Conclusion' to *Studies in the History of the Renaissance* (1873) was criticised for defending hedonism and his career was jeopardised by the near-exposure of his homosexuality in 1874. Rachel O'Connell notes that, from then on, in both his professional and social life, Pater pursued 'a project of self-effacement' and 'transformed himself into a bland, uncommunicative, punctiliously conventional figure'.[79] Once characterised by flamboyant dress and outspoken opinions, he became obsessively reserved in both his public persona and his published writings. The older Pater continued to defend individualism with qualifications and did not always shy away from controversial subjects in his writing.[80] Nonetheless, he removed his notorious Conclusion from later editions of *The Renaissance* and restored it only after publishing *Marius*, which he claimed vindicated the Conclusion's intended moral orthodoxy.[81] Sebastian Lecourt contends that *Marius*'s protagonist achieves self-realisation, paradoxically, by 'eschewing choice and decision' in favour of 'surrendering to the determining influences of history'.[82] Turning away from his youthful materialism, the Roman becomes fascinated by Christianity. Marius's de facto conversion to this religion reflects a receptivity so strong that he seems to lose any personal agency, following, in the narrator's words, 'the impulse to surrender himself, in perfectly liberal inquiry about it, to anything that, as a matter of fact, attracted or impressed him strongly'. Christianity impresses Marius less by its theological cogency than its satisfying synthesis of ancient traditions and instinctive needs. It represents 'the conjoint efforts of human mind through many generations', combining 'images of hope, snatched sometimes even from that jaded pagan world ... the consoling images it had thrown off, of succour, of regeneration, of escape from death'.[83] This vision de-radicalises Paterian individualism, framing it as the refinement of eternal, unifying tendencies rather than disruptive deviation. Marius stands out from the conventions of his time only to blend in with an imagined eternal 'system' of values.

This shift from standing out to blending in was also mirrored in Pater's lectures on Plato, which Edward Dowden claimed reflected Pater's change from a radical 'Heraclitean' to a conservative defender of social stability.[84] Prefiguring Gummere's language of literary evolution, Pater identified (via Plato) opposing 'centrifugal' and 'centripetal' tendencies in society, which had to be finely balanced. However, despite Pater's rhetorical contortions, Platonic social harmony was fundamentally at odds with Pater's earlier individualism. Pater depicts Plato's republic as the culmination of artistic self-control: citizens select which objects and sensations will influence them, surrounding themselves with 'symmetry, aesthetic fitness, tone' and banishing degrading 'vulgarities'.[85] Yet this process also involves a diminution of individuality. To enforce social–mental harmony, art must be homogenised, following 'the maintenance of a standard' rather than idiosyncratic whims. 'In the matter of art, of poetry, of taste in all its varieties', Pater writes, citizens must 'make, and sternly keep, a "self-denying ordinance"'. Plato's citizens prove their individuality by *not* expressing it, subordinating self-expression to the collective expression of their society. Hence, in art, 'Alternations will be few and far between . . . We shall allow no musical innovations.' Pater is forced to acknowledge the diminution of individuality in this vision, even as he tries to downplay it, commenting:

> We are to become – like little pieces in a machine! you may complain. – No, like performers rather, individually, it may be, of more or less importance, but each with a necessary and inalienable part, in a perfect musical exercise which is well worth while, or in some sacred liturgy; or like soldiers in an invincible army, invincible because it moves as one man. We are to find, or be put into, and keep, every one his natural place; to cultivate those qualities which will secure mastery over ourselves, the subordination of the parts to the whole, musical proportion.[86]

As the orchestral analogy demonstrates, unity overrides individualism. Mastery over one's self gives way to 'mastery over ourselves'. Pater finally imagines the transcendence of mindless imitation through the dissolution of the individual. His qualified individualism leads, paradoxically, to self-obliteration. It would be left to his pupil Wilde to pursue cryptophobic individualism to its logical, socially disruptive conclusion.

Eluding 'Resemblance' and 'Recognition': Oscar Wilde's Artistic Crypsis

It may seem contradictory to figure Wilde as a writer who sought to transcend imitation when he was frequently accused of derivativeness and even outright plagiarism (although some critics have defended his borrowings as illustrations of his theory of influence).[87] Nonetheless, in his late writings on aesthetics, Wilde, like Pater, conceptualised originality as conscious self-definition in contrast to mindless conventionality. Instead of reflecting their surroundings, Wilde's individualists (like Pater's) developed their art and personalities according to select, eclectic sources. They grew their unique imaginative worlds regardless of society's conventions, like organisms evolving new features. Yet this model of art as individual self-realisation was complicated by Wilde's simultaneous sense that art lived in its effects upon audiences. He imagined art attaining individuality by dividing audiences with ambiguous suggestiveness, resisting straightforward interpretation. In this sense, Wilde envisaged the escape from primitive imitation and homogeneity as not self-revelation but self-concealment. Artistic individualism consisted of eluding not only 'resemblance' to others but also 'recognition' by them. Viewing art as a vehicle for enhancing individuality, Wilde made a virtue of obscurity, associating it with imaginative creativity. Art with clear meanings seemed to him mechanical, trapped in the same cycle of display and recognition as the rest of the organic world. By suggesting many things and signifying nothing definite, Wilde's ideal of art disrupted this cycle, producing chains of imaginative association that spread out infinitely beyond its time and place of production.

From his student days onward, Wilde was well versed in evolutionary ideas, and he likely kept abreast of such discussions through the 1880s and 1890s as he published in the *Nineteenth Century*, which also carried essays by Spencer, Huxley and Stephen.[88] Scientific naturalism's reduction of phenomena to fixed laws caused him to characterise primitive life by homogeneity and automatism. As a young man, he wrote facetiously in a notebook: 'Nature kills off all those who do not believe in the Uniformity of Nature and the Law of Causation.'[89] His later critical work seems to echo this sentiment, conflating the uniformity of nature's laws with uniformity among its products. In the dialogue 'The Decay of Lying' (1889), the speaker Vivian complains of nature's 'extraordinary monotony' and dismisses its supposed 'infinite variety' as 'pure myth'. Variety, Vivian claims, exists only in human 'imagination' and art which, instead of passively mirroring life, 'takes life as part of her rough material, recreates it, and refashions it in fresh forms'.[90] Humans' conscious, mental life enables them to break with nature's homogeneous automatism, innovating instead of merely replicating.

Wilde suggested that thought was agential while action was determinist, since all action derived from biological necessity. As the speaker Gilbert comments in Wilde's dialogue 'The Critic as Artist' (1891), 'The scientific principle of Heredity' has revealed 'the absolute mechanism of all action ... It has shown us that we are never less free than when we try to act.' However, Wilde imagined mental individualism as less the opposite of nature than a higher development of it. His reading of Spencer gave him a model of development through 'differentiation', which he used in an early essay to present 'individualism' as the end point of evolution. Minds differentiated from each other the same as organs, Wilde claimed, because 'thought' and 'matter' were subject to the same law of 'progress'.[91] Wilde can also be seen to merge mental individualism with material evolution through the words of Lord Henry in *Dorian Gray*: 'The aim of life is self-development. To realize one's own nature perfectly.'[92] The same sentiment is voiced in 'The Critic as Artist', when Gilbert asserts: 'Nature is matter struggling into mind.'[93] Wilde imagined the organic universe as both the source of mechanical homogeneity and the means of transcending it.

Like Pater, Wilde envisaged primitive automatism and homogeneity permeating society through uncritical conventionality. Without conscious criticism, Gilbert asserts, 'art is ... confined to the reproduction of formal types'. Artistic creation turns out to be unconscious imitation. It is critical engagement with existing art, Gilbert states, 'that invents fresh forms', unlike the mechanistic 'mere creative instinct' (144–145). Wilde further identified conventionality with homogenous automatism in 'The Soul of Man under Socialism' (1891). 'Thought', he writes, is 'dangerous' and 'Individualism is a disturbing and disintegrating force', since both undermine 'monotony of type, slavery of custom, tyranny of habit, and the reduction of man to the level of a machine'. He asserts that 'the modern stress of competition and struggle for place' exist in tandem with 'the immoral ideal of uniformity of type and conformity to rule'. Capitalism's struggle for existence compels people to mimic their neighbours so that most of them 'go through their lives in a sort of coarse comfort, like petted animals, without ever realising that they are probably thinking other people's thoughts, living by other people's standards ... and never being themselves for a single moment'.[94] The pressure to mindlessly blend in could be as pronounced in modern society as it was in nature.

Wilde envisaged the artist-individualist escaping this conformity by selecting influences from diverse, archaic sources and half-forgotten race memories, à la Pater. Gilbert sets out this strategy in 'Critic as Artist' as he envisages the individualist expanding outward, absorbing eclectic influences, instead of yielding to his immediate surroundings. This heroic non-conformist

> will seek for beauty in every age and in each school, and will never suffer himself to be limited to any settled custom of thought or stereotyped mode of looking at things. He will realise himself in many forms, and by a thousand different ways, and will ever be curious of new sensations and fresh points of view. Through constant change, and through constant change alone, he will find his true unity. (189)

Again, the crucial point is not resisting external influences but consciously selecting them, as opposed to just mirroring the conventions of one's time and place.

Yet, in contrast to Pater's compromise between the 'centripetal' and 'centrifugal', Wilde favoured the sacrifice of social unity for self-realisation. He likely consolidated his belief in the incompatibility of these tendencies through reading the philosopher David Ritchie's meditation on social evolution, *Darwinism and Politics* (1889). Ritchie argued that societies with strong central organisation paid for their national competitiveness by individual mediocrity. Although it defeated Athens on the battlefield, he wrote, 'Sparta never produced one really great man. How much more does the world owe to Athens which failed, than to Sparta which succeeded in the physical struggle for existence?'[95] Wilde praised Ritchie's book as 'extremely suggestive, and full of valuable ideas for the philosophic student of sociology', and echoed the dichotomy between mediocre survival and brilliant (but possibly doomed) individualism in 'Critic as Artist'.[96] Gilbert designates the centripetal and centrifugal forces as 'ethics' and 'aesthetics', which he views as civilisation's corollaries to natural and sexual selection. He states: 'Ethics, like natural selection, make existence possible. Aesthetics, like sexual selection, make life lovely and wonderful, fill it with new forms, and give it progress, and variety and change' (204). Ethics and natural selection represent conservatism, restricting individual variations that threaten the stability of a wider system. Conversely, aesthetics and sexual selection embody individual development, irrespective of wider, containing structures.

Gilbert exposes the contradiction in equating individuality with societal 'health', observing, 'The security of society lies in custom and unconscious instinct, and the basis of the stability of society, as a healthy organism, is the complete absence of any intelligence amongst its members' (183). Society's unthinking conformity is underlined for Gilbert by the rise of popular journalism. Darwinian market forces push out original 'literature',

172   Blending in and Standing out, I

he claims, as dull readers promote unchallenging work in a 'survival of the vulgarest' (135). Conversely, in 'Soul of Man', Wilde comments that the true artist works 'without any reference to his neighbours, without any interference ... solely for his own pleasure ... We have been able to have fine poetry in England because the public do not read it, and consequently do not influence it'.[97] Similarly as extravagant individual traits are usually contrary to the interests of the species, individuated, self-conscious literature opposes the coherence or 'health' of society. Wilde was not always consistent in his formulation of individualism as decadent. In 'Soul of Man', he envisaged individualism evolving in tandem with socialism to 'restore society to its proper condition of a thoroughly healthy organism'. He argues that the more individuated society's members become, the more they will also be united by a 'large, healthy and spontaneous' sympathy.[98] Individualism seems morbid, he suggests, only due to its current association with competitive capitalism. However, Wilde's utopian vision is vague and ignores the presumable tension between self-development and the centralised control required for the redistribution of property.

Further, it is difficult to square his rhetoric of individualist socialism with his arguments elsewhere for individualism independent of external moral and social responsibilities. Wilde had noted the tension between individual development and social cohesion in an 1886 article on poetry, commenting: 'The fact is that most modern poetry is so artificial in its form, so individual in its essence and so literary in its style, that the people as a body are little moved by it, and when they have grievances against the capitalist or the aristocrat they prefer strikes to sonnets and rioting to rondels.'[99] The image places the refined poet in an ambiguous position: while not the direct target of the revolting masses, he does not enjoy their sympathy either. Cutting a weak figure amid the coming class war, Wilde's poet seems liable to perish in the crossfire like Allen's journalist (see Chapter 3). The passage resonates with Wilde's earlier claim that '[t]he artist has always been, and will always be, an exquisite exception'. This point was proved, he wrote, by the public hounding of 'every great poet and thinker' of Athens, demonstrating that no populace had ever been in sympathy with original minds.[100] John Wilson Foster has noted an 'analogy' 'between Wilde's over-cultivation as an aesthete (a too-great differentiation from his moral environment and other, hypocritically moral individuals) and the fate that natural selection visits upon those organisms that exhibit its counterpart in nature (unadaptable and self-damaging overspecialization)'.[101] Wilde's tension between mimetic homogeneity and individualism coheres with this model, suggesting that the latter will be

Oscar Wilde's Artistic Crypsis   173

attained not in tandem with physical fitness but in opposition to it. Fitness implies subordination to external standards, and Wilde's individuals are laws unto themselves. While Pater avoided such decadent implications, Wilde gleefully highlights them.

The maladaptation of Wilde's individualism is linked with its conspicuousness. Similarly as natural selection tends to enforce dull, assimilative patterns and sexual selection conjures eye-catching (sometimes maladaptive) ones, Wilde's individualists stand out not only from their immediate society but also from their eclectic sources. While mimetic animals and humans blend with their models, individualists treat theirs as materials to react against, enhancing differences. Gilbert's critic-creator 'treats the work of art simply as a starting-point for a new creation' (157). Recontextualisation can stamp such material with striking new aspects, reflecting the unique personality of the appropriator. Hence, Gilbert states, 'the critic reproduces the work that he criticizes in a mode that is never imitative, and part of whose charm may really consist in the rejection of resemblance' (161). Indeed, Gilbert continues, artists grow more distinct by reworking the examples of others, 'just as it is only by contact with the art of foreign nations that the art of a country gains that individual and separate life that we call nationality' (164). Unlike primitive mimicry, which conflates identities, conscious artistic appropriation differentiates them in a Hegelian dialectic. Art progresses as a multiplication of differences.

Wilde's vision of artistic individualism also drew on adaptive appearance by approaching art as a product of audience interpretation rather than authorial self-expression. Although Wilde often wrote of the artist's 'personality' permeating his works, he also emphasised the gulf between the creator of a work and its effects on viewers or readers.[102] His preface to *Dorian Gray* declared:

> To reveal art and conceal the artist is art's aim ... All art is at once surface and symbol. Those who go beneath the surface do so at their peril. Those who read the symbol do so at their peril. It is the spectator, and not life, that art really mirrors. Diversity of opinion about a work of art shows that the work is new, complex, and vital.[103]

Wilde constructs art as a stimulant to viewers' varying imaginative tendencies. It thrives upon eluding straightforward interpretation, provoking diverse reactions. Wilde's epigrams accord with Gilbert's assertion in 'Critic as Artist' that art transcends not only 'the low standard of imitation or resemblance' but also the 'faculty of recognition' that resemblance appeals to. Artworks fail, Gilbert states, when they are 'too intelligible' and, thus, 'do not stir the imagination, but set definite bounds to it'. Conversely, the highest artworks 'possess the subtle quality of suggestion', inducing uncanny impressions of familiarity and strangeness. This effect is observable in 'the flowerless carpets of Persia', on which 'tulip and rose blossom indeed, and are lovely to look on, though they are not reproduced in visible shape or line' (159–161).

Wilde's dichotomy between 'recognition' and 'suggestion' resonated with contemporary efforts among evolutionary theorists to distinguish human consciousness from lower cognition. Wallace had argued that gregarious animals such as hares carried 'markings' of 'recognition and identification' on their bodies, which enabled them to coordinate with each other.[104] Such 'recognition' needed no conscious reflection, however, as Romanes clarified in his model of animal 'recepts' (see the Introduction). These mental associations, Romanes claimed, were spontaneous and based on mechanical 'recognition'. A predator might learn to chase certain patterns associated with its prey, but the association would hold only while the stimulus was physically present. By contrast, humans developed abstract 'concepts' that existed independently of the sensory world and could be intentionally compared and combined as 'symbolic representations'.[105]

Wilde read Romanes's work, and its model of progressive mental abstraction cohered with Wilde's view of art as liberation from one's immediate surroundings.[106] While receptual recognition is determined by the organism's environment, the symbolic imagination has a life of its own, generating infinite chains of association from finite stimuli. Wilde's Gilbert thus rails against Naturalism's 'shackles of verisimilitude', which restrict art to the 'obvious' (154, 160). Like nature's resemblances, such artworks 'have but one message to deliver, and having delivered it become dumb and sterile' (161). Verisimilitude, be it through a mimetic animal or a realist painting, generates no new mental phenomena; it only repeats. By contrast, symbolism stimulates novel suggestions, causing audiences to 'brood and dream and fancy', envisioning things never witnessed externally (160). Wilde further emphasises art's self-fertilisation through his speaker Vivian in 'Decay of Lying'. Vivian asserts that 'misrepresentation', like resemblance, is 'sterile', merely reproducing pre-existing forms, whereas artistic 'lying' produces novel moods and images. Art, he states, 'has flowers that no forests know of, birds that no woodland possesses. She makes and unmakes many worlds.'[107] In Wilde's vision, transcending nature's homogeneous automatism involves transcending representation, conjuring imaginative works with no referents in the material universe.

Oscar Wilde's Artistic Crypsis

Wilde's vision of art escaping cosmic automatism made a virtue of the gap between expression and interpretation. The more individuated people became, he suggested, the less they would convey clear, unambiguous meanings to each other. Straightforward mutual understanding implied sameness and simplicity, while differentiated minds would produce subtle, opaque art and find infinitely varied connotations in it. Gilbert comments:

> the meaning of any beautiful created thing is, at least, as much in the soul of him who looks at it, as it was in the soul who wrought it. Nay, it is rather the beholder who lends to the beautiful things its myriad meanings ... For when the work is finished it has, as it were, an independent life of its own, and may deliver a message far other than that which was put into its lips to say. (157)

Wilde imagines art escaping nature's mechanistic cycle of resemblance and recognition through its endless suggestiveness and indeterminacy. As Gilbert states, 'obvious' representations possess only one meaning, while true artworks 'make all interpretations true, and no interpretation final' (161). Gilbert's quip – 'I live in terror of not being misunderstood' – underlines how Wilde imagined individualism as a derailment of significa-tion (136). Associating individualism with obscurity led Wilde to avoid expressing his theory too directly, lest he become an example of vulgar obviousness. In a letter of 1889, Wilde explained that he used the dialogue form in order 'to put my new views on art, and particularly on the relations of art and history, in a form that they [the public] could not under-stand'.[108] By voicing his most expansive statements on aesthetics via fictional characters, Wilde framed them as ironic provocations that perhaps meant more than they said.[109] As Gilbert states with dramatic irony, dialogue is attractive to the artist-critic because, through it, 'he can both reveal and conceal himself' (186). Wilde used such dialogic self-concealment even when writing in his own authorial voice, such as in the final paragraph which he added to 'The Truth of Masks' (1886) in the collection *Intentions* (1891). Having defended the use of historically accur-ate dress and décor on stage, Wilde abruptly states: 'Not that I agree with everything that I have said in this essay. There is much with which I entirely disagree. The essay simply represents an artistic standpoint.'[110] Cultivating individualism for Wilde meant commanding attention while eluding 'recognition', since the latter implied dependence on external referents.

This attitude dovetailed with Wilde's avoidance of identifying as a homosexual. Lawrence Danson contends that, in fin-de-siècle England, 'there was a semantic grey zone between effeminacy and sodomy', and that '[t]hat is the zone Wilde publicly inhabited and exploited. He intended people to think something they could not know.'[111] Ironically, Wilde's conviction for homosexual acts stemmed from efforts to deny the label of homosexual. He was tried only after attempting to sue the Marquess of Queensberry for libelling him as a 'sodomite' (or, as Queensberry claimed to have written it, accusing him of 'posing as a sodomite').[112] Wilde's evasiveness about his sexuality was no doubt partly strategic, given the risks of imprisonment and ostracism. Further, Jonathan Dollimore has argued that Wilde exemplified heteronormative 'interpellation', conforming to conventional sexual morals by expressing regret for his 'perverse pleasures' while in prison.[113] However, Michael Doylen observes that Wilde's 'ethics of self-invention' were incompatible with defending homosexuality if such a defence demanded placing it at the centre of his identity. Wilde saw his 'same-sex passions' as parts of his self-invention, Doylen claims, but did not consider them to 'speak the truth of his essential being'.[114] Indeed, for Wilde to define himself as homosexual would have been to compromise his individualist philosophy, yielding to primitive 'resemblance' and 'recognition'.

Wilde reflected this conflict in his repeated appeals for 'obscurity' when involved with the magazine *The Chameleon*, which published content sympathetic to homosexuality. In his 'Phrases and Philosophies for the Use of the Young' (1894), which Wilde contributed to the magazine, he asserted, 'Only the great masters of style ever succeed in being obscure.'[115] In spite of its name, however, *The Chameleon*'s homoeroticism proved dangerously obvious, such as in a story by John Francis Bloxam of a love affair between a boy and a priest. This content formed part of the evidence used against Wilde in his trial. Prior to publication, Wilde had objected to the transparent purpose of Bloxam's story, commenting: 'God and other artists are always a little obscure.'[116] Three years later, writing 'De Profundis' in his prison cell, Wilde remained committed to his ideal of an individualism that eluded classification and assimilation to external standards. 'Most people are other people', he wrote. 'Their thoughts are someone else's opinions, their lives a mimicry, their passions a quotation.' By contrast, Wilde defined himself as 'a born antinomian', 'made for exceptions, not for laws'.[117] To subsume one's identity under any label would have seemed to Wilde slavishly mimetic, even a label as outré as homosexual. The only time that Wilde submitted to such a label was when he petitioned the Home Secretary for compassionate release on the grounds that his crimes arose from a 'sexual madness' that required medical treatment rather than punishment. Citing Nordau, who had used him as a case study in *Degeneration*, Wilde temporarily embraced the classification of degenerate, seemingly in an opportunistic bid for freedom.[118] What seemed like self-revelation was really pragmatic adaptation to others' perceptions, much like animal crypsis.

Like adaptive appearance, Wilde's artistic individualism focussed on intersubjective effects as much as the authentic expression of internal essences. Yet it also sought the transcendence of nature's predictable cycle of resemblance and recognition. Wilde's commitment to artistic autonomy rendered semantic clarity a sort of conformity. The more explainable art was, as either realist mimesis or moral teaching, the more it seemed to reflect society's conventions instead of the unique imagination of its producer. Wilde envisaged art escaping such automatism through a kind of crypsis, hiding its author's intentions behind ambiguous suggestion. Too much clarity denoted a lack of independence, as yielding to explanation seemed to correlate with subjugation, much like Foucault's concept of 'compulsory visibility'. To be fully understandable to others was to echo convention, while ambiguity and misreading generated fresh resonances and unpredictable associations. Other critics who took inspiration from adaptive appearance usually glossed over its destabilising implications for language and culture. Wilde, however, boldly confronted the subjective, interpretive nature of meaning that adaptive appearance illustrated. His critical writings recognised that the refinement of individual expression was necessarily antagonistic to language's function as a social stabiliser. Wilde's celebration of artistic concealment thus prefigured Modernist valorisations of 'difficulty' and 'obscurity'.[119]

These case studies show that theories of adaptive appearance energised fin-de-siècle discourse on artistic and intellectual individualism in diverse ways. The mimeophobia and cryptophobia exemplified in late Victorian cultural criticism was rooted in a desire for authenticity and autonomy, and a fear of the semiotic instability that was implicit in adaptive appearance. However, evolutionary models of crypsis and conspicuousness might be applied to the identities of groups as well as individuals. The next chapter explores how these tropes were used to rethink the position of Jews and women in western society at the turn of the century, and how they produced similar conflicts between authentic expression and inauthentic semiosis.

CHAPTER 6

Blending in and Standing out, II
Mimicry, Display and Identity Politics in the Literary Activism of Israel Zangwill and Charlotte Perkins Gilman

This chapter argues that evolutionary theories of crypsis and display served as models for thinking through the positions of disempowered, marginalised groups at the turn of the century. Similarly as critics in the last chapter invoked protective mimicry as a watchword for intellectual and creative inadequacy, Israel Zangwill sometimes used it to decry Jewish assimilation as the degenerate defence mechanism of helpless dependents. Zangwill's wish for Jews to be strong enough to stand out from Gentiles was fundamental to his argument for a Jewish state. Charlotte Perkins Gilman also used adaptive appearance to make sense of women's perceived weakness, but via the conspicuous display of sexual selection. Gilman argued that women's eye-catching, impractical clothes reflected their feeble dependence on men. Barred from providing for themselves by patriarchal society, Gilman's women survived by seizing the attention of prospective husbands. Gilman consequently associated women's liberation with a diminution of feminine conspicuousness.

Through their rhetoric of standing out and blending in, both authors sought to recover the imagined authentic essence of their group identity, which regimes of Gentile or male surveillance had repressed. Like Nietzsche's pauper who had 'become a coat', Zangwill and Gilman suggested that Jews and women had been reduced to reflective surfaces, unable to display their true selves. The biological categories of race and sex seemed to offer routes to this *real* being beneath the masquerade of self-conscious social life. Unlike social identities, which had to be contrived and mediated by substitutive signs, race and sex simply *were*. In this sense, both authors exemplify the Edwardian culture of 'Biotopia' described by Jim Endersby: an optimistic trust that biological concepts and science could offer tools to improve the lot of humanity in general and specific groups.[1]

Yet, although Zangwill and Gilman framed self-realisation in opposition to inauthentic, social appearances, they also imagined this self-realisation being asserted through visual display. Discussing American Jewishness, Ken Koltun-Fromm observes that authentic identity is a public performance, writing: 'American Jews cannot just be authentic: they have to appear, embody, be seen, or look in ways that are, so they claim, visually authentic modes of being Jewish in America.'[2] While Zangwill exemplified this trend with his rhetoric of Jews distinguishing themselves from Gentiles, Gilman would seem to deviate from it, associating female liberation with a loss of visibility. However, she also envisaged empowered women standing out, only through their humanity instead of their femininity. Authentic identities had to be displayed; yet the intersubjectivity of display rendered it inherently inauthentic, mediated by arbitrary symbols. This contradiction caused Zangwill's vision of Jewish self-realisation to vacillate between essentialism and anti-essentialism, between a return to pure origins and progression toward open-ended, heterogeneous identity. Gilman's vision similarly vacillated between the restoration of a primordial female 'modesty' and the progressive transcendence of visible sex distinctions. She imagined women realising themselves and displaying their self-realisation through a unisex 'true beauty', which, while downplaying their sexual difference from men, would visually manifest their physical and mental autonomy. Gilman imagined such beauty as true identity, beneath the inauthentic play of arbitrary signs by which the male gaze constructed femininity. However, her ideal was riven with contradictions. As in Zangwill's writing, the biological theory that Gilman appropriated undermined the idea of fixed origins or essences, and the validity of appearance as a mode of knowledge. Moreover, her vision of authentic self-display was torn between making women homogenous, transparent objects, perfectly adapted to their environments, and agential subjects who consciously shaped their appearances to express their individuality.

Israel Zangwill and the Mimetic Jew

Israel Zangwill was the son of émigrés from the Russian Empire and spent most of his formative years in the cosmopolitan Jewish community of Whitechapel in London's East End. He began his writing career as a humourist, collaborating with Jerome K. Jerome before winning international fame with his novel of Jewish London life *Children of the Ghetto* (1892). His other best-remembered work was his play *The Melting-Pot* (1909), which explored the experience of immigrants to the United States and won plaudits from no less than Theodore Roosevelt. At the turn of the century, Zangwill was 'probably the most famous Jew in the

180 Blending in and Standing out, II

English-speaking world', and he used his celebrity to advocate for the establishment of a Jewish homeland, first in Palestine then in some other, uninhabited territory.[3] He was on personal terms with leading literary voices of the time from Nordau to Pater, and also mixed with scientific authorities such as Raphael Meldola, an entomologist and theorist of crypsis.[4] It was perhaps his contact with Meldola that inspired Zangwill to repeatedly describe Jewish assimilation as 'protective mimicry'. His use of this trope reflected his conflicted views of Jewish identity as he both celebrated his people's adaptability and worried that such mimicry was linked with weakness and degeneracy. Writing in a context of rising anti-Semitism and pogroms, Zangwill stressed Jews' common humanity with Gentiles and sometimes hoped for the transcendence of racial divisions. However, he also emphasised Jews' difference to Gentiles and imagined that their evolutionary progress would involve cultivating and making more conspicuous this difference. From this perspective, assimilation could seem even worse than persecution, threatening to wipe Jews out of existence once and for all. Zangwill's 'melting-pot' vision of different races synthesising clashed with a mimeophobic view of assimilation as a zero-sum game between dominant majorities and submissive (and thus mimetic) minorities.

Zangwill was preceded by a broad chorus of commentators (both Jewish and Gentile) who regarded the newly emancipated Jew as peculiarly mimetic. The anti-Semite Frederick Millingen (writing under the pseudonym Osman Bey) claimed that Jews were able to assume the 'Mask' of any nationality, being 'a rare sort of human chameleons, as many colored in their scales as in their principles'.[5] Jay Geller notes that such images of the imitative Jew existed in a dichotomy with the supposed 'authentic, virile, original genius of the Gentile'.[6] For example, Eduard von Hartmann wrote that Jews excelled in theatre and all of the arts in which 'no more than reproduction is required ... Everywhere they step first into the foreground when non-Jews have creatively built up the field sufficiently so that only the reproduction of existing models is left to be done'.[7] Among Jewish commentators who also linked Jewishness with mimicry was the anthropologist Joseph Jacobs, who was a friend of Zangwill. Examining the history of Jewish surnames, Jacobs observed that many a British-sounding name 'may have been adopted by a kind of "mimicry" so that its bearers might escape that instant identification as Jews which is usual with the more pronounced surnames'. Hence, the name *Davids* had given way to *Davis*, while Jews from Germany brought with them 'perfectly Teutonic surnames' which 'have in most cases been made and have not grown'.

Israel Zangwill and the Mimetic Jew

Jacobs emphasised the specifically Darwinian nature of such mimicry by explaining that he used the word in the sense of 'natural science to express the devices by which insects and small animals adopt colours and forms resembling their surroundings so as to escape the notice of their enemies'.[8] Jacobs's language evokes the familiar organicist dichotomy between vigorous, fertile creation and weak, sterile copying: while Gentiles originate, Jews mimic.

Toward the turn of the century, the Zionist movement, reinvigorated by Theodor Herzl, replicated this rhetoric of emasculating mimicry to criticise Jewish assimilation. At the First Zionist Congress in 1897, Nordau declared that assimilation had failed to protect Jews from anti-Semitism, since Gentile racialism still marked them out as other. Despite his 'true mimicry' of European nations, Nordau claimed, the assimilated Jew's 'countrymen repel him when he wishes to associate with them. He has no ground under his feet and he has no community to which he belongs as a full member'. However, Nordau's rhetoric was often less concerned with the danger of failing to blend in than the imagined degradation of doing so, which he depicted as emasculating. He wrote that the emancipated Jew's 'best powers are exhausted in the suppression, or at least in the difficult concealment of his own real character . . . He becomes an inner cripple, and externally unreal, and thereby always ridiculous and hateful to all higher feeling men, as is everything that is unreal.'[9] Treating authenticity as a measure of survival value, Nordau interpreted Jews' 'ethnic mimicry' as a sign of looming extinction, lamenting that 'instead of their being originals worthy of their existence, this striving at imitation will mould them into mediocre or wretched copies of foreign models'.[10] Nordau contrasted this abjection with the Jew in the old days of the Ghetto who, for all his persecution, could at least be himself. 'The Jew without any rights did not love the prescribed yellow Jewish badge on his coat', Nordau stated. 'But voluntarily he did much more to make his separate nature more distinct even than the yellow badge could do . . . In the Ghetto, the Jew had his own world . . . Here all specific Jewish qualities were esteemed, and through their special development that admiration was to be obtained which is the sharpest spur to the human mind.'[11] Nordau frames persecution as the price, and perhaps also test, of Jewish authenticity. As with conspicuous animals, contrasting strongly with one's environment invites persecution; yet it also demonstrates strength and autonomy. Unlike the assimilated Jew, the Ghetto Jew was spiritually (if not physically) robust enough to withstand Gentile oppression without suppressing his unique nature and heritage. He subsisted as

182 Blending in and Standing out, II

part of a tight-knit, self-sufficient unit, while the assimilated Jew is an isolated, empty vessel depending on outsiders for material survival and spiritual meaning.

Zangwill often echoed this view in his writings, presenting assimilation as the presage of a racial twilight. His proem to *Children of the Ghetto* elegises pre-emancipation times when 'all Israel were brethren', and before

> Judaea prostrated itself before the Dagon of its hereditary foe, the Philistine, and respectability crept on to freeze the blood of the Orient with its frigid finger, and to blur the vivid tints of the East into the uniform gray of English middle-class life. In the period within which our story moves, only vestiges of the old gaiety and brotherhood remained.[12]

The images of homogenisation and absorption are paralleled by depictions of assimilative Judaism as a cluster of sterile reproductions and appropriations. Even within the relative protection of the ghetto, Zangwill worried that the Jewish character had suffered degenerative mimicry, such as in the emergence of Yiddish. The narrator describes this language as 'the most hopelessly corrupt and hybrid jargon ever evolved'.[13] Zangwill's diction frames Yiddish as an adulteration of ancient Hebrew, which, by contrast, is imagined as having evolved from the Jewish people's unique racial character, without external influences. In speeches and articles through the 1890s and 1900s, he also echoed the rhetoric of physical degeneration caused by reliance on mimicry and concealment in Jewish diasporic history. Jews' long-term survival, he commented, was partly owing to 'the cunning inevitably developed in the struggle of the weak with the strong'. Forced to live in cities and by mercantile work, he remarked, they had grown

> out of touch with nature, out of harmony with woods and waters, out of affinity with art; the brain growing subtler and subtler, and the body punier and punier, till at this day a tall Jew is as rare as a dull Jew. What wonder if Israel changed in the course of two thousand years from the agricultural, military people we read about in the Bible to a meek, commercial people.[14]

Zangwill seems to replicate the anti-Semitic rhetoric of Jews as parasites who mimic Gentiles due to innate feebleness and unoriginality.

However, Zangwill also challenged such anti-Semitism by arguing that Jews' imitativeness resulted from external forces suppressing their essential nature, which was dynamic and original. The inter-racial influence had been mutual, he claimed, and much to the benefit of Gentiles. Diasporic Jews were not only 'tinged by' but also 'tinged in turn, the colours of every environment'. Their 'biological' relationship to Gentiles, Zangwill

Israel Zangwill and the Mimetic Jew

asserted, had consisted of not parasitism but 'symbiosis, by which members of different species ... render each other mutual service in the struggle for existence'.[15] He suggested that Jews had only been losing their distinctiveness, gradually in the Ghetto and then rapidly with emancipation, because they were subsumed within much larger Gentile nations. Assimilative 'mimicry', Zangwill complained in 1893, had rendered Jews 'backboneless', incapable of 'asserting their individuality' from their Gentile neighbours.[16] When some Jews expressed scepticism of Zionism's feasibility, Zangwill interpreted their sentiments as only further demonstrations of the degradation wrought by adaptive mimicry. In 1903, he declared that Jews' status as 'the middlemen of the world' derived from their having been so long 'permitted to live [only] for the benefit of their neighbours, and so pliantly did they adapt themselves to the service of mankind that the natural human instinct for political independence was finally atrophied'.[17] Zangwill therefore supported Zionism as a means to replace 'symbiosis' with 'autobiosis': autonomous survival, which would enable Jews to develop their distinctive character without restraints. Such nation-building, Zangwill concluded in his 'Ghetto' speech, was the Jew's 'only chance, since only a deep-rooted, native, independent character has the strength to survive in the struggle and the interaction of the races'.[18] He envisaged the Jews' emergence from the shadows as a reversal of their former degeneration, writing, 'Already the swift development of physical manliness under new open air conditions promises to bring back the ancient Maccabean type.'[19] If environmental pressures had robbed Jews of their vigorous distinctiveness, then, perhaps, a new environment, without incentives for mimicry, could restore it.

Zangwill's model of racial mimicry conceives of diasporic Jewish identity as a zero-sum game in which Jews either assimilate to Gentiles or Gentiles assimilate to them. 'For the Jew's only value to the world', he declared in the 'Ghetto' speech, 'his only justification for persistence, is his spiritual originality, and not his repetition of borrowed formulae'.[20] Any Jewish appropriation of Gentile manners, he suggested, equated to a diminution of the unique Jewish racial essence. He thus described the tendency of emancipated Jews to follow Gentile fashions as a 'surrender to contemporary civilization'.[21] In a 1911 address to the Universal Races Congress in London, Zangwill claimed that assimilated Jews were neurotically over-patriotic, representing an unequivocal gain to their adoptive nations and a loss to the Jewish one. 'There are no Ottomans so Young Turkish as the Turkish Jews', he asserted, 'no Americans so spread-eagle as the American Jews, no section of Britain so Jingo as the Anglo-Jewry ...

184   Blending in and Standing out, II

[F]ortunate must be accounted the peoples which have at hand so gifted and serviceable a race, proud to wear their livery'.[22] Zangwill frames this reinforcement of Gentile nations as a weakening of Israel, removing its 'best and strongest' members, who would normally support 'the weakest' and, thus, maintain the integrity of the national organism. Zangwill also implies that Jews disbelieve in their ability to form a state partly because many of their people's achievements have been appropriated by Gentile nations. After listing illustrious Jewish-European philosophers, scholars and scientific investigators, he states: 'one wonders what the tale would be both for yesterday and today if every Jew wore a yellow badge and every crypto-Jew came out into the open, and every half-Jew were as discoverable as Montaigne or the composer of "The Mikado"'.[23] Zangwill's rhetoric depicts art and ideas as exclusive racial property, formed by the innate collective genius of one's people. In such passages, European-Jewishness can mean only the imposition of one identity or culture upon another, or the dispossession of one by another. Like mimeophobic individualism, Zangwill's model of racial mimicry rests on essentialist foundations. Art, thought and social manners seem manifestations of racial essence, which either dominates or is usurped by a foreign essence, reducing the race from an autotelic force to a passive instrument.

Zangwill's racial mimeophobia would seem to be sharply contradicted by his own life as a secular Jew and his celebration of America's multiracial 'melting-pot'. Far from preserving Jewish tradition, Zangwill married a Gentile, spurned religious orthodoxy and refused to have his son circumcised. He supported progressive secular causes such as pacifism and women's suffrage, and sometimes presented Jewish intermixture with Gentiles as part of humanity's advancement. In *The Melting-Pot*, the Russian-Jewish émigré David, who has fled the Kishinev pogroms, hails American identity as a way of transcending ethnic hostilities. He declares: 'America is God's Crucible, the great Melting-Pot where all the races of Europe are melting and re-forming! ... Germans and Frenchmen, Irishmen and Englishmen, Jews and Russians – into the Crucible with you all! God is making the American.'[24] David illustrates this process by marrying a Russian immigrant, even though her father was responsible for the slaughter of his family. David envisions American identity 'melt[ing] up all race-differences' and with them all of the past 'vendettas'.[25]

The play's apparent celebration of racial homogenisation resonates with Zangwill's sporadic efforts to downplay fixed race differences and frame identity through the more open prism of social experience. In his Races

Congress speech, he stressed the 'comparative superficiality' of biological differences between humans and asserted that the great distinctions between groups lay primarily in 'the geographical and spiritual heritage – the national autocosm, as I have called it – into which the child is born that makes out of the common human element the specific Frenchman, American or Dutchman'.[26] *The Melting-Pot* demonstrates this flexibility of identity through not only its lovers but also the Irish maid Kathleen. Through serving David's family, Kathleen transitions from anti-Semitic hostility to her masters to sympathetic identification with them. By the play's last act, she is speaking Yiddish to David's grandmother and comically referring to 'we Jews'.[27] Such moments in Zangwill's play and statements in his speeches suggest that eternal racial essences, on which racial mimeophobia depended, are illusions that needlessly divide and isolate peoples.

On one level, Zangwill's writings were simply contradictory, caught between a Zionist-Territorialist desire for racial distinction and a pacifist, cosmopolitan ideal of human unity. Yet he also groped toward a reconciliation of these aims by sometimes invoking a non-essentialist vision of identity. Zangwill seems to have developed this more nuanced view partly through engaging with Pater and Wilde, expanding their Hegelian models of individual development to the scale of races. In an essay on Italian rural life, he mused:

> It is, in fact, impossible for us moderns, educated in a long literary tradition, to live our lives as naturally and naïvely as the unlettered of to-day, or the people of the preliterary geological epoch ... [W]e are all to some extent remoulded in imitation of the Booklanders, and this is the truth in the 'decadent' paradox that nature copies art. There is a drop of ink in the blood of the most natural of us; we are all hybrids, crossed with literature, and Shakespeare is as much the author of our being as either of our parents.[28]

Zangwill's Wildean language frames a world in which modern literacy and cosmopolitanism have undermined belief in authentic identities. Instead, identities are recognised as mediated through an eclectic, transnational canon of literature and art. The mimetic inauthenticity which Zangwill elsewhere presented as the special fate of Jews seems here applicable to all civilised nations. Zangwill exemplifies this point with an anecdote of some 'cold-blooded artistic English' friends who came close to witnessing a murder at Fiesole. Finding a track of blood and a band of villagers excitedly narrating the tale of a fatal fight over personal honour, these spectators 'felt no answering throb of sympathy – it was still a scene in a play to them, still

186   Blending in and Standing out, II

a *coup de theatre* – they had lost the primary human instincts, corrupted by a long course of melodrama and comic opera'.[29] Zangwill's jaded travellers experience the world as a tissue of textual allusions that stretches across national borders and heritages. Frames of reference and, by extension, identity appear less 'natural' than constructed by 'imitation of the Book-landers'. One's identity proceeds as much from what one reads as whom one's ancestors were. Zangwill's inclusion of himself in the heritage of Shakespeare demonstrates literature's potential to cross heritages, uniting Jews with Anglo-Saxons, while theatre unites Europeans in general. Like Pater's poet-scholar, Zangwill sees himself as a 'hybrid', absorbing influences from diverse sources.

This attitude resonates with Gilles Deleuze and Felix Guattari's concept of 'minor literature', which refers to minorities appropriating the language of the majority and making it strange. By reworking the acquired tongue to reflect its users' position between cultures, minor literature detaches language from essentialist discourses of race and nation.[30] Zangwill's notion of literary hybridity also coheres with Homi Bhaba's observation that mimetic relations between coloniser and colonised expose the lack of 'essence' and 'presence' behind the 'mask' of identity. While the native might seem degraded by mimicking the coloniser, his mimicry also highlights the inauthenticity and instability of the coloniser's identity.[31] Zangwill sometimes seems to have vaguely recognised these dynamics, such as when discussing the popularisation of 'Jewish' styles of humorous writing. Noting that critics had misidentified his collaborator Jerome K. Jerome as Jewish, Zangwill joked, 'Well, after all, Mr. Jerome's style has Jewish discursiveness, and I am afraid if he does not modify it he will incur similar suspicion.'[32] In such moments, Zangwill appears to acknowledge the inevitable inauthenticity and impurity of group identities, suggesting that they are realised, and constantly reshaped, through interaction with each other.

Zangwill sometimes celebrated Jewish hybridity as a sign of Spencerian advancement instead of degradation, indexing their complexity and heterogeneity. Jews' status as the 'middlemen of the world', he declared in 1911, might represent the attainment of their destiny. As a 'born intermediary', he wrote, the Jew was uniquely placed 'to be the medium and missionary' of 'an ultimate unification of mankind'.[33] Zangwill's vision blended race destiny with universal human destiny, hailing the invention of Esperanto by a Jew as the latest stage in the progression. Such rhetoric surpassed the zero-sum games of mimeophobic anti-Semitism and Zionism, reconceptualising identity as open and cumulative. Yet his rhetoric also, paradoxically, salvaged a sense of Jewish distinctiveness by framing Jews' openness to and absorption of outside influences as unique or, at least, uniquely developed. He argued that Jews' special ability to see beyond national–racial divisions derived from their unmatched hybridity, which had widened their worldview. 'What wonder that Jews are the chief ornaments of the stage, that this chameleon quality finds its profit in artistic mimicry as well as in biological!' Zangwill declared. 'For, when the Jew grows out of his own ghetto without narrowing into his neighbour's, he must necessarily possess a superior sense of perspective.'[34] Zangwill thus inverted the anti-Semitic trope of Jews as parasitic mimics into a more positive image of global synthesisers.

Arguing for both Jews' common humanity and their essential specificity, he vacillated between depicting them as the vanguard of humanity's general evolution and, conversely, as a discrete race following their own path (albeit one which overlapped with the paths of other races). This desire to retain (and perhaps even intensify) racial differences simultaneously with humankind's unification is hinted at in *The Melting-Pot*, which avoids equating unity with homogeneity. David imagines Americanness as not the obliteration of different identities but their 'fusion' into new forms, perhaps exemplified in the Hebraised Irishwoman Kathleen. Neil Larry Shumsky has noted that David's statements about the need to reject old Jewish separatism are countered by 'a strong attachment to his native culture'.[35] David struggles with his romantic attachment to a woman whose relatives abetted the pogroms, rejecting her before a final reconciliation. Shumsky argues that the reconciliation is contrived and inconsistent with David's previous motivations.[36] After discovering what he calls 'a river of blood' between his family and that of his fiancée, David claims to have heard 'always a small, still voice calling me back' to his people, which he had previously ignored but now overwhelms him.[37] The play thus reflects the tensions in Zangwill's idea of progress between racial unification and differentiation.

Zangwill would acknowledge this tension in a 1917 lecture, admitting that his 'ideal' was also an insoluble 'problem': 'how to maintain the virtues of tribalism without losing the wider vision; how to preserve the brotherhood of Israel without losing the brotherhood of man; how to secure that, though there *shall* be both Jew and Greek, there shall yet be neither'.[38] His ambivalence derived from competing views of identity as, on the one hand, internal and essential, and, on the other, external and acquired. While the first view nurtured mimeophobia, the second challenged it, valuing accumulation of influences instead of essential purity.

Zangwill downplayed this contradiction by locating Jews' racial essence in a uniquely pronounced openness to others' influences. By seeming to become like other peoples, Zangwill's Jews became truly themselves. In Zangwill's hazy vision of the future, racial differences seem to both dissolve and harden. These paradoxes show the enduring power of mimeophobia over his imagination. Although Zangwill engaged with views of identity as a social acquisition, he remained attached to the notion of an internal, racial essence beneath such changeable mimicries. He sought to invalidate anti-Semitic denigrations of Jews as parasitic imitators by exposing the fallaciousness of racial essentialism. Yet these efforts were undercut by a parallel desire to restore Jewish racial pride by depicting an essential Jewish genius and destiny. Zangwill's example shows how crypsis could be used to figure the precariousness of oppressed groups, in contrast to empowering conspicuousness. I will now consider an opposing discourse that identified conspicuousness with the subjection of women, and forms of invisibility with their liberation.

Charlotte Perkins Gilman: Conspicuous Display and the Patriarchal Gaze

Charlotte Perkins Gilman was an American social reformer who won prominence for her feminist writings and lecture tours. She is now most famous for her short story of female madness induced by patriarchal medicine, 'The Yellow Wallpaper' (1891), and her novella of a utopian women's society, *Herland* (1915). From her youth, Gilman was fascinated by evolutionary theory, and she sought to harness this authoritative paradigm in the service of women's liberation.[39] Contra widespread contemporary assertions that biology showed women's natural inferiority, Gilman argued that it proved their natural predominance. She thus criticised modern women's economic dependence on men as an artificial imposition. In writings spanning from the 1880s through the First World War and beyond, Gilman repeatedly identified this socially generated inadequacy with women's appearances. However, unlike previous authors discussed, Gilman located the degeneracy in exaggerated visibility instead of obscurity. She sometimes used the term 'protective mimicry' to satirise sartorial dishonesties such as washable starch collars (which enabled a single shirt to be passed off as several) or the priest's cassock (which resembled women's clothing at a distance and, thus, Gilman argued, marked the clergy as non-combatants).[40] However, her main focus was

Charlotte Perkins Gilman

how women had come to signal such helplessness and be so visually distinct in the first place.

Gilman's answer was sexual selection, which had sacrificed women's fitness for the sake of attractiveness. She proposed that, forced to rely on men's favour to survive, women had developed increasingly showy, impractical surface traits from excessive blushing to garish, constrictive clothes, all to signal femininity. Following a Spencerian model of progress as increasing racial efficiency, she depicted such excessive display as wasteful and maladaptive.[41] Her reformist rhetoric envisaged women's clothes and bodies becoming less distinctive as their growing independence obviated sexual attention-seeking. Women's appearances would reflect their authentic being instead of men's arbitrary aesthetic preferences. However, this vision of authentic womanhood was conflicted, caught between an imagined natural femaleness that was distinct from maleness (although not flamboyantly so) and the almost total transcendence of visible sexual differences.[42] Leaning, ultimately, toward the latter goal, Gilman envisaged future women demonstrating their strength and authenticity by standing out, but as humans rather than as women. Viewing femininity as mostly an inauthentic imposition, Gilman sought to cultivate 'human' identity, which would be displayed through a unisex beauty of body and dress.

Gilman imagined such 'true beauty' as closing the gap between outer appearance and inner being: through their appearances, women would display their true, individual characters instead of the unreal, man-made phantasm of femininity. At the same time, Gilman elided authenticity with biological fitness, framing 'true beauty' as a visual manifestation of health, unlike maladaptive, inauthentic 'sex beauty'. However, this elision was contradicted by the science of adaptive appearance, which constructed appearance as inevitably semiotic. Further, Gilman's notion of 'true beauty' was based on a contradictory metaphysics of presence. On the one hand, women's bodies would display their nature transparently and unconsciously, while, on the other, women would express themselves by consciously manipulating their appearance. Gilman's wish for women to be masters of their appearance meant that they would also be alienated from it, reviving the vortex of inauthentic, substitutive signs that she wished them to escape. Gilman held these contradictions in abeyance by avoiding depicting her ideal future women in much visual detail. Authentic self-display turned into a paradoxical disappearing-act.

Gilman developed her ideas about display and female biology through her interests in dress reform and physical culture. She became committed to the latter movement as a schoolgirl in Providence, Rhode Island, adopting a rigorous exercise regimen and lobbying successfully for the establishment of the city's first women's gymnasium.[43] Gilman kept records of her athletic development, and her commitment to bodily fitness cohered with new models of womanhood in nineteenth-century North America that emphasised strength and independence. Frances Cogan claims that the mid-century saw the emergence of an ideal of 'Real Womanhood', which revered female 'physical fitness and health, self-sufficiency' and 'economic self-reliance'.[44] The idea of attaining autonomy through discipline and enhancement of the muscular body intersected with arguments for dress reform, which often hinged on the issues of health, practicality and self-responsibility.[45] In her first published intervention in the dress reform debate in 1886, Gilman depicted traditional women's clothes as not only restrictive but degenerative. They stifled women's development and reduced them to weak invalids, she wrote, inducing 'a crowd of diseases, heavy and light, a general condition of feebleness and awkwardness and total inferiority as an animal organism'.[46] To attain independence, Gilman implied, women had to evolve, physically as well as mentally. Traditional female dress represented an environmental condition that obstructed this development and, therefore, needed to be renounced.

Why, though, had women acquired such impractical, enervating attire in the first place? A possible answer came through the rise of secular anthropology since the mid-century, which had mooted the idea of pre-historic society being matriarchal.[47] John Ferguson McLennan in Britain and Lewis Henry Morgan in the United States had argued that, before marriage developed as an institution, humans had been promiscuous and family purely matrilineal.[48] They thus concluded that marriage had evolved in tandem with increasing patriarchal power, a process that Spencer claimed had increased sexual dimorphism. As women had become men's vassals, Spencer wrote, their strength and intelligence had diminished through disuse. Women's new dependence on men's favour had enhanced their 'ability to please, and the concomitant love of approbation', as well as 'their powers of disguising their feelings'.[49] This argument would be extended into the history of clothes by Lester Ward, who became an important intellectual ally to Gilman. Men's dominance, Ward wrote, had enabled them to prioritise 'utility' in their dress, evolving 'a comparatively convenient and at the same time comely habit' fit for 'the demands of active life'. Conversely, women's 'conditions' of life emphasised 'embellishment' since they survived by attracting male protectors.[50]

Charlotte Perkins Gilman 191

Such evolutionary logic could be used to oppose dress reform by making loud, impractical female clothes seem inevitable. In 1885, the novelist Charles Dudley Warner wrote that eye-catching feminine dress was a necessary part of humanity's development since the sexes had dimorphised, and, therefore, 'beauty is a duty women owe to society'.[51] Perhaps nature had intended women to appear rather than to act. Ward opposed such complacency, though, on the grounds that women's enforced conspicuousness created a degenerative feedback loop. A woman's dress, he wrote, had become 'a means of loading her with ornaments', which impeded physical activity and 'threaten[ed] to work a permanent physical deterioration of the race'.[52] The model of development from matriarchy to patriarchy also emphasised the possibility of social transformation. If women had been diminished by androcentric social relations, then new relations could empower them. Ward wrote: 'We see in the progress of true civilization the unmistakable tendency toward the ultimate restoration of the primeval state of nature.'[53] Empowering women, Ward suggested, would restore their rightful position as sexual selectors (at which they were supposedly more judicious than men due to a lower sex drive) and make them stronger, more intelligent and productive. The reorientation of women's fashion from embellishment to practicality would, therefore, be both a catalyst and an effect of their sociobiological advancement.

Ward's example shows how Victorian evolutionary psychology, so often used to justify gender inequalities, could also be adapted to challenge them, although not without problems.[54] The Lamarckian logic of women's socially engineered inferiority becoming hereditary suggested that many generations might have to pass before the effect would be reversed. Ward still assumed that men had evolved to be innately more intelligent than women, irrespective of patriarchal society. Nonetheless, Gilman found much to agree with in Ward's arguments, and was similarly eager to exploit the authority of science for the cause of dress reform and women's liberation.[55]

Gilman first did this at length in her 1898 book *Women and Economics*, which argued that female subjection jeopardised the biological progress of women and humanity in general. It was a law of nature, Gilman asserted, that males and females of any species must have more similarities than differences, because both had to survive in the same environments. While sexual selection encouraged dimorphism, she wrote, this process was checked by natural selection, which prevented sex-specific traits from becoming so pronounced that they hindered survival. Invoking Darwin's most famous example of a secondary sexual character, Gilman explained:

'If the peacock's tail were to increase in size and splendor till it shone like the sun and covered an acre, . . . he would die, and his tail-tendency would perish with him.' Equally, although the peahen tended to be smaller than the peacock, 'if she should grow so small and dull as to fail to keep herself and her young fed and defended, then she would die'.[56] Gilman argued that patriarchal society had removed this check on sexual dimorphism through women's 'total economic dependence' on men (5). Primordially, she asserted, 'woman belongs to a tall, vigorous, beautiful animal species, capable of great and varied exertion'. However, millennia of male-dominated sexual selection and exclusion from productive activities had produced increasing 'smallness and feebleness' in women, accompanied by 'comparative inability to stand, walk, run, jump, climb, and perform other race-functions common to both sexes'. Gilman warned that women were in danger of becoming like 'those insects where the female, losing economic activity and modified entirely to sex, becomes a mere egg-sac, an organism with no powers of self-preservation' (59). Like Ward, Gilman conflated the physical body with its dress, contrasting practical male clothes with a woman's 'garments whose main purpose is unmistakably to announce her sex', sacrificing bodily fitness to this end. Showy feminine costume, Gilman implied, both exemplified and reinforced women's total dependence upon men as 'excessive sex-distinction' rendered them incapable of providing for themselves.

Gilman developed this argument further in relation to clothes and conspicuousness in the 1900s, partly, perhaps, through her engagement with the sociologist Thorstein Veblen's concept of 'conspicuous consumption'. Veblen contended that, under capitalism, social status was asserted through the display of overpriced commodities, notably clothes. Gilman invoked this theory in a 1905 article, 'Symbolism in Dress', commenting that clothes expressed 'the "conspicuous consumption" of Veblen'. However, Gilman argued that such wasteful, unproductive conspicuousness was far more pronounced in women's dress than men's, which had been checked by the practical demands of a 'life of a thousand activities'. While women's dress 'mutilates and deforms the body', and served only the purpose of 'symbolism', male costume was adapted to the wearer's environment and motions.[57] In another article of the same year, Gilman speculated, that, in the barbaric past, 'a conspicuously distinctive dress was a natural protection to women', preventing them from being mistaken for men and so killed. Recognisably feminine clothes served for 'marking one's self a non-combatant, a helpless thing'. Women had been reduced to ciphers of sexual difference, valued for what they symbolised instead of what they did. Gilman lamented that a woman's dress 'may or may not be healthful, may or may not be beautiful, may or may not be useful, may or may not be economical; but it must be "feminine" above all!'[58] Gilman further emphasised society's division of men and women into agents and cynosures in 1915, demanding: 'Do women not notice that in the perennial love story the heroine is still described, for the most part, in terms of physical beauty?' She continued: 'The man is required to do something, to show character, action. The woman, in spite of all our rational progress, is still most emphasized as something to look at.'[59] Such statements evoke later feminist theories of the objectifying male gaze.[60] If women were vigorous and self-sufficient, Gilman wrote, they would not need to seize men's attention through 'loud devices of ultra-feminine charms'.[61] Liberation would seem to require a reduction in saliency as women would be defined by their actions instead of their appearance.

So how unremarkable should women become? Gilman sometimes portrayed this change as the restoration of an original femaleness, characterised by visual understatement, as opposed to the complete obliteration of visible sex distinctions. Melyssa Wrisley argues that, at least in her earlier career, Gilman advocated for a balance of practicality and attractiveness in women's dress, and sought to combine these aims in her own clothing.[62] As a public lecturer, she typically appeared in simple 'long gowns, lace collars and trim' with her 'hair pulled neatly back', and news reports often mentioned the 'old-fashioned' simplicity of her dress.[63] This style fitted with Gilman's view of women as primordially plain in contrast to men, whose 'efflorescence' had guided women to select the most vigorous mates. Males' naturally high sex drives obviated female display, Gilman explained, allowing the female of most species to be 'dull in color, simple in form, quiet in demeanor. She is in herself the attraction, the eternal drawing power; for her and to her come the males, numerous, varied, ardent, venting their superfluous energies in a thousand gaudy decorations, strutting and battling before her'. Females were distinctive and attractive, Gilman suggested, by virtue of their contrast with eye-catching, forward males. 'The demure withdrawal of the female', she wrote, 'is her form of sex-attraction and on exactly the same level as the blustering advance of the male.'[64] Gilman thus appealed to a supposed female essence, which showed its authenticity by its lack of showiness. Woman, she declared, 'has been false to the most inherent laws of her sex and adopted this essentially masculine function of sex-decoration ... [I]t is most obviously unfeminine, being an essentially male characteristic in all species'.[65]

Paradoxically, Gilman implied that women ought, by nature, to stand out and attract men by their relative inconspicuousness.

This paradoxical logic continued with Gilman's claims that, in a state of nature, females stood out from males by virtue of their averageness. Gilman was channelling a popular view of the time that males varied more than females in all biological traits.[66] In a 1910 article, Gilman stated that, among most animals, 'the beauty of the female is mainly that of race'. While the lion with its mane tended toward excessive display, she wrote, 'The lioness is a more appreciable working type of feline power', its body sculpted for practical needs.[67] In contrast to the divergent appearances forced on women by society, she contended, females' natural beauty consisted of their strong adherence to 'the normal', which denoted health. Women were destined to return to this natural averageness, Gilman argued, by entering all fields of work, which would lead to them converging with men in strength and size. She wrote: 'The human woman, now so rapidly developing, will regain the wholesome natural beauty that belongs to her as a human being; will hold, of course, the all-powerful attraction of her womanhood; but will leave to the male of her species; – to whom it properly belongs, the effort of conscious display.'[68] Gilman seemed to imply that her ideal future women would remain visually distinct from men through the 'all-powerful attraction' they would exhibit. She was unclear, though, about what this attractiveness would consist of. This ambivalence resonates with Sander Gilman's observation that, historically, aesthetic surgery typically aimed for a paradoxical '(in)visibility' through the removal of salient deformities and deviations from 'the normal'.[69] Aesthetic enhancement was conceptualised as at once standing out and blending in.

Despite the emancipatory rhetoric, representations of women as naturally modest and 'normal' could easily shade into patriarchal ideas of them belonging in the domestic sphere, out of public view, and with little individuality to develop. Gilman had experienced the consequences of such attitudes in her unhappy first marriage, and she acknowledged that invisibility was as much a factor in women's subjection as hyper-visibility. 'Harriet Martineau must conceal her writing under her sewing when callers came, because "to sew" was a feminine verb, and "to write" a masculine one', she wrote in *Women and Economics*. 'Mary Somerville must struggle to hide her work from even relatives, because mathematics was a "masculine" pursuit' (53). In a later essay collection, Gilman lamented that women had been 'veiled and swathed, hidden in harems, kept to the tent or house, and confined to the activities of a house-servant'.[70] In her study of women and visual media in the 1920s, Liz Conor argues that the 'magnified visibility' of women in this era was not only objectifying but also integral to the growth of women's 'cultural presence and political representation'.[71] Gilman also considered the possibility that female visibility was not inherently repressive, and sometimes depicted women's liberation as enriching their appearance rather than diminishing it. 'The differences we now find in the ever-revolving wheel of changing fashions we might still have', Gilman wrote of her programme for dress reform. 'Now we are all alike in one kind of foolish dress, until we are all alike in another. Then we could all be different, as different as in a fancy dress ball, if we so preferred'. The crucial change, she suggested, would be less about visibility than agency and authenticity. Instead of dressing to please men, women would dress 'to strike out for oneself; to cultivate an original distinctive personal taste; to invent for oneself'. Individual 'reason' and 'judgment' would take the place of 'brainless obedience' to fashion.[72] Such statements seem to contradict the rhetoric of modesty, associating independence with vivid display.

These different strains of argument might be reconciled, though, if we appreciate that Gilman wished for women to stand out, but as humans rather than as a sex. She came to view humanity as a progressive development that transcended primitive sex differences. This sentiment can be gauged in statements attributed to her in a 1914 article that discussed disagreements between so-called human feminists and female feminists. In contrast to other activists who celebrated specifically female experience, Gilman identified as a human feminist. Such a feminist, she was quoted as stating, 'holds that sex is a minor department of life; that the main lines of human development have nothing to do with sex, and that what women need most is the development of human characteristics'.[73] Men had already progressed some way along this path, Gilman claimed, as the growth of civilisation had curbed excessive male traits such as aggression, selfishness and erotic obsession. As a result, she wrote in *Women and Economics*, '[i]n the growth of industry, commerce, science, manufacture, government, art, religion, the male of our species has become human, far more than male' (43). Echoing Spencer, Gilman defined progress as increasing complexity and versatility. This model framed sex distinctions as primitive because they emphasised only one, sporadic activity at the expense of other capacities. Modern men were identified primarily as functional parts of a larger social organism, and Gilman sought a similarly de-sexualised humanness for women. 'Humanity', she asserted, 'is a relation far higher than sex, and that dress suitable for the service of humanity

Blending in and Standing out, II

need not carry any other label ... Any special costume necessary to a special human process is a human dress, and not a mark of sex.'[74] When deciding whether to wear a hat, she wrote, a woman should first 'put it on a man's head' to judge whether it was appropriate or ridiculous.[75] Gilman thus emphasised sexual similitude over difference, positioning men and women as mirrors instead of foils.

Gilman's contradictory discourse of inconspicuous femininity permeates her utopian novella *Herland*, in which a male narrator, Van, and two other explorers discover an advanced, exclusively female society. The men's first encounters with the Herlandians are characterised by perceptual uncertainty as they struggle to sexually categorise the people. In her criticism of feminine hyper-visibility, Gilman had noted, 'On the level plains of our great West a common measure of a mile is "as far as you can tell a man from a woman"'.[76] By contrast, Van struggles to sexually identify the first Herlandians he sees from a distance, commenting that 'still there had not been one man that we were certain of.[77] Spotting three in closer vicinity up a tree, Van's description foregrounds the figures' resistance to such classification:

> There among the boughs overhead was something – more than one something – that clung motionless, close to the great trunk at first, and then, as one and all we started up the tree, separated into three swift-moving figures and fled upward ... [W]e rested awhile, eagerly studying our objects of pursuit ... They were girls, of course, no boys could ever have shown that sparkling beauty, and yet none of us was certain at first. (14–15)

Van's narration vacillates between presenting the Herlandians' appearance as distinctively female and sexually indeterminate. The 'sparkling beauty' that supposedly marks them out as 'girls' remains untied to any definite physical traits. The short-haired Herlandians are as tall and strong as their male guests, often more so, forcing Van to sometimes describe them in conventionally masculine terms. The women in the trees are 'erect, serene, standing sure-footed and light as any pugilist' (20). Yet, far from being mannish, the Herlandians are desexualised humans, as Van remarks, they 'had eliminated not only certain masculine characteristics ... but so much of what we had always thought essentially feminine' (57). When the men don the Herlandians' 'sexless costume', the two groups visually converge with 'only our beards to distinguish us' (84, 45). At the same time, though, Gilman suggests that Herland has revived women's primordial plainness through the male visitors reverting, by contrast, to primordial efflorescence. Van reports that, after the men were allowed to choose garments

Charlotte Perkins Gilman 197

'according to our personal taste', they 'were surprised to find, on meeting large audiences, that we were the most highly decorated' (84). On balance, however, the Herlandians have transcended sex more than returned to a primordial form of it, given that they now reproduce by parthenogenesis. Although the men fall in love while visiting Herland, they are superfluous to the race's survival. Conceiving children from unfertilised ova, the Herlandians embody a fantasy of desexualisation.

This desexualisation illustrated Gilman's radical belief that human nature was fundamentally epicene and sex distinctions were mostly artificial impositions. Although the feminist theoretical distinction between sex and gender was not available to her, Gilman foreshadowed such thinking by presenting sex distinctions as generally semiotic, based on arbitrary, conventional signs. The difference between Gilman and later gender theorists such as Judith Butler was that while the latter viewed identity as always already semiotic, Gilman believed that authentic identity was possible, beneath the play of signs. She conceptualised non-semiotic identity as essential to women's empowerment: women would use signs to express themselves instead of *being* signs. Gilman wrote that contemporary women's fashion used 'the body as a conventional shape to convey a feeling or idea, making a sort of ideograph of it; a conventionalized symbol of a living form!'[78] Conspicuous woman sacrificed her range of action so that her body could 'cry aloud to all beholders, "I am a female – don't forget it!"'[79] Gilman viewed modern men's identities as less semiotic than women's', which gave them a more agential, individuated and authentic presence. They 'stand out from one another by personal distinction', she wrote, rather than garish advertisements of maleness: 'The Man is noted rather than the clothes.'[80] Instead of expressing themselves through their appearance, Gilman's feminine women are twisted and swaddled into symbols of male erotic fantasy.

Gilman equated authentic self-display to biological health and semiotic identity to degenerative sickness. Bodily semiosis led to arbitrary signs being valued over the real traits for which they substituted. Gilman framed this tendency as degenerative by presenting communication as an environmental adaptation that helped humans only as long as it connected them reliably with material reality. Language had emerged, she wrote, 'From need and use . . . like all organic functions', and had consisted originally of 'concrete terms and immediate practical ideas'.[81] Such language of 'facts' was 'healthy', Gilman wrote, because it was tied closely to the external world. Conversely, an opposing tendency toward 'fancy' twisted words to evoke people's subjective mental associations, playing on '[t]hat natural variance in minds by reason of which no two persons get precisely the same idea from the same facts'. Instead of describing the world truthfully, linguistic 'fancy' sought 'to please' and was manifested in the aesthetic movement: 'the un-moral literary craftsmen, who hold that literature is an Art – and exists for its own sake, knowing no laws of use or ethics'. For Gilman, language is purely instrumental, and playing with words for subjective 'gratification', à la AESTHETICISM, disrupts the wider social body.[82] Instead of connecting people with the real world, fanciful language alienates them from it, conjuring fantasies based on words' connotations rather than their denotations.

Gilman argued that sex attraction worked in the same way, twisting women's bodies into conventional fantasies of femininity, which bore no relation to real-world biological fitness. Like most words, she claimed, sexual symbols lacked natural links to their referents and arose from chance associations. 'We know how arbitrary, how changeable, how helplessly associative, is the "beauty sense"', Gilman lamented in 1910: 'no sensation is more erratic'.[83] She elaborated on this arbitrariness in 1915, writing that men had come to value degenerative physical features in women through

> a principle which seems to be inherent in the action of the human mind; namely – conventionalization. We recognize the beauty of certain lines and proportion in various objects, and then, subconsciously, we add them together and get their average; we seek for a common denominator; we make, from the natural object, a conventionalized design . . . This tendency has acted steadily upon the dress of women, and even upon the modifications of her living body. We have seized upon certain salient outlines and proportions; and from them projected a fixed outline, representing 'woman', not pictorially, but as a conventionalized decorative design.[84]

Gilman traced this alienation from biological reality in the development of high-heeled shoes. Appreciating the naturally beautiful 'curving outline' of a woman's foot, she wrote, the artist's 'fancy' had 'increase[d] these curves, at pleasure', until the toes were 'utterly forgotten in the slim point which covers them', and in the place of the normally flat sole of the foot 'we now have this languid luxuriance of graceful line'.[85] Although women's physical differences to men, such as shorter stature, were transmitted biologically, Gilman insisted that they were inauthentic, imposed by arbitrary male preferences instead of emerging from adaptation to environments. Bodies had been adapted to arbitrary fashions instead of clothes adapting to the objective demands of organic fitness.

Gilman thus articulated the inauthenticity of women's fashion as a pathological inversion of expression: artificial outside had shaped natural inside instead of vice-versa. Railing against fabrics and designs that gave 'shape' to the figure, she instructed her readers: '*You* are the shape', so that a healthy dress 'will have your shape, and has no business to have any other'. Gilman presented such sartorial dishonesty as part and parcel of women's degraded position as signal-bearers, unable to simply be themselves. She lamented: 'You can not wear lies on your outside and not feel it in your soul.'[86] By symbolising beauty instead of embodying it, Gilman wrote, 'We are content to live in fat or meagre, unwholesome, ill made bodies, which are a burden and a mask to the spirit, instead of the perfect vehicle of thought and feeling they should be.' In contrast to such mendacious displays, Gilman revered unisex 'human beauty' or 'true beauty' as transparent, objective fitness. Unlike arbitrary symbols of femininity, true beauty reflected laws of geometric regularity. Gilman wrote that beautiful bodies were 'well proportioned, vigorous, active' and of 'relative size and strength', exemplifying species norms.[87] This notion of beauty as a healthy mean is exemplified by the Herlandians, whom the narrator describes as 'physically ... more alike than we, as they lacked all morbid or excessive types' (77). Gilman suggested that fitness visually announced itself in fixed, unmistakable forms, beyond arbitrary semiosis. Bodies were beautiful and healthy because they were transparent, as Gilman declared: 'beauty and goodness and truth are one'.[88] Gilman also envisaged clothes evolving to reflect such 'true beauty' by the expulsion of symbolism, sexual or otherwise. 'The primal laws of design and our pleasure in them reach deeper and higher than sex', she wrote in 1915. 'From simple repetition and alternation, on through symmetry, radiation, and the rest, we respond to regularity, to balance, to the lifting and soothing effect of line, form, color.'[89] Dress would reveal the perfection of its wearers. 'True beauty' seemed to seal the gap between body and soul, signifier and signified.

Gilman's vision of health and fitness finding visual embodiment in mathematical order was undermined, though, by her simultaneous equation of 'true beauty' with environmental adaptation. 'No ship could be beautiful', she wrote, 'the lines and general structures of which prevented her from sailing', and the same rule applied to bodies.[90] The Herlandians' bodies seem to be infinitely adaptive, enabling them to climb trees like monkeys and run and jump 'like deer' (32). Yet these different animal comparisons point to the Darwinian reality that there is no ideal body but only different adaptations to different conditions and activities. Gilman admitted as much in *Women and Economics*, writing, 'Every quality of every creature is relative to its condition', so that 'creatures that live in trees cannot be so big as creatures that live on the ground' (59–60). However, the Herlandians somehow manage to be both large, muscular ground-dwellers and light tree-climbers, representing ideal bodily perfection rather than adaptive fitness. The tension between perfection and adaptation also emerges in Gilman's contradictory comments on the future of women's clothes. Amid her strict pronouncements on sartorial beauty, Gilman denied that there would be 'some revelation of A Perfect Dress . . . Clothes must differ as people differ.' In the dress of the future, she continued, 'the major note will be adaptation to the human body and its activities'.[91] Although she repeatedly asserted its beauty, Gilman was rather vague about what her future dress would look like, and this visual vagueness is reflected in Herlandian clothes. Although Van calls them 'richly beautiful', their appearance is barely described (81). Van records some practical details of costumes such as 'a one-piece cotton undergarment, thin and soft, that reached over the knees and shoulders, something like the one-piece pajamas some fellows wear, and a kind of half-hose, that came up to just under the knee' (26). However, more space is devoted to the garments' comfort and flexibility than their visual features. Gilman's faith in a union of beauty and goodness (in the sense of fitness) depended on an ideality that her own Darwinian rhetoric undercut.

Gilman's model of transparent bodily fitness was further undermined by her interest in hereditary diseases, which often hid under seemingly healthy bodily surfaces. In her early utopian novel *Moving the Mountain* (1911), Gilman depicts a near-future society in which 'the birth of defectives and degenerates' has been prevented through careful sexual selection by women. However, when selecting mates, these women avoid relying on mere personal attraction or even cold assessment of men's appearances. Instead, a 'Department of Eugenics' records every patient with sexually transmitted diseases and allows women to check its 'list' of contaminated men. Laws now require 'a clean bill of health with every marriage license'.[92] Gilman's narrative thus frames biological fitness as an invisible quality that can be estimated only indirectly through long-term bureaucratic surveillance.

In the same year, Gilman published another novel, *The Crux*, which depicts a doomed romance between a young woman, Vivian, and her sweetheart, Morton, who becomes degenerate after moving to the city and contracting syphilis. Syphilis formed a locus for conflicting ideas about the visibility and invisibility of disease in the period. Discourse on syphilis often vacillated between emphasising the hideousness of its full-blown symptoms and the lack of clear, visible signs during much of its progress.[93]

Charlotte Perkins Gilman

This vacillation is echoed in Gilman's text, which sometimes suggests that Morton's degeneracy is legible in his features, triggering instinctive revulsion in the viewer. Although charmed by Morton when he returns from the city, Vivian is also repelled by 'his coarsened complexion' and 'a certain look about the eyes' that he lacked previously. The narrator observes that Vivian registered that 'something seemed vaguely wrong' about him. When Morton lights a cigarette in the dark, his illuminated face gives her 'a sudden displeasure'.[94] However, Morton's disease is revealed only after the former madam of a brothel, now a servant, recognises him at a reunion and informs Vivian's doctor that Morton had liaisons with infected women. Vivian receives the news with disbelief, picturing Morton's 'handsome face', which has bewitched her. The doctor notes that 'it takes a long microscopic analysis to be sure' of such diseases, reinforcing the body's opacity.[95] Gilman's view of biological fitness as visibly evident clashed with an alternative view of the body as a mask capable of conjuring impressions quite contrary to its internal state.

The failure of fitness to display itself transparently similarly haunted Gilman's writing on dress. Conscious that her programme for dress reform did not meet universal approval, Gilman envisaged making sartorial beauty an educational topic. Children could learn the history of clothes, she suggested, since '[w]e shall never be competent to judge the merits of costume until we have full knowledge of its bases'. She proposed lectures in which 'models of distinct personal types' could parade upon stage in various clothes, embodying possible forms of 'becomingness' such as 'special power and dignity of bearing', 'soft grace' and 'dainty roundness'.[96] Yet the notion that one needed to be taught to perceive 'true beauty' contradicted its supposed naturalness. If such beauty was self-evident, surely it ought to be recognised automatically? True beauty was, perhaps, as much a system of arbitrary signs as 'sex-beauty'. Gilman's wish for transparent bodily surfaces (extended through dress) clashed with the associative nature of perception constructed by empiricist psychology, which rendered all vision necessarily semiotic. Even if consistent rules of beauty could be found, such as in symmetry, such beauty was still only a subjective experience for the perceiver, as George Santayana had written in 1896: beauty was 'pleasure objectified'.[97] A person's appearance was, perhaps, always an object of interpretation and never simply an authentic manifestation of their inner character or worth.

The imagined transparent fitness of Gilman's 'true beauty' also conflicted with her rhetoric of dress as autonomous personal expression. Although she claimed that future clothes would 'differ as people differ', such differences often seem more like mindless organic variations than agential choices. Clothing, Gilman wrote, was 'a sort of social skin', and its 'origin, development, and variation' could be studied 'as we would study the same processes in the vegetable or animal world'.[98] This elision of dress with organic growths emphasised its authenticity in the sense of being uncontrived but undermined its authenticity as conscious, personal expression. Gilman scornfully compared women worrying about the appearance of their clothes to 'a hen saying to her chickens, "go away, you'll muss my feathers!"'[99] The geometric harmonies and optimal adaptation of Gilman's future dress hollowed out its wearers' subjectivity, reducing them to passive instruments of racial efficiency. Gilman was sometimes forced to acknowledge this point, predicting that, '[i]n the interests of comfort and convenience in ordinary work, women will become largely similar in dress through business hours'. She tried to preserve space for creative agency by arguing that women would still be free to express themselves decoratively in leisure time, adding: 'But when working hours are over, at home, or at play, the whole world of women could blossom out to their heart's content, in beauty as varied as the flowers.'[100] However, Gilman's evolutionary credo denied such a separation of labouring and leisurely self. Humans were, supposedly, wholly products of their work (or exclusion from it). It is ironic that Gilman should use flowers as a simile for the varied beauty produced in the leisure hours of her future women. Darwin had, of course, analysed flowers' colours as environmental adaptations, attracting animals to spread pollen, and, therefore, in Gilman's terms, as a form of 'work'. Her portrayal of women's collective self-realisation as a biological inevitability proceeding along fixed lines clashed with her notion of women developing into autonomous individuals.[101] Having lamented sex attraction's reduction of women to symbols, Gilman threatened to reduce them to spokes in the natural machine critiqued by Pater and Wilde.

Gilman downplayed the contradictions in her vision of authentic self-display by shifting between imagery of visible presence and invisible soul or mind. Despite her sometimes rigid design prescriptions for clothes, she also asserted: 'The coming change in the Dress of Women is not so much a change of costume as a change of mind.' In such moments, she stressed abstract qualities over material ones, asserting: 'The majesty of womanhood will shine out in a far nobler splendor when she drops forever her false decoration, and learns that beauty lies in truth, in dignity, in full expression of our highest human powers.'[102] The fixed visual forms of 'true beauty' seem to give way to invisible expressive agency, which is

Charlotte Perkins Gilman 203

inferred indirectly through a woman's actions. Gilman suggested as much, writing that the crux of the matter lay in 'not the effect of the fashion ordered, but the effect of obeying the orders'.[103] Gilman was more concerned with internal self-consciousness and agency than superficial visible differentiation. The seemingly great variety of women's current fashion only reinforced for her its 'brainless obedience', as disempowered women pathetically sought male attention through 'a frantic shadow-dance after constantly changing patterns' instead of following their own judgement and taste.[104]

The extravisuality of authentic, liberated womanhood is also reflected in *Herland* through Van's courtship of the Herlandian Ellador. Despite earlier assertions of her and other Herlandians' visual beauty, Van narrates the process of falling in love with Ellador as a mental–spiritual process. He states: 'The "long suit" in most courtships is sex attraction, of course. Then gradually develops such comradeship as the two temperaments allow ... Here everything was different. There was no sex-feeling to appeal to, or practically none' (91–92). Instead, Van and Ellador's love grows from a meeting of minds. He explains: 'We discussed – everything. And, as I traveled farther and farther, exploring the rich, sweet soul of her, my sense of pleasant friendship became but a broad foundation for such height, such breadth, such interlocked combination of feeling as left me fairly blinded with the wonder of it' (90). The lack of visual details in Van's description accentuates the irrelevance of bodily appearance. Ellador's beauty and value subsists in her psychical life which seems to have no relation to her appearance. Gilman's extravisual language suggests that human worth, like biology's fundamental processes, exists beyond what can be seen.

As with Zangwill, the contradictions in Gilman's vision derived from her essentialist approach to identity, which clashed with emergent notions of identity as produced by social interactions. Gilman attacked sexual essentialism, arguing that the visible marks of femininity often considered as eternal were androcentric impositions, composed of arbitrary, conventional symbols. In this way, Gilman prefigures Simone de Beauvoir's later existential argument that femininity was a social construct used to restrict women to second-class status.[105] Indeed, her image of feminine appearance as 'a frantic shadow-dance' of imitations even evokes Judith Butler's radical view of femininity as a performance.[106] However, Gilman rejected essentialism on the sexual level only to revive it on a 'human' one. Conflating identity with biological progress, she viewed authentic appearance as a telos of personal and racial development. This evolutionary trajectory framed the mediation of identity by signs as a disease rather than an inevitable condition of life. Yet Gilman's ideal of authentic appearance was destabilised by goals that were both internally contradictory and incompatible with each other. The idea of displaying biological fitness ran counter to the open-endedness of environmental adaptation and extravisuality of nature's processes. Conversely, subjecthood involved becoming alienated from one's appearance, consciously manipulating its significations rather than ridding it of any. Gilman was able to rescue her ideal of authentic womanhood, torn between transparency and opacity, only by reframing it in non-visual terms. Although her ideal women were never invisible, they could be remarkably elusive.

Zangwill and Gilman's engagements with the biology of crypsis and display show how these concepts energised discussions about authentic identity even as they also problematised it. Both authors viewed society's play of substitutive signs and imitations as symptomatic of the weakness and degradation of their respective group identities. Crypsis and sexual display offered a scientifically authoritative language for diagnosing this perceived degeneration and its causes, and for articulating an alternative of strength and autonomy through authentic appearance. Zangwill and Gilman located the perceived enfeeblement of Jews and women in the suppression of their true characters due to Gentile persecution or male economic domination. They therefore depicted the emancipation of their groups as a casting off of contrived exteriors to display their true, inner essences. However, the science through which they elaborated this rhetoric also undermined it. Their presentation of semiotic identity as a morbid aberration framed authentic appearance as the natural order of life, in contrast to society's unreal representations. Yet biological mimicry and display collapsed this dichotomy, revealing semiosis as a ubiquitous phenomenon permeating all levels of life. The idea of stripping identity back to authentic origins in physical bodies and racial essences relied on a naive view of animal life as innocent and transparent which biological research increasingly contradicted. From the perspectives of Darwinian biology and early social psychology, Zangwill's mimetic Jews and Gilman's symbolic women would have seemed more normal than aberrant. Both authors' search for an authentic identity outside the play of semiosis only led them into further chains of substitutive signs and semantic deferral.

Conclusion
Adaptive Appearance and Cultural Theory

This study has shown that adaptive appearance responded to and reshaped various wider discussions in Victorian and Edwardian culture, and these interactions can be traced by analysis of scientific and literary texts. Adaptive appearance problematised scientific objectivity, the anthropocentric gaze and the Cartesian binary of hermeneutic humans versus non-human automatons. It suggested new ways of imagining the roles of appearance in human life from individual selfhood and competition to group identity and artistic expression. The Victorian and Edwardian discourse of adaptive appearance thus speaks to contemporary discussions in cultural theory: current debates about non-human signification and subjectivity can be enriched and further complicated by considering how nineteenth-century authors grappled with similar issues. *Mimicry and Display* also intervenes in long-running cultural–theoretical discussions about power and identity, showing that the stakes of mimicry, essentialism, vision and visibility are ecological as well as societal. The work offers a new angle on the historical separation (or interpenetration) of science and the humanities, objective and subjective knowledge. It also invites further reflection on the afterlives of adaptive appearance as a discourse in later twentieth- and twenty-first-century culture.

Let us return to the opening claim that, for Bates, Wallace and Darwin, appearances mattered. Their theories suggested that appearance and being needed to be redefined, not as opposites but as parts of a single whole. Appearances mattered not just in the sense of determining survival but also in that of being material phenomena, produced by organismic interrelations. Far from being extrinsic to physical life, perception, signs and meanings had grown from and influenced it. This idea would be formulated most systematically in the late nineteenth and early twentieth centuries by the American philosopher Charles Sanders Peirce.[1] The meaning of a sign, Peirce argued, lay purely in its 'interpretant', or effect, upon an audience. He proposed that all perceptions were signs and that 'thought'

205

emerged through sensory–semiotic interactions with the world, decentring signification from humans. However, Peirce's semiotic theory received little exposure during his lifetime, and was not widely discussed until the mid-twentieth century.[2] Notions of biological semiosis developed more in the interwar years through the work of the Baltic German zoologist Jakob von Uexküll, who investigated animals' sensory capacities and behaviours. Uexküll concluded that every organism possessed a perceptual inner world or *Umwelt* based on its sensations. An organism's environment, he suggested, existed as subjective 'marks' (*Merkmalträger*) or 'carriers of significance' (*Bedeutungsträger*), rendering every interaction with its surroundings an act of interpretation.[3] Since the 1960s, linguists and theoretical biologists have built on Peirce's and Uexküll's ideas to develop the interdisciplinary field of zoosemiotics. As the Introduction mentioned, such work approaches relations between animals as semiotic activity, mediated by their respective *Umwelten*. Zoosemiotics fits into the wider field of biosemiotics, which studies all biology as semiotic systems from plant communication to DNA code.[4]

Such theoretical paradigms contrast starkly with a long western tradition of presenting semiosis as a uniquely human activity. Wendy Wheeler traces this tradition to the dualism of William of Ockham and René Descartes, which confined meaning and interpretation to the realm of metaphysical, exclusively human, mind.[5] Such dualism, in John Berger's words, 'emptied' non-humans 'of experience and secrets' while suppressing the materiality of human subjectivity and communication.[6] The dichotomy continues in the 'physicalism' of much mainstream biology, which tends to treat signs and codes in non-human contexts as mere metaphors for deterministic physical processes. Dario Martinelli notes that this determinism is realised in the paradigm of bio-mathematical 'information', which 'presupposes that information is an entity that can be measured objectively', and its effects predicted.[7] Non-humans' communicative interactions are thus reduced to 'a rigid stimulus-response scheme'.[8] Scientific depictions of animal communication as predictable signalling systems replicate Descartes's image of animals as machines.

Theorists of zoosemiotics and biosemiotics present their approaches as correctives to such anthropocentric reductionism, reconfiguring semiosis from a barrier between humans and non-humans into a bridge. Jesper Hoffmeyer thus proposes that the line from animal to human communication might be conceptualised as a spectrum of increasing 'semiotic freedom' instead of the binary presence or absence of Cartesian mind.[9] These studies have inspired cultural theorists such as Donna Haraway to

Conclusion 207

suggest approaching animals as beings embedded in 'material-semiotic nodes or knots in which diverse bodies and meanings coshape one another'.[10] Timo Maran observes that ecological literary criticism (or ecocriticism) might utilise biosemiotics to analyse 'communicative and sign relations between human cultural activities and other [non-human] semiotic subjects and their representation in literature'.[11] Such theory intersects with a broader turn toward 'New Materialism', which seeks to reconceptualise agency in non-anthropocentric terms, questioning binaries between discourse and matter.[12]

This study suggests that such concepts of non-human and cross-species semiosis are less new than they may seem.[13] As Chapter 1 shows, Victorian studies of adaptive appearance involved extending subjecthood to animals and imagining the world through their eyes. However, the Victorian context also prefigured current physicalist views as zoologists theorised patterns of perception and reaction on large scales, framing animal behaviour as mechanically predictable. My findings problematise posthumanist celebrations of the supposed collapsing of the human/non-human binary, showing that this binary can be reinscribed at the same time as it seems to be loosened. Designating animals as interpreters does not rule out the possibility of them being machine-like.[14] Machines might be described as interpreters, such as computers that process programming languages (or Charles Baggage's calculating machines, in the Victorian context).[15] Indeed, for Victorians and Edwardians, collapsing the human/non-human binary was as likely to mechanise humans as to extend subjecthood to animals.

This study also questions associations sometimes drawn in cultural theory between biosemiotics and progressive politics. Wheeler argues that biosemiotic perspectives cohere with environmentalism, animal liberation, socialism and general anti-essentialism.[16] In the Victorian and Edwardian context, however, the biology of crypsis and display seem more ideologically equivocal. Although the naturalists and authors discussed here found common psychological ground with non-humans, this mostly did not lead them to question hunting, vivisection or exploitation of nature as a resource.[17] Adaptive appearance energised Grant Allen's socialism, enabling him to frame capitalism as a primitive masquerade akin to that seen in nature. Yet this biological prism also dampened Allen's socialism, nudging him toward the pessimistic conclusion that, as products of nature, humans inevitably replicated the former's deceptions. Like evolution in general, biosemiotic thought seems to be ideologically ambiguous and pliable.

My case studies have shown that, as a cultural trope, adaptive appearance could both undermine and reinforce essentialist views of identity,

208 Conclusion

much like Bhaba's analysis of colonial mimicry. Bhaba wrote that mimicry 'alienates' identity from 'essence', revealing the former's performative nature. Yet it could also stress the rigidity of identities, shown by Bhaba's example of the mimetic colonial subject who remains 'almost the same but not quite' as his master.[18] Michael Taussig similarly notes that mimicry implicitly supports transcendental concepts of origins and authenticity by acting as their opposites.[19] Chapters 5 and 6 show writers invoking crypsis and sexual display as pejorative figures for a lack of individuality, originality or authenticity, thereby reinforcing these essentialist ideals. While Stephen, Pater and others recognised that adaptive appearance threatened the dogma of the autonomous individual, they still appealed to it in defence of this ideal. Similarly, Zangwill and Gilman sometimes drew on adaptive appearance to question fixed racial and sexual identities, suggesting that what seemed immutable was really a matter of changeable surface signs. Yet both also railed against identity based on appearance, reifying race and sex (or a sexless humanness) as authentic realities, even though the details of the science they invoked undermined authentic identities. Again, as with evolution in general, literary invocations of adaptive appearance could depart widely from the details of the theory.

More broadly, this study's discussions of visibility, recognition and appearance suggest new ways of approaching the politics of the gaze. Literary critics have applied Foucault's model of 'compulsory visibility' to the Victorian realist novel, arguing that the genre enacts the panoptical gaze through multi-perspectival, omniscient narration.[20] The subjection of visibility figures invisibility as contrastingly empowering powerful and subversive.[21] My textual close readings sometimes reinforce this model, such as in Allen's tales of chameleonic criminals whose invisibility can be threatening and even anarchistic. However, some also contradict the dynamic of visibility-as-subjection, such as in the writings of Stephen, Watts-Dunton and Zangwill that associated invisibility (or, rather, indistinctiveness) with weak dependence and conspicuousness with autonomy. Judith Butler's notion of gender performativity similarly constructs self-presentation as a means of social control, arguing that people are compelled to constantly perform conventional signs of maleness or femaleness.[22] In this sense, freedom and subversion might exist less in invisibility than inscrutability, that is, self-display that resists conventional interpretation. Wilde's ideas about eluding recognition exemplify such subversive inscrutability, offering a model of enigmatic conspicuousness. Hiding in plain sight might consist of standing out as well as blending in.

Mimicry and Display also intervenes in long-running feminist discussions of the ideological stakes of female visibility. The concept of the 'male gaze', coined by Laura Mulvey, posits that androcentric traditions of representation construct women as hyper-visible objects of male desire.[23] Conversely, in other contexts, critics have identified women's subjection with forced invisibility.[24] Gilman's evolutionary approach to female visibility and invisibility pre-echoes this contrast. Her protests against attention-seeking female dress resonate, in some ways, with later critiques of the androcentric gaze. Her frequent association of female empowerment with the loss of visible distinctions from men also contrasted with the aforementioned motif of self-sufficient conspicuousness linked with manhood. This inconsistency shows that visibility could be made to signify different traits in different contexts: strength and weakness, presence and absence, masculinity and femininity. Nonetheless, I have shown that Gilman also sometimes envisaged her future, emancipated women as highly conspicuous, wearing diverse, beautiful clothes. Her example shows that female visibility could be envisaged as alternately empowering and disempowering, depending on whether it was defined as an external (male) imposition or internal expression of selfhood and agency.

This study throws new light on historical conceptions of science and the arts or humanities as linked or separate enterprises. Eric Mielants argues that the humanities emerged as a self-conscious orientation toward knowledge in the nineteenth century through resistance to the expanding authority of physical science. Such humanistic culture opposed the wishes of philosophers such as Auguste Comte to reduce moral questions to Baconian induction and systemic, Newtonian precision, defending the value of imagination and interpretation.[25] Lorraine Daston and Peter Galison also argue that science and art were increasingly discussed as oppositional activities through the nineteenth century onward, the former identified with systematic method and the latter with intuitive tact.[26] Conversely, Smith has contended that Victorians often conceived of knowledge as a combination of 'fact and feeling', method and imagination, which could be applied to the arts as well as sciences.[27] Similarly, Philipp Erchinger suggests that art in the period was sometimes conceived as continuous with nature (instead of separate from it) and productive of material knowledge (instead of being only guided by it).[28] My study shows that adaptive appearance further resisted the divergence of objective and subjective knowledge through researchers drawing on their embodied perceptions to infer those of other species. They also used the techniques of art and literature to recreate these perceptions for readers. Adaptive appearance's tendency to blur the subjective and objective and, thus, also art and science, can be seen to continue beyond the scope of this study, such as in Hugh Cott's *Adaptive Coloration in Animals* (1940). Cott begins by invoking Ruskin's 'innocence of eye', encouraging readers to challenge their customary perceptions of nature and to interrogate its visual forms afresh.[29] Future research might further explore how representations of crypsis and display resisted the supposed 'Two Cultures' trajectory of the mid- to late twentieth century.

Such research could trace Modernist uses of adaptive appearance to meditate upon art and the human mind. Roger Caillois was fascinated by animal mimicry and camouflage, and argued that they showed that artistic creation and the Freudian death drive were deep biological forces.[30] Walter Benjamin argued that human representation was the culmination of a cross-species 'mimetic faculty'.[31] Conversely, Jacques Lacan seized upon crypsis to mark the animal–human boundary, claiming that, while animals could represent things, only humans could consciously 'play' with representations.[32] Although Jacques Derrida would later critique this binary, Luce Irigaray used it to frame women's liberation as a matter of 'play[ing] with mimesis', changing women from objects of the male gaze to representational agents (as in Gilman's writing).[33] Parallels might also be drawn between Victorian associations of concealment with weakness and later texts such as D. H. Lawrence's poem 'Self-Protection'. Lawrence's speaker dismisses theories of crypsis, declaring that the triumphant creatures of the wild 'give themselves away in flash and sparkle/ And gay flicker of joyful life', while 'the dodo' probably 'looked like a clod', its extinction foretold in its dull plumage.[34] Vladimir Nabokov's engagements with insect mimicry further resonate with Kingsley's and Thayer's depictions of nature as a text or artwork. Nabokov's claims that insect resemblances exemplified 'artistic perfection', too perfect to have occurred by chance, continue Kingsley's earlier efforts to find transcendent purpose in adaptive appearance.[35] Nabokov also repeated Victorian comparisons between adaptive appearance and art, commenting, 'Every writer is a great deceiver, but so is that arch-cheat Nature ... The writer of fiction only follows Nature's lead.'[36]

The use of 'protective mimicry' as a trope of social assimilation might be further pursued among later writers who depicted the experiences of racial and sexual minorities. Reflecting on the Harlem Renaissance of the 1920s, Alain LeRoy Locke associated the flowering of African American literature with emancipation from the 'masks of protective mimicry'.[37] As in Zangwill's writings on the Jewish diaspora, adaptive appearance gave

Conclusion 211

Locke a language to express the historic silencing of black voices and their restoration with growing economic empowerment. Alternatively, the mid-century American novelist Frederic Prokosch described his habit of wearing tennis clothes as 'protective mimicry' to conceal his (supposedly visible) homosexuality, framing effeminate physicality as athletic gracefulness.[38] More recently, Mylène Dressler's novel *The Deadwood Beetle* (2002) drew on Batesian mimicry as a figure for expressing post-war immigrant assimilation in the United States.[39] Researchers might inquire whether such invocations of adaptive appearance involve similarly problematic notions of authentic identity as Zangwill's and Gilman's writings do.

Future studies could explore the significance of adaptive appearance in the genre of the realistic animal story, which emerged at around the turn of the twentieth century in North America. Authors such as Ernest Thompson Seton, William J. Long and Jack London published narratives of animal characters, supposedly informed by zoological knowledge of such creatures' behaviours in the wild. Focalising animals' perspectives frequently caused such narratives to explore the roles of perceptions and intersubjectivities in their survival. For example, in *Wild Animals I Have Known* (1898), Seton describes a rabbit learning 'the signs by which to know all his foes and then the way to baffle them. For hawks, owls, foxes, hounds, curs, minks, weasels, cats, skunks, coons, and – men, each have a different plan of pursuit, and for each and all of these evils he was taught a remedy.'[40] Seton's choice of words accentuates the book's anthropomorphism, implying that rabbits infer other beings' intentions in a manner analogous to humans. Such anthropomorphism would be attacked by the nature writer John Burroughs, who argued that zoological research did not support advanced animal cognition. 'Animals practice concealment', he wrote, 'but not deception, as man does. They do not use lures or disguises, or traps or poison.'[41] It is interesting that such criticism of anthropomorphic literature often ran in tandem with scepticism of adaptive appearance more broadly. Burroughs doubted many claimed examples of crypsis, particularly protective mimicry.[42] Similarly, his friend Roosevelt attacked 'Nature Fakers' like Seton at the same time as he excoriated Thayer's theories of animal camouflage.[43] Hostility to the idea of mental commonality between humans and animals seems sometimes to have correlated with resistance to zoosemiotics in general (although, as I have shown, zoosemiotic logic did not necessarily level humans and animals either).

Scholars might also consider how adaptive appearance has featured in retrospective depictions of Victorian society and culture. In the late

212 Conclusion

twentieth century, pastiches of Victorian fiction sometimes seized upon theories of crypsis and sexual display as reflections of the era's obsessions with public image and respectability. In John Fowles's *The French Lieutenant's Woman* (1969), the narrator explains a character's tendency to vary his manners in different company 'biologically by Darwin's phrase: *cryptic coloration*, survival by learning to blend with one's surroundings – with the unquestioned assumptions of one's age or social caste . . . Very few Victorians chose to question the virtues of such cryptic coloration.'[44] Crypsis and display receive more sustained thematic treatment in A. S. Byatt's novella 'Morpho Eugenia' (1992), in which the fictional naturalist William Adamson studies insect display like Bates (whom he counts as a correspondent). William's discourses on mimicry and sexual advertisement punctuate his encounters with his love interest Eugenia, whose pale skin and colourful outfits fascinate him. William wins Eugenia's hand by arranging a dazzling 'cloud' of live butterflies in a conservatory, appropriating their bright patterns to produce his own sexually attractive display, while Eugenia's dress draws many insects, which mistake her for a flower.[45] Yet William is warned by a servant that '[t]hings are not what they seem', and Eugenia's beauty and grace conceal scandalous secrets that he discovers only after marrying her.[46] Such fiction frames the science of adaptive appearance as a kind of unconscious self-revelation by which Victorian society pointed obliquely (or, rather, *cryptically*) to its own anxieties and suppressions.

Victorian ideas of mental evolution as incremental interpretive detachment could also be traced through later theories of art and literature. The twentieth-century British psychologist Edward Bullough argued that art was inherently 'antirealistic' due to its dependence on the observer's 'psychical distance' from sensory stimuli.[47] As in Wilde's reverence of artistic obscurity, Bullough claimed that art functioned by evoking sensory realities while remaining distinct from them. Ruskinian notions of optical innocence might be linked with Formalist art theory, which stressed the automaticity of perception and often approached art as an evolutionary phenomenon.[48] Bertolt Brecht's theatrical theory of *Verfremdungseffekt* similarly emphasised critical distance from emotions, on the part of both actors and audiences, a theory developed in dialogue with science and Darwinism.[49] The association of interpretive detachment with scientific authority might be further linked with mid-century New Criticism's rejection of sentimental and emotional readings of literature, as well as unfalsifiable claims about authorial intentions.[50]

We might wonder whether recent theorisations in literary criticism of 'literary Darwinism', 'distant reading' or 'surface reading' appeal to the

Conclusion 213

same ideal of interpretive detachment that has its roots in Victorian scientific culture. 'Literary Darwinism' applies concepts from evolutionary biology and psychology to literary criticism, claiming to replace Poststructuralist relativism with objective scientific laws.[51] 'Surface reading' seeks empirical robustness by focussing on the extant verbal content of texts and avoiding 'symptomatic' readings based on what they supposedly omit or repress (traditionally associated with approaches such as Marxism or psychoanalysis).[52] Conversely, 'distant reading' uses digital technology to discover macro-patterns in textual networks, partly replacing human hermeneutics with mechanical quantification.[53] Such approaches suggest that credibility derives from avoidance or minimisation of subjective interpretation. Their rhetoric can frame texts as landscapes of empirical facts to be identified and measured. In an era when empirical and, particularly, quantitative data have never enjoyed higher prestige, literary criticism, like Victorian studies of adaptive appearance, sometimes seems caught between seeking the richness of free interpretation and the certainty of restrained fact-gathering. Indeed, as the humanities in higher education are constantly pressured to demonstrate value, might not critics who associate their methods with science be accused of 'protective mimicry' like Stephen's Victorian theologians? In any case, adaptive appearance undermines the simplistic view of science reducing the organic world to a body of definite, quantitative facts. Like language and literature, the living world involves infinite networks of imperceptible relations, which must be inferred before investigators can seek ways of verifying them. Similarly as language functions holistically, not elementally, the living world consists of irreducible interconnections that evade objective measurement perhaps, ultimately, as much as the meanings of texts. The implicit assumption that science must progress toward a God-like view-from-nowhere in which uncertain interpretation gives way to factual certainty seems the height of teleological delusion. Although, as a species, we have gained much abstract knowledge of the world, we remain embedded in its processes, making sense of our surroundings, like any other organism, to gain not transcendent truth but adaptive advantage.[54]

This last point highlights another question to be explored: in an age of looming anthropogenic eco-catastrophe, how might environmentalist politics take account of the biologization of semiosis and display? Timothy Morton observes that the agency of 'pure appearance' in the living world implies that a place must be found for 'art' in 'evolutionary biology'.[55] Yet the Anthropocene also involves human art and culture encroaching upon non-humans' lives, sometimes with grave consequences. This encroachment is crystallised in the artist Chris Jordan's work 'Midway: Message from the Gyre' (2009). The photographic series depicts the decaying carcasses of albatross chicks, whose open stomachs are full of plastic rubbish.[56] The bright colours of these objects, from bottle caps and netting to cigarette lighters, would have likely drawn the attention of the chicks' parents as they searched for food. The garish surfaces designed to attract human consumers have also fatally seduced animals. By foregrounding these artificial objects' literal entanglement with the birds, Jordan shows that our relations with non-humans are at once material and semiotic. Yet the fact that human cultural productions can, in a sense, speak to non-humans, does not render such interspecies communication sympathetic, or even intentional. The semiotic worlds of humans and non-humans intersect in chaotic, unexpected ways, much like the networks of significance between non-humans. Discussions about non-human communication have often revolved around the possibility of animals learning to understand language or possessing faculties analogous to it.[57] Yet adaptive appearance illustrates the narrow anthropocentrism of this approach as we seek in other species reflections of ourselves (or, rather, idealisations of ourselves as self-expressive free agents). Instead, adaptive appearance invites us to view signification as a process that works through all life forms, shaped by chance circumstances, not transcendent intentions. Ecology is a web of not only physical dependencies but also signs and suggestions. Some Victorians concluded that humanity progressed via ever-widening altruism, and more recent philosophers have argued that our moral responsibilities should be extended to other species.[58] If we are to build such an interspecies ethics, it must take into account not only our physical relations with non-humans but also our semiotic ones. If we are to be caretakers of the living Earth, we are obliged to try to interpret it on its own terms, and consider how it might interpret us.

Notes

Introduction

1 Lorraine Daston and Peter Galison, *Objectivity* (New York: Zone Books, 2007), pp. 122–124; Daston and Elizabeth Lunbeck, 'Introduction: Observation Observed', in *Histories of Scientific Observation*, ed. Lorraine Daston and Elizabeth Lunbeck (London: University of Chicago Press, 2011), 1–10, pp. 3–4.
2 Henry Walter Bates, 'Contributions to an Insect Fauna of the Amazon Valley. Lepidoptera: Heliconidæ', *Transactions of the Linnean Society of London*, 23 (1862), 495–566, p. 507.
3 For an overview of current knowledge of crypsis, see Martin Stevens, *Cheats and Deceits: How Animals and Plants Exploit and Mislead* (Oxford: Oxford University Press, 2016).
4 The term *aposematism* was coined by Edward Bagnall Poulton in *The Colours of Animals* (London: Kegan Paul, Trench, Trübner & Co., 1890), p. 337. Subsequent quotations are referenced in the text.
5 Fritz Müller, 'Über die Vortheile der Mimicry bei Schmetterlingen', *Zoologischer Anzeiger*, 1 (1875), 54–55. See also 'Ituna and Thyridia: A Remarkable Case of Mimicry in Butterflies', trans. Raphael Meldola, *Proceedings of the Entomological Society of London* (1879), 20–29.
6 Charles Darwin, *On the Origin of Species* (London: John Murray, 1859), pp. 87–90. Darwin discussed sexual selection with Bates: see Letter, Darwin to Bates, 4 April 1861, *Darwin Correspondence Project*, www.darwinproject.ac.uk/letter/DCP-LETT-3109.xml <accessed 4/25/2018>. Darwin elaborated his theory of sexual selection in *The Descent of Man* (1871).
7 Darwin, 'Contributions to an Insect Fauna of the Amazon Valley. By Henry Walter Bates, Esq. Transact. Linnean Soc. Vol. XXIII. 1862, p. 495', *Natural History Review*, 3 (1863), 219–224, pp. 220–221.
8 Alfred Russel Wallace, 'Mimicry, and Other Protective Resemblances among Animals', *Westminster and Foreign Quarterly Review*, 32:1 (1867), 1–43, p. 40.
9 Christopher Herbert, *Victorian Relativity: Radical Thought and Scientific Discovery* (London: University of Chicago Press, 2001), pp. 3–6.
10 Jane Goodall, *Performance and Evolution in the Age of Darwin: Out of the Natural Order* (London: Routledge, 2007), p. 7; Kirsten Shepherd-Barr,

216   *Notes on pages 3–4*

Theatre and Evolution from Ibsen to Beckett (New York: Columbia University Press, 2015), pp. 5, 10.

11 See Gillian Beer, *Darwin's Plots: Evolutionary Narrative in Darwin, George Eliot and Nineteenth-Century Fiction*, 3rd ed. (Cambridge: Cambridge University Press, 2009); *Open Fields: Science in Cultural Encounter* (Oxford: Oxford University Press, 1996); George Levine, *Darwin and the Novelists: Patterns of Science in Victorian Fiction* (London: University of Chicago Press, 1991); *Darwin the Writer* (Oxford: Oxford University Press, 2011); Sally Shuttleworth, *Charlotte Brontë and Victorian Psychology* (Cambridge: Cambridge University Press, 1996); *The Mind of the Child: Child Development in Literature, Science, and Medicine, 1840–1900* (Oxford: Oxford University Press, 2010); Laura Otis, *Membranes: Metaphors of Invasion in Nineteenth-Century Literature, Science, and Politics* (Baltimore, MD: Johns Hopkins University Press, 2000); *Networking: Communicating with Bodies and Machines in the Nineteenth Century* (Ann Arbor, MI: University of Michigan Press, 2001). For recent overviews of literature and science as a field, see Martin Willis, *Literature and Science: A Reader's Guide to Essential Criticism* (London: Palgrave, 2015), and *The Routledge Research Companion to Nineteenth-Century British Literature and Science*, ed. John Holmes and Sharon Ruston (London: Routledge, 2017).

12 Beer, *Plots*, p. 5.

13 On popular contortions of evolutionary theory, see Peter J. Bowler, *Evolution: The History of an Idea* (Berkeley, CA: University of California Press, 2009), and *The Non-Darwinian Revolution: Reinterpreting a Historical Myth* (Baltimore, MD: Johns Hopkins University Press, 1988); Bernard Lightman, *Victorian Popularizers of Science: Designing Nature for New Audiences* (Chicago, IL: University of Chicago Press, 2007); Piers J. Hale, *Political Descent: Malthus, Mutualism, and the Politics of Evolution in Victorian England* (London: University of Chicago Press, 2014).

14 Greg Garrard, *Ecocriticism*, 2nd ed. (London: Routledge: 2012), p. 8.

15 Cheryl Lousley, 'Ecocriticism and the Politics of Representation', in *The Oxford Handbook of Ecocriticism*, ed. Greg Garrard (Oxford: Oxford University Press, 2014), 155–171, pp. 156–157.

16 Timo Maran, 'Biosemiotic Criticism', in *Handbook of Ecocriticism*, 260–275; Aaron M. Moe, *Zoopoetics: Animals and the Making of Poetry* (Lanham, MD: Lexington Books, 2014).

17 Jerome J. McGann, *The Romantic Ideology: A Critical Investigation* (London: University of Chicago Press, 1983).

18 See, for example, the use of 'chameleon' as an insult in Shakespeare's *The Two Gentlemen of Verona*, ed. Norman Sanders (London: Penguin, 2005), pp. 26, 30.

19 Beer, *Plots*, p. 74. On metaphor, comparison and analogy in Victorian science, see Devin Griffiths, *The Age of Analogy: Science and Literature between the Darwins* (Baltimore, MD: Johns Hopkins University Press, 2016), pp. 182–205.

Notes on pages 5–6

20 See Anne DeWitt, *Moral Authority: Men of Science, and the Victorian Novel* (Cambridge: Cambridge University Press, 2013), pp. 3–8.

21 On the history of the 'one culture' approach to Victorian science and literature, see Alice Jenkins, 'Beyond Two Cultures: Science, Literature and Disciplinary Boundaries', in *The Oxford Handbook of Victorian Literary Culture*, ed. Juliet John (Oxford: Oxford University Press, 2016), 401–415, pp. 404–411.

22 See Caroline Levine, *The Serious Pleasures of Suspense: Victorian Realism and Narrative Doubt* (London: University of Virginia Press, 2003); Charlotte Sleigh, *Literature and Science* (Basingstoke: Palgrave Macmillan, 2011), pp. 27–55; Peter Garratt, *Victorian Empiricism: Self, Knowledge, and Reality in Ruskin, Bain, Lewes, Spencer, and George Eliot* (Madison, NJ: Fairleigh Dickinson University Press, 2010); Adelene Buckland, *Novel Science: Fiction and the Invention of Nineteenth-Century Geology* (Chicago, IL: University of Chicago Press, 2013).

23 Catherine Gallagher, 'George Eliot: Immanent Victorian', *Representations*, 90:1 (2005), 61–74.

24 Pamela K. Gilbert, *Victorian Skin: Surface, Self, History* (London: Cornell University Press, 2019), p. 7.

25 On the history of crypsis theory, see Stanislav Komárek, *Mimicry, Aposematism, and Related Phenomena: Mimetism in Nature and the History of Its Study* (Munich: Lincom Europa, 2009), and Peter Forbes, *Dazzled and Deceived: Mimicry and Camouflage* (London: Yale University Press, 2011). On cultural traffic between military and animal camouflage (mainly in the twentieth century), see Hanna Rose Shell, *Hide and Seek: Camouflage, Photography, and the Media of Reconnaissance* (New York: Zone Books, 2012), and Ann Dirouhi Elias, *Camouflage Australia: Art, Nature, Science and War* (Sydney: Sydney University Press, 2011). See also Hillel Schwartz, *The Culture of the Copy: Striking Likenesses, Unreasonable Facsimiles*, 2nd ed. (New York: Zone Books, 2014), pp. 145–157, 168–169; and Matthew Brower, *Developing Animals: Wildlife and Early American Photography* (Minneapolis, MN: University of Minnesota Press, 2011), pp. 135–190.

26 See Evelleen Richards, *Darwin and the Making of Sexual Selection* (Chicago, IL: University of Chicago Press, 2017); Erika Lorraine Milam, *Looking for a Few Good Males: Female Choice in Evolutionary Biology* (Baltimore, MD: Johns Hopkins University Press, 2011); David Rothenberg, *Survival of the Beautiful: Art, Science and Evolution* (London: Bloomsbury, 2013); Barbara Jean Larson and Fae Brauer (eds.), *The Art of Evolution: Darwin, Darwinisms, and Visual Culture* (Hanover, NH: Dartmouth College Press, 2009); Barbara Larson and Sabine Flach (eds.), *Darwin and Theories of Aesthetics and Cultural History* (Farnham: Ashgate, 2013); Diana Donald and Jane Munro (eds.), *Endless Forms: Charles Darwin, Natural Science and the Visual Arts* (New Haven, CT: Yale University Press, 2009); Benjamin Morgan, *The Outward Mind: Materialist Aesthetics in Victorian Science and Literature* (London: University of Chicago Press, 2017).

218   *Notes on pages 6–8*

27 Margot Norris, *Beasts of the Modern Imagination: Darwin, Nietzsche, Kafka, Ernst, and Lawrence* (Baltimore, MD: Johns Hopkins University Press, 1985).

28 Sleigh, *Six Legs Better: A Cultural History of Myrmecology* (Baltimore, MD: Johns Hopkins University Press, 2007), pp. 163–218.

29 Srdjan Smajić, *Ghost-Seers, Detectives, and Spiritualists: Theories of Vision in Victorian Literature and Science* (Cambridge: Cambridge University Press, 2010); Martin Willis, *Vision, Science and Literature: Ocular Horizons* (London: Pickering & Chatto, 2011).

30 Jonathan Smith, *Charles Darwin and Victorian Visual Culture* (Cambridge: Cambridge University Press, 2006); George Levine, *Realism, Ethics and Secularism: Essays on Victorian Literature and Science* (Cambridge: Cambridge University Press, 2008).

31 Anne Helmreich, *Nature's Truth: Photography, Painting, and Science in Victorian Britain* (University Park, PA: Pennsylvania State University Press, 2016), p. 165.

32 Tiffany Watt-Smith, *On Flinching: Theatricality and Scientific Looking from Darwin to Shell Shock* (Oxford: Oxford University Press, 2014).

33 Edward Bagnall Poulton, 'Mimicry in Butterflies of the Genus Hypolimnas and Its Bearing on Older and More Recent Theories of Mimicry', *Proceedings of the American Association for the Advancement of Science*, 46 (1897), 242–244, p. 242.

34 Allen, 'False Pretences', in *In Nature's Workshop* (London: George Newnes, 1901), 29–59, p. 29.

35 Translators have, however, quibbled over this phrase, with Daniel W. Graham arguing that 'Nature is hidden' comes closer to the original 'φύσις κρύπτεσθαι φιλεῖ'; see 'Does Nature Love to Hide? Heraclitus B123 DK', *Classical Philology*, 98:2 (2003), 175–179. On Aristotle and Pliny, see Komárek, *Mimicry*, pp. 17–18.

36 See, for example, Oliver Goldsmith, *A History of the Earth, and Animated Nature*, 3 vols. (London: William Charlton Wright, 1824), II, pp. 23–24.

37 Christian Konrad Sprengel, *Das entdeckte Geheimnis der Natur im Bau und der Befruchtung der Blumen* (Berlin: F. Vieweg, 1793). This work would influence Charles Darwin's *On the Various Contrivances by Which British and Foreign Orchids Are Fertilised by Insects* (London: John Murray, 1862), p. 3.

38 Erasmus Darwin, *Zoonomia; or, The Laws of Organic Life*, 2 vols. (London: J. Johnson, 1794), I, p. 509.

39 Muriel Blaisdell, *Darwinism and Its Data: The Adaptive Coloration of Animals* (London: Garland Publishing, 1992), p. 5.

40 See William Paley, *Natural Theology; or, Evidences of the Existence and Attributes of the Deity* (London: J. Faulder, 1809), pp. 1–8. On structural idealism in natural history, see Ron Amundson, 'Typology Reconsidered: Two Doctrines on the History of Evolutionary Biology', *Biology and Philosophy*, 13 (1998), 153–177.

41 Robert J. O'Hara, 'Diagrammatic Classifications of Birds, 1819–1901: Views of the Natural System in 19th-Century British Ornithology', in *Acta XIX*

Notes on pages 8–10

219

Congressus Internationalis Ornithologici, ed. H. Ouellet (Ottawa: National Museum of Natural Sciences, 1988), 2746–2759, pp. 2749–2751.

42 Diana Donald, *Picturing Animals in Britain, 1750–1850* (New Haven, CT: Yale University Press, 2007), pp. 27–37; Wendy Wheeler, *Expecting the Earth: Life, Culture, Biosemiotics* (London: Lawrence and Wishart, 2016), p. 20.

43 John Oliver French, 'An Inquiry Respecting the True Nature of Instinct, and of the Mental Distinctions between Brute Animals and Man', *Zoological Journal*, 1 (1824), 1–32, pp. 1–2.

44 Susan E. Lorsch, *Where Nature Ends: Literary Responses to the Designification of Landscape* (London: Associated University Presses, 1983), pp. 13–14.

45 John Locke, *An Essay Concerning Human Understanding*, 3 vols. (Edinburgh: Mundell & Sons, 1801), III, pp. 59–60.

46 On comparative philology and Victorian culture, see Will Abberley, *English Fiction and the Evolution of Language, 1850–1914* (Cambridge: Cambridge University Press, 2015); Brigitte Nerlich, *Semantic Theories in Europe, 1830–1930: From Etymology to Contextuality* (Amsterdam: John Benjamins, 1992); Christine Ferguson, *Language, Science and Popular Fiction in the Victorian Fin-de-Siècle: The Brutal Tongue* (Aldershot: Ashgate, 2006); Linda Dowling, *Language and Decadence: Language and Decadence in the Victorian Fin de Siècle* (Princeton, NJ: Princeton University Press, 1986).

47 Benjamin Humphrey Smart, *An Outline of Sematology* (London: John Richardson, 1831), p. 210. Dugald Stewart expressed a similar view; see 'On the Tendency of Some Late Philological Speculations', in *The Works of Dugald Stewart*, 7 vols. (Cambridge: Hilliard and Brown, 1829), IV, 141–180, pp. 141–143.

48 Smart, *Outline*, p. 184.

49 Wallace, 'Mimicry', p. 17.

50 Smart, *Outline*, pp. 182, 220.

51 Lord Henry Brougham, *Dissertations on Subjects of Science Connected with Natural Theology*, 2 vols. (London: C. Knight & Co., 1839), I, p. 196. For a longer historical view of animals as rhetorical addressees, see Debra Hawhee, *Rhetoric in Tooth and Claw: Animals, Language, Sensation* (London: University of Chicago Press, 2016).

52 On Darwin's engagements with Smart and Brougham, see Darwin, 'Old and Useless Notes about the Moral Sense & Some Metaphysical Points' (1838–1840), ed. Paul H. Barrett, *Darwin Online*, http://darwin-online.org .uk/content/frameset?pageseq=1&itemID=CUL-DAR91.4-55&viewtype=text <accessed 14/05/2018>; and *Darwin on Man*, ed. Howard Gruber and Paul Barrett (London: Wildwood House, 1974), p. 342. See also Beer, 'Darwin and the Growth of Language Theory', in *Open Fields: Science in Cultural Encounter* (Oxford: Oxford University Press, 1996), 95–114.

53 Darwin, *The Descent of Man*, 2 vols. (London: John Murray, 1871), I, p. 46.

54 Alexander Bain, 'Animal Instincts and Intelligence', in *Chambers' Papers for the People*, vol. XI (William and Robert Chambers: Edinburgh, 1850), 1–32, p. 1.

220   *Notes on pages 10–13*

55 Ibid., pp. 2, 24.
56 W. J. T. Mitchell, *Picture Theory: Essays on Verbal and Visual Representation* (London: University of Chicago Press, 1995), p. 336.
57 Jonathan Culler, *Literary Theory: A Very Short Introduction* (Oxford: Oxford University Press, 2011), p. 9.
58 Mitchell, *Picture Theory*, p. 339.
59 George Romanes, *Mental Evolution in Man: Origin of Human Faculty* (London: Kegan Paul, Trench & Co., 1888), p. 176.
60 See Martin Rudwick, 'The Emergence of a Visual Language for Geological Science 1760–1840', *History of Science*, 14 (1976), 149–195; James Krasner, *The Entangled Eye: Visual Perception and the Representation of Nature in Post-Darwinian Narrative* (Oxford: Oxford University Press, 1992).
61 See Jonathan Crary, *Techniques of the Observer: On Vision and Modernity in the Nineteenth Century* (London: MIT Press, 1990); Lindsay Smith, *Victorian Photography, Painting and Poetry: The Enigma of Visibility in Ruskin, Morris and the Pre-Raphaelites* (Cambridge: Cambridge University Press, 1995); Kate Flint, *Victorians and the Visual Imagination* (Cambridge: Cambridge University Press, 2000), pp. 26–31; Smajić, *Ghost-Seers*; Willis, *Horizons*.
62 Willis, *Horizons*, pp. 2, 5.
63 Smajić, *Ghost-Seers*, pp. 67–71.
64 Herbert Spencer, *First Principles of a New System of Philosophy* (London: Williams and Norgate, 1862), p. 228.
65 G. H. Lewes, *Problems of Life and Mind*, First Series, 2 vols. (Boston: James R. Osgood, 1875), II, p. 108. See Sue Zemka, *Time and the Moment in Victorian Literature and Society* (Cambridge: Cambridge University Press, 2012), pp. 30–31.
66 Fanny Mayne, 'The Literature of the Working Classes', *Englishwoman's Magazine and Christian Mother's Miscellany*, NS 5 (October 1850), 619–622, p. 619.
67 H. L. Mansel, 'Sensation Novels', *Quarterly Review*, 113 (1863), 481–514, p. 357.
68 Gustave Le Bon, *The Crowd: A Study of the Popular Mind* (New York: Macmillan, 1896), p. 12.
69 On idolatry and science, see Peter Harrison, *The Bible, Protestantism, and the Rise of Natural Science* (Cambridge: Cambridge University Press, 1998), pp. 30–31.
70 E. B. Tylor, *Primitive Culture*, 2 vols. (London: John Murray, 1871), II, p. 344.
71 Norman Triplett, 'The Psychology of Conjuring Deceptions', *American Journal of Psychology*, 11:4 (1900), 439–510, pp. 440–447.
72 Ibid., p. 440.
73 Wallace, 'Mimicry', p. 26.
74 Edith Wharton, 'The Eyes', *Tales of Men and Ghosts* (New York: Charles Scribner's Sons, 1910), 241–274, p. 261.

Notes on pages 14–17 221

75 Spencer, *First Principles*, pp. 77, 79, 161.
76 On the cultural history of altruism, see Thomas Dixon, *The Invention of Altruism: Making Moral Meanings in Victorian Britain* (Oxford: Oxford University Press, 2008).
77 Darwin, *Descent*, I, p. 162.
78 Spencer, 'The Morals of Trade', *Westminster Review*, 71 (April 1859), 357–390, p. 384.
79 Lionel Trilling, *Sincerity and Authenticity* (Cambridge, MA: Harvard University Press, 1971), p. 110.
80 Ibid., pp. 388–389.
81 Darwin, letter to Charles Lyell, 4 May 1860, *Darwin Correspondence Project*, www.darwinproject.ac.uk/letter/DCP-LETT-2782.xml <accessed 4/25/2018>. See Hale, *Political Descent*, p. 24.
82 Darwin, *Descent*, I, p. 95.
83 Triplett, 'Conjuring Deceptions', p. 440.
84 J. G. Wood, *Sketches and Anecdotes of Animal Life* (London: Routledge, 1854), p. 4.
85 C. H. Powell, 'The Invisibility of the Soldier', *Blackwood's Edinburgh Magazine*, 166 (December 1899), 836–846, pp. 836–837.
86 Henry Rider Haggard, *King Solomon's Mines* (Oxford: Oxford University Press, 2008). See Brian V. Street, *The Savage in Literature: Representations of 'Primitive' Society in English Fiction, 1858–1920* (London: Routledge and Kegan Paul, 1975), pp. 60–63.
87 See Tim Christensen, 'The Unbearable Whiteness of Being: Misrecognition, Pleasure, and White Identity in Kipling's *Kim*', *College Literature*, 39:2 (2012), 9–30, pp. 23–27.
88 Rudyard Kipling, *The Jungle Book* (New York: The Century Co., 1894), pp. 80, 85.
89 See Geoffrey Russell Searle, *Morality and the Market in Victorian Britain* (Oxford: Clarendon Press, 1998), pp. 91–97; William D. Brewer, *Staging Romantic Chameleon Imposters* (Basingstoke: Palgrave Macmillan, 2015); Rohan McWilliam, 'Unauthorized Identities: The Imposter, the Fake and the Secret History in Nineteenth-Century Britain', in *Legitimacy and Illegitimacy in Nineteenth-Century Law, Literature and History*, ed. Margot C. Finn, Michael Lobban and Jenny Bourne Taylor (Basingstoke: Palgrave Macmillan, 2010), 67–92.
90 P. T. Barnum, *The Humbugs of the World* (New York: Carleton, 1866), p. 11.
91 Eliot, *Middlemarch* (London: Penguin, 1994), p. 409.
92 See Friedrich Nietzsche, 'On Truth and Lie in a Nonmoral Sense', in *On Truth and Untruth: Selected Writings*, trans. and ed. Taylor Carman (London: HarperCollins, 2010), 15–50.
93 John Kucich, *The Power of Lies: Transgression in Victorian Fiction* (London: Cornell University Press, 1994), pp. 1–4. See also Alexander Welsh, *George Eliot and Blackmail* (Cambridge, MA: Harvard University Press, 1985).

222 *Notes on pages 17–21*

94 Henry Sidgwick, *Methods of Ethics* (London: Macmillan & Co., 1874), pp. 291–296; John Morley, *On Compromise* (London: Macmillan & Co., 1874), pp. 168–176.

95 ETHICS [Samuel Butler], 'A Clergyman's Doubts', *Examiner*, 8 March 1879, 303–304, p. 304. See Henry Festing Jones, *The Note-Books of Samuel Butler* (New York: E. P. Dutton & Co., 1917), p. 304.

96 See Patrick Brantlinger, *The Reading Lesson: The Threat of Mass Literacy in Nineteenth-Century British Fiction* (Bloomington, IN: Indiana University Press, 1998), pp. 13–19.

97 Benjamin Kidd, *Social Evolution*, 2nd ed. (London: Macmillan & Co., 1894), p. 102.

98 H. G. Wells, *Love and Mr Lewisham* (London: Penguin, 2005), p. 134.

99 Friedrich Nietzsche, *The Dawn of Day*, trans. Johanna Volz (London: T. F. Unwin, 1903), p. 22.

100 Thomas Henry Huxley, 'Evolution and Ethics – Prolegomena', in *Collected Essays*, 9 vols. (New York: Appleton, 1897), IX, 1–45, p. 28.

101 See David Hume, *A Treatise of Human Nature* (London: John Noon, 1739), p. 335.

102 Otis, *Membranes*, p. 6.

103 Charles Taylor, *Sources of the Self: The Making of the Modern Identity* (Cambridge: Cambridge University Press, 1992), p. 376.

104 Jean Jacques Rousseau, 'Discourse on the Origin of Inequality', in *The Social Contract and Other Discourses*, trans. G. D. H. Cole (London: Dent, 1973), 27–113, p. 104.

105 See Harold Bloom, *The Anxiety of Influence: A Theory of Poetry*, 2nd ed. (Oxford: Oxford University Press, 1997).

106 John Stuart Mill, *On Liberty* (Indianapolis, IN: Bobbs-Merrill, 1956), p. 70.

107 See Thomas Carlyle, *On Heroes, Hero-Worship and the Heroic in History* (London: James Fraser, 1841).

108 Norris, *Beasts*, pp. 53–72. See also Elias, *Camouflage Australia*, pp. 97–98.

109 Nietzsche, *The Gay Science*, trans. Walter Kaufmann (New York: Vintage, 1974), p. 316. See Norris, *Beasts*, p. 61.

110 Gina Lombroso, *Criminal Man According to the Classification of Cesare Lombroso Briefly Summarized by His Daughter Gina Lombroso* (New York: G. P. Putnam, 1911), p. 276.

111 G. W. F. Hegel, *The Phenomenology of Spirit*, trans. A. V. Miller (Oxford: Oxford University Press, 1977).

112 Darwin, *Descent*, II, p. 97. See Milam, *Good Males*, pp. 9–28.

113 See Franz Fanon, *Black Skin, White Masks*, trans. Charles L. Markmann (London: Pluto Press, 1986); Schwartz, *Copy*, pp. 186–190.

114 Romanes, 'Mental Differences between Men and Women', *Nineteenth Century*, 31 (May 1887), 383–401, p. 384.

115 James Hunt, 'On the Negro's Place in Nature', *Journal of the Anthropological Society of London*, 2 (1864), xv–lvi, p. xvi.

Notes on pages 21–29

116 Eva Figes, *Patriarchal Attitudes: Women in Society* (New York: Perses Books, 1970), p. 124. On the association between female dissimulation and mimicry, see Geoffrey C. Bunn, *The Truth Machine: A Social History of the Lie Detector* (Baltimore, MD: Johns Hopkins University Press, 2012), pp. 53–59.

117 Jaine Chemmachery, 'Lies and Self-Censorship in Kipling's Indian Stories', *Kipling Journal*, 88:353 (2014), 32–44, p. 36.

118 George Bernard Shaw, 'John Bull's Other Island', in *John Bull's Other Island and Major Barbara* (New York: Brentano's, 1908), 1–26, p. 25.

119 Alice Stopford Green, *A Woman's Place in the World of Letters* (London: Macmillan, 1913), p. 5.

120 Charles Dickens, 'The Battle of Life', in *A Christmas Carol, and Other Christmas Books* (London: J. M. Dent, 1907), 247–328, p. 251.

121 Griffiths, *Age of Analogy*, pp. 34–36.

122 See William Kirby and William Spence, *An Introduction to Entomology*, 4 vols. (London: Longman, Rees, Orme, Brown, and Green, 1815–1826); Westwood, *An Introduction to the Modern Classification of Insects*, 2 vols. (London: Longman, Orme, Brown, Green, and Longmans, 1839).

123 See Hugh B. Cott, *Adaptive Coloration in Animals* (London: Methuen, 1940). On crypsis and Modernism, see Joyce Cheng, 'Mask, Mimicry, Metamorphosis: Roger Caillois, Walter Benjamin and Surrealism in the 1930s', *Modernism/Modernity*, 16:1 (2009), 61–86; David Lomas, 'Artist–Sorcerers: Mimicry, Magic and Hysteria', *Oxford Art Journal*, 35:3 (2012), 363–388.

Chapter 1

1 Ruskin, *The Eagle's Nest* [1872], in *Works*, XXII, 115–292, p. 201.

2 Poulton, 'Notes upon, or Suggested by, the Colours, Markings, and Protective Attitudes of Certain Elpidopterous Larvae and Pupae, and of a Phytophagous Hymenopterous Larva', *Transactions of the Entomological Society of London*, 32:1 (1884), 27–60, pp. 52–53.

3 Bates, 'Contributions', p. 513.

4 Michel Foucault, *The Order of Things: An Archaeology of the Human Sciences*, trans. Alan Sheridan Smith (London: Tavistock Publications, 1970), 157–160.

5 Galileo Galilei, *The Essential Galileo*, ed. and trans. Maurice A. Finocchiaro (Cambridge: Hackett Publishing Company, 2008), pp. 185–189; Locke, *Essay*, I, p. 113.

6 George Berkeley, *An Essay towards a New Theory of Vision* (Dublin: J. Pepyat, 1709).

7 Immanuel Kant, *Critique of Judgment*, trans. J. H. Bernard (New York: Hafner Press, 1951); Johann Wolfgang von Goethe, *Theory of Colours*, trans. Charles Lock Eastlake (Cambridge, MA: MIT Press, 1982).

8 Alexander von Humboldt, *Views of Nature*, trans. E. C. Otté and Henry G. Bohn (London: Henry G. Bohn, 1850), p. 154.

224   *Notes on pages 30–33*

9 Jason Howard Lindquist, 'A "Pure Excess of Complexity": Tropical Surfeit, the Observing Subject, and the Text, 1773–1871', PhD thesis (Indiana University, 2008), pp. 183–184.

10 Humboldt, *Personal Narrative of Travels to the Equinoctial Regions of the New Continent, during the Years 1799–1804*, trans. Helen Maria Williams, 7 vols. (London: Longman, Hurst, Rees, Orme & Brown, 1814–1829), III, pp. 36–37.

11 Humboldt, *Cosmos: Sketch of a Physical Description of the Universe*, vol. 2, trans. Edward Sabine (London: John Murray, 1849), p. 74.

12 See Rachel Teukolsky, *The Literate Eye: Victorian Art Writing and Modernist Aesthetics* (Oxford: Oxford University Press, 2009), pp. 34–42.

13 Qtd. in Charles Robert Leslie, *Memoirs of the Life of John Constable* (London: Longman, Brown, Green, and Longmans, 1845), p. 355; see Teukolsky, *Eye*, p. 34.

14 Ruskin, *Modern Painters, III* [1856], in *Works*, V, 1–430, p. 387. On Ruskin and science, see Mark Frost, 'The Circles of Vitality: Ruskin, Science, and Dynamic Materiality', *Victorian Literature and Culture*, 39:2 (2011), 367–383; Frederick Kirchoff, 'A Science against Sciences: Ruskin's Floral Mythology', in *Nature and the Victorian Imagination*, ed. U. C. Knoepflmacher and G. B. Tennyson (London: University of California Press, 1977), 246–258.

15 See Linda M. Shires, 'Color Theory – Charles Lock Eastlake's 1840 Translation of Johann Wolfgang von Goethe's Zur Farbenlehre (Theory of Colours)', *Branch*, www.branchcollective.org/?ps_articles=linda-m-shires-color-theory-charles-lock-eastlakes-1840-translation-of-johann-wolfgang-von-goethes-zur-farbenlehre-theory-of-colours <accessed 18/05/2018>.

16 Ruskin, *The Elements of Drawing* [1857], in *Works*, XV, 1–232, p. 27.

17 Ibid., p. 28.

18 Ibid., p. 27.

19 C. Levine, *Suspense*, pp. 60–61.

20 Ruskin, *Eagle's Nest*, p. 197.

21 Ruskin, *Proserpina* [1875], in *Complete Works*, XXV, 191–552, p. 263.

22 Birch, 'Ruskin', p. 141.

23 Ruskin, *The Queen of the Air* [1869] in *Works*, XIX, 283–426.

24 Paul Smethurst, *Travel Writing and the Natural World, 1768–1840* (Basingstoke: Palgrave Macmillan, 2013), pp. 43, 50.

25 Krasner, *Entangled Eye*, p. 47.

26 Darwin, *Charles Darwin's Beagle Diary Charles Darwin's Beagle Diary*, ed. Richard Darwin Keynes (Cambridge: Cambridge University Press, 1988), p. 42. Qtd. in Krasner, *Entangled Eye*, p. 48.

27 George Cuvier, 'Analyse d'un ouvrage de M. Humboldt intitulé: Tableaux de la nature ou considérations sur les deserts, sur la physionomie des végétaux et sur les cataractes de l'Orenoque' (Library of the Institut de France, Paris, Fonds Cuvier, MS 3159), p. 6. Qtd. in Dorinda Outram, 'New Spaces in Natural History', in *Cultures of Natural History*, ed. N. Jardine, James Secord and E. C. Spary (Cambridge: Cambridge University Press, 1996), 249–265, pp. 259–261.

28 Outram, 'New Spaces', p. 262.

Notes on pages 33–41 225

29 See Robert E. Kohler, *Landscapes and Labscapes: Exploring the Lab-Field Border in Biology* (Chicago: University of Chicago Press: 2002), pp. 2–7.

30 Anne Secord, 'Botany on a Plate: Pleasure and the Power of Pictures in Promoting Early Nineteenth-Century Scientific Knowledge', *Isis*, 93:1 (2002), 28–57, pp. 36–37.

31 Lightman, *Popularizers*, pp. 138–139; Rudwick, 'Emergence', pp. 149–152.

32 Ann Shelby Blum, *Picturing Nature: American Nineteenth-Century Zoological Illustration* (Princeton, NJ: Princeton University Press, 1993), pp. 318–319.

33 See Daston, 'Scientific Objectivity with and without Words', in *Little Tools of Knowledge: Historical Essays on Academic and Bureaucratic Practices* (Ann Arbor: University of Michigan Press, 2000), 259–284.

34 Joseph E. Harmon and Alan G. Gross, *The Scientific Literature: A Guided Tour* (London: University of Chicago Press, 2007), p. 118.

35 William Whewell, *The Philosophy of the Inductive Sciences, Founded upon their History*, 2 vols. (London: J. W. Parker, 1840), I, p. xlviii.

36 See Nigel Leask, *Curiosity and the Aesthetics of Travel Writing 1770–1840* (Oxford: Oxford University Press, 2002), p. 6.

37 Darwin, letter to Bates, 25 September 1861, *Darwin Correspondence Project*, www.darwinproject.ac.uk/letter/DCP-LETT-3266.xml <accessed 4/25/2018>.

38 Matthew Arnold, 'The Study of Poetry', in *Essays in Criticism*, ed. Susan. S. Sheridan (Boston: Allyn & Bacon, 1896), 1–31, p. 1.

39 Ruskin, *The Stones of Venice* [1851], in *Works*, IX–XI, XI, pp. 47–48.

40 Frank Evers Beddard, *Animal Coloration* (London: Swan Sonnenschein & Co., 1892), pp. 109–110.

41 For the origin of this term, see Steven Shapin and Simon Schaffer, *Leviathan and the Air-Pump: Hobbes, Boyle, and the Experimental Life* (Princeton, NJ: Princeton University Press, 2011), pp. 60–65.

42 Bates, 'Contributions', p. 507.

43 Bates, 'Excursion to St. Paulo, Upper Amazons', *The Zoologist*, 16 (1858), 6160–6169, pp. 6165–6166.

44 Bates, 'Contributions', pp. 507–508.

45 Bates, 'Excursion', p. 6166.

46 Bates, 'Contributions', p. 507.

47 Ibid., p. 509.

48 Bates, *The Naturalist on the River Amazons*, 2 vols. (London: J. Murray, 1863), I, p. 185. Subsequent quotations are referenced in the text.

49 Bates, 'Contributions', p. 509.

50 Wallace, *The Malay Archipelago*, 2 vols. (London: Macmillan & Co., 1869), I, p. 130. Subsequent quotations are referenced in the text.

51 Wallace, 'Mimicry', pp. 11–12.

52 Wallace, *Science and the Supernatural* (London: F. Farrah, 1866), pp. 10–14.

53 Wallace, *Darwinism: An Exposition of the Theory of Natural Selection with Some of Its Applications* (London: Macmillan & Co., 1889), p. 210.

54 Wallace, *Supernatural*, pp. 6, 9.

226 *Notes on pages 42–53*

55 Wallace, 'Mimicry', p. 5.
56 Ibid., p. 6.
57 Ibid., p. 8.
58 Packard, 'The Origin of the Markings of Organisms (Pœcilogenesis) Due to the Physical Rather than to the Biological Environment; With Criticisms of the Bates–Müller Hypotheses', *Proceedings of the American Philosophical Society*, 43:178 (1904), 393–450.
59 Ibid., p. 397.
60 Ibid., p. 405.
61 Ruskin, 'The Light of the World' [1854], in *Works*, XII, 328–332, p. 331.
62 See Andrea Kennecy, 'The Beauty of Victorian Beasts: Illustration in the Reverend J. G. Wood's *Homes without Hands*', *Archives of Natural History*, 40:2 (2013), 193–212, p. 201.
63 On natural history illustration as a meeting point of different Victorian identities, see Geoffrey Belknap, 'Illustrating Natural History: Images, Periodicals, and the Making of Nineteenth-Century Scientific Communities', *British Journal for the History of Science*, 51:3 (2018), 395–422.
64 Qtd. in Hall Caine, 'The Influence of Ruskin', *Bookman*, 35:205 (1908), 26–34, p. 30.
65 Wallace, 'The Disguises of Insects', in *Studies Scientific and Social*, 2 vols. (London: Macmillan & Co., 1900), I, 185–198, p. 189.
66 See Poulton, *John Viriamu Jones and Other Oxford Memories* (London: Longmans, 1911), pp. 247, 244–246.
67 Ruskin, *Proserpina*, p. 267.
68 See Andrew Murray, *On the Disguises of Nature; Being an Inquiry into the Laws Which Regulate External Form and Colour in Plants and Animals* (Edinburgh: Neill & Co., 1859); 'Mimicry and Hybridisation', *Nature*, 3:60 (1870), 154–156; David Sharp, 'Natural Selection', *Athenaeum* (15 December 1866), 796–797.
69 J. O. Westwood, 'Mimicry in Nature', *Athenæum* (8 December 1866), 753–754, p. 753.
70 Samuel Wilberforce, '[Review of] *On the Origin of Species, by Means of Natural Selection*', *Quarterly Review*, 108 (1860), 225–264, p. 250.
71 Paul White, 'The Experimental Animal in Victorian Britain', in *Thinking with Animals: New Perspectives on Anthropomorphism*, ed. Lorraine Daston and Gregg Mitman (New York: Columbia University Press, 2005), 59–82.
72 John Lubbock, *The Pleasures of Life* (Philadelphia: Henry Altemus, 1894), pp. 310–311.
73 Ariane Dröscher, 'Pioneering Studies on Cephalopod's Eye and Vision at the Stazione Zoologica Anton Dohrn (1883-1977)', *Frontiers in Physiology*, 7:618 (2016), www.ncbi.nlm.nih.gov/pmc/articles/PMC5179557/ <accessed 14 May 2019>.
74 Beddard, *Coloration*, p. 110.
75 See J. Jenner Weir, 'On Insects and Insectivorous Birds', *Transactions of the Entomological Society of London* (1869), 21–26. For a historic overview, see

Notes on pages 53–58

Mary Alice Evans, 'Mimicry and the Darwinian Heritage', *Journal of the History of Ideas*, 26:2 (1965), 211–220, pp. 217–218. For studies which questioned Batesian crypsis, see Packard, *A Text-Book of Entomology* (London: Macmillan & Co., 1898), pp. 201–210.

76 'Naïves croyances', 'le monster qui ... se confondait avec un bloc de rocher, un tronc d'arbre, un fagot de ramée' [my translation], Jean-Henri Fabre, *Souvenirs Entomologiques: Etudes sur l'instinct et les moeurs des insects, troisième série* [1886] (Paris: Librarie Delagrave, 1923), p. 83.

77 Lee Waldo McAtee, 'The Experimental Method of Testing the Efficiency of Warning and Cryptic Coloration in Protecting Animals from Their Enemies', *Proceedings of the Academy of Natural Sciences of Philadelphia*, 64 (1912), 281–364, p. 303; qtd in Forbes, *Dazzled and Deceived*, pp. 55–56.

78 See William C. Kimler, 'Mimicry: Views of Naturalists and Ecologists before the Modern Synthesis', in *Dimensions of Darwinism: Themes and Counter-themes in Twentieth-Century Evolutionary Theory*, ed. Marjorie Grene (Cambridge: Cambridge University Press, 1983), 97–128, pp. 98, 109–113.

79 See Poulton, 'The Experimental Proof of the Protective Value of Colour and Markings in Insects', *Proceedings of the Zoological Society of London*, 55:2 (1887), 191–274.

80 For in-depth discussion of Thayer's theories, see Sharon Kingsland, 'Abbott Thayer and the Protective Coloration Debate', *Journal of the History of Biology*, 11:2 (1978), 223–244; Alexander Nemerov, 'Vanishing Americans: Abbott Thayer, Theodore Roosevelt, and the Attraction of Camouflage', *American Art*, 11:2 (1997), 50–81; Brower, *Developing Animals*, pp. 135–192; Shell, *Hide and Seek*, 25–76; Rothenberg, *Survival*, pp. 132–144; and Maggie M. Cao, 'Abbott Thayer and the Invention of Camouflage', *Art History*, 39:3 (2016), 486–511.

81 Cao, 'Invention', p. 490.

82 Abbott Handerson Thayer, 'The Law Which Underlies Protective Coloration', *The Auk*, 13:2 (1896), 124–129, pp. 125–126.

83 Ibid., p. 126.

84 Thayer, 'Protective Coloration in Its Relation to Mimicry, Common Warning Colours, and Sexual Selection', *Transactions of the Entomological Society of London*, 51:4 (1903), 553–569, p. 554.

85 Ibid., p. 555.

86 See Poulton, 'A Brief Discussion of A. H. Thayer's Suggestions as to the Meaning of Colour and Pattern in Insect Bionomics', *Transactions of the Entomological Society of London*, 51 (1903), 570–575.

87 Thayer, 'Protective Coloration in Its Relation', p. 553.

88 A. H. Thayer, 'Introduction', in Gerald Handerson Thayer and Abbott Handerson Thayer, *Concealing-Coloration in the Animal Kingdom* (New York: Macmillan, 1909), 3–12, p. 3.

89 Thayer, 'Protective Coloration in Its Relation', p. 569.

90 Thayer and Thayer, *Concealing-Coloration*, p. 40.

228 *Notes on pages 58–65*

91 On the development of wildlife photography, see Stefan Bargheer, *Moral Entanglements: Conserving Birds in Britain and Germany* (London: Chicago University Press, 2018), p. 85.

92 *Thayer and Thayer, Concealing-Coloration.*

93 Ibid., p. 67.

94 Ibid., caption to plate 3.

95 Ibid., p. 3.

96 Thomas Barbour and John C. Phillips, 'Concealing Coloration Again', *The Auk*, 28:2 (1911), 179–188, p. 180.

97 Ibid., p. 184.

98 Theodore Roosevelt, 'Revealing and Concealing Coloration in Birds and Mammals', *Bulletin of the American Museum of Natural History*, 30 (1911), 119–231, p. 123.

99 Ibid., p. 132.

100 Ibid., p. 136.

101 Ibid., p. 122.

102 Barbour and Philips, 'Coloration', p. 184.

103 J. A. Allen, 'Roosevelt's "Revealing and Concealing Coloration in Birds and Mammals"', *The Auk*, 28:4 (1911), 472–480, p. 479.

104 George F. Hampson, 'Protective- and Pseudo-Mimicry', *Nature*, 57 (17 February 1898), 364.

105 Francis H. Allen, 'Remarks on the Case of Roosevelt vs. Thayer, with a Few Independent Suggestions on the Concealing Coloration Question', *The Auk*, 29:4 (1912), 489–507, p. 489.

106 Ibid., p. 506.

107 Ibid., p. 502.

108 Kingsland, 'Abbott Thayer', pp. 238–240.

109 Barbour, 'A Different Aspect of the Case of Roosevelt vs. Thayer', *The Auk*, 30:1 (1913), 81–91, p. 88.

110 See note in J. A. Allen, 'The Concealing Coloration Question', *The Auk*, 30:2 (1913), 311–317, p. 317.

111 Brower, *Developing Animals*, p. 161.

112 See Shell, *Hide and Seek*, pp. 63–76.

113 E. R. Lankester, *Science from an Easy Chair* (London: Metheuen & Co., 1910), pp. 312–313.

Chapter 2

1 Philip Henry Gosse, *Omphalos: An Attempt to Untie the Geological Knot* (London: Van Voorst, 1857), p. 336.

2 Charles Kingsley, qtd. in Edmund Gosse, *The Life of Philip Henry Gosse* (London: Kegan Paul, 1890), pp. 280–281.

3 See René Descartes, *Meditations on First Philosophy*, trans. Michael Moriarty (Oxford: Oxford University Press, 2008), pp. 18–20.

Notes on pages 65–68 229

4 Charles Kingsley, *Charles Kingsley: His Letters and Memories of His Life*, ed. F. Kingsley, 2 vols. (London: King, 1877), I, p. 377.

5 Barbara T. Gates and Ann B. Shteir argue that the latter mode displaced the former in the 1850s; see 'Introduction: Charting the Tradition', in *Natural Eloquence: Women Reinscribe Science*, eds. Gates and Shteir (Madison, WI: University of Wisconsin Press, 1997), 3–24, pp. 5–15. Bernard Lightman claims that natural theology survived for longer, although in different forms; see *Popularizers of Science*, pp. 39–43. Aileen Fyfe and Jonathan Topham contend that 'natural theology' was increasingly replaced by a 'theology of nature' that celebrated nature as God's creation without relying on it as evidence of God; see Fyfe, *Science and Salvation: Evangelical Popular Science Publishing in Victorian Britain* (Chicago, IL: University of Chicago Press, 2004), p. 7; Topham, 'Natural Theology and the Sciences', in *The Cambridge Companion to Science and Religion*, ed. Peter Harrison (Cambridge: Cambridge University Press, 2010), 59–79, p. 60.

6 Harrison, *Bible*, p. 4.

7 Smith, *Visual Culture*, pp. 292–293.

8 See Alister E. McGrath, *Darwinism and the Divine: Evolutionary Thought and Natural Theology* (Oxford: Wiley-Blackwell, 2010), pp. 155–182; David Fergusson, 'Natural Theology after Darwin', in *Darwinism and Natural Theology*, ed. Andrew Robinson (Newcastle: Cambridge Scholars, 2012), 78–95.

9 Roger Luckhurst, *The Invention of Telepathy, 1870–1901* (Oxford: Oxford University Press, 2002), p. 21.

10 William Kirby, *The Seventh Bridgewater Treatise on the Power, Wisdom, and Goodness of God as Manifested in the Creation: The History, Habits and Instincts of Animals*, 2 vols. (London: William Pickering, 1835), I, p. xvii.

11 Kirby and Spence, *Entomology*, I, p. 12.

12 Anthony Pilkington, '"Nature" as Ethical Norm in the Enlightenment', in *Languages of Nature: Critical Essays in Science and Literature*, ed. Ludmilla Jordanova (London: Free Association Books, 1986), 51–85, pp. 61–62.

13 Qtd. in A. W. W. Dale, 'George Dawson', in *Nine Famous Birmingham Men*, ed. J. Muirhead (Birmingham: Cornish, 1909), 75–108, p. 90.

14 George Dawson, 'Things Unseen', in *Shakespeare and Other Lectures*, ed. George St. Claire (London: Kegan Paul, 1888), 393–428, pp. 414–423.

15 Ruskin, *The Seven Lamps of Architecture* [1849], *in The Complete Works of John Ruskin*, ed. E. T. Cook and Alexander Wedderburn, 39 vols. (London: George Allen, 1903–1912), VIII, p. 61.

16 Thomas Paine, *The Age of Reason* (London: Freethought, 1880), p. 21.

17 David Hume, *Dialogues Concerning Natural Religion* (London: Blackwood, 1907), pp. 133–134.

18 On the tensions between natural and revealed religion, see Topham, 'Theology', pp. 65–69; and John Hedley Brooke, *Science and Religion: Some Historical Perspectives* (Cambridge: Cambridge University Press, 1991), pp. 168–173, 181–189.

230 *Notes on pages 68–71*

19 Kingsley, 'The Natural Theology of the Future', in *Scientific Lectures and Essays* (London: Macmillan, 1880), 313–336, p. 315.

20 Philip Henry Gosse, *Evenings at the Microscope* (New York: Appleton, 1860), p. 407.

21 Gosse, *The Aquarium: An Unveiling of the Wonders of the Deep Sea* (London: John Van Voorst, 1856), p. 204.

22 Frederick Denison Maurice, *What Is Revelation?* (Cambridge: Macmillan, 1859), pp. 89–97. See Jeremy Morris, *F. D. Maurice and the Crisis of Christian Authority* (Oxford: Oxford University Press, 2005), pp. 169–173.

23 Ruskin, *Queen*. pp. 359.

24 See Friedrich Max Müller, *A History of Ancient Sanskrit Literature so Far as It Illustrates the Primitive Religion of the Brahmans* (London: Williams and Norgate, 1860).

25 Thomas Carlyle, *Sartor Resartus* (Philadelphia: James Munroe & Co., 1837), pp. 261–262.

26 For overviews of Kingsley's life and work, see J. M. I. Klaver, *The Apostle of the Flesh: A Critical Life of Charles Kingsley* (Boston, MA: Brill, 2006); and Susan Chitty, *The Beast and the Monk: A Life of Charles Kingsley* (London: Hodder & Stoughton, 1974).

27 Kingsley, *Letters*, I, p. 88. On Kingsley and science, see Buckland, *Novel Science*, pp. 179–220; Piers Hale, 'Monkeys into Men and Men into Monkeys: Chance and Contingency in the Evolution of Man, Mind and Morals in Charles Kingsley's *Water Babies*', *Journal of the History of Biology*, 46:4 (2013), 551–597; and 'Darwin's Other Bulldog: Charles Kingsley and the Popularisation of Evolution in Victorian England', *Science and Education*, 21:7 (2012), 977–1013; Christopher Hamlin, 'Charles Kingsley: From Being Green to Green Being', *Victorian Studies*, 54:2 (2012), 255–282; Francis O'Gorman, 'Victorian Natural History and the Discourses of Nature in Charles Kingsley's *Glaucus*', *Worldviews: Environment, Culture, Religion*, 2:1 (1998), 21–35; John C. Hawley, 'Charles Kingsley and the Book of Nature', *Anglican and Episcopal History*, 60:4 (1991), 461–479; Charles H. Muller, 'Spiritual Evolution and Muscular Theology: Lessons from Kingsley's Natural Theology', *University of Cape Town Studies in English*, 15 (1986), 24–34; A. J. Meadows, 'Kingsley's Attitude to Science', *Theology*, 78 (1975), 15–22.

28 Kingsley, *Yeast: A Problem* (London: J. W. Parker, 1851), p. 95.

29 See Trilling, *Sincerity*, pp. 1–23.

30 Kingsley, *Letters*, I, p. 178.

31 See Charles Kingsley and John Henry Newman, *Mr. Kingsley and Dr. Newman: A Correspondence on the Question Whether Dr. Newman Teaches That Truth Is No Virtue?* (London: Longman, Green, Longman, Roberts and Green, 1864).

32 See Klaver, *Apostle*, pp. 2–3.

33 Kingsley, *Yeast*, p. 312.

34 Kingsley, 'On English Composition', in *Literary and General Lectures and Essays* (London: Macmillan, 1898), 229–244, pp. 230–231.

Notes on pages 71–79 231

35 Kingsley, *Glaucus: Wonders of the Shore* (London: Macmillan, 1890), pp. 221–222. Subsequent quotations are referenced in the text.

36 Amy M. King, 'Reorienting the Scientific Frontier: Victorian Tide Pools and Literary Realism', *Victorian Studies*, 47:2 (2005), 153–163, pp. 159–162.

37 Ruskin, *Modern Painters, II* [1846], in *Works*, IV, 25–218, p. 42.

38 See Hamlin, 'Kingsley', p. 269.

39 Kingsley, *Letters*, I, p. 486.

40 Such pseudo-economic justification of seemingly horrid animal phenomena was common in natural-theological tradition. See Sheila Wille, 'The Ichneumon Fly and the Equilibration of British Natural Economies in the Eighteenth Century', *British Society for the History of Science*, 48:4 (2015), 639–660.

41 Romanes, *Thoughts on Religion* (London: Longmans, Green and Co., 1896), p. 83.

42 On Kingsley's providential view of history, see Jonathan Conlin, 'An Illiberal Descent: Natural and National History in the Work of Charles Kingsley', *History*, 96 (2011), 167–187.

43 See Michael J. Murray, *Nature Red in Tooth and Claw: Theism and the Problem of Animal Suffering* (Oxford: Oxford University Press, 2008).

44 Thomas Chalmers, *The First Bridgewater Treatise on the Power, Wisdom, and Goodness of God as Manifested in the Creation: On the Adaptation of External Nature to the Moral and Intellectual Constitution of Man* (London: William Pickering, 1833), pp. 187–188.

45 Kingsley, 'The Value of Law', in *Sermons on National Subjects* (London: Macmillan, 1880), 265–275, pp. 267, 273.

46 Kingsley, *Yeast*, p. 44.

47 Ibid., pp. 142–143.

48 Adam Sedgwick, *A Discourse on the Studies of the University* (Cambridge: Deighton, 1835), pp. 12–14.

49 John Tyndall, 'On the Study of Physics', in *Fragments of Science*, 2 vols. (London: Longmans, 1879), I, 333–355, p. 344.

50 Kingsley, 'The Study of Natural History', in *Scientific Lectures*, 181–200, p. 186.

51 Kingsley, *The Water-Babies* (New York: Cromwell, 1895), p. 260. Subsequent quotations referenced in the text.

52 Hamlin, 'Robert Warington and the Moral Economy of the Aquarium', *Journal of the History of Biology*, 19:1 (1986), 131–153, p. 81.

53 See Emma Griffin, *Blood Sport: Hunting in Britain since 1066* (New Haven: Yale University Press, 2007), pp. 144–146.

54 Kirby, *Bridgewater Treatise*, II, pp. 517–518.

55 On Kingsley's degeneration imagery, see Hamlin, 'Kingsley', pp. 269–271; and Hale, 'Monkeys', pp. 552–555.

56 Kingsley, *Letters*, II, p. 107.

57 See Matthew Arnold, *Literature and Dogma: An Essay towards a Better Apprehension of the Bible* (London: T. Nelson & Sons, 1873), pp. 181–200.

232 *Notes on pages 80–84*

58 Stephen Jay Gould, 'Nonoverlapping Magisteria', *Natural History*, 106:3 (1997), 16–22, p. 19.
59 Baden Powell, 'On the Study of the Evidence of Christianity', in *Essays and Reviews*, ed. John William Parker (London: J. W. Parker, 1860), 94–144, pp. 97, 100.
60 On scientific identity and professionalisation, see Frank Turner, *Contesting Cultural Authority: Essays in Victorian Intellectual Life* (Cambridge: Cambridge University Press, 1993), pp. 176–190; Ruth Barton '"Men of Science": Language, Identity and Professionalization in the Mid-Victorian Scientific Community', *History of Science*, 41:1 (2003), 73–119, pp. 73–80.
61 Levine, *Realism*, pp. 75–80.
62 Kingsley, *Letters*, II, p. 174–175.
63 Ibid., II, p. 175.
64 Spencer, *Social Statics* (London: Chapman, 1851), p. 58
65 See Hawley, 'Book', p. 470; Klaver, *Apostle*, pp. 477–483; Hale, 'Bulldog', p. 991. On Huxley's moralisation of nature, see DeWitt, *Moral Authority*, pp. 36–37.
66 Huxley, *Life and Letters of Thomas Henry Huxley*, ed. Leonard Huxley, 3 vols. (London: Macmillan, 1903), I, p. 317.
67 Ibid., I, p. 319.
68 Huxley, 'A Liberal Education and Where to Find It', *Essays*, III, 76–110, p. 85.
69 Kingsley, *The Gospel of the Pentateuch* (London: Parker, 1863), pp. x–xi.
70 Ibid., p. xi.
71 Ibid., p. 3.
72 Kingsley, *Letters*, II, p. 181.
73 Kingsley, *Gospel*, p. 2.
74 Huxley, 'Evolution and Ethics', in *Essays*, IX, 46–116, p. 81.
75 Huxley, *Letters*, I, p. 345.
76 Dixon, *Invention of Altruism*, pp. 175–176.
77 Kingsley, 'President's Address', *Report and Transactions of the Devonshire Association for the Advancement of Science, Literature and Art*, 4:1 (1871), 377–395, p. 383. See Hale, 'Monkeys', p. 587.
78 Kingsley, *Letters*, II, p. 173.
79 Kingsley, 'Natural Theology', p. 329. See also his earlier book for children, *Madame How and Lady Why* (London: Macmillan, 1869).
80 Kingsley, 'Natural Theology', pp. 334–335.
81 Kingsley, 'Bio-Geology', in *Scientific Lectures*, 155–180, pp. 174–176.
82 On Victorian typology, see George P. Landow, *Victorian Shadows: Biblical Typology in Victorian Literature, Art, and Thought* (London: Routledge, 1980).
83 Kingsley, *Letters*, II, p. 318.
84 Hawley, 'Book', p. 479.
85 Louise Lee, 'Voicing, De-voicing and Self-Silencing: Charles Kingsley's Stuttering Christian Manliness', *Journal of Victorian Culture*, 13:1 (2008), 1–17.

Notes on pages 84–91 233

86 Kingsley, *Letters*, II, p. 44. See Buckland, *Novel Science*, p. 182.
87 Henry Drummond, *Natural Law in the Spirit World* (New York: J. Pott, 1884), p. 319.

Chapter 3

1 Allen, 'Strictly Incog.', *Cornhill Magazine*, 8:44 (February 1887), 142–157, pp. 150, 152.
2 On the history of crime statistics, see Christian Borch, *Foucault, Crime and Power: Problematisations of Crime in the Twentieth Century* (Abingdon: Routledge, 2015), pp. 24–28; and Ian Hacking, *The Taming of Chance* (Cambridge: Cambridge University Press, 1990), pp. 1–10, 115–124, 170–179.
3 Gilbert, *Victorian Skin*, pp. 7–8, 21.
4 Allen, 'Masquerades and Disguises', in *Nature's Workshop*, 88–115, p. 95.
5 On knowledge and perspective in Victorian fiction, see Audrey Jaffe, *Vanishing Points: Dickens, Narrative, and the Subject of Omniscience* (Berkeley, CA: University of California Press, 1991), p. 13; and, more recently, Cristina Richieri Griffin, 'Omniscience Incarnate: Being in and of the World in Nineteenth-Century Fiction', PhD thesis (University of California, Los Angeles, 2015), pp. 6–12.
6 Foucault, *Discipline and Punish: The Birth of the Prison*, trans. Alan Sheridan (New York: Vintage, 1979), p. 187.
7 Mark Seltzer, *Henry James and the Art of Power* (Ithaca, NY: Cornell University Press, 1984), p. 41. See also D. A. Miller, *The Novel and the Police* (Berkeley, CA: University of California Press, 1988), pp. 17–32.
8 Peter Morton, *The Busiest Man in England: Grant Allen and the Writing Trade, 1875–1900* (Basingstoke: Palgrave Macmillan, 2005), p. 3.
9 Allen, *Physiological Aesthetics* (New York: Garland, 1877), pp. 155–156.
10 Allen, 'Masquerades and Disguises', p. 115.
11 Allen wrote an obituary of Bates, praising him as 'one of the profoundest scientific intellects I have ever known'; see 'Bates of the Amazons', *Fortnightly Review*, 58 (December 1892), 798–809, p. 798. See his correspondence with Wallace below. Allen criticized M. C. Cooke for conflating mimicry with mere 'adaptive similarity' (chance resemblances with no deceptive utility); see 'Science. *Freaks and Marvels of Plant Life* by M. C. Cooke', *The Academy*, 21 (4 February 1882), 85–86, p. 86.
12 Allen, 'Mimicry', *Encyclopædia Britannica*, 9th ed., 25 vols. (1875–1880), XVI.
13 Allen, 'Personal Reminiscences of Herbert Spencer', *Forum*, 35 (April 1904), 610–628, p. 610.
14 Allen, 'Masquerades', p. 106.
15 Allen, 'The New Hedonism', *Fortnightly Review*, 55 (March 1894), 377–392, p. 391.
16 Ibid., p. 380.
17 Allen, 'Sight and Smell in Vertebrates', *Mind*, 6 (October 1881), 453–471, p. 470.

234 *Notes on pages 91–96*

18 Allen, *The Colour-Sense: Its Origin and Development* (London: Trübner & Co., 1879), p. 244.

19 Lester Ward, *Dynamic Sociology* (New York: D. Appleton & Co., 1883), pp. 502–503.

20 Allen, '[Review of] *Dynamic Sociology, or Applied Social Science, as Based upon Statical Sociology and the Less Complex Sciences* by Lester F. Ward', *Mind*, 9 (April 1884), 305–311, p. 308.

21 Allen, 'False Pretences', p. 158.

22 Allen, 'Strictly Incog.', p. 157.

23 See James Sully, '[Review of] Grant Allen, *The Colour-Sense*', *Mind*, 4 (1879), 415–416; see William James's correspondence with Allen in William James, *The Correspondence of William James*, ed. Ignas K. Skrupskelis and Elizabeth M. Berkley, 12 vols. (Charlottesville, VA: University Press of Virginia, 1997), V, pp. 158–159.

24 Sully, *Illusions: A Psychological Study* (New York: Appleton, 1881), p. 68.

25 James, *Principles of Psychology*, 2 vols. (London: Macmillan, 1891), II, p. 95.

26 Allen, 'Our Scientific Observations on a Ghost', in *Strange Stories* (London: Chatto and Windus, 1884), 321–340, pp. 336–337.

27 Allen, 'Novels without a Purpose', *North American Review*, 163 (August 1896), 223–235, pp. 231, 233.

28 Allen, 'Fiction and Mrs. Grundy', *Novel Review*, 2 (1892), 294–315, p. 295.

29 Letter from Allen to George Croom Robertson, 23 February 1885, Robertson Papers, University College Library, University of London, MS.Add.88/12.

30 Allen, 'Grundy', p. 297.

31 Allen, 'The Trade of Author', *Fortnightly Review*, 51:45 (February 1889), 261–274, p. 269.

32 '"Colin Clout" at Home. An Interview with Mr. Grant Allen', *Pall Mall Gazette* (4 November 1889), 1–2, p. 2.

33 Eliot, 'The Morality of Wilhelm Meister', in *Selected Essays, Poems and Other Writings*, ed. A. S. Byatt and Nicholas Warren (Harmondsworth: Penguin, 1991), 307–310, p. 308. On the complexity of Victorian attitudes to poetic justice, see Sharon Marcus, 'Comparative Sapphism', in *The Literary Channel: The International Invention of the Novel*, ed. Margaret Cohen and Carolyn Dever (Princeton, NJ: Princeton University Press, 2002), 251–285, pp. 267–270; and Thomas Vargish, *The Providential Aesthetic in Victorian Fiction* (Charlottesville, VA: University Press of Virginia, 1985), pp. 3–9.

34 See Andrew Mangham, *Violent Women and Sensation Fiction* (London: Palgrave Macmillan, 2007), pp. 49–86; Bridget Walsh, *Domestic Murder in Nineteenth-Century England: Literary and Cultural Representations* (Farnham: Ashgate, 2014), pp. 1–10.

35 See Linden Peach, *Masquerade, Crime and Fiction: Criminal Deceptions* (Basingstoke: Palgrave Macmillan, 2006), pp. 2–3.

36 Allen, 'The Curate of Churnside', in *Strange Stories*, 66–99, p. 99. Unless otherwise stated, subsequent quotations refer to this version.

Notes on pages 96–101

37 See James Cowles Prichard, *A Treatise on Insanity and Other Disorders Affecting the Mind* (London: Sherwood, Gilbert and Piper, 1835), pp. 4–6; Cary Federman, Dave Holmes and Jean Daniel Jacob, 'Deconstructing the Psychopath: A Critical Discursive Analysis', *Cultural Critique*, 72 (2009), 36–65, pp. 46–48.

38 Thomas Griffiths Wainewright, *Essays and Criticisms*, ed. Carew Hazlitt (London: Reeves & Turner, 1880); Oscar Wilde, 'Pen, Pencil and Poison: A Study in Green', *Fortnightly Review*, 45 (1889), 41–54.

39 See Morton, *Busiest Man*, p. 133.

40 Leslie Stephen, 'The Decay of Murder', *Cornhill Magazine*, 20 (December 1869), 722–733, p. 725. See Ian Burney, *Poison, Detection and the Victorian Imagination* (Manchester: Manchester University Press, 2006), pp. 11–12. On Allen's relationship with Stephen, see Morton, *Busiest Man*, pp. 79, 194.

41 Wilde, *The Picture of Dorian Gray*, in *The Complete Works of Oscar Wilde*, general ed. Ian Small, 8 vols. (Oxford: Oxford University Press, 2000–2017), III, 1–357, p. 168.

42 William De Quincey, 'On Murder Considered as One of the Fine Arts', *Blackwood's Magazine*, 20 (February 1827), 199–213.

43 In Mary Elizabeth Braddon's *Henry Dunbar*, 3 vols. (London: John Maxwell & Co., 1864), one character states: 'I am something of Shakespeare's opinion; I cannot but believe that "murder will out", somehow or other, sooner or later' (II, pp. 187–188). See the line, 'murder cannot be hid long . . . truth will out', in William Shakespeare, *The Merchant of Venice*, ed. M. M. Mahood (Cambridge: Cambridge University Press, 2003), p. 97.

44 Shuttleworth, *Charlotte Brontë*, p. 49.

45 Allen, 'The Curate of Churnside', *Cornhill Magazine*, 3:15 (September 1884), 225–258, p. 254.

46 Brooke Taylor, 'Accounting for Mysteries: Narratives of Intuition and Empiricism in the Victorian Novel', PhD thesis (Washington University, 2010), pp. 72, 76.

47 Allen, 'Woman's Intuition', *Forum*, 10 (1890), 333–340, p. 338. On Allen's gendering of different forms of detection, see Chris Willis, 'The Detective's *Doppelgänger*: Conflicting States of Female Consciousness in Grant Allen's Detective Fiction', in *Grant Allen: Literature and Politics at the Fin de Siècle*, ed. William Greenslade and Terence Rodgers (Aldershot: Ashgate, 2005), 143–153.

48 Allen, 'The Curate', *Cornhill Magazine*, p. 258.

49 Allen, *The Devil's Die* (New York: F. M. Lupton, 1890), p. 143. Subsequent quotations are referenced in the text.

50 Stephen, 'An Attempted Philosophy of History', *Fortnightly Review* (April 1880), 672–695, p. 682.

51 Allen, 'The Human Face Divine', *New Quarterly Magazine*, 2 (July 1879), 166–182, pp. 181–82.

52 On Allen and race, see Morton, *Busiest Man*, pp. 36–39.

236 *Notes on pages 101–114*

53 Allen, 'Human Face', p. 182.
54 On 'passing' in literature, see Elaine K. Ginsberg (ed.), 'Introduction: The Politics of Passing', in *Passing and the Fictions of Identity* (London: Duke University Press, 1996), 1–18.
55 G. B. Shaw, 'Mr. Grant Allen's New Novel', *Pall Mall Gazette* (24 April 1888), 3.
56 Allen, 'The Next Presentation', in *Sir Theodore's Guest and Other Stories* (Bristol: J. W. Arrowsmith, 1902), 237–276, p. 237. Subsequent quotations are referenced in the text.
57 Henry Maudsley, *Body and Will* (London: Kegan Paul, Trench & Co., 1883), pp. 251–252. Allen cites Maudsley's work in *Physiological Aesthetics*, p. 3.
58 Conan Doyle helped Allen to complete his final novel *Hilda Wade* (1899) while Allen was on his deathbed. See Morton, *Busiest Man*, p. 182.
59 Allen, *An African Millionaire* (London: G. Richards, 1898), pp. 158, 272. Further references are given in the text.
60 Allen, 'Masquerades', pp. 105, 107.
61 Ibid., p. 106.
62 Allen, 'Natural Inequality', in *Hand and Brain*, ed. Elbert Hubbard (New York: Roycroft, 1898), 65–86, pp. 66.
63 Allen, 'False Pretences', pp. 151–153.
64 Allen, 'Democracy and Diamonds', *Contemporary Review*, 59 (May 1891), 666–677, pp. 670–71.
65 Allen, 'The Monopolist Instincts', in *Post-Prandial Philosophy* (London: Chatto & Windus, 1894), 79–86, p. 80.
66 Allen, *Colour-Sense*, p. 237.
67 Allen, 'Diamonds', p. 668.
68 On the role of the 'naive narrator' in the development of detective fiction, see Dennis Porter, *The Pursuit of Crime: Art and Ideology in Detective Fiction* (London: Yale University Press, 1981), pp. 36–38.
69 Peach, *Deception*, p. x.
70 Christopher Pittard, *Purity and Contamination in Late Victorian Detective Fiction* (Farnham: Ashgate, 2011), pp. 126–127; see Emile Durkheim, *The Rules of Sociological Method* (New York: Free Press, 1938), p. 66.
71 Allen, '*Dynamic Sociology*', pp. 310–311.
72 Allen, *The British Barbarians* (London: G. P. Putnam's Sons, 1895), p. 24.
73 Allen, letter to Wallace (24 April 1899), British Library, Manuscripts, Add. MS.46441, f. 188.
74 Allen, 'False Pretences', p. 32.
75 Qtd. in Grant Richards, 'Mr. Grant Allen and His Work', *Novel Review*, 1:3 (June 1892), 261–268, p. 267.
76 Allen, 'A Scribbler's Apology', *Cornhill Magazine*, 47 (May 1883), 538–550, pp. 542, 538, 543.
77 See Morton, *Busiest Man*, pp. 137–143, 193–196.

Notes on pages 116–120 237

Chapter 4

1 Thomas Hardy, *The Life and Work of Thomas Hardy*, ed. Michael Millgate (London: Macmillan, 1984), p. 224.

2 Ibid., p. 102.

3 Qtd. in Raymond Blathwayt, 'A Chat with the Author of *Tess*', *Black and White*, 4 (27 August 1892), 238–240, p. 240.

4 Hardy, 'The Science of Fiction', in *Thomas Hardy's Personal Writings*, ed. Harold Orel (Basingstoke: Palgrave Macmillan, 1990), 134–138, p. 136.

5 Hardy, 'Candour in English Fiction', in *Personal Writings*, 125–133, p. 127.

6 Kucich, *Power of Lies*, p. 201.

7 Ibid., p. 207.

8 On Darwinism in Hardy, see Beer, *Plots*, pp. 220–241; Roger Ebbatson, *The Evolutionary Self: Hardy, Forster, Lawrence* (Sussex: Harvester Press, 1982), pp. 1–58; Anna West, *Thomas Hardy and Animals* (Cambridge: Cambridge University Press, 2017); Otis, *Organic Memory*, pp. 158–179; Pamela Gossin, *Thomas Hardy's Novel Universe: Astronomy, Cosmology, and Gender in the Post-Darwinian World* (Aldershot, UK: Ashgate, 2007); John Glendenning, *The Evolutionary Imagination in Late-Victorian Novels: An Entangled Bank* (Aldershot: Ashgate, 2007), pp. 69–106; Angelique Richardson, *The Politics of Thomas Hardy: Biology, Culture and Environment* (Oxford: Oxford University Press, forthcoming).

9 Elisha Cohn similarly claims that moral agency for Hardy depends on the 'separateness' of human consciousness from nature's processes: '"No insignificant creature": Thomas Hardy's Ethical Turn', *Nineteenth-Century Literature*, 64:4 (2010), 494–520, p. 519.

10 On pastoral innocence, see Paul Alpers, *What Is Pastoral?* (London: University of Chicago Press, 1996), pp. 32–33. On Hardy's complex relationship with pastoral, see Indy Clark, *Thomas Hardy's Pastoral: An Unkindly May* (Basingstoke: Palgrave Macmillan, 2015).

11 In 1868, Hardy wrote that the chapter on individuality in Mill's *On Liberty* was one of his 'cures for despair'; *Life*, p. 59.

12 Hardy, 'The Profitable Reading of Fiction', *Personal Writings*, 110–124, p. 124.

13 Qtd. in Blathwayt, 'A Chat', p. 240.

14 On urban alienation in Hardy, see Keith Wilson, 'Thomas Hardy of London', in *A Companion to Thomas Hardy*, ed. Keith Wilson (Oxford: Wiley-Blackwell, 2009), 146–161, pp. 151–155; Patricia McKee, *Reading Constellations: Urban Modernity in Victorian Fiction* (Oxford: Oxford University Press, 2014), pp. 100–128.

15 Hardy, *A Pair of Blue Eyes*, ed. Pamela Dalziel (London: Penguin, 1998), pp. 7–8, 254. Subsequent quotations are referenced in the text.

16 Hardy, *Far from the Madding Crowd*, eds. Rosemarie Morgan and Shannon Russell (London: Penguin, 2000), p. 10. Subsequent quotations are referenced in the text.

238 *Notes on pages 121–127*

17 Hardy, *The Woodlanders*, ed. Dale Kramer (Oxford: Oxford University Press, 2005), p. 58. Subsequent quotations are referenced in the text.
18 On Hardy and naturalism, see William A. Newton, 'Hardy and the Naturalists: Their Use of Physiology', *Modern Philology*, 49:1 (1951), 28–41; Norman Page, 'Art and Aesthetics', *The Cambridge Companion to Thomas Hardy*, ed. Dale Kramer (Cambridge: Cambridge University Press, 1999), 38–53.
19 Hardy, 'Science', p. 134; *Life*, p. 228.
20 Hardy, 'Science', p. 134.
21 Hardy, *The Literary Notebooks of Thomas Hardy*, ed. Lennart A. Bjork, 2 vols. (Basingstoke: Palgrave Macmillan), I, p. 132. See Stephen, 'Attempted Philosophy'.
22 Hardy, *Notebooks*, I, pp. 33, 92.
23 Hardy, *Life*, p. 182.
24 Darwin, *Descent*, II, p. 122
25 Hardy, *Notebooks*, I, p. 201.
26 Maudsley, *Natural Causes and Supernatural Seemings* (London: K. Paul, Trench & Co., 1886), p. 315.
27 Eliot, 'The Natural History of German Life', *Westminster Review*, 66 (July 1856), 51–79, pp. 53–54.
28 On Eliot's possible influence on Hardy, see Hardy, *Literary Notebooks*, I, p. 381.
29 Hardy, *The Return of the Native*, ed. Simon Gatrell (Oxford: Oxford University Press, 2005), p. 64. Subsequent quotations are referenced in the text.
30 On anthropological concepts of the primitive in Hardy, see Andrew Radford, *Thomas Hardy and the Survivals of Time* (Aldershot: Ashgate, 2003); and Michael A. Zeitler, *Representations of Culture: Thomas Hardy's Wessex and Victorian Anthropology* (Oxford: Peter Lang, 2007).
31 Hardy, *Tess of the d'Urbervilles*, ed. Tim Dolin (London: Penguin, 1998), p. 277. Subsequent quotations are referenced in the text.
32 For records of Hardy's reading of both authors, see Hardy, *Notebooks*, I, pp. 185, 219; II, p. 31.
33 Arthur Schopenhauer, *The World as Will and Idea*, trans. R. B. Haldane and J. Kemp, 3 vols. (London: Trübner & Co., 1886), III, p. 341.
34 Eduard von Hartmann, *The Philosophy of the Unconscious*, trans. William Chatterton Coupland (London: Routledge, Trench, Trübner & Co., 1931), p. 219.
35 Hardy, *Life*, p. 158.
36 Francis Galton, *Inquiries into Human Faculty and Its Development* (London: Macmillan, 1883), pp. 56–57. On Galton's influence on Hardy, see Richardson, '"Some Science underlies all Art": The Dramatization of Sexual Selection and Racial Biology in Thomas Hardy's *A Pair of Blue Eyes* and *The Well-Beloved*', *Journal of Victorian Culture*, 3:2 (1998), 302–338.
37 Hardy, *Notebooks*, II, p. 31. See Schopenhauer, *Studies in Pessimism*, trans. T. Bailey Saunders (London: Swan Sonnenschein & Co., 1893), p. 110. On Hardy's complex treatment of gender, see Margaret R. Higonnet (ed.),

Notes on pages 128–136

239

The Sense of Sex: Feminist Perspectives on Hardy (Chicago, IL: University of Illinois Press, 1993); Shanta Dutta, *Ambivalence in Hardy: A Study of His Attitude to Women* (Basingstoke: Palgrave Macmillan, 2000); and Patricia Ingham, *Thomas Hardy* (Oxford: Oxford University Press, 2003).

38 Hardy, *Life*, p. 283.

39 Ibid., p. 235. On Hardy's belief in the natural origins of morality, see Richardson, 'Hardy and the Place of Culture', in Wilson, *Companion to Hardy*, 54–70, pp. 63–65. On Hardy's interest in theories of altruism, see T. R. Wright, 'Positivism: Comte and Mill', in *Thomas Hardy in Context*, ed. Philip Mallett (Cambridge: Cambridge University Press, 2013), 296–305.

40 See J. O. Bailey, 'Evolutionary Meliorism in the Poetry of Thomas Hardy', *Studies in Philology*, 60:3 (1963), 569–587; George Wooton, *Thomas Hardy: Towards a Materialist Criticism* (Totowa, NJ: Barnes & Noble, 1985), p. 6; Virginia R. Hyman, *Ethical Perspective in the Novels of Thomas Hardy* (Port Washington, NY: National University Publishers, 1975).

41 See Spencer, *The Data of Ethics* (London: Williams & Norgate, 1879), pp. 201–218.

42 See Wallace, 'The Colours of Animals and Plants. I. – The Colours of Animals', *Macmillan's Magazine*, 36 (September 1877), 384–408, p. 388.

43 Hardy, *A Laodicean*, ed. John Schad (London: Penguin, 1997), 81–82. Subsequent quotations are referenced in the text.

44 Hardy, *Desperate Remedies*, ed. Patricia Ingham (Oxford: Oxford University Press, 2003), p. 233.

45 Hardy, *Jude the Obscure*, ed. Dennis Taylor (London: Penguin, 1998), p. 42. Subsequent quotations are referenced in the text.

46 Hardy once recommended 'the works of Herbert Spencer' as 'a provisional view of the universe' for a religious correspondent disturbed by nature's cruelty: Hardy, *The Collected Letters of Thomas Hardy*, ed. Richard Little Purdy, Michael Millgate and Keith Wilson, 8 vols. (Oxford: Clarendon Press, 1878–2012), I, p. 174.

47 Hardy, *Life*, p. 275.

48 Richard A. Kaye, *The Flirt's Tragedy: Desire without End in Victorian and Edwardian Fiction* (London: University of Virginia Press, 2002). Kaye's title echoes Hardy's poem of the same name in which the speaker seeks revenge on a woman who jilted him by employing a womanizer to seduce and jilt her.

49 Hardy, *Letters*, II, p. 92.

50 Hardy, *Notebooks*, II, p. 73. Quoting Auguste Comte, *System of Positive Polity: Social Dynamics*, trans. Harriet Martineau, 3 vols. (London: Longmans, Green & Co., 1876), III, p. 519.

51 See Tess O'Toole, *Genealogy and Fiction in Hardy: Family Lineage and Narrative Lines* (Basingstoke: Macmillan, 1997); Sophie Gilmartin, *Ancestry and Narrative in Nineteenth-Century British Literature: Blood Relations from Edgeworth to Hardy* (Cambridge: Cambridge University Press, 1998), pp. 195–245; Graeme Tytler, '"Know how to Decipher a Countenance": Physiognomy in Thomas Hardy's Fiction', *Thomas Hardy Year Book*,

240 *Notes on pages 136–145*

27 (1998), 43–60; Sharrona Pearl, *About Faces: Physiognomy in Nineteenth-Century Britain* (London: Harvard University Press, 2010), pp. 78–81.

52 O'Toole, *Genealogy*, pp. 1–2.

53 See Trish Ferguson, *Thomas Hardy's Legal Fictions* (Edinburgh: Edinburgh University Press, 2013), pp. 132–156.

54 Hardy, *Thomas Hardy's 'Facts' Notebook*, ed. William Greenslade (New York: Routledge, 2016), pp. 72–73.

55 Galton, 'Personal Identification and Description', *Nature*, 38 (21 and 28 June 1888), 173–177, 201–202, p. 202.

56 'Squire Petrick's Lady', in *A Group of Noble Dames* (London: Macmillan & Co., 1903), 171–186.

57 'Heredity', in *Thomas Hardy: The Complete Poems*, ed. James Gibson (Basingstoke: Palgrave Macmillan, 2001), 434.

58 Hardy, 'The Pedigree', in *Poems*, 460–461, p. 461.

59 Galton, 'Personal Identification', p. 202.

60 See Bowler, *Evolution*, pp. 260–273.

61 Maudsley, *The Pathology of Mind* (New York: D. Appleton & Co., 1880), p. 118.

62 Johann Caspar Lavater, *Essays on Physiognomy*, trans. Thomas Holcroft (London: W. Tegg, 1862), p. 149.

63 Hardy, *The Mayor of Casterbridge*, ed. Dale Kramer (Oxford: Oxford University Press, 2004), p. 118.

64 Hardy, 'For Conscience' Sake', in *Life's Little Ironies* (London: Harper & Brothers, 1920), 55–74, pp. 67–68.

65 O'Toole, *Genealogy*, p. 14.

66 Hardy, *Mayor*, p. 118.

67 Hardy, 'The Marchioness of Stonehenge', in *Noble Dames*, 107–128, p. 126.

68 Ibid., pp. 126–127.

69 Hardy, 'Lady Mottisfont', in *Noble Dames*, 129–152, p. 142.

70 Ibid., p. 148.

71 Henry Sumner Maine, *Ancient Law: Its Connection with the Early History of Society and Its Relation to Modern Ideas* (London: John Murray, 1861), p. 27. See Mary Jean Corbett, *Family Likeness: Sex, Marriage, and Incest from Jane Austen to Virginia Woolf* (London: Cornell University Press, 2008), pp. 86–89.

72 Hardy, 'An Imaginative Woman', in *Life's Little Ironies*, 3–31, p. 31.

73 On maternal impressions in Victorian fiction, see Martha Stoddard Holmes, *Fictions of Affliction: Physical Disability in Victorian Culture* (Ann Arbor, MI: University of Michigan Press, 2004), pp. 64–66.

74 See August Weismann, *Essays upon Heredity and Kindred Biological Problems*, 2 vols. (Oxford: Clarendon Press, 1889–1892); Hardy, *Life*, I, p. 240.

75 Hardy, 'Imaginative Woman', p. 31.

76 The novel was a rewrite of his earlier serial *The Pursuit of the Well-Beloved* (1892).

Notes on pages 145–152 241

77 Hardy, *The Well-Beloved*, in *The Pursuit of the Well-Beloved and The Well-Beloved*, ed. Patricia Ingham (London: Penguin, 1997), 169–338, pp. 240, 244. Subsequent quotations are referenced in the text.
78 Hardy further emphasized the generational differences (which Pierston ignores) in his 1897 revision of the tale by naming Avice's daughter Ann Avice (which Pierston quickly shortens to just 'Avice'; p. 237).
79 Annette Federico, 'Thomas Hardy's *The Well-Beloved*: Love's Descent', *English Literature in Transition, 1880–1920*, 50:3 (2007), 269–290, p. 275.
80 Hardy, *Life*, p. 169.
81 Hardy, 'The Pedigree', p. 461.
82 On Hardy and self-deception, see *Literary Notebooks*, II, p. 161.

Chapter 5

1 Norris, *Beasts*, pp. 53–72.
2 See Regenia Gagnier, *Individualism, Decadence and Globalization: On the Relationship of Part to Whole, 1859–1920* (London: Palgrave Macmillan, 2010), pp. 1–10, 28–60; Luke Philip Plotica, *Nineteenth-Century Individualism and the Market Economy: Individualist Themes in Emerson, Thoreau, and Sumner* (Cham, Switzerland: Palgrave Macmillan, 2018), pp. 5–8, 29–41.
3 Steven Lukes, *Individualism* (Oxford: Blackwell, 1973), pp. 17, 32.
4 Alexis Harley, *Autobiologies: Charles Darwin and the Natural History of the* Self (Lewisburg, PA: Bucknell University Press, 2015), pp. 11–15.
5 Gagnier, *Individualism*, p. 88; Martin A. Danahay, *A Community of One: Masculine Autobiography and Autonomy in Nineteenth-Century Britain* (Albany, NY: State University of New York Press, 1993), pp. 1–38.
6 Williamson, *British Masculinity in the 'Gentleman's Magazine', 1731 to 1815* (Basingstoke: Palgrave Macmillan, 2016), p. 10.
7 Trilling, *Sincerity*, pp. 15, 20.
8 See Daniel Shanahan, *Toward a Genealogy of Individualism* (Amherst, MA: University of Massachusetts Press, 1992), pp. 99–107.
9 Williams Landels, *How Men Are Made* (London: J. Heaton, 1859), pp. 8–9; qtd. in John Tosh, *A Man's Place: Masculinity and the Middle-Class Home in Victorian England* (London: Yale University Press, 2007), p. 111.
10 Marilyn Randall, *Pragmatic Plagiarism: Authorship, Profit and Power* (Toronto: University of Toronto Press, 2003), p. 47.
11 Robert Macfarlane, *Original Copy: Plagiarism and Originality in Nineteenth-Century Literature* (Oxford: Oxford University Press, 2007), p. 33.
12 Carlyle, 'Corn-Law Rhymes', *Edinburgh Review*, 55 (July 1832), 338–361, p. 351.
13 Spencer, 'The Social Organism', in *Essays: Scientific, Political, Speculative, Second Series* (London: Williams & Norgate, 1863), 143–184, p. 146.
14 See Dowling, *Language and Decadence*, pp. 46–64.
15 Tylor, *Primitive Culture*, I, p. 2.

242   *Notes on pages 152–160*

16 Macfarlane, *Original Copy*, pp. 67–70, 8.
17 Walter Bagehot, *Physics and Politics* (London: Kegan Paul, 1881), pp. 108–109, 100.
18 James Mark Baldwin, *The Individual and Society; or, Psychology and Sociology* (Boston: Badger, 1911), p. 21.
19 Kidd, *Social Evolution*, pp. 243–287.
20 Qtd. in Havelock Ellis, 'A Note on Paul Bourget', in *Views and Reviews* (Boston: Houghton Mifflin, 1932), 48-60, p. 52.
21 Max Nordau, *Degeneration* (London: Heinemann, 1895), p. 58.
22 Cesare Lombroso, 'Nordau's "Degeneration": Its Value and Its Errors', *The Century*, 50 (May–October 1895), 936–940, pp. 937–938.
23 Francis B. Gummere, 'Originality and Convention in Literature', *Quarterly Review*, 204 (January 1906), 26–44, pp. 34–35.
24 Ibid., p. 26.
25 Ibid., p. 38.
26 Jason Camlot, *Style and the Nineteenth-Century British Critic: Sincere Mannerisms* (Aldershot: Ashgate, 2008), p. 5.
27 For an overview of Stephen's work, see Noel G. Annan, *Leslie Stephen: The Godless Victorian* (London: Weidenfeld and Nicolson, 1984).
28 Stephen, *Social Rights and Duties*, 2 vols. (London: Swan Sonnenschein, 1896), I, p. 28.
29 Stephen, 'Darwinism and Divinity', *Fraser's Magazine*, 5:28 (1872), 409–421, p. 416.
30 Ibid., p. 417. See John Henry Newman, *An Essay in Aid of a Grammar of Assent*, ed. Ian Ker (Oxford: Clarendon, 1985), pp. 73–78.
31 Stephen, *History of English Thought in the Eighteenth Century*, 2 vols. (London: Smith, Elder & Co., 1876), I, p. 17.
32 Stephen, *Social Rights*, I, p. 30.
33 Stephen, *The Science of Ethics* (London: Smith, Elder & Co., 1882), p. 123.
34 Stephen, 'Darwinism', p. 421.
35 Stephen, *English Thought*, I, p. 19.
36 Ibid., I, p. 169.
37 Stephen, 'Darwinism', p. 421.
38 See Annan, *Godless Victorian*, pp. 67–69.
39 Stephen, *Social Rights*, II, p. 146.
40 Ibid., I, pp. 7, 30.
41 Ibid., I, p. 9.
42 See Norris, *Beasts*, pp. 56–57.
43 For the sake of consistency, I will refer to him throughout by the later name.
44 Theodore Watts, 'Lord Tennyson', *Athenaeum* (8 October 1892), 482–483, p. 482.
45 Watts, 'Joseph and His Brethren', *Examiner* (6 May 1876), 515–517, p. 515.
46 Watts, '*A Book of Rhyme* by Augusta Webster', *Athenaeum* (20 August 1881) [attributed to Watts in *The Life and Letters of Theodore Watts-Dunton*, ed.

Notes on pages 160–165

Thomas Hake and Arthur Compton-Rickett, 2 vols. (London: T. C. & E. C. Jack, 1916), II, p. 283], 229–230, p. 230.

47 Watts, 'Joseph', p. 517.

48 Ibid., p. 516.

49 Watts-Dunton, 'Letters of Dante Gabriel Rossetti to William Allingham, 1855–1870', *Athenaeum* (26 March 1898), 395–397, p. 395.

50 Watts, 'Book of Rhyme', p. 230.

51 Watts, 'Tennyson', p. 483.

52 Watts-Dunton, '*Alfred, Lord Tennyson: A Memoir*', *Athenaeum* (9 October 1897), 481–484, p. 481.

53 Watts, 'Tennyson', p. 482.

54 Watts-Dunton, 'Bret Harte', *Athenaeum* (24 May 1902), 658–660, pp. 658–659.

55 Watts-Dunton, 'Edgar Poe', *Athenaeum* (2 September 1876), 306.

56 Watts, 'Ebenezer Jones', *Athenaeum* (28 September 1878), 401–403, p. 403.

57 Watts, 'The Poetical Works of Percy Bysshe Shelley' [unsigned, attributed in *Life and Letters*, II, p. 281], *Athenaeum* (29 September 1877), 396–400, p. 397.

58 Watts, '*Englishmen of Letters – Landor* by Sidney Colvin', *Athenaeum* (6 August 1881), 165–167, p. 167.

59 Gerald Massey had written that Dobell 'appears to select his subject, and the point of treatment, for their remoteness from all ordinary reality, and then to refine upon these until they are intangible to us'; 'Poetry – The Spasmodists', *North British Review*, 28:55 (1858), 231–250, p. 245.

60 Watts-Dunton, *Poetry and the Renascence of Wonder* (New York: E. P. Dutton, 1916), pp. 281–282.

61 Ibid., p. 7.

62 Algernon Charles Swinburne, 'Victor Hugo: L'Année Terrible', in *Essays and Studies* (London: Chatto & Windus, 1875), 17–59, p. 41.

63 Watts-Dunton, '*The Water of the Wondrous Isles. By William Morris*', *Athenaeum* (4 December 1897), 777–779, p. 777.

64 Camille Paglia writes that AESTHETICISM 'is predicated on a swerve from nature'; *Sexual Personae: Art and Decadence from Nefertiti to Emily Dickinson* (New York: Vintage Books 1991), p. 523.

65 On the possible influence of Spencer on Pater, see Yannis Kanarakis, 'The Aesthete as Scientist: Walter Pater and Nineteenth-Century Science', *Victorian Network*, 2:1 (2010), 88–105, pp. 3–4.

66 Kant, *Critique of Judgment*, p. 148.

67 Walter Pater, 'Coleridge', in *Appreciations* (London: Macmillan & Co., 1889), 64–106, p. 80.

68 Pater, *Plato and Platonism* (London: Macmillan & Co., 1893), pp. 245–246.

69 Pater, 'Coleridge', p. 66.

70 Pater, *The Renaissance: Studies in Art and Poetry*, 3rd ed. (London: Macmillan, 1888), p. 250.

244   *Notes on pages 165–169*

71 Pater, 'Wordsworth', in *Appreciations*, 37–63, p. 62.
72 Pater, 'Coleridge', p. 67.
73 Pater, *Renaissance*, p. 210. See Matthew Potolsky, 'Pale Imitations: Walter Pater's Decadent Historiography', in *Perennial Decay: On the Aesthetics and Politics of Decadance*, ed. Liz Constable, Dennis Denisoff and Matthew Potolsky (Philadelphia, PA: University of Pennsylvania Press, 1999), 235–253.
74 Pater, *Plato*, p. 253.
75 Pater, 'Style', in *Appreciations*, 1–36, pp. 9, 12–13.
76 Pater, *Marius the Epicurean: His Sensations and Ideas* (London: Macmillan & Co., 1885), p. 98.
77 On the history of such etymological 'organicism', see Abberley, *Evolution of Language*, pp. 91–127. On Pater's engagement with fin-de-siècle linguistic thought, see Dowling, *Language and Decadence*, pp. 110–139.
78 Pater, 'Style', p. 13.
79 Rachel O'Connell, 'Reparative Pater: Retreat, Ecstasy, and Reparation in the Writings of Walter Pater', *ELH*, 82:3 (2015), 969–986, p. 970. For more on Pater's sexuality, see Dowling, *Hellenism and Homosexuality in Victorian Oxford* (Ithaca, NY: Cornell University Press, 1996), pp. 97–114; Heather Love, *Feeling Backward: Loss and the Politics of Queer History* (Cambridge, MA: Harvard University Press, 2007), pp. 53–71.
80 See Matthew Kaiser, 'Marius at Oxford: Paterian Pedagogy and the Ethics of Seduction', in *Walter Pater: Transparencies of Desire*, ed. Lesley Higgins Brake and Carolyn Williams (Greensboro, NC: ELT Press, 2002), 189–201.
81 See Pater, *Renaissance*, p. 246.
82 Sebastian Lecourt, '"To surrender himself, in perfectly liberal inquiry": Walter Pater, Many-Sidedness, and the Conversion Novel', *Victorian Studies*, 53:2 (2011), 231–253, p. 233.
83 Pater, *Marius*, pp. 340, 346.
84 Edward Dowden, 'Walter Pater', in *Essays: Modern and Elizabethan* (London: J. M. Dent, 1910), 1–25, p. 21. See William F. Shuter, *Rereading Walter Pater* (Cambridge: Cambridge University Press, 1997), p. 61.
85 Pater, *Plato*, p. 242.
86 Ibid., pp. 244, 247, 246.
87 See Macfarlane, *Original Copy*, pp. 158–192; Florina Tufescu, *Oscar Wilde's Plagiarism: The Triumph of Art over Ego* (Dublin: Irish Academic Press, 2008); Paul Saint-Amour, *The Copywrights: Intellectual Property and the Literary Imagination* (Ithaca, NY: Cornell University Press, 2003), pp. 90–120; Joseph Bristow and Rebecca N. Mitchell, *Oscar Wilde's Chatterton: Literary History, Romanticism, and the Art of Forgery* (New Haven, CT: Yale University Press, 2015), pp. 160–213.
88 On Wilde's engagements with scientific naturalism, see Bruce Haley, 'Wilde's "Decadence" and the Positivist Tradition', *Victorian Studies*, 28:2 (1985), 215–229; John Wilson Foster, 'Against Nature? Science and Oscar Wilde', *University of Toronto Quarterly*, 63:2 (1993/1994), 328–346; Michael

Notes on pages 169–176

Wainwright, 'Oscar Wilde, the Science of Heredity, and *The Picture of Dorian Gray*', *English Literature in Transition, 1880–1920*, 54:4 (2011), 494–522; Caroline Sumpter, '"No Artist Has Ethical Sympathies": Oscar Wilde, Aesthetics, and Moral Evolution', *Victorian Literature and Culture*, 44:3 (2016), 623–640.

89 Wilde, *Oscar Wilde's Oxford Notebooks*, ed. Philip E. Smith II and Michael S. Helfand (Oxford: Oxford University Press, 1989), p. 121.

90 Wilde, 'The Decay of Lying', in *Works*, IV, 72–103, pp. 73, 84.

91 Wilde, 'Historical Criticism', in *Works*, IV, 3–70, p. 61.

92 Wilde, *Dorian Gray*, p. 183.

93 Wild, 'The Critic as Artist', in *Works*, IV, 123–206, p. 176. Subsequent quotations are referenced in the text.

94 Wilde, 'The Soul of Man under Socialism', in *Works*, IV, 231–268, p. 250.

95 David George Ritchie, *Darwinism and Politics* (London: Swan Sonnenschein, 1889), p. 15.

96 Wilde, 'Some Literary Notes' [May 1889], in *Works*, VII, 207–214, p. 211.

97 Wilde, 'Soul of Man', p. 249. Never a slave to consistency, Wilde, of course, enjoyed much financial success as a writer and thought a great deal about courting audiences: see Ian Small and Josephine M. Guy, *Oscar Wilde's Profession: Writing and the Culture Industry in the Late Nineteenth Century* (Oxford University Press, 2000).

98 Wilde, 'Soul of Man', p. 265. See Sumpter, 'Moral Evolution', p. 636.

99 Wilde, 'Béranger in England', in *Works*, VI, 73–74.

100 Wilde, 'Lecture to Art Students', in *Essays and Lectures* (London: Methuen & Co., 1913), 197–212, pp. 202, 204.

101 Foster, 'Against Nature?', pp. 336–337.

102 Norbert Kohl, *Oscar Wilde: The Works of a Conformist Rebel*, trans. David Henry Wilson (Cambridge: Cambridge University Press, 1989), pp. 83–95.

103 Wilde, *Dorian Gray*, pp. 167–168.

104 See Wallace, 'Colours of Animals', pp. 406–407.

105 Romanes, *Mental Evolution*, p. 75.

106 See Wilde, *Oxford Notebooks*, p. 81.

107 Wilde, 'Decay of Lying', p. 90.

108 Wilde, *The Letters of Oscar Wilde*, ed. Rupert Hart-Davis (London: Hart-Davis, 1962), p. 236.

109 William E. Buckler, 'Wilde's "Trumpet against the Gate of Dullness": "The Decay of Lying"', *English Literature in Transition, 1880–1920*, 33:3 (1990), 311–323, p. 314.

110 Wilde, 'The Truth of Masks', in *Works*, IV, 207–228, p. 228.

111 Lawrence Danson, *Wilde's Intentions: The Artist in His Criticism* (Oxford: Clarendon Press, 1997), p. 34.

112 See ibid., p. 107.

113 Jonathan Dollimore, *Sexual Dissidence: Augustine to Wilde, Freud to Foucault* (Oxford: Clarendon, 1991).

246   *Notes on pages 176–181*

114 Michael R. Doylen, 'Oscar Wilde's *De Profundis*: Homosexual Self-Fashioning on the Other Side of Scandal', *Victorian Literature and Culture*, 27:2 (1999), 547–566, p. 550.

115 Wilde, 'Phrases and Philosophies for the Use of the Young', *The Chameleon*, 1 (1894), 1–3, p. 3.

116 Wilde, *Letters*, p. 379.

117 Wilde, 'De Profundis', in *Works*, II, 157–193, p. 165.

118 Wilde, *Letters*, 401–405, pp. 402. See Stephen Karschay, *Degeneration, Normativity and the Gothic at the Fin de Siècle* (Palgrave Macmillan, 2015), pp. 1–3. For an alternative view that, post-trial, Wilde partly accepted the diagnosis of degenerate, see Dominic James, 'Oscar Wilde, Sodomy, and Mental Illness in Late Victorian England', *Journal of the History of Sexuality*, 23:1 (2014), 79–95.

119 See Leonard Diepeveen, *The Difficulties of Modernism* (Abingdon: Routledge, 2003), pp. 1–42; Allon White, *The Uses of Obscurity: Fiction of Early Modernism* (London: Routledge & Kegan Paul, 1981), pp. 13–29.

Chapter 6

1 Jim Endersby, 'A Visit to Biotopia: Genre, Genetics and Gardening in the Early Twentieth Century', *British Journal for the History of Science*, 51:3 (2018), 423–455.

2 Ken Koltun-Fromm, *Imagining Jewish Authenticity: Vision and Text in American Jewish Thought* (Bloomington: Indiana University Press, 2015), p. 6.

3 Meri-Jane Rochelson, *A Jew in the Public Arena: The Career of Israel Zangwill* (Detroit, MI: Wayne State University Press, 2008), p. 1.

4 Meldola and Zangwill were both members of the London Jewish learned society the Maccabaeans.

5 Major Osman Bey, *The Conquest of the World by the Jews*, trans. F. W. Mathias (St. Louis, MO: St. Louis Book Club & News Company, 1878), pp. 34, 66.

6 Jay Geller, *The Other Jewish Question: Identifying the Jew and Making Sense of Modernity* (New York: Fordham University Press, 2011), p. 265.

7 'Auf allen Gebieten, wo nicht mehr als Reproduction verlangt wird … überall treten sie erst dann in den Vordergrund, wenn die Nichtjuden das Feld zur Genüge schöpferisch bearbeitet haben, so dass nur die Reproduction der vorhandenen Vorbilder übrig bleibt' [my translation], Eduard von Hartmann, *Das Judentum in Gegenwart und Zukunft* (Berlin: Wilhelm Friedrich, 1885), p. 168.

8 Joseph Jacobs, *Studies in Jewish Statistics, Social, Vital and Anthropometric* (London: D. Nutt, 1891), pp. 33–34.

9 Nordau, 'Max Nordau's Address on the Situation of the Jews throughout the World' [1897], *The Jubilee of the First Zionist Congress, 1897–1947* (Jerusalem: The Executive of the Zionist Organization, 1947), 56–62, p. 59–60.

Notes on pages *181–187*

10 Nordau, *Zionism: Its History and Aims* (New York: Federation of American Zionists, 1905), p. 6.

11 Nordau, 'Address', pp. 58–59.

12 Israel Zangwill, *Children of the Ghetto* (London: Macmillan & Co., 1895), p. xviii.

13 Ibid., p. 30.

14 Zangwill, 'The Ghetto' [undated], in *Speeches, Articles and Letters of Israel Zangwill*, ed. Maurice Simon (London: Soncino Press, 1937), 3–27, pp. 19, 26.

15 Ibid., p. 3.

16 Zangwill, 'The Maccabaeans' [1893], in *Speeches, Articles and Letters*, 42–46, p. 44.

17 Zangwill, 'The Future of the Jewish People' [1903], in *Speeches, Articles and Letters*, 71–74, p. 72.

18 Zangwill, 'The Ghetto', p. 27.

19 Zangwill, 'The Future of the Jew', *Daily Mail* (8 September 1903), 4.

20 Zangwill, 'The Ghetto', p. 27.

21 Zangwill, 'The New Jew' [1898], in *Speeches, Articles and Letters*, 54–63, p. 56.

22 Zangwill, 'The Jewish Race' [1911], in *Speeches, Articles and Letters*, 82–97, p. 89.

23 Ibid., p. 92.

24 Zangwill, *The Melting-Pot: A Drama in Four Acts* (New York: Macmillan, 1909), p. 37. On the wider cultural context of this rhetoric, see Aviva F. Taubenfeld, *Rough Writing: Ethnic Authorship in Theodore Roosevelt's America* (New York: New York University Press, 2008), pp. 16–30.

25 Zangwill, *The Melting-Pot*, p. 193.

26 Zangwill, 'Jewish Race', pp. 92–93.

27 Zangwill, *The Melting-Pot*, p. 183.

28 Zangwill, 'Fiesole and Florence', in *Without Prejudice* (New York: Century Co., 1896), 294–298, p. 297.

29 Ibid., pp. 294–295.

30 Gilles Deleuze and Felix Guattari, *Kafka: Toward a Minor Literature*, trans. Dana Polan (Minneapolis, MN: University of Minnesota Press, 1986), pp. 16–17.

31 Homi Bhaba, *The Location of Culture* (New York: Routledge, 2004), p. 126.

32 Zangwill, 'Hebrew, Jew and Israelite' [1892], in *Speeches, Articles and Letters*, 28–41, p. 40.

33 Zangwill, 'Jewish Race', pp. 90, 82.

34 Ibid., pp. 89-90.

35 Neil Larry Shumsky, 'Zangwill's "The Melting Pot": Ethnic Tensions on Stage', *American Quarterly*, 27:1 (1975), 29–41, p. 32.

36 Ibid., p. 35.

37 Zangwill, *The Melting-Pot*, pp. 166, 170.

38 Zangwill, *The Principle of Nationalities: Conway Memorial Lecture* (London: Watts & Co., 1917), p. 89; see Rochelson, *Public Arena*, p. 189.

248 *Notes on pages 188–192*

39 See Judith Allen, *The Feminism of Charlotte Perkins Gilman: Sexualities, Histories, Progressivism* (London: University of Chicago Press, 2009), pp. 76–77, 104–109; Cynthia J. Davis, *Charlotte Perkins Gilman: A Biography* (Stanford, CA: Stanford University Press, 2010), pp. 122–126.

40 See Gilman, 'Modesty: Feminine and Other', *Independent*, 58 (29 June 1905), 1447–1450; 'Symbolism in Dress', *Independent*, 58 (8 June 1905), 1294–1297.

41 In her autobiography, Gilman wrote, 'From Spencer I learned wisdom and applied it'; see *The Living of Charlotte Perkins Gilman* (New York: Harper & Row, 1975), p. 154.

42 In this discussion, I will refer to *sex* rather than *gender* since the latter term is a product of post-war feminist discourse that clearly separates culture from biology – a separation that Gilman frequently did not make.

43 See Jane Lancaster, '"I Could Easily Have Been an Acrobat": Charlotte Perkins Gilman and the Providence Ladies' Sanitary Gymnasium, 1881–1884', *American Transcendental Quarterly*, 8:1 (1994), 33–52.

44 Frances B. Cogan, *All-American Girl: The Ideal of Real Womanhood in Mid-Nineteenth-Century America* (Athens, GA: University of Georgia Press, 1989), p. 4.

45 See Melyssa Wrisley, 'Fashioning a New Femininity: Charlotte Perkins Gilman and Discourses of Dress, Gender and Sexuality, 1875–1930', PhD thesis (Binghamton University, 2008), p. 27.

46 Gilman, 'Why Women Do Not Reform Their Dress', *Woman's Journal* (23 October 1886), 338.

47 Cynthia Eller, 'Sons of the Mother: Victorian Anthropologists and the Myth of Matriarchal Prehistory', *Gender & History*, 18:2 (2006), 285–310.

48 John Ferguson McLennan, *Primitive Marriage* (Edinburgh: Adam & Charles Black, 1865), pp. 182–184; Lewis Henry Morgan, *Ancient Society* (New York: Henry Holt & Co., 1878), pp. 393–394.

49 Spencer, 'Psychology of the Sexes', *Popular Science Monthly*, 4 (November 1873), 30–38, p. 33.

50 Ward, *Dynamic Sociology*, p. 643.

51 Charles Dudley Warner, 'How Shall Women Dress?', *North American Review*, 140 (June 1885), 557–564, p. 563.

52 Ward, *Dynamic Sociology*, p. 643.

53 Ibid., p. 615.

54 Bernice L. Hausman argues that Gilman's writing 'both incorporated and resisted evolutionary arguments concerning sexual difference'; see 'Sex before Gender: Charlotte Perkins Gilman and the Evolutionary Paradigm of Utopia', *Feminist Studies*, 24: 3 (1998), 488–510, p.493. On other 'New Woman' authors' engagements with evolutionary theory, see Angelique Richardson, *Love and Eugenics in the Late Nineteenth Century: Rational Reproduction and the New Woman* (Oxford: Oxford University Press, 2003).

55 See Allen, *Feminism of Charlotte Perkins Gilman*, 87–96.

56 Gilman, *Women and Economics* (Boston: Small, Maynard & Co., 1898), p. 35. Subsequent quotations are referenced in the text.

Notes on pages 192–198 249

57 Gilman, 'Symbolism', pp. 1295–1297.
58 Gilman, 'Modesty', p. 1448.
59 Gilman, 'Her "Charms"', *Forerunner*, 6:1 (1915), 26.
60 See Laura Mulvey, 'Visual Pleasure and Narrative Cinema', *Screen*, 16:3 (1975), 6–18; Anke Gleber, 'Women on the Screens and Streets of Modernity: In Search of the Female Flaneur', in *The Image in Dispute: Art and Cinema in the Age of Photography*, ed. Dudley Andrew (Austin: University of Texas Press, 1997), 55–85.
61 Gilman, 'Modesty', p. 1450.
62 Wrisley, *Femininity*, p. 4.
63 Ibid., pp. 180–182.
64 Gilman, 'Modesty', pp. 1448, 1450.
65 Ibid., p. 1449.
66 See Stephanie Shields, 'The Variability Hypothesis: History of a Biological Model of Sex Differences in Intelligence', *Signs: Journal of Women in Culture and Society*, 7 (1982), 769–797.
67 Gilman, 'The Beauty Women Have Lost', *Forerunner*, 1:11 (1910), 22–23, p. 22.
68 Ibid., p. 23.
69 Sander S. Gilman, *Creating Beauty to Cure the Soul: Race and Psychology in the Shaping of Aesthetic Surgery* (London: Duke University Press, 1998), p. 4.
70 Gilman, *The Man-Made World* (New York: Charlton Co., 1914), p. 51.
71 Liz Conor, *The Spectacular Modern Woman: Feminine Visibility in the 1920s* (Bloomington: Indiana University Press, 2004), p. 16.
72 Gilman, *The Dress of Women: A Critical Introduction to the Symbolism and Sociology of Clothing* [collected from articles in *The Forerunner*], ed. Michael R. Hill and Mary Jo Deegan (Westport, CA: Greenwood Press, 2002), pp. 122, 138.
73 Qtd. in 'The Conflict between "Human" and "Female" Feminism', *Current Opinion*, 56 (April 1914), 291–292. See Wrisley, *Femininity*, pp. 210–211.
74 Gilman, 'Modesty', p. 1449.
75 Gilman, *Dress of Women*, p. 68.
76 Gilman, 'Modesty', p. 1448.
77 Gilman, *Herland* (New York: Pantheon, 1979), p. 13. Subsequent quotations are referenced in the text.
78 Gilman, 'Symbolism', p. 1296.
79 Gilman, 'Modesty', p. 1448.
80 Gilman, *Dress of Women*, p. 53.
81 Gilman, 'Our Brains and What Ails Them', *The Forerunner*, 3:5 (May 1912), 133–139, pp. 133–134. See also Lou-Ann Matossian, 'A Woman-Made Language: Charlotte Perkins Gilman and *Herland*', *Women and Language*, 10:2 (1987), 16–20.
82 Gilman, 'Our Brains', pp. 136–137, 133. On Gilman's opposition to AESTHETICISM, see Ann Heilmann, 'Overwriting Decadence: Charlotte Perkins Gilman, Oscar Wilde, and the Feminization of Art in "The Yellow

Wallpaper"', in *The Mixed Legacy of Charlotte Perkins Gilman*, eds. Catherine J. Golden and Joanna Schneider Zangrando (London: Associated University Presses, 2000), 175–188.

83 Gilman, 'The Beauty', p. 22.

84 Gilman, *Dress of Women*, p. 45.

85 Ibid., pp. 46–47.

86 Gilman, 'The Shape of Her Dress', *Woman's Journal*, 35 (16 July 1904), 226.

87 Gilman, 'Beauty', p. 23.

88 Gilman, 'Shape'.

89 Gilman, *Dress of Women*, p. 10.

90 Ibid., p. 44.

91 Gilman, *Dress of Women*, pp. 133, 59.

92 Gilman, *Moving the Mountain* (New York: Charlton Co., 1911), pp. 132, 108–109.

93 Monika Pietrzak-Franger, *Syphilis in Victorian Literature and Culture: Medicine, Knowledge and the Spectacle of Victorian Invisibility* (Basingstoke: Palgrave Macmillan, 2017), pp. 7–8. See also Elaine Showalter, 'Syphilis, Sexuality, and the Fiction of Fin de Siècle', in *Sex, Politics, and Science in the Nineteenth-Century Novel: Selected Papers from the English Institute, 1983–1984*, ed. Ruth Bernard Yeazell (Baltimore: Johns Hopkins University Press, 1990), 88–115.

94 Gilman, *The Crux* (New York: Charlton Co., 1911), pp. 141, 131, 205.

95 Ibid., pp. 222–223.

96 Gilman, *Dress of Women*, pp. 124–126.

97 George Santayana, *The Sense of Beauty* (New York: C. Scribner's Sons, 1896), p. 52.

98 Gilman, *Dress of Women*, pp. 4, 15.

99 Gilman, 'Shape'.

100 Gilman, *Dress of Women*, p. 138.

101 On determinism (and its tensions) in Gilman's evolutionary sociology, see Brian Lloyd, 'Feminism, Utopian and Scientific: Charlotte Perkins Gilman and the Prison of the Familiar', *American Studies*, 39:1 (1998), 93–113, pp. 94–96.

102 Gilman, *Dress of Women*, pp. 140–141.

103 Ibid., p. 122.

104 Ibid., p. 116.

105 Simone de Beauvoir, *The Second Sex*, trans. E. M. Parshley (New York: Vintage, 1973).

106 Judith Butler, *Gender Trouble* (New York: Routledge, 1990).

Conclusion

1 Similar notions would also be developed by the British philosopher Victoria, Lady Welby, who corresponded with Peirce and, like him, was somewhat on the margins of Edwardian intellectual culture. See Welby, *What Is Meaning? Studies in the Development of Significance* (London: Macmillan & Co., 1903),

Notes on pages 206–207

and Charles S. Peirce, *Semiotic and Significs: The Correspondence between Charles S. Peirce and Victoria, Lady Welby*, ed. Charles S. Hardwick (Bloomington, IN: Indiana University Press, 1977).

2 See Nathan Houser, 'The Fortunes and Misfortunes of the Peirce Papers', in *Signs of Humanity*, ed. Michel Balat and Janice Deledalle-Rhodes, 3 vols. (Berlin: Mouton de Gruyter, 1992), III, 1259–1268.

3 Jakob von Uexküll, *A Foray into the Worlds of Animals and Humans: With a Theory of Meaning*, trans. Joseph D. O'Neil (Minneapolis: University of Minnesota Press, 2010), pp. 48–53, 139–146. See also Giorgio Agamben, *The Open: Man and Animal*, trans. Kevin Attell (Stanford, CA: Stanford University Press, 2004), pp. 39–47.

4 For overviews of biosemiotics and its history, see Jesper Hoffmeyer, *Biosemiotics: An Examination into the Signs of Life and the Life of Signs* (Scranton, PA: University of Scranton Press, 2008); and John Deely, *Four Ages of Understanding* (Toronto: University of Toronto Press, 2001). In 2005, the International Society for Biosemiotic Studies was founded and the journal *Biosemiotics* launched in 2008.

5 Wheeler, *Expecting the Earth*, pp. 21–22.

6 John Berger, 'Why Look at Animals?', in *About Looking* (New York: Pantheon, 1980), 3–28, p. 12.

7 Dario Martinelli, *A Critical Companion to Zoosemiotics: People, Paths, Ideas* (Dordrecht: Springer, 2010), p. 30.

8 Ibid., p. 8.

9 Hoffmeyer, 'Semiotic Freedom: An Emerging Force', in *Information and the Nature of Reality: From Physics to Metaphysics*, ed. Paul Davies and N. H. Gregersen (Cambridge: Cambridge University Press, 2010), 185–204, p. 164.

10 Donna Haraway, *When Species Meet* (Minneapolis: University of Minnesota Press, 2008), p. 4. See also Cary Wolfe, *What Is Posthumanism?* (Minneapolis, MN: University of Minnesota Press, 2010); Timothy Morton, *The Ecological Thought* (Cambridge, MA: Harvard University Press, 2010).

11 Maran, 'Biosemiotic Criticism', p. 262.

12 See Karen Barad, *Meeting the Universe Halfway: Quantum Physics and the Entanglement of Matter and Meaning* (Durham, NC: Duke University Press, 2007); Jane Bennett, *Vibrant Matter: A Political Ecology of Things* (Durham, NC: Duke University Press, 2010).

13 Scholars have also questioned the supposed historic pervasiveness of Cartesian dualism: see Keith Thomas, *Man and the Natural World: Changing Attitudes in England 1500–1800* (London: Allen Lane, 1983), pp. 33–36; and Rob Boddice, *A History of Attitudes and Behaviours toward Animals in Eighteenth- and Nineteenth-Century Britain: Anthropocentrism and the Emergence of Animals* (Lampeter, Ceredigion: Edwin Mellen Press, 2008), pp. 5–10.

14 Sleigh, for example, shows that 'cybernetic' models of communication based on studies of ants caused the latter to become associated with the loss of individuality in the 1930s. See *Six Legs Better*, pp. 165–166.

252   *Notes on pages 207–210*

15 On technological hermeneutics, see Don Ihde, *Postphenomenology and Technoscience: The Peking University Lectures* (Albany NJ: SUNY Press, 2009), pp. 63–74.

16 Wheeler, *The Whole Creature: Complexity, Biosemiotics and the Evolution of Culture* (London: Lawrence & Wishart, 2006), pp. 44–47, 101–102.

17 Alfred Russel Wallace was an exception here, denouncing vivisection in his later life, as well as promoting some socialist policies. See Martin Fichman, *An Elusive Victorian: The Evolution of Alfred Russel Wallace* (Chicago, IL: University of Chicago Press, 2004), pp. 126, 250–257.

18 Bhaba, *Location of Culture*, pp. 122, 89.

19 Michael Taussig, *Mimesis and Alterity: A Particular History of the Senses* (London: Routledge, 1993), xviii. See also Schwartz, *Culture of the Copy*, p. 11.

20 See Miller, *Novel and Police*, pp. 17–27.

21 Philip Ball, *Invisible: The Dangerous Allure of the Unseen* (London: Bodley Head, 2014), pp. 2–5.

22 Butler, *Gender Trouble*.

23 Mulvey, 'Visual Pleasure', pp. 6–18.

24 Kath Woodward, *The Politics of In/Visibility* (Basingstoke: Palgrave Macmillan, 2015), pp. 12–15.

25 Eric Mielants, 'Reaction and Resistance: The Natural Sciences and the Humanities, 1789–1945', in *Overcoming the Two Cultures: Science versus the Humanities in the Modern World-System*, ed. Richard E. Lee and Immanuel Wallerstein (New York: Routledge, 2016), 34–54, pp. 34–38.

26 Daston and Galison, *Objectivity*, pp. 229–231.

27 Smith, *Fact and Feeling: Baconian Science and the Nineteenth-Century Literary Imagination* (Madison, WI: University of Wisconsin Press, 1994).

28 Philipp Erchinger, *Artful Experiments: Ways of Knowing in Victorian Literature and Science* (Edinburgh: Edinburgh University Press, 2018).

29 Cott, *Adaptive Coloration*, p. 2.

30 Roger Caillois, 'Mimicry and Legendary Psychasthenia' [1935], trans. John Shepley, *October*, 31 (1984), 16–32; *The Mask of Medusa*, trans. George Ordish (London: Victor Gollancz, 1964). On biological mimicry in the mid-twentieth-century, see Cheng, 'Mask, Mimicry, Metamorphosis'; Lomas, 'Artist-Sorcerers'.

31 Walter Benjamin, 'On the Mimetic Faculty', in *Selected Writings, 1926–1934*, trans. Edmund Jephcott, ed. Michael W. Jennings, Howard Eiland and Gary Smith, 4 vols. (Cambridge, MA: Belknap Press, 1999), II, 720–722.

32 Jacques Lacan, *The Four Fundamental Concepts of Psychoanalysis*, trans. A. Sheridan (London: Penguin, 1977), p. 107.

33 Jacques Derrida, *The Animal That Therefore I Am*, trans. David Wills (New York: Fordham University Press, 2008), pp. 119–125; Luce Irigaray, *This Sex Which Is Not One* (Ithaca, NY: Cornell University Press, 1985), p. 76.

34 D. H. Lawrence, 'Self-Protection', in *The Complete Poems of D. H. Lawrence*, ed. Vivian de Sola Pinto and F. Warren Roberts, 3 vols. (New York: Viking, 1964), 523.

Notes on pages 210–213

35 Vladimir Nabokov, *Nabokov's Butterflies*, ed. Brian Boyd and Robert Pyle (New York: Beacon Press, 2000), p. 85. See Victoria N. Alexander, 'Nabokov, Teleology, and Insect Mimicry', *Nabokov Studies*, 7 (2002/2003), 177–213.

36 Nabokov, *Lectures on Literature*, ed. Fredson Bowers (London: Harvest, 1982), p. 5.

37 Alain LeRoy Locke, 'Sterling Brown: The New Negro Folk-Poet', in *Voices from the Harlem Renaissance*, ed. Nathan Irvin Huggins (Oxford: Oxford University Press, 1976), 251–259, p. 253.

38 Robert Greenfield, *Dreamer's Journey: The Life and Writings of Frederic Prokosch* (Newark: University of Delaware Press, 2010), p. 65.

39 Mylène Dressler, *The Deadwood Beetle* (New York: Penguin, 2002), pp. 13–14.

40 Ernest Thompson Seton, *Wild Animals I Have Known* (New York: Scribner, 1898), p. 108. On the realistic animal story, see Ralph H. Lutts, *The Nature Fakers: Wildlife, Science and Sentiment* (Charlottesville: University of Virginia Press, 2001).

41 John Burroughs, *Ways of Nature* (New York: Houghton, Mifflin & Co., 1905), p. 73.

42 Ibid., pp. 248–250.

43 Roosevelt, 'Nature Fakers', *Everybody's Magazine*, 17:3 (1907), 423–427.

44 John Fowles, *The French Lieutenant's Woman* (London: Vintage, 1996), pp. 145–146. Although Darwin described examples of cryptic coloration in *Origin*, he did not actually use this phrase.

45 A. S. Byatt, 'Morpho Eugenia', in *Angels & Insects* (London: Vintage, 1995), 1–160, pp. 19–21, 49–54.

46 Ibid., p. 119.

47 Edward Bullough, 'Psychical Distance as a Factor in Art and an Aesthetic Principle', *British Journal of Psychology*, 5:2 (1912), 87–118, p. 99.

48 See Rad Borislavov, 'Revolution Is Evolution: Evolution as a Trope in Šklovskij's Literary History', *Russian Literature*, 69:2 (2012), 209–238.

49 See Hugh Ridley, *Darwin Becomes Art: Aesthetic Vision in the Wake of Darwin: 1870–1920* (New York: Rodopi, 2014), pp. 203–208.

50 See, for example, William K. Wimsatt and Monroe C. Beardsley, 'The Intentional Fallacy' and 'The Affective Fallacy', in *The Verbal Icon: Studies in the Meaning of Poetry* (Lexington, KY: University Press of Kentucky, 1954), 3–20, 21–40.

51 See Joseph Carroll, *Reading Human Nature: Literary Darwinism in Theory and Practice* (Albany, NY: SUNY Press, 2011); Brian Boyd, *On the Origin of Stories: Evolution, Cognition, and Fiction* (Cambridge, MA: Harvard University Press, 2009).

52 Stephen Best and Sharon Marcus, 'Surface Reading: An Introduction', *Representations*, 108:1 (2009), 1–21, pp. 3–6.

53 See Franco Moretti, *Distant Reading* (London: Verso, 2013).

54 As Donald D. Hoffman comments, 'Perception has not evolved to report truth, but instead to guide adaptive behavior within a niche': 'The

Construction of Visual Reality', in *Hallucinations: Research and Practice*, eds. Jan Dirk Blom and Iris E. C. Sommer (New York: Springer, 2012), 7–15, abstract.

55 Morton, *Ecological Thought*, p. 18.

56 Chris Jordan, 'Midway: Message from the Gyre' (2009), www.chrisjordan .com/gallery/midway/ <accessed 20/04/2018>.

57 See Wolfe, *Posthumanism*, pp. 31–48.

58 See Peter Singer, *Animal Liberation: A New Ethics for Our Treatment of Animals* (London: Jonathan Cape, 1990).

Bibliography

PRIMARY SOURCES

Allen, Francis H. 'Remarks on the Case of Roosevelt vs. Thayer, with a Few Independent Suggestions on the Concealing Coloration Question', *The Auk*, 29:4 (1912), 489–507.

Allen, Grant. *An African Millionaire* (London: G. Richards, 1898).

'Bates of the Amazons', *Fortnightly Review*, 58 (December 1892), 798–809.

The British Barbarians (London: G. P. Putnam's Sons, 1895).

The Colour-Sense: Its Origin and Development (London: Trübner & Co., 1879).

'The Curate of Churnside', *Cornhill Magazine*, 3:15 (September 1884), 225–258.

'The Curate of Churnside', in *Strange Stories* (London: Chatto and Windus, 1884), 66–99.

'Democracy and Diamonds', *Contemporary Review*, 59 (May 1891), 666–677.

The Devil's Die (New York: F. M. Lupton, 1890).

'[Review of] *Dynamic Sociology, or Applied Social Science, as Based upon Statical Sociology and the Less Complex Sciences* by Lester F. Ward', *Mind*, 9 (April 1884), 305–311.

The Evolutionist at Large (London: Chatto & Windus, 1881).

'False Pretences', in *In Nature's Workshop* (London: George Newnes, 1901), 29–59.

'Fiction and Mrs. Grundy', *Novel Review*, 2 (1892), 294–315.

'The Human Face Divine', *New Quarterly Magazine*, 2 (July 1879), 166–182.

Letter to George Croom Robertson, 23 February 1885, Robertson Papers, University College Library, University of London, MS.Add.88/12.

Letter to Wallace, 24 April 1899, British Library, Manuscripts, Add. MS.46441, f. 188.

'Masquerades and Disguises', in *Nature's Workshop*, 88–115.

'Mimicry', in *Encyclopædia Britannica*, 9th ed., 25 vols. (1875–1880), XVI.

'The Monopolist Instincts', in *Post-Prandial Philosophy* (London: Chatto & Windus, 1894), 79–86.

'Natural Inequality', in *Hand and Brain*, ed. Elbert Hubbard (New York: Roycroft, 1898), 65–86.

'The New Hedonism', *Fortnightly Review*, 55 (March 1894), 377–392.

'The Next Presentation', in *Sir Theodore's Guest and Other Stories* (Bristol: J. W. Arrowsmith, 1902), 237–276.

'Novels without a Purpose', *North American Review*, 163 (August 1896), 223–235.

'Personal Reminiscences of Herbert Spencer', *Forum*, 35 (April 1904), 610–628.

Physiological Aesthetics (New York: Garland, 1877).

'Science. *Freaks and Marvels of Plant Life* by M. C. Cooke', *The Academy*, 21 (4 February 1882), 85–86.

'Our Scientific Observations on a Ghost', in *Strange Stories* (London: Chatto and Windus, 1884), 321–340.

'A Scribbler's Apology', *Cornhill Magazine*, 47 (May 1883), 538–550.

'Sight and Smell in Vertebrates', *Mind*, 6 (October 1881), 453–471.

'Strictly Incog.', *Cornhill Magazine*, 8:44 (February 1887), 142–157.

'The Trade of Author', *Fortnightly Review*, 51:45 (February 1889), 261–274.

'Woman's Intuition', *Forum*, 10 (1890), 333–340.

Allen, J. A. 'The Concealing Coloration Question', *The Auk*, 30:2 (1913), 311–317.

'Roosevelt's "Revealing and Concealing Coloration in Birds and Mammals"', *The Auk*, 28:4 (1911), 472–480.

Arnold, Matthew. *Literature and Dogma: An Essay towards a Better Apprehension of the Bible* (London: T. Nelson & Sons, 1873).

'The Study of Poetry', in *Essays in Criticism*, ed. Susan. S. Sheridan (Boston: Allyn & Bacon, 1896), 1–31.

Bagehot, Walter. *Physics and Politics* (London: Kegan Paul, 1881).

Bain, Alexander. 'Animal Instincts and Intelligence', *Chambers' Papers for the People*, vol. XI (Edinburgh: William and Robert Chambers, 1850), 1–32.

Baldwin, James Mark. *The Individual and Society; or, Psychology and Sociology* (Boston: Badger, 1911).

Barbour, Thomas. 'A Different Aspect of the Case of Roosevelt vs. Thayer', *The Auk*, 30:1 (1913), 81–91.

Barbour, Thomas and Phillips, John C. 'Concealing Coloration Again', *The Auk*, 28:2 (1911), 179–188.

Barnum, P. T. *The Humbugs of the World* (New York: Carleton, 1866).

Bates, Henry Walter. 'Contributions to an Insect Fauna of the Amazon Valley. Lepidoptera: Heliconidæ', *Transactions of the Linnean Society of London*, 23 (1862), 495–566.

'Excursion to St. Paulo, Upper Amazons', *The Zoologist*, 16 (1858), 6160–6169.

The Naturalist on the River Amazons, 2 vols. (London: J. Murray, 1863).

Beddard, Frank Evers. *Animal Coloration* (London: Swan Sonnenschein & Co., 1892).

Bey, Major Osman. *The Conquest of the World by the Jews*, trans. F. W. Mathias (St. Louis, MO: St. Louis Book Club & News Company, 1878).

Blathwayt, Raymond. 'A Chat with the Author of *Tess*', *Black and White*, 4 (27 August 1892), 238–240.

Bibliography

Bon, Gustave Le. *The Crowd: A Study of the Popular Mind* (New York: Macmillan, 1896).

Braddon, Mary Elizabeth. *Henry Dunbar*, 3 vols. (London: John Maxwell & Co., 1864).

Brougham, Lord Henry. *Dissertations on Subjects of Science Connected with Natural Theology*, 2 vols. (London: C. Knight & Co., 1839).

Bullough, Edward. 'Psychical Distance as a Factor in Art and an Aesthetic Principle', *British Journal of Psychology*, 5:2 (1912), 87–118.

Burroughs, John. *Ways of Nature* (New York: Houghton, Mifflin & Co., 1905).

[Butler, Samuel] ETHICS, 'A Clergyman's Doubts', *Examiner*, 8 March 1879, 303–304.

Byatt, A. S. 'Morpho Eugenia', in *Angels & Insects* (London: Vintage, 1995), 1–160.

Caine, Hall. 'The Influence of Ruskin', *Bookman*, 35:205 (1908), 26–34.

Carlyle, Thomas. 'Corn-Law Rhymes', *Edinburgh Review*, 55 (July 1832), 338–361.

    On Heroes, Hero-Worship and the Heroic in History (London: James Fraser, 1841).

    Sartor Resartus (Philadelphia: James Munroe & Co., 1837).

Chalmers, Thomas. *The First Bridgewater Treatise on the Power, Wisdom, and Goodness of God as Manifested in the Creation: On the Adaptation of External Nature to the Moral and Intellectual Constitution of Man* (London: William Pickering, 1833).

Chemmachery, Jaine. 'Lies and Self-Censorship in Kipling's Indian Stories', *Kipling Journal*, 88:353 (2014), 32–44.

'"Colin Clout" at Home. An Interview with Mr. Grant Allen', *Pall Mall Gazette* (4 November 1889), 1–2.

'The Conflict between "Human" and "Female" Feminism', *Current Opinion*, 56 (April 1914), 291–292.

Cott, Hugh B. *Adaptive Coloration in Animals* (London: Methuen, 1940).

Dale, A. W. W. 'George Dawson', in *Nine Famous Birmingham Men*, ed. J. Muirhead (Birmingham: Cornish, 1909), 75–108.

Darwin, Charles. *Charles Darwin's Beagle Diary*, ed. Richard Darwin Keynes (Cambridge: Cambridge University Press, 1988).

    'Contributions to an Insect Fauna of the Amazon Valley. By Henry Walter Bates, Esq. Transact. Linnean Soc. Vol. XXIII. 1862, p. 495', *Natural History Review*, 3 (1863), 219–224.

    Darwin on Man, ed. Howard Gruber and Paul Barrett (London: Wildwood, 1974).

    The Descent of Man, 2 vols. (London: John Murray, 1871).

    Letter to Henry Walter Bates, 4 April 1861, *Darwin Correspondence Project*, www.darwinproject.ac.uk/letter/DCP-LETT-3109.xml <accessed 14/05/2018>.

Bibliography

Letter to Bates, 25 September 1861, *Darwin Correspondence Project*, www .darwinproject.ac.uk/letter/DCP-LETT-3266.xml <accessed 4/25/2018>.

Letter to Charles Lyell, 4 May 1860, *Darwin Correspondence Project*, www .darwinproject.ac.uk/letter/DCP-LETT-2782.xml <accessed 14/05/2018>.

'Old and Useless Notes about the Moral Sense & Some Metaphysical Points' (1838–1840), ed. Paul H. Barrett, *Darwin Online*, http://darwin-online.org .uk/content/frameset?pageseq=1&itemID=CUL-DAR91.4-55&viewtype= text <accessed 14/05/2018>.

On the Origin of Species (London: John Murray, 1859).

On the Various Contrivances by Which British and Foreign Orchids Are Fertilised by Insects (London: John Murray, 1862).

Darwin, Erasmus. *Zoonomia; or, The Laws of Organic Life*, 2 vols. (London: J. Johnson, 1794).

Dawson, George. 'Things Unseen', in *Shakespeare and Other Lectures*, ed. George St. Claire (London: Kegan Paul, 1888), 393–428.

De Quincey, William. 'On Murder Considered as One of the Fine Arts', *Blackwood's Magazine*, 20 (February 1827), 199–213.

Descartes, René. *Meditations on First Philosophy*, trans. Michael Moriarty (Oxford: Oxford University Press, 2008).

Dickens, Charles. 'The Battle of Life', in *A Christmas Carol, and Other Christmas Books* (London: J. M. Dent, 1907), 247–328.

Dowden, Edward. 'Walter Pater', in *Essays: Modern and Elizabethan* (London: J. M. Dent, 1910), 1–25.

Dressler, Mylène. *The Deadwood Beetle* (New York: Penguin, 2002).

Drummond, Henry. *Natural Law in the Spirit World* (New York: J. Pott, 1884).

Durkheim, Emile. *The Rules of Sociological Method* (New York: Free Press, 1938).

Eliot, George. *Middlemarch* (London: Penguin, 1994).

'The Morality of Wilhelm Meister', in *Selected Essays, Poems and Other Writings*, ed. A. S. Byatt and Nicholas Warren (Harmondsworth: Penguin, 1991), 307–310.

'The Natural History of German Life', *Westminster Review*, 66 (July 1856), 51–79.

Ellis, Havelock. 'A Note on Paul Bourget', in *Views and Reviews* (Boston: Houghton Mifflin, 1932), 48–60.

Fabre, Jean-Henri. *Souvenirs entomologiques: Etudes sur l'instinct et les moeurs des insects, troisième série* [1886] (Paris: Librarie Delagrave, 1923).

Fowles, John. *The French Lieutenant's Woman* (London: Vintage, 1996).

French, John Oliver. 'An Inquiry Respecting the True Nature of Instinct, and of the Mental Distinctions between Brute Animals and Man', *Zoological Journal*, 1 (1824), 1–32.

Galilei, Galileo. *The Essential Galileo*, ed. and trans. Maurice A. Finocchiaro (Cambridge: Hackett Publishing Company, 2008).

Galton, Francis. *Inquiries into Human Faculty and Its Development* (London: Macmillan, 1883).

'Personal Identification and Description', *Nature*, 38 (21 and 28 June 1888), 173–177, 201–202.

Gilman, Charlotte Perkins. 'The Beauty Women Have Lost', *Forerunner*, 1:11 (1910), 22–23.

The Crux (New York: Charlton Co., 1911).

The Dress of Women: A Critical Introduction to the Symbolism and Sociology of Clothing [collected from articles in *The Forerunner*], ed. Michael R. Hill and Mary Jo Deegan (Westport, CA: Greenwood Press, 2002).

'Her "Charms"', *Forerunner*, 6:1 (1915), 26.

Herland (New York: Pantheon, 1979).

The Living of Charlotte Perkins Gilman (New York: Harper & Row., 1975).

The Man-Made World (New York: Charlton Co., 1914).

'Modesty: Feminine and Other', *Independent*, 58 (29 June 1905), 1447–1450.

Moving the Mountain (New York: Charlton Co., 1911).

'Our Brains and What Ails Them', *The Forerunner*, 3:5 (May 1912), 133–139.

'The Shape of Her Dress', *Woman's Journal*, 35 (16 July 1904), 226.

'Symbolism in Dress', *Independent*, 58 (8 June 1905), 1294–1297.

'Why Women Do Not Reform Their Dress', *Woman's Journal* (23 October 1886), 338.

Women and Economics (Boston: Small, Maynard & Co., 1898).

Goldsmith, Oliver. *A History of the Earth, and Animated Nature*, 3 vols. (London: William Charlton Wright, 1824).

Gosse, Edmund. *The Life of Philip Henry Gosse* (London: Kegan Paul, 1890).

Gosse, Philip Henry. *The Aquarium: An Unveiling of the Wonders of the Deep Sea* (London: John Van Voorst, 1856).

Evenings at the Microscope (New York: Appleton, 1860).

Omphalos: An Attempt to Untie the Geological Knot (London: Van Voorst, 1857).

Green, Alice Stopford. *A Woman's Place in the World of Letters* (London: Macmillan, 1913).

Gummere, Francis B. 'Originality and Convention in Literature', *Quarterly Review*, 204 (January 1906), 26–44.

Haggard, Henry Rider. *King Solomon's Mines* (Oxford: Oxford University Press, 2008).

Hampson, George F. 'Protective- and Pseudo-Mimicry', *Nature*, 57 (17 February 1898), 364.

Hardy, Thomas. 'Candour in English Fiction', in *Thomas Hardy's Personal Writings*, ed. Harold Orel (Basingstoke: Palgrave Macmillan, 1990), 125–133.

The Collected Letters of Thomas Hardy, ed. Richard Little Purdy, Michael Millgate and Keith Wilson, 8 vols. (Oxford: Clarendon Press, 1878–2012).

Desperate Remedies, ed. Patricia Ingham (Oxford: Oxford University Press, 2003).

Far from the Madding Crowd, ed. Rosemarie Morgan and Shannon Russell (London: Penguin, 2000).

260 *Bibliography*

'For Conscience' Sake', in *Life's Little Ironies* (London: Harper & Brothers, 1920), 55–74.

'Heredity', in *Thomas Hardy: The Complete Poems*, ed. James Gibson (Basingstoke: Palgrave Macmillan, 2001).

'An Imaginative Woman', in *Life's Little Ironies*, 3–31.

Jude the Obscure, ed. Dennis Taylor (London: Penguin, 1998).

'Lady Mottisfont', in *A Group of Noble Dames* (London: Macmillan & Co., 1903), 129–152.

A Laodicean, ed. John Schad (London: Penguin, 1997), 81–82.

The Life and Work of Thomas Hardy, ed. Michael Millgate (London: Macmillan, 1984).

The Literary Notebooks of Thomas Hardy, ed. Lennart A. Bjork, 2 vols. (Basingstoke: Palgrave Macmillan).

'The Marchioness of Stonehenge', in *Noble Dames*, 107–128.

The Mayor of Casterbridge, ed. Dale Kramer (Oxford: Oxford University Press, 2004).

A Pair of Blue Eyes, ed. Pamela Dalziel (London: Penguin, 1998).

'The Pedigree', in *Poems*, 460–461.

'The Profitable Reading of Fiction', in *Personal Writings*, 110–124.

The Return of the Native, ed. Simon Gatrell (Oxford: Oxford University Press, 2005).

'The Science of Fiction', *Personal Writings*, 134–138.

'Squire Petrick's Lady', *Noble Dames*, 171–186.

Tess of the d'Urbervilles, ed. Tim Dolin (London: Penguin, 1998).

Thomas Hardy's 'Facts' Notebook, ed. William Greenslade (New York: Routledge, 2016).

The Well-Beloved, in *The Pursuit of the Well-Beloved and The Well-Beloved*, ed. Patricia Ingham (London: Penguin, 1997), 169–338.

The Woodlanders, ed. Dale Kramer (Oxford: Oxford University Press, 2005).

Hartmann, Eduard von. *Das Judentum in Gegenwart und Zukunft* (Berlin: Wilhelm Friedrich, 1885).

The Philosophy of the Unconscious, trans. William Chatterton Coupland (London: Routledge, Trench, Trübner & Co., 1931).

Hegel, G. W. F. *The Phenomenology of Spirit*, trans. A. V. Miller (Oxford: Oxford University Press, 1977).

Hume, David. *Dialogues Concerning Natural Religion* (London: Blackwood, 1907).

A Treatise of Human Nature (London: John Noon, 1739).

Hunt, James. 'On the Negro's Place in Nature', *Journal of the Anthropological Society of London*, 2 (1864), xv–lvi.

Huxley, Thomas Henry. 'Evolution and Ethics', in *Collected Essays*, 9 vols. (New York: Appleton, 1897), IX, 46–116.

'Evolution and Ethics – Prolegomena', in *Essays*, IX, 1–45.

'A Liberal Education and Where to Find It', in *Essays*, III, 76–110.

Bibliography

Life and Letters of Thomas Henry Huxley, ed. Leonard Huxley, 3 vols. (London: Macmillan, 1903).

Jacobs, Joseph. *Studies in Jewish Statistics, Social, Vital and Anthropometric* (London: D. Nutt, 1891).

James, William. *The Correspondence of William James*, ed. Ignas K. Skrupskelis and Elizabeth M. Berkley, 12 vols. (Charlottesville, VA: University Press of Virginia, 1997).

Principles of Psychology, 2 vols. (London: Macmillan, 1891).

Jones, Henry Festing. *The Note-Books of Samuel Butler* (New York: E. P. Dutton & Co., 1917).

Kant, Immanuel. *Critique of Judgment*, trans. J. H. Bernard (New York: Hafner Press, 1951).

Kidd, Benjamin. *Social Evolution*, 2nd ed. (Macmillan & Co., 1894).

Kingsley, Charles. 'Bio-Geology', in *Scientific Lectures and Essays* (London: Macmillan, 1880), 155–180.

Charles Kingsley: His Letters and Memories of His Life, ed. F. Kingsley, 2 vols. (London: King, 1877).

Glaucus: Wonders of the Shore (London: Macmillan, 1890).

The Gospel of the Pentateuch (London: Parker, 1863).

'How to Study Natural History', in *Scientific Lectures*, 289–312.

Madame How and Lady Why (London: Macmillan, 1869).

'The Natural Theology of the Future', in *Scientific Lectures*, 313–336.

'On English Composition', in *Literary and General Lectures and Essays* (London: Macmillan, 1898), 229–244.

'President's Address', *Report and Transactions of the Devonshire Association for the Advancement of Science, Literature and Art*, 4:1 (1871), 377–395.

'The Study of Natural History', in *Scientific Lectures*, 181–200.

'The Value of Law', in *Sermons on National Subjects* (London: Macmillan, 1880), 265–275.

The Water-Babies (New York: Cromwell, 1895).

Yeast: A Problem (London: J. W. Parker, 1851).

Kingsley, Charles and Newman, John Henry. *Mr. Kingsley and Dr. Newman: A Correspondence on the Question Whether Dr. Newman Teaches That Truth Is No Virtue?* (London: Longman, Green, Longman, Roberts and Green, 1864).

Kipling, Rudyard. *The Jungle Book* (New York: The Century Co., 1894).

Kirby, William. *The Seventh Bridgewater Treatise on the Power, Wisdom, and Goodness of God as Manifested in the Creation: The History, Habits and Instincts of Animals*, 2 vols. (London: William Pickering, 1835).

Kirby, William and Spence, William. *An Introduction to Entomology*, 4 vols. (London: Longman, Rees, Orme, Brown and Green, 1815–1826).

Landels, William. *How Men Are Made* (London: J. Heaton, 1859).

Lankester, E. R. *Science from an Easy Chair* (London: Metheuen & Co., 1910).

Latham, G. R. *The Natural History of the Varieties of Man* (London: John Van Voorst, 1850).

262 *Bibliography*

Lavater, Johann Caspar. *Essays on Physiognomy*, trans. Thomas Holcroft (London: W. Tegg, 1862).

Lawrence, D. H. 'Self-Protection', in *The Complete Poems of D. H. Lawrence*, ed. Vivian de Sola Pinto and F. Warren Roberts, 3 vols. (New York: Viking, 1964), 523.

Lewes, G. H. *Problems of Life and Mind, First Series*, 2 vols. (Boston: James R. Osgood, 1875).

Locke, Alain LeRoy. 'Sterling Brown: The New Negro Folk-Poet', in *Voices from the Harlem Renaissance*, ed. Nathan Irvin Huggins (Oxford: Oxford University Press, 1976), 251–259.

Locke, John. *An Essay Concerning Human Understanding*, 3 vols. (Edinburgh: Mundell & Sons, 1801).

Lombroso, Cesare. 'Nordau's "Degeneration": Its Value and its Errors', *The Century*, 50 (May–October 1895), 936–940.

Lombroso, Gina. *Criminal Man According to the Classification of Cesare Lombroso Briefly Summarized by His Daughter Gina Lombroso* (New York: G. P. Putnam, 1911).

Lubbock, John. *The Pleasures of Life* (Philadelphia: Henry Altemus, 1894).

Maine, Henry Sumner. *Ancient Law: Its Connection with the Early History of Society and Its Relation to Modern Ideas* (London: John Murray, 1861).

Mansel, H. L. 'Sensation Novels', *Quarterly Review*, 113 (1863), 481–514.

Massey, Gerald. 'Poetry – The Spasmodists', *North British Review*, 28:55 (1858), 231–250.

Maudsley, Henry. *Body and Will* (London: Kegan Paul, Trench, & Co., 1883).
Natural Causes and Supernatural Seemings (London: K. Paul, Trench & Co., 1886).
The Pathology of Mind (New York: D. Appleton & Co., 1880).

Maurice, Frederick Denison. *What Is Revelation?* (Cambridge: Macmillan, 1859).

Mayne, Fanny. 'The Literature of the Working Classes', *Englishwoman's Magazine and Christian Mother's Miscellany*, NS 5 (October 1850), 619–622.

McAtee, Lee Waldo. 'The Experimental Method of Testing the Efficiency of Warning and Cryptic Coloration in Protecting Animals from Their Enemies', *Proceedings of the Academy of Natural Sciences of Philadelphia*, 64 (1912), 281–364.

McLennan, John Ferguson. *Primitive Marriage* (Edinburgh: Adam & Charles Black, 1865).

Mill, John Stuart. *On Liberty* (Indianapolis, IN: Bobbs-Merrill, 1956).

Morgan, Lewis Henry. *Ancient Society* (New York: Henry Holt & Co., 1878).

Morley, John. *On Compromise* (London: Macmillan & Co., 1874).

Müller, Friedrich Max. *A History of Ancient Sanskrit Literature so Far as It Illustrates the Primitive Religion of the Brahmans* (London: Williams and Norgate, 1860).

Müller, Fritz. 'Ituna and Thyridia: A Remarkable Case of Mimicry in Butterflies', trans. Raphael Meldola, *Proceedings of the Entomological Society of London* (1879), 20–29.

Bibliography

'Über die Vortheile der Mimicry bei Schmetterlingen', *Zoologischer Anzeiger*, 1 (1875), 54–55.

Murray, Andrew. 'Mimicry and Hybridisation', *Nature*, 3:60 (1870), 154–156.

On the Disguises of Nature; Being an Inquiry into the Laws Which Regulate External Form and Colour in Plants and Animals (Edinburgh: Neill & Co., 1859).

Nabokov, Vladimir. *Lectures on Literature*, ed. Fredson Bowers (London: Harvest, 1982).

Nabokov's Butterflies, ed. Brian Boyd and Robert Pyle (New York: Beacon Press, 2000).

Newman, John Henry. *An Essay in Aid of a Grammar of Assent*, ed. Ian Ker (Oxford: Clarendon, 1985).

Nietzsche, Friedrich. *The Dawn of Day*, trans. Johanna Volz (London: T. F. Unwin, 1903).

The Gay Science, trans. Walter Kaufmann (New York: Vintage, 1974).

'On Truth and Lie in a Nonmoral Sense', in *On Truth and Untruth: Selected Writings*, trans. and ed. Taylor Carman (London: HarperCollins, 2010), 15–50.

Nordau, Max. *Degeneration* (London: Heinemann, 1895).

'Max Nordau's Address on the Situation of the Jews throughout the World' [1897], in *The Jubilee of the First Zionist Congress, 1897–1947* (Jerusalem: The Executive of the Zionist Organization, 1947), 56–62.

Zionism: Its History and Aims (New York: Federation of American Zionists, 1905).

Packard, Alpheus Spring. 'The Origin of the Markings of Organisms (Pœcilogenesis) Due to the Physical Rather than to the Biological Environment; With Criticisms of the Bates-Müller Hypotheses', *Proceedings of the American Philosophical Society*, 43:178 (1904), 393–450.

A Text-Book of Entomology (London: Macmillan & Co., 1898).

Paine, Thomas. *The Age of Reason* (London: Freethought, 1880).

Paley, William. *Natural Theology; or, Evidences of the Existence and Attributes of the Deity* (London: J. Faulder, 1809).

Pater, Walter. 'Coleridge', in *Appreciations* (London: Macmillan & Co., 1889), 64–106.

Marius the Epicurean: His Sensations and Ideas (London: Macmillan & Co., 1885).

Plato and Platonism (London: Macmillan & Co., 1893).

The Renaissance: Studies in Art and Poetry, 3rd ed. (London: Macmillan, 1888).

'Style', in *Appreciations*, 1–36.

'Wordsworth', in *Appreciations*, 37–63.

Peirce, Charles S. *Semiotic and Significs: The Correspondence between Charles S. Peirce and Victoria, Lady Welby*, ed. Charles S. Hardwick (Bloomington: Indiana University Press, 1977).

Poulton, Edward Bagnall. 'A Brief Discussion of A. H. Thayer's Suggestions as to the Meaning of Colour and Pattern in Insect Bionomics', *Transactions of the Entomological Society of London*, 51 (1903), 570–575.

Bibliography

The Colours of Animals (London: Kegan Paul, Trench, Trübner & Co., 1890).

'The Experimental Proof of the Protective Value of Colour and Markings in Insects', *Proceedings of the Zoological Society of London*, 55:2 (1887), 191–274.

John Viriamu Jones and Other Oxford Memories (London: Longmans, 1911).

'Mimicry in Butterflies of the Genus Hypolimnas and Its Bearing on Older and More Recent Theories of Mimicry', *Proceedings of the American Association for the Advancement of Science*, 46 (1897), 242–244.

'Notes upon, or Suggested by, the Colours, Markings, and Protective Attitudes of Certain Elpidopterous Larvae and Pupae, and of a Phytophagous Hymenopterous Larva', *Transactions of the Entomological Society of London*, 32:1 (1884), 27–60.

Powell, Baden. 'On the Study of the Evidence of Christianity', in *Essays and Reviews*, ed. John William Parker (London: J. W. Parker, 1860), 94–144.

Powell, C. H. 'The Invisibility of the Soldier', *Blackwood's Edinburgh Magazine*, 166 (December 1899), 836–846.

Prichard, James Cowles. *A Treatise on Insanity and Other Disorders Affecting the Mind* (London: Sherwood, Gilbert, and Piper, 1835).

Richards, Grant. 'Mr. Grant Allen and His Work', *Novel Review*, 1:3 (June 1892), 261–268.

Ritchie, David George. *Darwinism and Politics* (London: Swan Sonnenschein, 1889).

Romanes, George. 'Mental Differences between Men and Women', *Nineteenth Century*, 31 (May 1887), 383–401.

Mental Evolution in Man: Origin of Human Faculty (London: Kegan Paul, Trench & Co., 1888).

Thoughts on Religion (London: Longmans, Green and Co., 1896).

Roosevelt, Theodore. 'Nature Fakers', *Everybody's Magazine*, 17:3 (1907), 423–427.

'Revealing and Concealing Coloration in Birds and Mammals', *Bulletin of the American Museum of Natural History*, 30 (1911), 119–231.

Rousseau, Jean-Jacques. 'Discourse on the Origin of Inequality', in *The Social Contract and Other Discourses*, trans. G. D. H. Cole (London: Dent, 1973), 27–113.

Ruskin, John. The Eagle's Nest [1872], in *The Complete Works of John Ruskin*, ed. E. T. Cook and Alexander Wedderburn, 39 vols. (London: George Allen, 1903–1912), XXII, 115–292.

The Elements of Drawing [1857], in *Works*, XV, 1–232.

'The Light of the World' [1854], in *Works*, XII, 328–332.

Modern Painters, II [1846], in *Works*, IV, 25–218.

Modern Painters, III [1856], in *Works*, V, 1–430.

Proserpina [1875], in *Works*, XXV, 191–552.

The Queen of the Air [1869], in *Works*, XIX, 283–426.

The Seven Lamps of Architecture [1849], in *Works*, VIII.

The Stones of Venice [1851], in *Works*, IX–XI.

Bibliography

Santayana, George. *The Sense of Beauty* (New York: C. Scribner's Sons, 1896).

Schopenhauer, Arthur. *Studies in Pessimism*, trans. T. Bailey Saunders (London: Swan Sonnenschein & Co., 1893).

The World as Will and Idea, trans. R. B. Haldane and J. Kemp, 3 vols. (London: Trübner & Co., 1886).

Seton, Ernest Thompson. *Wild Animals I Have Known* (New York: Scribner, 1898).

Shakespeare, William. *The Two Gentlemen of Verona*, ed. Norman Sanders (London: Penguin, 2005).

Sharp, David. 'Natural Selection', *Athenaeum* (15 December 1866), 796–797.

Shaw, George Bernard. 'John Bull's Other Island', in *John Bull's Other Island and Major Barbara* (New York: Brentano's, 1908), 1–26.

'Mr. Grant Allen's New Novel', *Pall Mall Gazette* (April 24, 1888), 3.

Sidgwick, Henry. *Methods of Ethics* (London: Macmillan & Co., 1874).

Smart, Benjamin Humphrey. *An Outline of Sematology* (London: John Richardson, 1831).

Spencer, Herbert. *The Data of Ethics* (London: Williams & Norgate, 1879).

First Principles of a New System of Philosophy (London: Williams & Norgate, 1862).

'The Morals of Trade', *Westminster Review*, 71 (April 1859), 357–390.

'Psychology of the Sexes', *Popular Science Monthly*, 4 (November 1873), 30–38.

'The Social Organism', in *Essays: Scientific, Political, Speculative, Second Series* (London: Williams & Norgate, 1863), 143–184.

Social Statics (London: Chapman, 1851).

Sprengel, Christian Konrad. *Das entdeckte Geheimnis der Natur im Bau und der Befruchtung der Blumen* (Berlin: F. Vieweg, 1793).

Stephen, Leslie. 'An Attempted Philosophy of History', *Fortnightly Review* (April 1880), 672–695.

'Darwinism and Divinity', *Fraser's Magazine*, 5:28 (1872), 409–421.

'The Decay of Murder', *Cornhill Magazine*, 20 (December 1869), 722–733.

History of English Thought in the Eighteenth Century, 2 vols. (London: Smith, Elder & Co., 1876).

The Science of Ethics (London: Smith, Elder & Co., 1882).

Social Rights and Duties, 2 vols. (London: Swan Sonnenschein, 1896).

Stewart, Dugald. 'On the Tendency of some Late Philological Speculations', in *The Works of Dugald Stewart*, 7 vols. (Cambridge: Hilliard and Brown, 1829), IV, 141–180.

Strickland, Hugh Edwin. 'On the Method of Discovering the Natural System in Zoology and Botany', *Annals and Magazine of Natural History*, 6 (1841), 184–194.

Sully, James. '[Review of] Grant Allen, *The Colour-Sense*', *Mind*, 4 (1879), 415–416.

Illusions: A Psychological Study (New York: Appleton, 1881).

Swinburne, Algernon Charles. 'Victor Hugo: L'Année Terrible', in *Essays and Studies* (London: Chatto & Windus, 1875), 17–59.

266 *Bibliography*

Thayer, Abbott Handerson. 'Introduction', in Thayer and Thayer, *Concealing-Coloration*, 3–12.

'The Law Which Underlies Protective Coloration', *The Auk*, 13:2 (1896), 124–129.

'Protective Coloration in Its Relation to Mimicry, Common Warning Colours, and Sexual Selection', *Transactions of the Entomological Society of London*, 51:4 (1903), 553–569.

Thayer, Gerald and Thayer, Abbott Handerson. *Concealing-Coloration in the Animal Kingdom* (New York: Macmillan, 1909).

Triplett, Norman. 'The Psychology of Conjuring Deceptions', *American Journal of Psychology*, 11:4 (1900), 439–510.

Tylor, E. B. *Primitive Culture*, 2 vols. (London: John Murray, 1871).

Wainewright, Thomas Griffiths. *Essays and Criticisms*, ed. Carew Hazlitt (London: Reeves & Turner, 1880).

Wallace, Alfred Russel. 'The Colours of Animals and Plants. I. – The Colours of Animals', *Macmillan's Magazine*, 36 (September 1877), 384–408.

Darwinism: An Exposition of the Theory of Natural Selection with Some of Its Applications (London: Macmillan & Co., 1889).

'The Disguises of Insects', in *Studies Scientific and Social*, 2 vols. (London: Macmillan & Co., 1900), I, 185–198.

The Malay Archipelago, 2 vols. (London: Macmillan & Co., 1869).

'Mimicry, and Other Protective Resemblances among Animals', *Westminster and Foreign Quarterly Review*, 32:1 (1867), 1–43.

Science and the Supernatural (London: F. Farrah, 1866).

Ward, Lester. *Dynamic Sociology* (New York: D. Appleton & Co., 1883).

Warner, Charles Dudley. 'How Shall Women Dress?', *North American Review*, 140 (June 1885), 557–564.

Watts(-Dunton), Theodore. 'Alfred, Lord Tennyson: A Memoir', *Athenaeum* (9 October 1897), 481–484.

'A Book of Rhyme by Augusta Webster', *Athenaeum* (20 August 1881) [attributed to Watts in *Life and Letters*, II, p. 283], 229–230.

'Bret Harte', *Athenaeum* (24 May 1902), 658–660.

'Ebenezer Jones', *Athenaeum* (28 September 1878), 401–403.

'Edgar Poe', *Athenaeum* (2 September 1876), 306.

'*Englishmen of Letters – Landor* by Sidney Colvin', *Athenaeum* (6 August 1881), 165–167.

'Joseph and His Brethren', *Examiner* (6 May 1876), 515–517.

'Letters of Dante Gabriel Rossetti to William Allingham, 1855–1870', *Athenaeum* (26 March 1898), 395–397.

The Life and Letters of Theodore Watts-Dunton, ed. Thomas Hake and Arthur Compton-Rickett, 2 vols. (London: T. C. & E. C. Jack, 1916).

'Lord Tennyson', *Athenaeum* (8 October 1892), 482–483.

'The Poetical Works of Percy Bysshe Shelley' [attributed in *Life and Letters*, II, p. 281], *Athenaeum* (29 September 1877), 396–400.

Poetry and the Renascence of Wonder (New York: E. P. Dutton, 1916).

Bibliography

'*The Water of the Wondrous Isles*. By William Morris', *Athenaeum* (4 December 1897), 777–779.

Weir, J. Jenner. 'On Insects and Insectivorous Birds', *Transactions of the Entomological Society of London* (1869), 21–26.

Weismann, August. *Essays upon Heredity and Kindred Biological Problems*, 2 vols. (Oxford: Clarendon Press, 1889–92).

Welby, Lady Victoria. *What Is Meaning? Studies in the Development of Significance* (London: Macmillan & Co., 1903).

Wells, H. G. *Love and Mr Lewisham* (London: Penguin, 2005).

Westwood, J. O. *An Introduction to the Modern Classification of Insects*, 2 vols. (London: Longman, Orme, Brown, Green and Longmans, 1839).

'Mimicry in Nature', *Athenæum* (8 December 1866), 753–754.

Wharton, Edith. 'The Eyes', in *Tales of Men and Ghosts* (New York: Charles Scribner's Sons, 1910), 241–274.

Whewell, William. *The Philosophy of the Inductive Sciences, Founded upon Their History*, 2 vols. (London: J. W. Parker, 1840).

Wilberforce, Samuel. '[Review of] *On the Origin of Species, by Means of Natural Selection*', *Quarterly Review*, 108 (1860), 225–264.

Wilde, Oscar. 'Béranger in England', in *The Complete Works of Oscar Wilde*, general ed. Ian Small, 8 vols. (Oxford: Oxford University Press, 2000–2017), VI, 73–74.

'The Critic as Artist', in *Works*, IV, 123–206.

'The Decay of Lying', in *Works*, IV, 72–103.

'De Profundis', in *Works*, II, 157–193.

'Historical Criticism', in *Works*, IV, 3–70.

'Lecture to Art Students', in *Essays and Lectures* (London: Methuen & Co., 1913), 197–212.

The Letters of Oscar Wilde, ed. Rupert Hart-Davis (London: Hart-Davis, 1962).

Oscar Wilde's Oxford Notebooks, ed. Philip E. Smith II and Michael S. Helfand (Oxford: Oxford University Press, 1989).

'Pen, Pencil and Poison: A Study in Green', *Fortnightly Review*, 45 (1889), 41–54.

'Phrases and Philosophies for the Use of the Young', *The Chameleon*, 1 (1894), 1–3.

The Picture of Dorian Gray, in *Works*, III, 1–357.

'Some Literary Notes' [May 1889], in *Works*, VII, 207–214.

'The Soul of Man under Socialism', in *Works*, IV, 231–268.

'The Truth of Masks', in *Works*, IV, 207–228.

Wood, J. G. *Sketches and Anecdotes of Animal Life* (London: Routledge, 1854).

Zangwill, Israel. *Children of the Ghetto* (London: Macmillan & Co., 1895).

'Fiesole and Florence', in *Without Prejudice* (New York: The Century Co., 1896), 294–298.

'The Future of the Jew', *Daily Mail* (8 September 1903), 4.

'The Future of the Jewish People' [1903], in *Speeches, Articles and Letters of Israel Zangwill*, ed. Maurice Simon (London: Soncino Press, 1937), 71–74.

268 Bibliography

'The Ghetto' [undated], in Speeches, Articles and Letters, 3–27.
'Hebrew, Jew and Israelite' [1892], in *Speeches, Articles and Letters*, 28–41.
'The Jewish Race' (1911), in Speeches, Articles and Letters of Israel Zangwill, 82–97.
'The Maccabaeans' [1893], in *Speeches, Articles and Letters*, 42–46.
The Melting-Pot: A Drama in Four Acts (New York: Macmillan, 1909).
'The New Jew' [1898], in *Speeches, Articles and Letters*, 54–63.
The Principle of Nationalities: Conway Memorial Lecture (London: Watts & Co., 1917).

SECONDARY SOURCES

Abberley, Will. *English Fiction and the Evolution of Language, 1850–1914* (Cambridge: Cambridge University Press, 2015).

Agamben, Giorgio. *The Open: Man and Animal*, trans. Kevin Attell (Stanford, CA: Stanford University Press, 2004).

Alexander, Victoria N. 'Nabokov, Teleology, and Insect Mimicry', *Nabokov Studies*, 7 (2002/2003), 177–213.

Allen, Judith A. *The Feminism of Charlotte Perkins Gilman: Sexualities, Histories, Progressivism* (London: University of Chicago Press, 2009).

Alpers, Paul. *What Is Pastoral?* (London: University of Chicago Press, 1996).

Amundson, Ron. 'Typology Reconsidered: Two Doctrines on the History of Evolutionary Biology', *Biology and Philosophy*, 13 (1998), 153–177.

Annan, Noel G. *Leslie Stephen: The Godless Victorian* (London: Weidenfeld and Nicolson, 1984).

Bailey, J. O. 'Evolutionary Meliorism in the Poetry of Thomas Hardy', *Studies in Philology*, 60:3 (1963), 569–587.

Ball, Philip. *Invisible: The Dangerous Allure of the Unseen* (London: Bodley Head, 2014).

Barad, Karen. *Meeting the Universe Halfway: Quantum Physics and the Entanglement of Matter and Meaning* (Durham, NC: Duke University Press, 2007).

Bargheer, Stefan. *Moral Entanglements: Conserving Birds in Britain and Germany* (London: University of Chicago Press, 2018).

Barton, Ruth. '"Men of Science": Language, Identity and Professionalization in the Mid-Victorian Scientific Community', *History of Science*, 41:1 (2003), 73–119.

Beauvoir, Simone de. *The Second Sex*, trans. E. M. Parshley (New York: Vintage, 1973).

Beer, Gillian. *Darwin's Plots: Evolutionary Narrative in Darwin, George Eliot and Nineteenth-Century Fiction*, 3rd ed. (Cambridge: Cambridge University Press, 2009).

Open Fields: Science in Cultural Encounter (Oxford: Oxford University Press, 1996).

Bibliography

Belknap, Geoffrey. 'Illustrating Natural History: Images, Periodicals, and the Making of Nineteenth-Century Scientific Communities', *British Journal for the History of Science*, 51:3 (2018), 395–422.

Benjamin, Walter. 'On the Mimetic Faculty', in *Selected Writings, 1926–1934*, trans. Edmund Jephcott, eds. Michael W. Jennings, Howard Eiland and Gary Smith, 4 vols. (Cambridge, MA: Belknap Press, 1999), II, 720–722.

Bennett, Jane. *Vibrant Matter: A Political Ecology of Things* (Durham, NC: Duke University Press, 2010).

Berger, John. 'Why Look at Animals?', in *About Looking* (New York: Pantheon, 1980), 3–28.

Berkeley CA, George. *An Essay towards a New Theory of Vision* (Dublin: J. Pepyat, 1709).

Best, Stephen and Marcus, Sharon. 'Surface Reading: An Introduction', *Representations*, 108:1 (2009), 1–21.

Bhaba, Homi. *The Location of Culture* (London: Routledge, 1994).

Blaisdell, Muriel. *Darwinism and Its Data: The Adaptive Coloration of Animals* (London: Garland Publishing, 1992).

Bloom, Harold. *The Anxiety of Influence: A Theory of Poetry*, 2nd ed. (Oxford: Oxford University Press, 1997).

Blum, Ann Shelby. *Picturing Nature: American Nineteenth-Century Zoological Illustration* (Princeton, NJ: Princeton University Press, 1993).

Boddice, Rob. *A History of Attitudes and Behaviours toward Animals in Eighteenth- and Nineteenth-Century Britain: Anthropocentrism and the Emergence of Animals* (Lampeter, Ceredigion: Edwin Mellen Press, 2008).

Borch, Christian *Foucault, Crime and Power: Problematisations of Crime in the Twentieth Century* (Abingdon: Routledge, 2015).

Borislavov, Rad. 'Revolution Is Evolution: Evolution as a Trope in Šklovskij's Literary History', *Russian Literature*, 69:2 (2012), 209–238.

Bowler, Peter J. *Evolution: The History of an Idea* (Berkeley: University of California Press, 2009).

  The Non-Darwinian Revolution: Reinterpreting a Historical Myth (Baltimore, MD: Johns Hopkins University Press, 1988).

Boyd, Brian. *On the Origin of Stories: Evolution, Cognition, and Fiction* (Cambridge, MA: Harvard University Press, 2009).

Brantlinger, Patrick. *The Reading Lesson: The Threat of Mass Literacy in Nineteenth-Century British Fiction* (Bloomington, IN: Indiana University Press, 1998).

Brewer, William D. *Staging Romantic Chameleon Imposters* (Basingstoke: Palgrave Macmillan, 2015).

Bristow, Joseph and Mitchell, Rebecca N. *Oscar Wilde's Chatterton: Literary History, Romanticism, and the Art of Forgery* (New Haven, CT: Yale University Press, 2015).

Brooke, John Hedley. *Science and Religion: Some Historical Perspectives* (Cambridge: Cambridge University Press, 1991).

Bibliography

Brower, Matthew. *Developing Animals: Wildlife and Early American Photography* (Minneapolis, MN: University of Minnesota Press, 2011).

Buckland, Adelene. *Novel Science: Fiction and the Invention of Nineteenth-Century Geology* (Chicago, IL: University of Chicago Press, 2013).

Buckler, William E. 'Wilde's "Trumpet against the Gate of Dullness": "The Decay of Lying"', *English Literature in Transition, 1880–1920*, 33:3 (1990), 311–323.

Bunn, Geoffrey C. *The Truth Machine: A Social History of the Lie Detector* (Baltimore, MD: Johns Hopkins University Press, 2012).

Burney, Ian. *Poison, Detection and the Victorian Imagination* (Manchester: Manchester University Press, 2006).

Butler, Judith. *Gender Trouble* (New York: Routledge, 1990).

Caillois, Roger. *The Mask of Medusa*, trans. George Ordish (London: Victor Gollancz, 1964).

'Mimicry and Legendary Psychasthenia' [1935], trans. John Shepley, *October*, 31 (1984), 16–32.

Camlot, Jason. *Style and the Nineteenth-Century British Critic: Sincere Mannerisms* (Aldershot: Ashgate, 2008).

Cao, Maggie M. 'Abbott Thayer and the Invention of Camouflage', *Art History*, 39:3 (2016), 486–511.

Carroll, Joseph. *Reading Human Nature: Literary Darwinism in Theory and Practice* (Albany, NY: SUNY Press, 2011).

Cheng, Joyce. 'Mask, Mimicry, Metamorphosis: Roger Caillois, Walter Benjamin and Surrealism in the 1930s', *Modernism/Modernity*, 16:1 (2009), 61–86.

Chitty, Susan. *The Beast and the Monk: A Life of Charles Kingsley* (London: Hodder & Stoughton, 1974).

Christensen, Tim. 'The Unbearable Whiteness of Being: Misrecognition, Pleasure, and White Identity in Kipling's *Kim*', *College Literature*, 39:2 (2012), 9–30.

Clark, Indy. *Thomas Hardy's Pastoral: An Unkindly May* (Basingstoke: Palgrave Macmillan, 2015).

Cogan, Frances B. *All-American Girl: The Ideal of Real Womanhood in Mid-Nineteenth-Century America* (Athens, GA: University of Georgia Press, 1989).

Cohn, Elisha. '"No insignificant creature": Thomas Hardy's Ethical Turn', *Nineteenth-Century Literature*, 64.4 (2010), 494–520.

Comte, Auguste. *System of Positive Polity: Social Dynamics*, trans. Harriet Martineau, 3 vols. (London: Longmans, Green & Co., 1876).

Conlin, Jonathan. 'An Illiberal Descent: Natural and National History in the Work of Charles Kingsley', *History*, 96 (2011), 167–187.

Conor, Liz. *The Spectacular Modern Woman: Feminine Visibility in the 1920s* (Bloomington, IN: Indiana University Press, 2004).

Corbett, Mary Jean. *Family Likeness: Sex, Marriage, and Incest from Jane Austen to Virginia Woolf* (London: Cornell University Press, 2008).

Crary, Jonathan. *Techniques of the Observer: On Vision and Modernity in the Nineteenth Century* (London: MIT Press, 1990).

Bibliography

Culler, Jonathan. *Literary Theory: A Very Short Introduction* (Oxford: Oxford University Press, 2011).

Cuvier, George. 'Analyse d'un ouvrage de M. Humboldt intitulé: Tableaux de la nature ou considérations sur les deserts, sur la physionomie des végétaux et sur les cataractes de l'Orenoque', Library of the Institut de France, Paris, Fonds Cuvier, MS 3159.

Danahay, Martin A. *A Community of One: Masculine Autobiography and Autonomy in Nineteenth-Century Britain* (Albany, NY: State University of New York Press, 1993).

Danson, Lawrence. *Wilde's Intentions: The Artist in His Criticism* (Oxford: Clarendon Press, 1997).

Daston, Lorraine. 'Scientific Objectivity with and without Words', in *Little Tools of Knowledge: Historical Essays on Academic and Bureaucratic Practices* (Ann Arbor, MI: University of Michigan Press, 2000).

Daston, Lorraine and Galison, Peter. *Objectivity* (New York: Zone Books, 2007).

Daston, Lorraine and Lunbeck, Elizabeth. 'Introduction: Observation Observed', in *Histories of Scientific Observation*, eds. Lorraine Daston and Elizabeth Lunbeck (London: University of Chicago Press, 2011), 1–10.

Davis, Cynthia J. *Charlotte Perkins Gilman: A Biography* (Stanford, CA: Stanford University Press, 2010).

Deely, John. *Four Ages of Understanding* (Toronto: University of Toronto Press, 2001).

Deleuze, Gilles and Guattari, Felix. *Kafka: Toward a Minor Literature*, trans. Dana Polan (Minneapolis, MN: University of Minnesota Press, 1986).

Derrida, Jacques. *The Animal That Therefore I Am*, trans. David Wills (New York: Fordham University Press, 2008).

DeWitt, Anne. *Moral Authority: Men of Science, and the Victorian Novel* (Cambridge: Cambridge University Press, 2013).

Diepeveen, Leonard. *The Difficulties of Modernism* (Abingdon: Routledge, 2003).

Dixon, Thomas. *The Invention of Altruism: Making Moral Meanings in Victorian Britain* (Oxford: Oxford University Press, 2008).

Dollimore, Jonathan. *Sexual Dissidence: Augustine to Wilde, Freud to Foucault* (Oxford: Clarendon, 1991).

Donald, Diana. *Picturing Animals in Britain, 1750–1850* (New Haven, CT: Yale University Press, 2007).

Donald, Diana and Munro, Jane (eds.). *Endless Forms: Charles Darwin, Natural Science and the Visual Arts* (New Haven, CT: Yale University Press, 2009).

Dowling, Linda. *Hellenism and Homosexuality in Victorian Oxford* (Ithaca, NY: Cornell University Press, 1996).

Language and Decadence: *Language and Decadence in the Victorian Fin de Siècle* (Princeton, NJ: Princeton University Press, 1986).

Doylen, Michael R. 'Oscar Wilde's *De Profundis*: Homosexual Self-Fashioning on the Other Side of Scandal', *Victorian Literature and Culture*, 27:2 (1999), 547–566.

Dröscher, Ariane. 'Pioneering Studies on Cephalopod's Eye and Vision at the Stazione Zoologica Anton Dohrn (1883–1977)', *Frontiers in Physiology*, 7:618 (2016), www.ncbi.nlm.nih.gov/pmc/articles/PMC5179557/ <accessed 14 May 2019>.

Dutta, Shanta. *Ambivalence in Hardy: A Study of His Attitude to Women* (Basingstoke: Palgrave Macmillan, 2000).

Ebbatson, Roger. *The Evolutionary Self: Hardy, Forster, Lawrence* (Sussex: Harvester Press, 1982).

Elias, Ann Dirouhi. *Camouflage Australia: Art, Nature, Science and War* (Sydney: Sydney University Press, 2011).

Eller, Cynthia. 'Sons of the Mother: Victorian Anthropologists and the Myth of Matriarchal Prehistory', *Gender & History*, 18:2 (2006), 285–310.

Endersby, Jim. 'A Visit to Biotopia: Genre, Genetics and Gardening in the Early Twentieth Century', *British Journal for the History of Science*, 51:3 (2018), 423–455.

Erchinger, Philipp. *Artful Experiments: Ways of Knowing in Victorian Literature and Science* (Edinburgh: Edinburgh University Press, 2018).

Evans, Mary Alice. 'Mimicry and the Darwinian Heritage', *Journal of the History of Ideas*, 26:2 (1965), 211–220.

Fanon, Franz. *Black Skin, White Masks*, trans. Charles L. Markmann (London: Pluto Press, 1986).

Federico, Annette. 'Thomas Hardy's *The Well-Beloved*: Love's Descent', *English Literature in Transition, 1880–1920*, 50:3 (2007), 269–290.

Federman, Cary, Holmes, Dave and Jacob, Jean Daniel. 'Deconstructing the Psychopath: A Critical Discursive Analysis', *Cultural Critique*, 72 (2009), 36–65.

Ferguson, Christine. *Language, Science and Popular Fiction in the Victorian Fin-de-Siècle: The Brutal Tongue* (Aldershot: Ashgate, 2006).

Ferguson, Trish. *Thomas Hardy's Legal Fictions* (Edinburgh: Edinburgh University Press, 2013).

Fergusson, David. 'Natural Theology after Darwin', in *Darwinism and Natural Theology*, ed. Andrew Robinson (Newcastle: Cambridge Scholars, 2012), 78–95.

Fichman, Martin. *An Elusive Victorian: The Evolution of Alfred Russel Wallace* (Chicago: University of Chicago Press, 2004).

Figes, Eva. *Patriarchal Attitudes: Women in Society* (New York: Perses Books, 1970).

Flint, Kate. *Victorians and the Visual Imagination* (Cambridge: Cambridge University Press, 2000).

Forbes, Peter. *Dazzled and Deceived: Mimicry and Camouflage* (London: Yale University Press, 2011).

Foster, John Wilson. 'Against Nature? Science and Oscar Wilde', *University of Toronto Quarterly*, 63:2 (1993/1994), 328–346.

Foucault, Michel. *Discipline and Punish: The Birth of the Prison*, trans. Alan Sheridan (New York: Vintage, 1979).

Bibliography

The Order of Things: An Archaeology of the Human Sciences, trans. Alan Sheridan Smith (London: Tavistock Publications, 1970).

Frost, Mark. 'The Circles of Vitality: Ruskin, Science, and Dynamic Materiality', *Victorian Literature and Culture*, 39:2 (2011), 367–383.

Fyfe, Aileen. *Science and Salvation: Evangelical Popular Science Publishing in Victorian Britain* (Chicago: University of Chicago Press, 2004).

Gagnier, Regenia. *Individualism, Decadence and Globalization: On the Relationship of Part to Whole, 1859–1920* (London: Palgrave Macmillan, 2010).

Gallagher, Catherine. 'George Eliot: Immanent Victorian', *Representations*, 90:1 (2005), 61–74.

Garrard, Greg. *Ecocriticism*, 2nd ed. (London: Routledge: 2012).

Garratt, Peter. *Victorian Empiricism: Self, Knowledge, and Reality in Ruskin, Bain, Lewes, Spencer, and George Eliot* (Madison, WI: Fairleigh Dickinson University Press, 2010).

Gates, Barbara T. and Shteir, Ann B. 'Introduction: Charting the Tradition', in *Natural Eloquence: Women Reinscribe Science*, ed. Gates and Shteir (Madison: University of Wisconsin Press, 1997), 3–24.

Geller, Jay. *The Other Jewish Question: Identifying the Jew and Making Sense of Modernity* (New York: Fordham University Press, 2011).

Gilbert, Pamela K. *Victorian Skin: Surface, Self, History* (London: Cornell University Press, 2019).

Gilman, Sander S. *Creating Beauty to Cure the Soul: Race and Psychology in the Shaping of Aesthetic Surgery* (London: Duke University Press, 1998).

Gilmartin, Sophie. *Ancestry and Narrative in Nineteenth-Century British Literature: Blood Relations from Edgeworth to Hardy* (Cambridge: Cambridge University Press, 1998).

Ginsberg, Elaine K. 'Introduction: The Politics of Passing', in *Passing and the Fictions of Identity*, ed. Elaine K. Ginsberg (London: Duke University Press, 1996), 1–18.

Gleber, Anke. 'Women on the Screens and Streets of Modernity: In Search of the Female Flaneur', in *The Image in Dispute: Art and Cinema in the Age of Photography*, ed. Dudley Andrew (Austin: University of Texas Press, 1997), 55–85.

Glendenning, John. *The Evolutionary Imagination in Late-Victorian Novels: An Entangled Bank* (Aldershot: Ashgate, 2007).

Goethe, Johann Wolfgang von. *Theory of Colours*, trans. Charles Lock Eastlake (Cambridge, MA: MIT Press, 1982).

Goodall, Jane. *Performance and Evolution in the Age of Darwin: Out of the Natural Order* (London: Routledge, 2007).

Gossin, Pamela. *Thomas Hardy's Novel Universe: Astronomy, Cosmology, and Gender in the Post-Darwinian World* (Aldershot, Ashgate, 2007).

Gould, Stephen Jay. 'Nonoverlapping Magisteria', *Natural History*, 106:3 (1997), 16–22.

Graham, Daniel W. 'Does Nature Love to Hide? Heraclitus B123 DK', *Classical Philology*, 98:2 (2003), 175–179.

Bibliography

Greenfield, Robert. *Dreamer's Journey: The Life and Writings of Frederic Prokosch* (Newark, DE: University of Delaware Press, 2010).

Griffin, Cristina Richieri. 'Omniscience Incarnate: Being in and of the World in Nineteenth-Century Fiction', PhD thesis (University of California, Los Angeles, 2015).

Griffin, Emma. *Blood Sport: Hunting in Britain since 1066* (New Haven, CT: Yale University Press, 2007).

Griffiths, Devin. *The Age of Analogy: Science and Literature between the Darwins* (Baltimore, MD: Johns Hopkins University Press, 2016).

Hale, Piers J. 'Darwin's Other Bulldog: Charles Kingsley and the Popularisation of Evolution in Victorian England', *Science and Education*, 21:7 (2012), 977–1013.

'Monkeys into Men and Men into Monkeys: Chance and Contingency in the Evolution of Man, Mind and Morals in Charles Kingsley's *Water Babies*', *Journal of the History of Biology*, 46:4 (2013), 551–597.

Political Descent: Malthus, Mutualism, and the Politics of Evolution in Victorian England (London: University of Chicago Press, 2014).

Hamlin, Christopher. 'Charles Kingsley: From Being Green to Green Being', *Victorian Studies*, 54:2 (2012), 255–282.

Harley, Alexis. *Autobiologies: Charles Darwin and the Natural History of the Self* (Lewisburg, PA: Bucknell University Press, 2015).

Harrison, Peter. *The Bible, Protestantism, and the Rise of Natural Science* (Cambridge: Cambridge University Press, 1998).

Hawhee, Debra. *Rhetoric in Tooth and Claw: Animals, Language, Sensation* (London: University of Chicago Press, 2016).

Hawley, John C. 'Charles Kingsley and the Book of Nature', *Anglican and Episcopal History*, 60:4 (1991), 461–479.

Helmreich, Anne. *Nature's Truth: Photography, Painting, and Science in Victorian Britain* (University Park, PA: Pennsylvania State University Press, 2016).

Herbert, Christopher. *Victorian Relativity: Radical Thought and Scientific Discovery* (London: University of Chicago Press, 2001).

Holmes, John and Ruston, Sharon (eds.). *The Routledge Research Companion to Nineteenth-Century British Literature and Science* (London: Routledge, 2017).

Humboldt, Alexander von. *Cosmos: Sketch of a Physical Description of the Universe*, vol. 2, trans. Edward Sabine (London: John Murray, 1849).

Personal Narrative of Travels to the Equinoctial Regions of the New Continent, during the Years 1799–1804, trans. Helen Maria Williams, 7 vols. (London: Longman, Hurst, Rees, Orme & Brown, 1814–1829).

Views of Nature, trans. E. C. Otté and Henry G. Bohn (London: Henry G. Bohn, 1850).

Hacking, Ian. *The Taming of Chance* (Cambridge: Cambridge University Press, 1990).

Haley, Bruce. 'Wilde's "Decadence" and the Positivist Tradition', *Victorian Studies*, 28:2 (1985), 215–229.

'Robert Warington and the Moral Economy of the Aquarium', *Journal of the History of Biology*, 19:1 (1986), 131–153.

Haraway, Donna. *When Species Meet* (Minneapolis: University of Minnesota Press, 2008).

Harmon, Joseph E. and Gross, Alan G. *The Scientific Literature: A Guided Tour* (London: University of Chicago Press, 2007).

Hausman, Bernice L. 'Sex before Gender: Charlotte Perkins Gilman and the Evolutionary Paradigm of Utopia', *Feminist Studies*, 24:3 (1998), 488–510.

Heilmann, Ann. 'Overwriting Decadence: Charlotte Perkins Gilman, Oscar Wilde, and the Feminization of Art in "The Yellow Wallpaper"', in *The Mixed Legacy of Charlotte Perkins Gilman*, ed. Catherine J. Golden and Joanna Schneider Zangrando (London: Associated University Presses, 2000), 175–188.

Higonnet, Margaret R. (ed.). *The Sense of Sex: Feminist Perspectives on Hardy* (Chicago: University of Illinois Press, 1993).

Hoffman, Donald D. 'The Construction of Visual Reality', in *Hallucinations: Research and Practice*, ed. Jan Dirk Blom and Iris E. C. Sommer (New York: Springer, 2012), 7–15.

Hoffmeyer, Jesper. *Biosemiotics: An Examination into the Signs of Life and the Life of Signs* (Scranton, PA: University of Scranton Press, 2008).

'Semiotic Freedom: An Emerging Force', in *Information and the Nature of Reality: From Physics to Metaphysics*, ed. Paul Davies and N. H. Gregersen (Cambridge: Cambridge University Press, 2010), 185–204.

Holmes, Martha Stoddard. *Fictions of Affliction: Physical Disability in Victorian Culture* (Ann Arbor, MI: University of Michigan Press, 2004).

Houser, Nathan. 'The Fortunes and Misfortunes of the Peirce Papers', in *Signs of Humanity*, ed. Michel Balat and Janice Deledalle-Rhodes, 3 vols. (Berlin: Mouton de Gruyter, 1992), III, 1259–1268.

Hyman, Virginia R. *Ethical Perspective in the Novels of Thomas Hardy* (Port Washington, NY: National University Publishers, 1975).

Ihde, Don. *Postphenomenology and Technoscience: The Peking University Lectures* (Albany, NY: SUNY Press, 2009).

Ingham, Patricia. *Thomas Hardy* (Oxford: Oxford University Press, 2003).

Irigaray, Luce. *This Sex Which Is Not One* (Ithaca, NY: Cornell University Press, 1985).

Jaffe, Audrey. *Vanishing Points: Dickens, Narrative, and the Subject of Omniscience* (Berkeley, CA: University of California Press, 1991).

James, Dominic. 'Oscar Wilde, Sodomy, and Mental Illness in Late Victorian England', *Journal of the History of Sexuality*, 23:1 (2014), 79–95.

Jenkins, Alice. 'Beyond Two Cultures: Science, Literature and Disciplinary Boundaries', in *The Oxford Handbook of Victorian Literary Culture*, ed. Juliet John (Oxford: Oxford University Press, 2016), 401–415.

Jordan, Chris. 'Midway: Message from the Gyre' (2009), www.chrisjordan.com/gallery/midway/ <accessed 20/04/2018>.

Bibliography

Kaiser, Matthew. 'Marius at Oxford: Paterian Pedagogy and the Ethics of Seduction', in *Walter Pater: Transparencies of Desire*, ed. Lesley Higgins Brake and Carolyn Williams (Greensboro, NC: ELT Press, 2002), 189–201.

Kanarakis, Yannis. 'The Aesthete as Scientist: Walter Pater and Nineteenth-Century Science', *Victorian Network*, 2:1 (2010), 88–105.

Karschay, Stephen. *Degeneration, Normativity and the Gothic at the Fin de Siècle* (Palgrave Macmillan, 2015).

Kaye, Richard A. *The Flirt's Tragedy: Desire without End in Victorian and Edwardian Fiction* (London: University of Virginia Press, 2002).

Kennedy, Andrea. 'The Beauty of Victorian Beasts: Illustration in the Reverend J. G. Wood's *Homes without Hands*', *Archives of Natural History*, 40:2 (2013), 193–212.

Kimler, William C. 'Mimicry: Views of Naturalists and Ecologists before the Modern Synthesis', in *Dimensions of Darwinism: Themes and Counterthemes in Twentieth-Century Evolutionary Theory*, ed. Marjorie Grene (Cambridge: Cambridge University Press, 1983), 97–128.

King, Amy M. 'Reorienting the Scientific Frontier: Victorian Tide Pools and Literary Realism', *Victorian Studies*, 47:2 (2005), 153–163.

Kingsland, Sharon. 'Abbott Thayer and the Protective Coloration Debate', *Journal of the History of Biology*, 11:2 (1978), 223–244.

Kirchoff, Frederick. 'A Science against Sciences: Ruskin's Floral Mythology', in *Nature and the Victorian Imagination*, ed. U. C. Knoepflmacher and G. B. Tennyson (London: University of California Press, 1977), 246–258.

Klaver, J. M. I. *The Apostle of the Flesh: A Critical Life of Charles Kingsley* (Boston, MA: Brill, 2006).

Kohl, Norbert. *Oscar Wilde: The Works of a Conformist Rebel*, trans. David Henry Wilson (Cambridge: Cambridge University Press, 1989).

Kohler, Robert E. *Landscapes and Labscapes: Exploring the Lab-Field Border in Biology* (Chicago: University of Chicago Press: 2002).

Koltun-Fromm, Ken. *Imagining Jewish Authenticity: Vision and Text in American Jewish Thought* (Bloomington, IN: Indiana University Press, 2015).

Komárek, Stanislav. *Mimicry, Aposematism, and Related Phenomena: Mimetism in Nature and the History of Its Study* (Munich: Lincom Europa, 2009).

Krasner, James. *The Entangled Eye: Visual Perception and the Representation of Nature in Post-Darwinian Narrative* (Oxford: Oxford University Press, 1992).

Kucich, John. *The Power of Lies: Transgression in Victorian Fiction* (London: Cornell University Press, 1994).

Lacan, Jacques. *The Four Fundamental Concepts of Psychoanalysis*, trans. A. Sheridan (London: Penguin, 1977).

Lancaster, Jane. '"I Could Easily Have Been an Acrobat": Charlotte Perkins Gilman and the Providence Ladies' Sanitary Gymnasium, 1881–1884', *American Transcendental Quarterly*, 8:1 (1994), 33–52.

Landow, George P. *Victorian Shadows: Biblical Typology in Victorian Literature, Art, and Thought* (London: Routledge, 1980).

Bibliography

Larson, Barbara and Brauer, Fae (eds.). *The Art of Evolution: Darwin, Darwinisms, and Visual Culture* (Hanover, NH: Dartmouth College Press, 2009).

Larson, Barbara and Flach, Sabine (eds.). *Darwin and Theories of Aesthetics and Cultural History* (Farnham: Ashgate, 2013).

Leask, Nigel. *Curiosity and the Aesthetics of Travel Writing 1770–1840* (Oxford: Oxford University Press, 2002).

Lecourt, Sebastian. '"To Surrender Himself, in Perfectly Liberal Inquiry": Walter Pater, Many-Sidedness, and the Conversion Novel', *Victorian Studies*, 53:2 (2011), 231–253.

Lee, Louise. 'Voicing, De-voicing and Self-Silencing: Charles Kingsley's Stuttering Christian Manliness', *Journal of Victorian Culture*, 13:1 (2008), 1–17.

Leslie, Charles Robert. *Memoirs of the Life of John Constable* (London: Longman, Brown, Green and Longmans, 1845).

Levine, Caroline. *The Serious Pleasures of Suspense: Victorian Realism and Narrative Doubt* (London: University of Virginia Press, 2003).

Levine, George. *Darwin and the Novelists: Patterns of Science in Victorian Fiction* (London: University of Chicago Press, 1991).

  Darwin the Writer (Oxford: Oxford University Press, 2011).

  Realism, Ethics and Secularism: Essays on Victorian Literature and Science (Cambridge: Cambridge University Press, 2008).

Lightman, Bernard. *Victorian Popularizers of Science: Designing Nature for New Audiences* (Chicago: University of Chicago Press, 2007).

Lindquist, Jason Howard. 'A "Pure Excess of Complexity": Tropical Surfeit, the Observing Subject, and the Text, 1773–1871', PhD thesis (Indiana University, 2008).

Lloyd, Brian. 'Feminism, Utopian and Scientific: Charlotte Perkins Gilman and the Prison of the Familiar', *American Studies*, 39:1 (1998), 93–113.

Lomas, David. 'Artist-Sorcerers: Mimicry, Magic and Hysteria', *Oxford Art Journal*, 35:3, (2012), 363–388.

Lorsch, Susan E. *Where Nature Ends: Literary Responses to the Designification of Landscape* (London: Associated University Presses, 1983).

Lousley, Cheryl. 'Ecocriticism and the Politics of Representation', in *The Oxford Handbook of Ecocriticism*, ed. Greg Garrard (Oxford: Oxford University Press, 2014), 155–171.

Love, Heather. *Feeling Backward: Loss and the Politics of Queer History* (Cambridge, MA: Harvard University Press, 2007).

Luckhurst, Roger. *The Invention of Telepathy, 1870–1901* (Oxford: Oxford University Press, 2002).

Lukes, Steven. *Individualism* (Oxford: Blackwell, 1973).

Lutts, Ralph H. *The Nature Fakers: Wildlife, Science and Sentiment* (Charlottesville, VA: University of Virginia Press, 2001).

Macfarlane, Robert. *Original Copy: Plagiarism and Originality in Nineteenth-Century Literature* (Oxford: Oxford University Press, 2007).

Mangham, Andrew. *Violent Women and Sensation Fiction* (London: Palgrave Macmillan, 2007).

278   *Bibliography*

Maran, Timo. 'Biosemiotic Criticism', in *The Oxford Handbook of Ecocriticism*, ed. Greg Garrard (Oxford: Oxford University Press, 2014), 260–275.

Marcus, Sharon. 'Comparative Sapphism', in *The Literary Channel: The International Invention of the Novel*, ed. Margaret Cohen and Carolyn Dever (Princeton, NJ: Princeton University Press, 2002), 251–285.

Martinelli, Dario. *A Critical Companion to Zoosemiotics: People, Paths, Ideas* (Dordrecht: Springer, 2010).

Matossian, Lou-Ann. 'A Woman-Made Language: Charlotte Perkins Gilman and *Herland*', *Women and Language*, 10:2 (1987), 16–20.

McGann, Jerome J. *The Romantic Ideology: A Critical Investigation* (London: University of Chicago Press, 1983).

McGrath, Alister E. *Darwinism and the Divine: Evolutionary Thought and Natural Theology* (Oxford: Wiley-Blackwell, 2010).

McKee, Patricia. *Reading Constellations: Urban Modernity in Victorian Fiction* (Oxford: Oxford University Press, 2014).

McWilliam, Rohan. 'Unauthorized Identities: The Imposter, the Fake and the Secret History in Nineteenth-Century Britain', in *Legitimacy and Illegitimacy in Nineteenth-Century Law, Literature and History*, eds. Margot C. Finn, Michael Lobban and Jenny Bourne Taylor (Basingstoke: Palgrave Macmillan, 2010), 67–92.

Meadows, A. J. 'Kingsley's Attitude to Science', *Theology*, 78 (1975), 15–22.

Mielants, Eric. 'Reaction and Resistance: The Natural Sciences and the Humanities, 1789–1945', in *Overcoming the Two Cultures: Science versus the Humanities in the Modern World-System*, eds. Richard E. Lee and Immanuel Wallerstein (New York: Routledge, 2016), 34–54.

Milam, Erika Lorraine. *Looking for a Few Good Males: Female Choice in Evolutionary Biology* (Baltimore, MD: Johns Hopkins University Press, 2011).

Miller, D. A. *The Novel and the Police* (Berkeley, CA: University of California Press, 1988).

Mitchell, W. J. T. *Picture Theory: Essays on Verbal and Visual Representation* (London: University of Chicago Press, 1995).

Moe, Aaron M. *Zoopoetics: Animals and the Making of Poetry* (Lanham, MD: Lexington Books, 2014).

Moretti, Franco. *Distant Reading* (London: Verso, 2013).

Morgan, Benjamin. *The Outward Mind: Materialist Aesthetics in Victorian Science and Literature* (London: University of Chicago Press, 2017).

Morris, Jeremy. *F. D. Maurice and the Crisis of Christian Authority* (Oxford: Oxford University Press, 2005).

Morton, Peter. *The Busiest Man in England: Grant Allen and the Writing Trade, 1875–1900* (Basingstoke: Palgrave Macmillan, 2005).

Morton, Timothy. *The Ecological Thought* (Cambridge, MA: Harvard University Press, 2010).

Muller, Charles H., 'Spiritual Evolution and Muscular Theology: Lessons from Kingsley's Natural Theology', *University of Cape Town Studies in English*, 15 (1986), 24–34.

Bibliography

Mulvey, Laura. 'Visual Pleasure and Narrative Cinema', *Screen*, 16:3 (1975), 6–18.

Murray, Michael J. *Nature Red in Tooth and Claw: Theism and the Problem of Animal Suffering* (Oxford: Oxford University Press, 2008).

Nemerov, Alexander. 'Vanishing Americans: Abbott Thayer, Theodore Roosevelt, and the Attraction of Camouflage', *American Art*, 11:2 (1997), 50–81.

Nerlich, Brigitte. *Semantic Theories in Europe, 1830–1930: From Etymology to Contextuality* (Amsterdam: John Benjamins, 1992).

Newton, William A. 'Hardy and the Naturalists: Their Use of Physiology', *Modern Philology*, 49:1 (1951), 28–41.

Norris, Margot. *Beasts of the Modern Imagination: Darwin, Nietzsche, Kafka, Ernst, and Lawrence* (Baltimore, MD: Johns Hopkins University Press, 1985).

O'Connell, Rachel. 'Reparative Pater: Retreat, Ecstasy, and Reparation in the Writings of Walter Pater', *ELH*, 82:3 (2015), 969–986.

O'Gorman, Francis. 'Victorian Natural History and the Discourses of Nature in Charles Kingsley's *Glaucus*', *Worldviews: Environment, Culture, Religion*, 2:1 (1998), 21–35.

O'Hara, Robert J. 'Diagrammatic Classifications of Birds, 1819–1901: Views of the Natural System in 19th-Century British Ornithology', in *Acta XIX Congressus Internationalis Ornithologici*, ed. H. Ouellet (Ottawa: National Museum of Natural Sciences, 1988), 2746–2759.

Otis, Laura. *Membranes: Metaphors of Invasion in Nineteenth-Century Literature, Science, and Politics* (Baltimore, MD: Johns Hopkins University Press, 2000).
  Networking: Communicating with Bodies and Machines in the Nineteenth Century (Ann Arbor: University of Michigan Press, 2001).

O'Toole, Tess. *Genealogy and Fiction in Hardy: Family Lineage and Narrative Lines* (Basingstoke: Macmillan, 1997).

Outram, Dorinda. 'New Spaces in Natural History', in *Cultures of Natural History*, ed. N. Jardine, James Secord and E. C. Spary (Cambridge: Cambridge University Press, 1996), 249–265.

Page, Norman. 'Art and Aesthetics', in *The Cambridge Companion to Thomas Hardy*, ed. Dale Kramer (Cambridge: Cambridge University Press, 1999), 38–53.

Paglia, Camille. *Sexual Personae: Art and Decadence from Nefertiti to Emily Dickinson* (New York: Vintage Books 1991).

Peach, Linden. *Masquerade, Crime and Fiction: Criminal Deceptions* (Basingstoke: Palgrave Macmillan, 2006).

Pearl, Sharrona. *About Faces: Physiognomy in Nineteenth-Century Britain* (London: Harvard University Press, 2010).

Pietrzak-Franger, Monika. *Syphilis in Victorian Literature and Culture: Medicine, Knowledge and the Spectacle of Victorian Invisibility* (Basingstoke: Palgrave Macmillan, 2017).

Pilkington, Anthony. '"Nature" as Ethical Norm in the Enlightenment', in *Languages of Nature: Critical Essays in Science and Literature*, ed. Ludmilla Jordanova (London: Free Association Books, 1986), 51–85.

Bibliography

Pittard, Christopher. *Purity and Contamination in Late Victorian Detective Fiction* (Farnham: Ashgate, 2011).

Plotica, Luke Philip. *Nineteenth-Century Individualism and the Market Economy: Individualist Themes in Emerson, Thoreau, and Sumner* (Cham, Switzerland: Palgrave Macmillan, 2018).

Porter, Dennis. *The Pursuit of Crime: Art and Ideology in Detective Fiction* (London: Yale University Press, 1981).

Potolsky, Matthew. 'Pale Imitations: Walter Pater's Decadent Historiography', in *Perennial Decay: On the Aesthetics and Politics of Decadance*, eds. Liz Constable, Dennis Denisoff and Matthew Potolsky (Philadelphia: University of Pennsylvania Press, 1999), 235–253.

Radford, Andrew. *Thomas Hardy and the Survivals of Time* (Aldershot: Ashgate, 2003).

Randall, Marilyn. *Pragmatic Plagiarism: Authorship, Profit and Power* (Toronto: University of Toronto Press, 2003).

Richards, Evelleen. *Darwin and the Making of Sexual Selection* (Chicago: University of Chicago Press, 2017).

Richardson, Angelique. 'Hardy and the Place of Culture', in *A Companion to Thomas Hardy*, ed. Keith Wilson (Oxford: Wiley-Blackwell, 2009), 54–70.

Love and Eugenics in the Late Nineteenth Century: Rational Reproduction and the New Woman (Oxford: Oxford University Press, 2003).

'"Some Science underlies all Art": The Dramatization of Sexual Selection and Racial Biology in Thomas Hardy's *A Pair of Blue Eyes* and *The Well-Beloved*', *Journal of Victorian Culture*, 3:2 (1998), 302–338.

The Politics of Thomas Hardy: Biology, Culture and Environment (Oxford: Oxford University Press, forthcoming).

Ridley, Hugh. *Darwin Becomes Art: Aesthetic Vision in the Wake of Darwin: 1870–1920* (New York: Rodopi, 2014).

Rochelson, Meri-Jane. *A Jew in the Public Arena: The Career of Israel Zangwill* (Detroit, MI: Wayne State University Press, 2008).

Rothenberg, David. *Survival of the Beautiful: Art, Science and Evolution* (London: Bloomsbury, 2013).

Rudwick, Martin. 'The Emergence of a Visual Language for Geological Science 1760–1840', *History of Science*, 14 (1976), 149–195.

Saint-Amour, Paul. *The Copywrights: Intellectual Property and the Literary Imagination* (Cornell University Press, 2003).

Searle, Geoffrey Russell. *Morality and the Market in Victorian Britain* (Oxford: Clarendon Press, 1998).

Secord, Anne. 'Botany on a Plate: Pleasure and the Power of Pictures in Promoting Early Nineteenth-Century Scientific Knowledge', *Isis*, 93:1 (2002), 28–57.

Schwartz, Hillel. *The Culture of the Copy: Striking Likenesses, Unreasonable Facsimiles*, 2nd ed. (New York: Zone Books, 2014).

Bibliography

Sedgwick, Adam. *Discourse on the Studies of the University* (Cambridge: Deighton, 1835).

Seltzer, Mark. *Henry James and the Art of Power* (Ithaca, NY: Cornell University Press, 1984).

Shanahan, Daniel. *Toward a Genealogy of Individualism* (Amherst, MA: University of Massachusetts Press, 1992).

Shapin, Steven and Schaffer, Simon. *Leviathan and the Air-Pump: Hobbes, Boyle, and the Experimental Life* (Princeton, NJ: Princeton University Press, 2011).

Shell, Hanna Rose. *Hide and Seek: Camouflage, Photography, and the Media of Reconnaissance* (New York: Zone Books, 2012).

Shepherd-Barr, Kirsten. *Theatre and Evolution from Ibsen to Beckett* (New York: Columbia University Press, 2015).

Shields, Stephanie. 'The Variability Hypothesis: History of a Biological Model of Sex Differences in Intelligence', *Signs: Journal of Women in Culture and Society*, 7 (1982), 769–797.

Shires, Linda M. 'Color Theory – Charles Lock Eastlake's 1840 Translation of Johann Wolfgang von Goethe's Zur Farbenlehre (Theory of Colours)', *Branch*, www.branchcollective.org/?ps_articles=linda-m-shires-color-theory-charles-lock-eastlakes-1840-translation-of-johann-wolfgang-von-goethes-zur-farbenlehre-theory-of-colours <accessed 18/05/2018>.

Showalter, Elaine. 'Syphilis, Sexuality, and the Fiction of Fin de Siècle', in *Sex, Politics, and Science in the Nineteenth-Century Novel: Selected Papers from the English Institute, 1983–1984*, ed. Ruth Bernard Yeazell (Baltimore, MD: Johns Hopkins University Press, 1990), 88–115.

Shumsky, Neil Larry. 'Zangwill's "The Melting Pot": Ethnic Tensions on Stage', *American Quarterly*, 27:1 (1975), 29–41.

Shuter, William F. *Rereading Walter Pater* (Cambridge: Cambridge University Press, 1997).

Shuttleworth, Sally. *Charlotte Brontë and Victorian Psychology* (Cambridge: Cambridge University Press, 1996).

   The Mind of the Child: Child Development in Literature, Science, and Medicine, 1840–1900 (Oxford: Oxford University Press, 2010).

Singer, Peter. *Animal Liberation: A New Ethics for Our Treatment of Animals* (London: Jonathan Cape, 1990).

Sleigh, Charlotte. *Literature and Science* (Basingstoke: Palgrave Macmillan, 2011).

   Six Legs Better: A Cultural History of Myrmecology (Baltimore, MD: Johns Hopkins University Press, 2007).

Smajić, Srdjan. *Ghost-Seers, Detectives, and Spiritualists: Theories of Vision in Victorian Literature and Science* (Cambridge: Cambridge University Press, 2010).

Small, Ian and Guy, Josephine M. *Oscar Wilde's Profession: Writing and the Culture Industry in the Late Nineteenth Century* (Oxford University Press, 2000).

Smethurst, Paul. *Travel Writing and the Natural World, 1768–1840* (Basingstoke: Palgrave Macmillan, 2013).

Bibliography

Smith, Jonathan. *Charles Darwin and Victorian Visual Culture* (Cambridge: Cambridge University Press, 2006).

Fact and Feeling: Baconian Science and the Nineteenth-Century Literary Imagination (Madison, WI: University of Wisconsin Press, 1994).

Smith, Lindsay. *Victorian Photography, Painting and Poetry: The Enigma of Visibility in Ruskin, Morris and the Pre-Raphaelites* (Cambridge: Cambridge University Press, 1995).

Stevens, Martin. *Cheats and Deceits: How Animals and Plants Exploit and Mislead* (Oxford: Oxford University Press, 2016).

Street, Brian V. *The Savage in Literature: Representations of 'Primitive' Society in English Fiction, 1858–1920* (London: Routledge and Kegan Paul, 1975).

Sumpter, Caroline. '"No Artist has Ethical Sympathies": Oscar Wilde, Aesthetics, and Moral Evolution', *Victorian Literature and Culture*, 44:3 (2016), 623–640.

Taubenfeld, Aviva F. *Rough Writing: Ethnic Authorship in Theodore Roosevelt's America* (New York: New York University Press, 2008).

Taussig, Michael. *Mimesis and Alterity: A Particular History of the Senses* (London: Routledge, 1993).

Taylor, Brooke. 'Accounting for Mysteries: Narratives of Intuition and Empiricism in the Victorian Novel', PhD thesis (Washington University, 2010).

Taylor, Charles. *Sources of the Self: The Making of the Modern Identity* (Cambridge: Cambridge University Press, 1992).

Teukolsky, Rachel. *The Literate Eye: Victorian Art Writing and Modernist Aesthetics* (Oxford: Oxford University Press, 2009).

Thomas, Keith. *Man and the Natural World: Changing Attitudes in England 1500–1800* (London: Allen Lane, 1983).

Topham, Jonathan. 'Natural Theology and the Sciences', in *The Cambridge Companion to Science and Religion*, ed. Peter Harrison (Cambridge: Cambridge University Press, 2010), 59–79.

Tosh, John. *A Man's Place: Masculinity and the Middle-Class Home in Victorian England* (London: Yale University Press, 2007).

Trilling, Lionel. *Sincerity and Authenticity* (Cambridge, MA: Harvard University Press, 1971).

Tufescu, Florina. *Oscar Wilde's Plagiarism: the Triumph of Art over Ego* (Dublin: Irish Academic Press, 2008).

Turner, Frank. *Contesting Cultural Authority: Essays in Victorian Intellectual Life* (Cambridge: Cambridge University Press, 1993).

Tyndall, John. 'On the Study of Physics', in *Fragments of Science*, 2 vols. (London: Longmans, 1879).

Tytler, Graeme. '"Know How to Decipher a Countenance": Physiognomy in Thomas Hardy's Fiction', *Thomas Hardy Year Book*, 27 (1998), 43–60.

Uexküll, Jakob von. *A Foray into the Worlds of Animals and Humans: With a Theory of Meaning*, trans. Joseph D. O'Neil (Minneapolis: University of Minnesota Press, 2010).

Bibliography

Vargish, Thomas. *The Providential Aesthetic in Victorian Fiction* (Charlottesville: University Press of Virginia, 1985).

Wainwright, Michael. 'Oscar Wilde, the Science of Heredity, and *The Picture of Dorian Gray*', *English Literature in Transition, 1880–1920*, 54:4 (2011), 494–522.

Walsh, Bridget. *Domestic Murder in Nineteenth-Century England: Literary and Cultural Representations* (Farnham: Ashgate, 2014).

Watt-Smith, Tiffany. *On Flinching: Theatricality and Scientific Looking from Darwin to Shell Shock* (Oxford: Oxford University Press, 2014).

Welsh, Alexander. *George Eliot and Blackmail* (Cambridge, MA: Harvard University Press, 1985).

West, Anna. *Thomas Hardy and Animals* (Cambridge: Cambridge University Press, 2017).

Wheeler, Wendy. *Expecting the Earth: Life, Culture, Biosemiotics* (London: Lawrence and Wishart, 2016).

  The Whole Creature: Complexity, Biosemiotics and the Evolution of Culture (London: Lawrence & Wishart, 2006).

White, Allon. *The Uses of Obscurity: Fiction of Early Modernism* (London: Routledge & Kegan Paul, 1981).

White, Paul. 'The Experimental Animal in Victorian Britain', in *Thinking with Animals: New Perspectives on Anthropomorphism*, ed. Lorraine Daston and Gregg Mitman (New York: Columbia University Press, 2005), 59–82.

Wille, Sheila. 'The Ichneumon Fly and the Equilibration of British Natural Economies in the Eighteenth Century', *British Society for the History of Science*, 48:4 (2015), 639–660.

Williamson, Gillian. *British Masculinity in the 'Gentleman's Magazine', 1731 to 1815* (Basingstoke: Palgrave Macmillan, 2016).

Willis, Chris. 'The Detective's *Doppelgänger*: Conflicting States of Females Consciousness in Grant Allen's Detective Fiction', in *Grant Allen: Literature and Politics at the Fin de Siècle*, eds. William Greenslade and Terence Rodgers (Aldershot: Ashgate, 2005), 143–153.

Willis, Martin. *Literature and Science: A Reader's Guide to Essential Criticism* (London: Palgrave, 2015).

  Vision, Science and Literature: Ocular Horizons (London: Pickering & Chatto, 2011).

Wilson, Keith. 'Thomas Hardy of London', in *A Companion to Thomas Hardy*, ed. Keith Wilson (Oxford: Wiley-Blackwell, 2009), 146–161.

Wimsatt, William K. and Beardsley, Monroe C. 'The Affective Fallacy', in *The Verbal Icon: Studies in the Meaning of Poetry* (Lexington, KY: University Press of Kentucky, 1954), 21–40.

  'The Intentional Fallacy', in *Verbal Icon*, 3–20.

Wolfe, Cary. *What Is Posthumanism?* (Minneapolis, MI: University of Minnesota Press, 2010).

Woodward, Kath. *The Politics of In/Visibility* (Basingstoke: Palgrave Macmillan, 2015).

Bibliography

Wooton, George. *Thomas Hardy: Towards a Materialist Criticism* (Totowa, NJ: Barnes & Noble, 1985).

Wright, T. R. 'Positivism: Comte and Mill', in *Thomas Hardy in Context*, ed. Philip Mallett (Cambridge: Cambridge University Press, 2013), 296–305.

Wrisley, Melyssa. 'Fashioning a New Femininity: Charlotte Perkins Gilman and Discourses of Dress, Gender and Sexuality, 1875–1930', PhD thesis (Binghamton University, 2008).

Zeitler, Michael A. *Representations of Culture: Thomas Hardy's Wessex and Victorian Anthropology* (Oxford: Peter Lang, 2007).

Zemka, Sue. *Time and the Moment in Victorian Literature and Society* (Cambridge: Cambridge University Press, 2012).

Index

Abbot, John, 41
Abdul Hamid, Sultan, 13–14
adaptive appearance
  and creativity, 20, 25
  and cultural theory, 205–214
  definition of, 2–6
  and the human/animal binary, 3, 6, 9–11,
    205–207
  and identity, 19–22, 210–211
  as literary trope, 4, 21
  and meaning as reception instead of intention,
    84, 149
  in neo-Victorian fiction, 211–212
  politics of, 3–4
  polysemy of, 3
  pre-Victorian theories of, 2, 7–8, 24
  scepticism of, 42–43, 52–53, 61–63, 211
adulteration, 16
advertisement
  as biological phenomenon, 4, 63
  as metaphor for adaptive appearance, 6–7
aestheticism, 153
  and amorality, 95–96
  and biology, 164–165, 198
agnosticism, 80–81, 150, 154, 156–158
Allen, Francis, 62–63
Allen, Grant, 3, 5, 18, 22–23, 86–115
  An African Millionaire, 25, 87–88, 90,
    106–113
  The British Barbarians, 113
  The Colour-Sense, 90
  comparing human and non-human deception,
    7, 22
  and the concealment–detection arms race,
    86–87, 91–93, 115
  'The Curate of Churnside', 25, 87, 95,
    101
  The Devil's Die, 25, 95
  and fiction as adaptive appearance, 88
  and misdirection as narrative technique, 88,
    110–111

  and moral convention versus amoral nature,
    87, 94–105
  'The Next Presentation', 87, 95, 103–106
  'Our Scientific Observations on a Ghost', 93
  and pessimism, 88, 106, 207
  Physiological Aesthetics, 90
  and the popular print market, 90, 93–94,
    113–114
  and 'purposive' literature, 93
  and race, 101–102
  and social satire, 88, 92
  'Strictly Incog.', 86
  tensions in his evolutionary view of deception,
    18
  view of progress as transcendence of deceit,
    87, 89, 91, 106
  What's Bred in the Bone, 90
  The Woman Who Did, 90, 113
  writings on adaptive appearance, 88–92
Allen, J. A., 62
altruism
  as ethical alternative to honesty, 25, 117, 128,
    132–135, 147
  and evolution, 14–15, 18, 153, 214
  and science, 25, 75, 112
American Ornithologists' Union, 54
analogy, 23, 56
anecdotes, 5, 24, 29, 31
animism, 13
anthropology, 13, 39, 151, 156, 190
anthropomorphism, 52, 58, 63, 73, 83, 211
aposematism, 2, 5, 20, 22–23, 56
arbitrariness
  of signs, 9, 179, 189, 197–199, 201, 203
Arnold, Matthew, 33, 79
art
  as model of nature, 44, 49–51
  as a scientific resource, 58–61, 64
assimilation, 26, 178, 180–182, 210
Athenaeum, 159
The Auk, 54, 61, 63

285

Index

authenticity
  and group identity, 178–180
  idealisation of, 3, 7, 19, 21, 26
  as illusion, 97, 104, 141
  and literature, 149, 160, 177
  problematisation of, 26, 84, 150
  as socially disruptive force, 150–151, 162

Bagehot, Walter, 152
Bain, Alexander, 10
Baldwin, James Mark, 152
Barbour, Thomas, 61–63
Barnum, P. T., 16
Bates, Henry Walter, 6–7, 23–24, 205; see
    mimicry, protective
  and Amazonian natives, 38–40
  and anecdotes of adaptive appearance, 24,
    28–40, 63
  and animal vision/agency, 9, 12, 35–37
  'Contributions to an Insect Fauna of the
    Amazon Valley', 1–2, 44–45
  and the distanced eye of science, 37–38
  in fiction, 212
  and field observation, 24, 31, 35, 52, 54
  and Grant Allen, 90, 233
  and illustration, 43–47
  and Kingsley, 80
  The Naturalist on the River Amazons, 36–40,
    45–47
  on the persecution of conspicuous forms, 125,
    127
Beauvoir, Simone de, 203
Beddard, Frank Evers, 34, 43, 52–53, 61
Bell, Vanessa, 155
Benjamin, Walter, 210
Bentham, Jeremy, 89; see *utilitarianism*
Berkeley, George, 29
Bey, Osman, 180
Bhaba, Homi, 186, 208
biosemiotics, see *zoosemiotics*
Bloxham, John Francis, 176
bodies
  opacity of, 200–201
  as semiotic surfaces, 5, 23, 25, 87, 118
Bon, Gustave Le, 12, 18
Braddon, Mary Elizabeth, 95, 99
Brecht, Bertolt, 212
Brimley, George, 84
Brougham, Henry, 10
Bourget, Paul, 152
Bullough, Edward, 212
Burroughs, John, 211
Butler, Judith, 197, 203, 208
Byatt, A. S., 212

Caillois, Roger, 210
camouflage, 1, 3, 7, 16, 63
capitalism
  critiques of, 3, 106
  and deception, 16, 25
  and primitive perception, 109–112
Carlyle, Thomas, 19, 69–70, 151
chameleons, 4, 129
  and hypocrisy, 124
  Jews as, 180
  and politics, 13
  and sympathy, 18
The Chameleon, 176
Chalmers, Thomas, 74–75
Chartism, 70
Christian Socialism, 70–71
Class
  and crypsis, 19–20, 75, 119, 124, 136, 158
  and primitive interpretation, 12–13, 17, 154
Coleridge, Samuel Taylor, 161
Collins, Wilkie, 95
colonialism, see *imperialism*
Comte, Auguste, 135, 155, 157, 209
confidence men, 16
conjuring, 13, 39, 123, 163
Constable, John, 30
coquettes, 119, 130, 132
Cornhill Magazine, 86, 93, 95–96, 99
Cott, Hugh, 24, 210
creativity, see *originality*
crime
  criminal types, 101
  and crypsis, 20, 23, 75, 86–115
  fiction, 5, 25, 95
  and the justice system, 98, 101, 103
  public fear of, 95
Croom Robertson, George, 93–94
crypsis
  definition of, 1–2
  and group identities, 178–204
  and literary and cultural criticism, 5, 25–26,
    149–177
  as model for human concealment, 5, 13, 16,
    23
  textual representations of, 12
cryptic coloration, see *protective coloration*
cryptophobia, see *mimeophobia*
cuckoos, 23, 136–137
cunning
  of animals, 7, 73, 86
  and art, 122
  and civilisation, 16
  of 'nature', 21, 58, 73
  and primitiveness, 14, 75, 78, 123
  and weakness, 182

Index

287

Cuvier, Georges, 32, 35
cybernetics, 6

Darwin, Charles, 23, 49, 94, 122, 202
on adaptive appearance, 2, 20, 205, 212
on animal communication, 10
Beagle Diary, 32
and chance, 97, 99
The Descent of Man, 10, 83
on lying and truthfulness, 14–15, 91, 128
On the Origin of Species, 2, 52
and religion, 66–67, 83
and sex, 122, 127, 163, 191
and teleology, 18, 87, 91, 112
visualisations of evolution, 8, 11
on writing, 33
Darwin, Erasmus, 7
Dawson, George, 68
decadence, 152
deception
as biological phenomenon, 3, 117–118,
127–136
and civilisation, 15–18
and morality, 3, 17–18, 25, 65–85, 116–148
of self, 16, 136–148
degeneration, 3, 13, 19–20, 74
as excessive individuality, 153
and sexual selection, 189–190
deism, 68, 81, 157
De Quincey, William, 97
Derrida, Jacques, 210
Descartes, René, 65, 205–206
detective fiction, see *crime, fiction*
Dickens, Charles, 22
Dobell, Sidney, 162
Doyle, Arthur Conan, 95, 106
dress, 26, 104
Dressler, Mylène, 211
Drummond, Henry, 85

ecocriticism, 3–4, 207, 213–214
ekphrasis, 24, 29, 43–53, 58, 63
Eliot, George, 16, 94, 123
Encyclopedia Britannica, 159
essentialism, 26, 179, 203, 205
critiques of, 3, 188, 207
eugenics, 101, 113, 200
Examiner, 159

Fabre, Jean-Henri, 53
feigning injury, 17
Fiction
as a form of deception/adaptive appearance,
18, 84–85, 88, 116
Fielding, Henry, 161

forgery, 95–99, 108, 153
formalism, 212
Foucault, Michel, 89, 177, 208
Fowles, John, 212
French, John Oliver, 8

Galilei, Galileo, 29
Galton, Francis, 127, 137
geology, 11, 65
Gilman, Charlotte Perkins, 23–24, 26, 85,
188–204
contradictions in her feminist sociobiology,
194–195, 199–204
The Crux, 200–201
and dress reform, 189–190
The Dress of Women, 24, 193, 199
and evolutionary theory, 188–192, 202
and female 'modesty', 179, 193–195
and feminine attractiveness as degeneration,
189–192, 197–199, 204
her aversion to biosemiosis, 179, 197–199,
204
Herland, 24, 188, 196–197, 199–200, 203
and Lester Ward, 190–191
and the male gaze, 193
Moving the Mountain, 200
and sexual display as patriarchal bondage, 22,
178–179, 188
'Symbolism in Dress', 192
and unisex identity, 179, 189, 195–197
Women and Economics, 191–192, 194–195,
199
'The Yellow Wall-Paper', 188
Goethe, Johann Wolfgang, 29–30
Gosse, Philip Henry, *Omphalos*, 65, 68–70, 76
Green, Alice Stopford, 21
gullibility
of animals, 10, 148
and civilisation, 16–17
and egoism, 110, 118, 142
and morality, 18, 87, 106, 136, 147
of naturalists, 35
and savagery, 13, 38–40
Gummere, Francis, 153

Haggard, Henry Rider, 16
Hampson, George F., 62
Haraway, Donna, 206
Hardy, Thomas, 3, 18, 22
and biology, 23, 117, 122–123, 132, 144
and the biosemiotics of ancestry, 136–147
and civilization as progressive self-
concealment, 118–122
and criticism of familial favouritism, 118,
136–137, 142–147

288 *Index*

Hardy, Thomas (cont.)
  and criticism of religious morals, 135–136
  and deceit as an instinct, 25, 117–118, 127–136
  Desperate Remedies, 130–131
  and division of social causes, from biological ones, 134
  and familial misidentification, 5, 136–137, 141–142, 144
  Far from the Madding Crowd, 116, 120–121, 123–124, 129–130
  and female transparency/dissimulation, 120, 127, 130–132, 145
  'For Conscience' Sake', 138–139
  'God's Funeral', 148
  'Heredity', 137
  'An Imaginative Woman', 144–145
  and invisible humans, 125–126
  Jude the Obscure, 116, 131–136, 144
  'Lady Mottisfont', 143
  A Laodicean, 130, 140–142
  and literary insincerity, 116
  and literary realism, 122
  'The Marchioness of Stonehenge', 142–143
  The Mayor of Casterbridge, 138, 142
  and morality as a biological development, 117, 128, 148
  and nature as a trickster, 122–124, 144, 146
  and nature's uncertain moral status, 117, 132, 148
  A Pair of Blue Eyes, 119–120, 124, 129, 139–140
  and pastoral, 5, 25, 117–127, 148
  'The Pedigree', 137, 139, 147–148
  and physiognomy, 138–139
  and reading bodies, 22, 25, 118–120, 136–147
  The Return of the Native, 124–126, 137–138
  'Squire Petrick's Lady', 137
  Tess of the d'Urbervilles, 116, 126–127, 135–136
    and ancestry, 137, 139, 147
    and honesty, 131–133
  truthfulness as maladaptation, 132–134
  and the uncertain ethics of lying, 116–117, 135–136, 148
  The Well-Beloved, 145–147
  The Woodlanders, 121–123, 126
Hartmann, Eduard von, 127, 180
Hazlitt, William, 151
Heraclitus, 7
Herder, Johann Gottfried, 19
Herzl, Theodor, 181
higher criticism, 70, 79
homosexuality, 167, 175–176, 211

Humboldt, Alexander, 29–31
Hume, David, 68
Hunt, James, 21
Hunt, Leigh, 151
Huxley, Thomas Henry, 23, 80–83, 148, 169
hybridity, 52, 102, 182, 185–187
hypnotism, 13, 16, 128

idolatry, 13, 15
illusion
  and art, 31, 33, 36, 43, 48, 57
  and biology, 1–2, 24, 29, 39–40
  and geology, 65
  and kinship, 136–148
  and psychology, 92–93, 107, 110
illustration, 24, 29, 34, 43–49, 88, 107
  limitations of as data of adaptive appearance, 45, 47
  and scientific authority, 33
imperialism, 16, 21, 79, 208
imposters, 16, 22–23, 93, 106–112, 133
individualism, 19, 21, 25–26, 149–177, 184
  contradictions of, 150–153
insanity, 20
interpretation
  and art, 173, 175
  evolution of, 6–11, 13–14, 109–112, 212
  as a factor in biology, 2, 206
  and insanity, 98
  instability of, 8
  resistance to, 169, 173, 175, 208
  restraint of, 5, 213
interspecies empathy, 6, 10–11, 214
intuition
  foiling deception, 99, 102–103
  and science, 49
invisibility
  of animals, 31, 47, 51, 54, 58, 63
  of bodily features, 107, 138
  gender, 18, 194, 204, 209
  of humans, 15, 75, 86, 89, 95–106, 125–126
  misattribution of, 62
  of nature's processes, 62, 200
  and power, 208
  and the spiritual, 72, 83, 202
Irigaray, Luce, 210
Irishness, 21, 79, 185–187
is–ought problem, 18

Jacobs, Joseph, 180–181
James, Henry, 54
James, William, 92–93
Jerome, K. Jerome, 179, 186
Jews, 22, 26, 177–188
  and humour, 186

Index

289

as intermediaries, 186–187
and theatre, 180, 187
and Zionism, 181–183, 185–186
Jordan, Chris, 214
judgment
divine, 78
and gullibility, 10
suspension of, 24, 28
and taste, 195

Kant, Immanuel, 29, 135, 164
khaki, 15, 92; see *warfare, camouflage*
Kidd, Benjamin, 17, 152
Kingsley, Charles, 5, 8, 18, 64–85
and Biblical criticism, 82
'Bio-Geology', 84
and biology, 22–23
and class tensions, 17, 70, 75
and degeneration, 75, 78–79
'On English Composition', 71
formative influences, 68, 70–71
Glaucus: Wonders of the Shore, 24, 66, 71–78
The Gospel of the Pentateuch, 82
and 'the How' and 'the Why' of nature,
83–84
'The Natural Theology of the Future', 83
and nature's symbolism, 24–25, 66–68,
71–74, 77–79, 84–85
science as realisation of this, 74–77
and the theodicy of adaptive appearance,
65
and truthfulness as divine virtue, 65–66, 71
The Water-Babies, 66, 77–79, 147
Yeast, 67–75, 78
Kipling, Rudyard, 16
Kirby, William, 24, 67, 70, 77–78

Lacan, Jacques, 210
Landels, William, 151
language
analogies with organic world, 72, 213
and computer programming, 207
and degeneration/primitiveness, 13, 153, 182,
198
and the human–animal divide, 10, 214
and individuality, 163, 166–167, 177
and minorities, 186
and reality, 33, 197
theories of, 9, 71, 151, 161, 163
Lankester, E. R., 64, 128
Lavater, Johann Caspar, 138
Lawrence, D. H., 210
Lewes, G. H. 12
liberalism, 19, 158
Linnaeus, Carl, 28

Linnean Society, 1
literature
as adaptive appearance, 94, 113–114, 171
and biosemiotics, 207
and Darwinism, 212–213
and empiricism, 212–213
and health, 159–164, 172, 197
and insincerity, 116, 149
as model of divine creation, 71–72
and the organic world, 152–153, 159–172,
213
and political activism, 178–204
and popular print culture, 88, 153, 157
and psychology, 212
and science, 33; see science, and art/literature
and social progress, 93
Locke, Alain LeRoy, 210
Locke, John, 9–10, 29
Lombroso, Cesare, 20, 153
London, Jack, 211
Long, William J., 211
Lubbock, John, 52
lying, see *deception*

Machiavellianism, 7, 66
Macleay, William Sharp, 7–8
Maine, Henry, 143
Malthus, Thomas, 94, 104–105
Mansel, H. L., 12
Martineau, Harriet, 194
moral insanity, 96, 98, 101, 104
masculinity, 19, 21, 137, 150, 155, 193–196
mass culture, 4, 12
materialism, 4, 6, 12, 16, 87, 167
and art, 23
and ethics, 80, 83, 94
New Materialism, 207
and semiosis, 8, 11, 64
and theism, 57, 145, 157, 167
Maudsley, Henry
on ancestral features, 138
on madness as a spectrum, 104
on mendacity as mental illness, 122–123
Maurice, Frederick Denison, 69, 72
Mayne, Fanny, 12
McAtee, Waldo Lee, 53
McLennan, John Ferguson, 190
Meldola, Raphael, 180
Meredith, George, 116
Mill, John Stewart, 118, 155
Mivart, St. George Jackson, 155
modernism, 24, 149, 177, 210
Morgan, Lewis Henry, 190
Morris, William, 163
Mill, John Stuart, 19

Index

mimeophobia, 6, 19–21
  and Jewishness, 180, 184–188
  and literature, 149, 177
mimesis, 6, 154
  as exclusively human capacity, 11, 37
mimicry, 3
  and agency, 9
  aggressive, 2
  and creativity, 152
  in cultural theory, 26, 186, 208
  as death drive, 210
  fear of, see *mimeophobia*
  instability of, 64
  and instinct, 18–19
    opposition to, 56
  protective, 1, 13, 21
  and satire, 32, 188
  and weakness, 13, 20–22
Mind, 92
minor literature, 186
morality
  mimicry as source of, 18
  and nature, 7–8, 25, 64
Morley, John, 17
Müller, Friedrich Max, 69
Müller, Fritz, 2, 6; see *mimicry, aggressive*
murderers
  animals as, 73
  as artists, 95–96
  and invisibility, 86, 95–106
  as products of nature, 100, 104–105

Nabokov, Vladimir, 210
narration, 5
  and distance, 38, 40, 129
  and interspecies empathy, 76
  omniscient, 89–90, 95, 102, 114, 208
  unreliable, 88, 110–111, 146
naturalism (literary), 116–117, 122, 174
natural selection, 2, 28, 43, 49, 53, 55
  and conservatism, 171–173, 191
  scepticism of, 52
  and society, 83, 114, 117, 156, 160
natural theology, 8, 23–24
  decline of, 66–67
  and degeneration, 74
  endurance of, 69–70
  tensions with secular science, 80
new criticism, 212
Newman, John Henry, 71, 155–156
Nietzsche, Friedrich, 17–18, 149, 151
  on communication as weakness, 154, 158
  on the 'mimicry' of the poor, 19–20, 178
Nineteenth Century, 169
Nordau, Max, 153, 177, 180–181

objectivity, 1–2, 6, 11–12, 23, 205; see *truth*
  and altruism, 147
  versus experiential knowledge, 29, 32, 64
  of visual features, 51
obscurity
  as an artistic goal, 26, 169, 176–177, see
    Wilde
  as pathology, 153, 163
Ockham, William of, 206
originality, 21–22
  ambivalence of, 150, 153–154
  as an energy, 156
  and individualism, 150–151, 208
  as a measure of health, 159–161, 172
  problematisations of, 161, 163
  as a racial characteristic, 180–183
  and selection of influences, 166, 169
  and taste, 195

Packard, Alpheus Spring, 42–43
Paine, Thomas, 68
Paley, William, 8, 31, 68, 74, 78
parasitism
  in humans, 13–15, 39, 105, 112, 129
  and Jews, 180–183, 187–188
  and literature, 13, 113–114, 161
  and maladaptation, 19, 78
  in non-humans, 30, 68, 73, 84–85, 122
pastoral, 5, 25, 117–127
Pater, Walter, 21–23
  on the automatism of life, 164–165
    self-consciousness as an escape from this,
      164–167
  and conventionality, 154, 167–168
  and crypsis, 153
  on cultural influence, 26
  and eclecticism, 165–167
  on the inevitability of human mimicry and
    crypsis, 150, 164–165
  and language, 166–167
  Marius the Epicurean, 166–167
  Plato and Platonism, 164–165, 167–168
  Studies in the History of the Renaissance, 167
  'Style', 166–167
  and Zangwill, 180
patriarchy, 21
Payn, James, 93, 96
peacock, 20
Peirce, Charles Sanders, 205–206
Pengelly, William, 84
perception, see *illusion, interpretation*
  evolution of, 11
  problematising of, 6, 28, 32
philistinism, 106, 161
Phillips, John C., see Barbour, Thomas

Index

291

philology, 9, 151
photography, 11
  and adaptive appearance, 53–56, 58–59
  in art and literature, 107, 144, 214
plagiarism, 97, 168
Plato, 164–168
Pliny the Elder, 7, 10–12
Poe, Edgar Allan, 161
poetic justice, 5, 94–95, 98–100, 102, 105, 112
posthumanism, 3, 207, see *ecocriticism*
Poulton, Edward Bagnall, 6–7, 23–24
  on animal vision, 28
  The Colours of Animals, 49–52
  criticism of his theories, 52, 61
  on crypsis as aesthetic effects, 43–44, 49–51
  and empirical data, 52–54
  on nature's variety, 50–52
  and Ruskin, 49–50
  and Thayer, 56–57
Powell, Baden, 80
Powell, C. H., 15
Pre-Raphaelitism, 47
Prichard, J. C., 96
protective coloration, 22, 49, 54, 57–64, 212,
    see *camouflage*
providence, 81
  failure of, 87
  ironic invocation of, 105
psychology, 6, 12
  of crowds, 12
  and evolution, 191
  of illusions, 92–93
  and semiosis, 201, 204
Punch, 13–14

quinarianism, 8

race, 21, 23, 82, 101–102
  and dishonesty, 79
  and gullibility, 38–42
  and imitation, 159, 178–188, 210
realism, 5, 58, 87, 95–98, 122, 144
  and animals, 211
  and power, 208
  and psychology, 212
  sterility of, 174, 177
recognition
  as bondage, 150, 154, 168–177, 208
  and identity, 20
religion
  and adaptive appearance, 65–85
  and anthropology, 151, 155–156
  crisis of, 17
  as crypsis, 17, 26
  utility of, 157–158

rhetoric, 2, 6–11, 20
Ritchie, David, 171
Robinson, E. W., 45
Romanes, George, 11, 21, 74, 174
Romanticism, 3, 19, 150
Roosevelt, Theodore, 61–63, 179, 211
Rossetti, Dante Gabriel, 160
Rousseau, Jean-Jacques, 7, 19, 68
Ruskin, John, 28–29, 97–98
  and the aesthetics and epistemology of
    suspense, 30–32, 34, 43
  on art and science, 30, 33–34
  and the artist as seer, 5, 61
  and deceptive architecture, 68
  influence on biology of adaptive appearance,
    36, 42–43, 49–51, 54, 210
  and 'innocence of the eye', 6, 24, 30, 47, 63,
    165, 212
  opposition to Darwinism, 6, 32, 57, 80
  and spiritual view of nature, 16, 64, 69, 72

Santayana, George, 201
Schopenhauer, Arthur, 127
science
  and art/literature, 4–6, 23–24, 27–28, 64,
    205, 209–210
  as force for truth, 5, 14, 18, 75–77, 89,
    106
  and the imperceptible, 11–12
  uncertain boundaries of, 67
scientific naturalism, 6, 23, 91, 123, 169
  and intellectual history, 157
Scot, Walter, 161
Sedgwick, Adam, 75
seduction, 120–121, 129, 131
selfhood, 19–21
semiotics, 6
  as model for biology 20, see *zoosemiotics*
  precursors to, 9–10
sensation fiction, 12, 87, 93–94, 99
Seton, Ernest Thompson, 211
sexual display, see *sexual selection*
sexual selection, 2, 5, 22–24, 90
  and aesthetics, 171, 173
  and desire as a trick of nature, 127
  and humans, 117, 122, 124, 212
  and maladaptation, 20, 126, 134
  and the subjection of women, 26, 148, 178,
    189–204
shading, 50, 54, 62
Shaftesbury, Lord [Anthony Ashley Cooper],
  68
Shaw, George Bernard, 21, 103
Shelley, Percy Bysshe, 162
Sidgwick, Henry, 17

Index

sincerity
 idealisation of, 19, 71, 81, 150–151
 and literature, 84, 113, 116, 154
 problematisation of, 17, 114, 116–117, 129, 135
Smart, Benjamin Humphrey, 9–10
Smith, James Edward, see *Abbot, John*
Smollett, Tobias, 161
Social Darwinism, 85
socialism, 93, 109, 112–113
 and biology, 108, 114, 172, 207
 and biosemiotics, 207
Somerville, Mary, 194
Spasmodists, 162
Spencer, Herbert, 169
 and Grant Allen, 91
 and Hardy, 128, 132
 and honesty, 14–16, 18, 25, 74
 on semiosis, 12
 on sexual dimorphism, 190
 on societal evolution, 81, 112, 151, 155, 170, 195
Spence, William, 24, 67
spiritualism, 17, 40–41, 43
Sprengel, Christian Konrad, 7
Stephen, Leslie, 17, 21–23, 85, 169
 and crypsis, 153–158
 and Darwinism, 122
 on Deism, 157
 and freethinking, 155, 158
 and Hardy, 116
 his elitism, 156
 his fear of radicalism, 154–155, 158
 on intellectual history as an evolutionary struggle, 155–156
  contradictions of this concept, 156–158
 and murder, 96, 100
 and the role of mass emotions in the spread of ideas, 156–157
 on religious apologetics, 26, 150, 154–158
 and the utility of religion, 157–158
Stevenson, Robert Louis, 86
subjectivity, see *objectivity*
Sully, James, 92–93
surface reading, 212–213
Surrealism, 154
Swinburne, Algernon, 159–160, 163
symbolism
 in nature, 8, 20, 25, 66–68, 77–79
sympathy, 146
 appearance of, 97
 as mimetic instinct, 18
 and progress, 147
syphilis, 200

Tennyson, Alfred, 159, 161
Thackeray, William Makepeace, 161
Thayer, Abbott Handerson, 5, 16, 23–24, 53–64
 and animals as pictures of environments, 54, 56–57
 and art as a scientific resource, 58–61
 and the authority of the artist, 54, 57–58
 controversy of his claims, 29
 and counter-shading, 54–55
 and disruptive coloration, 54
 'The Law Which Underlies Protective Coloration', 54–56
Thayer, Gerald Handerson, 54, 57–61
theatre
 and adaptive appearance, 2, 8, 12, 180
telescopy, 11
Tichborne case, 16, 93, 136; see *imposters*
Triplett, Norman, 13, 15
trompe l'oeil, 11, 31; see *illusion*
truth
 capacity of animals to comprehend it, 11
 as the end of progress, 18
 as an illusion, 17–18
 rival conceptions of, 5–6
truthfulness
 as amoral adaptation, 83
 and civilisation, 16, 75, 79
 and divinity, 24–25, 75, 80, 83
 and Englishness, 15, 21
 instinctive, 132–134
 of nature, 7, 65–68, 71–72, 74
 and science, 66, 74–75, 77
Turner, J. M. W., 30, 49–50, 98
Twain, Mark, 54
Tylor, E. B., 13, 151
Tyndall, John, 75, 80

Uexküll, Jakob von, 205
utilitarianism, 68, 117, 128, 135

Veblen, Thorstein, 192
vivisection, 6
visibility
 as a biological factor, 32, 35, 54, 57, 205
 of diseases, 200
 politics of, 26, 89–90, 177, 208
 of women, 179, 188, 194–196, 209

Wainwright, Thomas Griffiths, 96
Wallace, Alfred Russel, 2, 23–24, 106, 205
 and bio-geography, 52, 54
 and birds, 126
 and Grant Allen, 90, 113
 The Malay Archipelago, 40–42, 47–48

Index

and mimetic maladaptation, 13, 19, 125, 127
'Mimicry, and other Protective Resemblances
    among Animals', 48–49
and polymorphism, 106
and recognition, 174
representing adaptive appearance, 24, 29–31,
    34, 40–43, 63
and spiritualism, 40–41, 43, 67
and Stephen, 155
and Thayer, 57
and the unintentionality of mimicry, 9
Ward, Lester, 92, 112, 190–191
Warner, Charles Dudley, 191
warning colours, see *aposematism*
Watts-Dunton, Theodore, 21–23, 85, 158–164
conservatism of, 154
and critics as selective breeders, 159, 161
and crypsis, 153
and excessive individuality as a social evil,
    159, 162–163
and literature as a biological development,
    159–161
and literature as a collective production,
    161–163
on literary originality and imitativeness, 26,
    150, 159–161
and the masses as primitive readers, 159–161
on the randomness of literary success, 160
scientific education, 159
Webster, Augusta, 160
Weismann, August, 144
Wells, Charles, 160
Wells, H. G., 17
West London Ethical Society, 155
Westwood, John Obadiah, 24, 52
Wharton, Edith, 13
Whewell, William, 33
Wilde, Oscar, 21–23, 168–177
accusations of plagiarism, 168
and art's amorality, 96
and audience interpretation, 173, 175
'The Critic as Artist', 170–175
and crypsis as artistic strategy, 26, 150, 154,
    169
'The Decay of Lying', 169, 174
'De Profundis', 176
and evolutionism, 169, 171–174

and homosexuality, 175–176
on nature's uniformity, 169
    art/thought as an escape from this,
        169–171, 173–174
and obscurity, 26, 169, 176–177
and originality as disease, 171–173
'Phrases and Philosophies for the Use of the
    Young', 176
The Picture of Dorian Gray, 97, 170, 173
and 'recognition' versus 'suggestion', 173–177
and socialism 170, 172
'The Soul of Man under Socialism', 170, 172
and theoretical radicalism, 154, 171–172
'The Truth of Masks', 175
Wolf, Joseph, 45–47
women, 21–22, 26, 177
and 'real womanhood', 190
and sexual display, 124
supposed natural deceitfulness of, 127
Wood, J. G., 15
Wood, T. W., 47–49
Woolf, Virginia, 155

Young Turks, 13

Zangwill, Israel, 22–23, 26, 85
Children of the Ghetto, 179, 182
and an essentialist Jewish identity, 179,
    183–184, 187
and the inauthenticity of literary modernity,
    185–186
links with theorists of protective mimicry, 180
and Jewish assimilation as protective mimicry,
    178–188
and Jewish assimilation as symbiosis, 183
    view of this as degenerative, 182–184
The Melting-Pot, 179, 184–185, 187
and a non-essentialist Jewish identity, 179,
    185–187
and a transracial human community,
    184–185, 188
and Zionism, 180, 185–186
Zionism, 180–181
Zola, Émile, 122
zoosemiotics, 3–4, 205–206, 211
zoopoetics, 3
Zwecker, Johann Baptist; see *Wolf, Joseph*

CAMBRIDGE STUDIES IN NINETEENTH-CENTURY
LITERATURE AND CULTURE

General editor
GILLIAN BEER, *University of Cambridge*

Titles published

1. *The Sickroom in Victorian Fiction: The Art of Being Ill*
MIRIAM BAILIN, *Washington University*

2. *Muscular Christianity: Embodying the Victorian Age* edited by
DONALD E. HALL, *California State University, Northridge*

3. *Victorian Masculinities: Manhood and Masculine Poetics in Early Victorian*
Literature and Art
HERBERT SUSSMAN, *Northeastern University, Boston*

4. *Byron and the Victorians*
ANDREW ELFENBEIN, *University of Minnesota*

5. *Literature in the Marketplace: Nineteenth-Century British Publishing and the*
Circulation of Books edited by
JOHN O. JORDAN, *University of California, Santa Cruz* and ROBERT L. PATTEN,
Rice University, Houston

6. *Victorian Photography, Painting and Poetry*
LINDSAY SMITH, *University of Sussex*

7. *Charlotte Brontë and Victorian Psychology*
SALLY SHUTTLEWORTH, *University of Sheffield*

8. *The Gothic Body: Sexuality, Materialism and Degeneration at the Fin de Siècle*
KELLY HURLEY, *University of Colorado at Boulder*

9. *Rereading Walter Pater*
WILLIAM F. SHUTER, *Eastern Michigan University*

10. *Remaking Queen Victoria* edited by
MARGARET HOMANS, *Yale University* and ADRIENNE MUNICH, *State University of*
New York, Stony Brook

11. *Disease, Desire, and the Body in Victorian Women's Popular Novels*
PAMELA K. GILBERT, *University of Florida*

12. *Realism, Representation, and the Arts in Nineteenth-Century Literature*
ALISON BYERLY, *Middlebury College, Vermont*

13. *Literary Culture and the Pacific*
VANESSA SMITH, *University of Sydney*

14. *Professional Domesticity in the Victorian Novel Women, Work and Home*
MONICA F. COHEN

15. *Victorian Renovations of the Novel: Narrative Annexes and the Boundaries of Representation*
SUZANNE KEEN, *Washington and Lee University, Virginia*

16. *Actresses on the Victorian Stage: Feminine Performance and the Galatea Myth*
GAIL MARSHALL, *University of Leeds*

17. *Death and the Mother from Dickens to Freud: Victorian Fiction and the Anxiety of Origin*
CAROLYN DEVER, *Vanderbilt University, Tennessee*

18. *Ancestry and Narrative in Nineteenth-Century British Literature: Blood Relations from Edgeworth to Hardy*
SOPHIE GILMARTIN, *Royal Holloway, University of London*

19. *Dickens, Novel Reading, and the Victorian Popular Theatre*
DEBORAH VLOCK

20. *After Dickens: Reading, Adaptation and Performance*
JOHN GLAVIN, *Georgetown University, Washington D C*

21. *Victorian Women Writers and the Woman Question* edited by
NICOLA DIANE THOMPSON, *Kingston University, London*

22. *Rhythm and Will in Victorian Poetry*
MATTHEW CAMPBELL, *University of Sheffield*

23. *Gender, Race, and the Writing of Empire: Public Discourse and the Boer War*
PAULA M. KREBS, *Wheaton College, Massachusetts*

24. *Ruskin's God*
MICHAEL WHEELER, *University of Southampton*

25. *Dickens and the Daughter of the House*
HILARY M. SCHOR, *University of Southern California*

26. *Detective Fiction and the Rise of Forensic Science*
RONALD R. THOMAS, *Trinity College, Hartford, Connecticut*

27. *Testimony and Advocacy in Victorian Law, Literature, and Theology*
JAN-MELISSA SCHRAMM, *Trinity Hall, Cambridge*

28. *Victorian Writing about Risk: Imagining a Safe England in a Dangerous World*
ELAINE FREEDGOOD, *University of Pennsylvania*

29. *Physiognomy and the Meaning of Expression in Nineteenth-Century Culture*
LUCY HARTLEY, *University of Southampton*

30. *The Victorian Parlour: A Cultural Study*
THAD LOGAN, *Rice University, Houston*

31. *Aestheticism and Sexual Parody 1840–1940*
DENNIS DENISOFF, *Ryerson University, Toronto*

32. *Literature, Technology and Magical Thinking, 1880–1920*
PAMELA THURSCHWELL, *University College London*

33. *Fairies in Nineteenth-Century Art and Literature*
NICOLA BOWN, *Birkbeck, University of London*

34. *George Eliot and the British Empire*
NANCY HENRY, *The State University of New York, Binghamton*

35. *Women's Poetry and Religion in Victorian England: Jewish Identity and Christian Culture*
CYNTHIA SCHEINBERG, *Mills College, California*

36. *Victorian Literature and the Anorexic Body*
ANNA KRUGOVOY SILVER, *Mercer University, Georgia*

37. *Eavesdropping in the Novel from Austen to Proust*
ANN GAYLIN, *Yale University*

38. *Missionary Writing and Empire, 1800–1860*
ANNA JOHNSTON, *University of Tasmania*

39. *London and the Culture of Homosexuality, 1885–1914*
MATT COOK, *Keele University*

40. *Fiction, Famine, and the Rise of Economics in Victorian Britain and Ireland*
GORDON BIGELOW, *Rhodes College, Tennessee*

41. *Gender and the Victorian Periodical*
HILARY FRASER, *Birkbeck, University of London* JUDITH JOHNSTON and
STEPHANIE GREEN, *University of Western Australia*

42. *The Victorian Supernatural* edited by
NICOLA BOWN, *Birkbeck College, London* CAROLYN BURDETT, *London Metropolitan University* and PAMELA THURSCHWELL, *University College London*

43. *The Indian Mutiny and the British Imagination*
GAUTAM CHAKRAVARTY, *University of Delhi*

44. *The Revolution in Popular Literature: Print, Politics and the People*
IAN HAYWOOD, *Roehampton University of Surrey*

45. *Science in the Nineteenth-Century Periodical: Reading the Magazine of Nature*
GEOFFREY CANTOR, *University of Leeds* GOWAN DAWSON, *University of Leicester*
GRAEME GOODAY, *University of Leeds* RICHARD NOAKES, *University of Cambridge*
SALLY SHUTTLEWORTH, *University of Sheffield* and JONATHAN R. TOPHAM,
University of Leeds

46. *Literature and Medicine in Nineteenth-Century Britain from Mary Shelley to George Eliot*
JANIS MCLARREN CALDWELL, *Wake Forest University*

47. *The Child Writer from Austen to Woolf* edited by
CHRISTINE ALEXANDER, *University of New South Wales* and JULIET
MCMASTER, *University of Alberta*

48. *From Dickens to Dracula: Gothic, Economics, and Victorian Fiction*
GAIL TURLEY HOUSTON, University of New Mexico

49. *Voice and the Victorian Storyteller*
IVAN KREILKAMP, *University of Indiana*

50. *Charles Darwin and Victorian Visual Culture*
JONATHAN SMITH, *University of Michigan-Dearborn*

51. *Catholicism, Sexual Deviance, and Victorian Gothic Culture*
PATRICK R. O'MALLEY, *Georgetown University*

52. *Epic and Empire in Nineteenth-Century Britain*
SIMON DENTITH, *University of Gloucestershire*

53. *Victorian Honeymoons: Journeys to the Conjugal*
HELENA MICHIE, *Rice University*

54. *The Jewess in Nineteenth-Century British Literary Culture*
NADIA VALMAN, *University of Southampton*

55. *Ireland, India and Nationalism in Nineteenth-Century Literature*
JULIA WRIGHT, *Dalhousie University*

56. *Dickens and the Popular Radical Imagination*
SALLY LEDGER, *Birkbeck, University of London*

57. *Darwin, Literature and Victorian Respectability*
GOWAN DAWSON, *University of Leicester*

58. *'Michael Field': Poetry, Aestheticism and the Fin de Siècle*
MARION THAIN, *University of Birmingham*

59. *Colonies, Cults and Evolution: Literature, Science and Culture in Nineteenth-Century Writing*
DAVID AMIGONI, *Keele University*

60. *Realism, Photography and Nineteenth-Century Fiction*
DANIEL A. NOVAK, *Louisiana State University*

61. *Caribbean Culture and British Fiction in the Atlantic World, 1780–1870*
TIM WATSON, *University of Miami*

62. *The Poetry of Chartism: Aesthetics, Politics, History*
MICHAEL SANDERS, *University of Manchester*

63. *Literature and Dance in Nineteenth-Century Britain: Jane Austen to the New Woman*
CHERYL WILSON, *Indiana University*

64. *Shakespeare and Victorian Women*
GAIL MARSHALL, *Oxford Brookes University*

65. *The Tragi-Comedy of Victorian Fatherhood*
VALERIE SANDERS, *University of Hull*

66. *Darwin and the Memory of the Human: Evolution, Savages, and South America*
CANNON SCHMITT, *University of Toronto*

67. *From Sketch to Novel: The Development of Victorian Fiction*
AMANPAL GARCHA, *Ohio State University*

68. *The Crimean War and the British Imagination*
STEFANIE MARKOVITS, *Yale University*

69. *Shock, Memory and the Unconscious in Victorian Fiction*
JILL L. MATUS, *University of Toronto*

70. *Sensation and Modernity in the 1860s*
NICHOLAS DALY, *University College Dublin*

71. *Ghost-Seers, Detectives, and Spiritualists: Theories of Vision in Victorian Literature and Science*
SRDJAN SMAJIĆ, *Furman University*

72. *Satire in an Age of Realism*
AARON MATZ, *Scripps College, California*

73. *Thinking About Other People in Nineteenth-Century British Writing*
ADELA PINCH, *University of Michigan*

74. *Tuberculosis and the Victorian Literary Imagination*
KATHERINE BYRNE, *University of Ulster, Coleraine*

75. *Urban Realism and the Cosmopolitan Imagination in the Nineteenth Century: Visible City, Invisible World*
TANYA AGATHOCLEOUS, *Hunter College, City University of New York*

76. *Women, Literature, and the Domesticated Landscape: England's Disciples of Flora, 1780–1870*
JUDITH W. PAGE, *University of Florida* Elise L. Smith, *Millsaps College, Mississippi*

77. *Time and the Moment in Victorian Literature and Society*
SUE ZEMKA, *University of Colorado*

78. *Popular Fiction and Brain Science in the Late Nineteenth Century*
ANNE STILES, *Washington State University*

79. *Picturing Reform in Victorian Britain*
JANICE CARLISLE, *Yale University*

80. *Atonement and Self-Sacrifice in Nineteenth-Century Narrative*
JAN-MELISSA SCHRAMM, *University of Cambridge*

81. *The Silver Fork Novel: Fashionable Fiction in the Age of Reform*
EDWARD COPELAND, *Pomona College, California*

82. *Oscar Wilde and Ancient Greece*
IAIN ROSS, *Colchester Royal Grammar School*

83. *The Poetry of Victorian Scientists: Style, Science and Nonsense*
DANIEL BROWN, *University of Southampton*

84. *Moral Authority, Men of Science, and the Victorian Novel*
ANNE DEWITT, *Princeton Writing Program*

85. *China and the Victorian Imagination: Empires Entwined*
ROSS G. FORMAN, *University of Warwick*

86. *Dickens's Style* edited by
DANIEL TYLER, *University of Oxford*

87. *The Formation of the Victorian Literary Profession*
RICHARD SALMON, *University of Leeds*

88. *Before George Eliot: Marian Evans and the Periodical Press*
FIONNUALA DILLANE, *University College Dublin*

89. *The Victorian Novel and the Space of Art: Fictional Form on Display*
DEHN GILMORE, *California Institute of Technology*

90. *George Eliot and Money: Economics, Ethics and Literature*
DERMOT COLEMAN, *Independent Scholar*

91. *Masculinity and the New Imperialism: Rewriting Manhood in British Popular Literature, 1870–1914*
BRADLEY DEANE, *University of Minnesota*

92. *Evolution and Victorian Culture* edited by
BERNARD LIGHTMAN, *York University, Toronto* and Bennett Zon, *University of Durham*

93. *Victorian Literature, Energy, and the Ecological Imagination*
ALLEN MACDUFFIE, *University of Texas, Austin*

94. *Popular Literature, Authorship and the Occult in Late Victorian Britain*
ANDREW MCCANN, *Dartmouth College, New Hampshire*

95. *Women Writing Art History in the Nineteenth Century: Looking Like a Woman*
HILARY FRASER *Birkbeck, University of London*

96. *Relics of Death in Victorian Literature and Culture*
DEBORAH LUTZ, *Long Island University, C. W. Post Campus*

97. *The Demographic Imagination and the Nineteenth-Century City: Paris, London, New York*
NICHOLAS DALY, *University College Dublin*

98. *Dickens and the Business of Death*
CLAIRE WOOD, University of York

99. *Translation as Transformation in Victorian Poetry*
ANNMARIE DRURY, *Queens College, City University of New York*

100. *The Bigamy Plot: Sensation and Convention in the Victorian Novel*
MAIA MCALEAVEY, *Boston College, Massachusetts*

101. *English Fiction and the Evolution of Language, 1850–1914*
WILL ABBERLEY, *University of Oxford*

102. *The Racial Hand in the Victorian Imagination*
AVIVA BRIEFEL, *Bowdoin College, Maine*

103. *Evolution and Imagination in Victorian Children's Literature*
JESSICA STRALEY, *University of Utah*

104. *Writing Arctic Disaster: Authorship and Exploration*
ADRIANA CRACIUN, *University of California, Riverside*

105. *Science, Fiction, and the Fin-de-Siècle Periodical Press*
WILL TATTERSDILL, *University of Birmingham*

106. *Democratising Beauty in Nineteenth-Century Britain: Art and the Politics of Public Life*
LUCY HARTLEY, *University of Michigan*

107. *Everyday Words and the Character of Prose in Nineteenth-Century Britain*
JONATHAN FARINA, *Seton Hall University, New Jersey*

108. *Gerard Manley Hopkins and the Poetry of Religious Experience*
MARTIN DUBOIS, *University of Newcastle upon Tyne*

109. *Blindness and Writing: From Wordsworth to Gissing*
HEATHER TILLEY, *Birkbeck College, University of London*

110. *An Underground History of Early Victorian Fiction: Chartism, Radical Print Culture, and the Social Problem Novel*
GREGORY VARGO, *New York University*

111. *Automatism and Creative Acts in the Age of New Psychology*
LINDA M. AUSTIN, *Oklahoma State University*

112. *Idleness and Aesthetic Consciousness, 1815–1900*
RICHARD ADELMAN, *University of Sussex*

113. *Poetry, Media, and the Material Body: Autopoetics in Nineteenth-Century Britain*
ASHLEY MILLER, *Albion College, Michigan*

114. *Malaria and Victorian Fictions of Empire*
JESSICA HOWELL, *Texas A&M University*

115. *The Brontës and the Idea of the Human: Science, Ethics, and the Victorian Imagination* edited by
ALEXANDRA LEWIS, *University of Aberdeen*

116. *The Political Lives of Victorian Animals: Liberal Creatures in Literature and Culture*
ANNA FEUERSTEIN, *University of Hawai'i-Manoa*

117. *The Divine in the Commonplace: Recent Natural Histories and the Novel in Britain*
AMY KING, *St John's University, New York*

118. *Plagiarizing the Victorian Novel: Imitation, Parody, Aftertext*
ADAM ABRAHAM, *Virginia Commonwealth University*

119. *Literature, Print Culture, and Media Technologies, 1880–1900: Many Inventions*
RICHARD MENKE, *University of Georgia*

120. *Aging, Duration, and the English Novel: Growing Old from Dickens to Woolf*
JACOB JEWUSIAK, *Newcastle University*

121. *Autobiography, Sensation, and the Commodification of Identity in Victorian Narrative: Life upon the Exchange*
SEAN GRASS, *Rochester Institute of Technology*

122. *Settler Colonialism in Victorian Literature: Economics and Political Identity in the Networks of Empire*
PHILLIP STEER, *Massey University, Auckland*

123. *Mimicry and Display in Victorian Literary Culture: Nature, Science and the Nineteenth-Century Imagination*
WILL ABBERLEY, *University of Sussex*